# LUPE VÉLEZ

# LUPE VÉLEZ

*The Life and Career of
Hollywood's "Mexican Spitfire"*

Michelle Vogel

*Foreword by Kevin Brownlow*

McFarland & Company, Inc., Publishers
*Jefferson, North Carolina, and London*

LIBRARY OF CONGRESS CATALOGUING-IN-PUBLICATION DATA

Vogel, Michelle, 1972–
Lupe Vélez : the life and career of Hollywood's "Mexican spitfire" /
Michelle Vogel ; foreword by Kevin Brownlow.
p.    cm.
Includes bibliographical references and index.
Includes filmography.

ISBN 978-0-7864-6139-4
softcover : acid free paper ∞

1. Vélez, Lupe, 1906–1944.    2. Motion picture actors and
actresses — United States — Biography.    3. Motion picture
actors and actresses — Mexico — Biography.    I. Title.
PN2287.V43V64 2012        791.4302'33092 — dc23        [B]        2012022490

BRITISH LIBRARY CATALOGUING DATA ARE AVAILABLE

On the cover: Lupe Vélez strikes a pose in a classic mid–1930s Hollywood
glamour portrait that showcases her beauty; background © 2012 Shutterstock

Manufactured in the United States of America

*McFarland & Company, Inc., Publishers
Box 611, Jefferson, North Carolina 28640
www.mcfarlandpub.com*

# Table of Contents

# Acknowledgments

A very special thank you to the people mentioned below, all of whom contributed to this project in some way. This book wouldn't be as thorough as it is without your input, support and enthusiasm to tell Lupe Vélez's story as it was meant to be told.

In no particular order, Jeff Stafford, G. D. Hamann, Craig Harvey, Bill Caffrey, Rick Egusquiza, Martín Caballero, Marielis Orom, Rosa Helia Villa, Andy Lauer, Paul Ginsberg, Dick Moore, Bill Cappello, Alistair Tremps, Robert Osborne, Laura Petersen Balogh, Viviana García-Besné, E. J. Fleming, Hugh Munro Neely, Gregg Nystrom, Dr. Levica Narine, Jared Case, Caroline Yeager, Hal Erickson, Kay Shackleton, Michael Ankerich, Billy Doyle, Diane Lussier, Joseph Worrell, Alex Monty Canawati, Stephanie Swengel, Antoinette Garza, Uwe Linnemueller, Jon Mirsalis, David L. Smith, William M. Drew, Kevin John Charbeneau, Kristine Krueger, Valerie Yaros, David Ybarra, Gor Megaera, University of Washington Libraries (Special Collections), the Library of Congress (Recorded Sound Reference Center), the Mary Pickford Institute, Turner Classic Movies, George Eastman House, 20th Century–Fox, Beverly Hills Police Department (archives), Our Lady of the Lake University (archive material), the Margaret Herrick Library (Special Collections), the Los Angeles Public Library and the Museum of Modern Art.

Academy Award–winning film historian Kevin Brownlow contributed the foreword. I'm humbled and honored for our names to share a book cover.

Paul Green is my fellow author and good friend. The all too often lonely road of assembling and writing a book is boosted greatly by our daily e-mail banter.

I thank Pedro Quintanilla Gómez-Noriega for his invaluable personal recollections and family photographs of his Villalobos-Reyes relatives, as well as many clarifications, translations and explanations of the Spanish language and Mexican culture in general. Without doubt, this book would be a lesser work if it weren't for his involvement and willingness to share personal stories for the benefit of the reader's better understanding of Lupe's early years.

Rogelio Agrasánchez Jr. and Xóchitl Fernández of the Agrasánchez Film Archive generously shared their vast collection of photographs and knowledge of Lupe Vélez and the Mexican film industry, as well as providing countless Spanish-to-English translations from vintage newspapers and magazines.

The usual suspects ... my parents, my big boys Josh and Reeve, my little boy Ryan, and my husband Matt, for tracking down several vintage film magazines that contained much of the information that was included within these pages. Thank you for your love and support, in all that I do.

"My life story? It is the story of a devil. And who wants to print the story of a devil? I am wild, I cannot help it." —Lupe Vélez in an unidentified newspaper clipping from around the 1930s.

# Foreword by Kevin Brownlow

In the beginning, there was no such thing as a film star. Financiers were anxious to avoid the mistakes they had made in the theater. Having given in to their actors' demands, having parted with staggering sums of money, they had had to surrender to further outrageous demands. One picture company, the Biograph, provided no cast list on their films, yet audiences preferred their players to any others. They named their favorite "The Biograph Girl" but it took another company to poach her and to make her real name known: Florence Lawrence. Her replacement was even more popular. Incredibly popular. Once the audiences knew *her* name — Mary Pickford — the star system had taken over, an integral part of the industry.

It was assumed the moment an idol was found to have feet of clay, audiences would desert the theaters and the industry would collapse. The early stars could thus rely on the police to conceal their peccadilloes. They may get fined for speeding but they could run someone over with impunity.

But then came a series of scandals that could not be covered up. Comedian Roscoe Arbuckle, accused of manslaughter, was put on trial and banned from the screen. Editorials expressed horror as more and more errant behavior — drugs, drink, sex — came to light. Women's clubs protested. Did this drive the audiences away? There had been a postwar slump already, and the industry had panicked, but people came back in ever-larger numbers. Arbuckle's trial sold more newspapers than the sinking of the *Lusitania*.

Reporters realized that the shenanigans of Hollywood made wonderful copy and sold thousands of papers — so long as the stories were true. If they were untrue, why, they would sell even more. What your average newspaperman prayed for was a gorgeous star with a wayward temperament. They had had Mabel Normand, a brilliant comedienne who was often "on" something, and then came Clara Bow, who was equally gifted but took her stimulus in other ways.

Lupe Vélez, "the Mexican Spitfire," was a combination of the two. Most audiences would first encounter her in an outstanding film with Douglas Fairbanks called *The Gaucho*. Dolores del Rio, also from Mexico, and famous for her role in *What Price Glory?*, had been Fairbanks's first choice as "The Wild Mountain Girl," but del Rio was already working on another picture. When someone (Eugene Pallette) pretended to kidnap Lupe's precious Chihuahua and Fairbanks heard of her fury launched on the unfortunate practical joker, a spirited audition followed and he cast her at once.

In an impressive feat of research, Michelle Vogel has unearthed a large number of press stories. As she points out, the reporters were taken aback to find that Mexican Lupe had a reasonable command of English, so they went away and hoked up her dialogue with a vaudeville accent. Newspapers were intended as much for entertainment as the movies, after

1

all. Remember those tough newspapermen in '30s films like *The Front Page*— cynical, jaded and ultimately ruthless? How could they resist such a prize specimen?

But for once, publicity couldn't match the real thing. The stars of that time seldom went to acting school — they had learned their craft in the School of Hard Knocks. And to put over a powerful personality on the screen, you needed a personality many times more powerful. Lupe had that charisma, but sometimes used it willfully.

Reading the papers each morning must have been agony for those in charge of her career. She was the original loose cannon, only too happy to reveal to reporters the secrets of her private life, to quote verbatim the latest row with her husband.

In the argot of the time, she was "nuts." Now we'd assume she was bi-polar, or manic-depressive. She was certainly violent. If she liked you, life could be tough enough. God help you if she loved you. Take the case of Gary Cooper. She stabbed him more than once; she even opened fire at him with a revolver. No wonder his mother, English-born, the wife of a judge, deplored the very thought of her. Mrs. Cooper had sent Gary to an English school in the hope that nothing like Lupe would ever happen to him. The charming manners with which he emerged appealed greatly to Lupe and while she loved him for the rest of her life, alas he was "the one that got away."

Or is this just one more example of the stereotype? Those who knew Lupe well insist that in private she was "genteel and intelligent," that she was as generous with ordinary people who needed medical help as the legendary Marion Davies. That she had a wonderful sense of humor. Yet she was one of Hollywood's tragedies. And during her career she made comparatively few worthwhile pictures, but to anyone who has seen her, she is hard to forget.

It is no secret that she committed suicide, and as a devout Catholic that must have taken more than the usual determination. Michelle Vogel's analysis is illuminating, although it can do little to alleviate the sadness. Lupe Vélez was a fine artist who found life a great deal harder than she could face. How ironic that upon her suicide note she should bid farewell to her friends "and to the American press that were always so nice to me."

*Author, film preservationist and filmmaker Kevin Brownlow received an Honorary Academy Award on November 13, 2010, for his years of tireless dedication to preserving film and cinematic history.*

# *Preface*

In the January 1941 issue of *Modern Screen*, Lupe Vélez* said, "I do not care what is printed about me, so long as it is the truth." So, while researching and writing her life story, I pasted that very line above my computer to constantly remind me to honor her wishes (and her memory) by telling the truth — just as she asked.

Decades before controversial author-filmmaker Kenneth Anger made Lupe Vélez infamous with his sordid account of her death, through sheer determination and a love of entertaining she worked her way from war-torn Mexico to Hollywood fame and fortune. She was recognized, both on screen and off, for many and varying reasons, all of which will be explored within the following chapters.

The Agrasánchez Film Archive has been instrumental in making this book the definitive guide to Lupe's life and career. Rare photographs and several Spanish-language articles that were reproduced and transcribed within the following pages were generously provided by the Archive.

Lupe's second cousin, Pedro Quintanilla Gómez-Noriega, has provided never-before-seen family photographs and recounted family stories that have never been publicly told — until now. As a result, Lupe's paternal ancestry is meticulously showcased throughout the following pages.

You'll find a comprehensive biographical account of Lupe's dramatic early life and theatrical days in Mexico, right through to her Hollywood career, which includes her turbulent love affairs, unpredictable social antics, her marriage (and divorce) to Johnny "Tarzan" Weissmuller, her role of Carmelita in the popular "Mexican Spitfire" film series (1939–1943) and her tragic, premature death by way of a self-inflicted barbiturate overdose on December 14, 1944.

*Screen Secrets*, a lesser-known monthly film magazine, published a four-part interview with Lupe in the March, April, May and June of 1929 issues. Starting with her childhood and continuing all the way through to her early Hollywood beginnings, Lupe tells her life story (to date), all in her own words.

The Gladys Hall Papers at the Margaret Herrick Library contained several in-depth interviews with Lupe. This material has been equally helpful in understanding Lupe's mind-

---

*Lupe's surname will be printed throughout with its traditional Spanish spelling of Vélez. For the purpose of clarity, hyphenated surnames printed throughout will denote both the father and mother's last names as the person's full surname. While the author is aware that a hyphen isn't traditionally used to link surnames in the Spanish-speaking world, it's a recent trend that has been adopted within America's Hispanic-Latino community to prevent mistaking the second name as a middle name. Additionally, many magazines and newspapers printed Lupe's words in broken English to play up her "character" and ethnicity. For historical purposes, in these instances, whenever she is quoted in this context, I have faithfully transcribed the entire quote in its original form, without error.

set almost a decade on from the *Screen Secrets* interviews of 1929. Both sources serve to give a well-rounded, autobiographical explanation of her life, all these years later ... as only *she* could tell it.

There is a meticulously detailed career record that covers her films made in both Hollywood and Mexico (1927–1944), noted stage work (1932–1944), noted radio work (1930–1940), as well as documented footage where she appears as herself (1928–1941). Lupe's long-standing and continuing influence in pop culture is also explored. As well, film and stage productions that she was once associated with, but for whatever reason didn't appear in, are all listed in "Lupe's Lost Productions."

Her eventful childhood, her early stage work in Mexico, her film and theater career, her tumultuous romances, her love-hate relationship with the media, her tragic death, and everything in between. It's all here.

Unfortunately, the passage of time muddies the facts, and in Lupe's case, fiction has morphed into fact on the grandest of scales. To this day, her death has taken on urban legend–type qualities. And she's become the butt of many Hollywood folklore-type jokes. Toilet humor — literally!

In 2009, Oscar-winning film historian Kevin Brownlow revealed Kenneth Anger's research methlods for his notorious *Hollywood Babylon* tome. Unbelievably, Anger's three-word response was even more shocking than anything ever written within the pages of his book. Asked how he did his research, Anger replied, "Mental telepathy, mostly" (*Karl Dane: A Biography and Filmography*, Laura Petersen Balogh, Jefferson, N.C., McFarland, 2009).

As a researcher and writer, it's been an exhaustive undertaking to find the buried facts within almost seven decades (since her death) of fiction. However, the existence of this book is the result of my determination to find those threads of truth and weave them cohesively together. Oh, the myths are addressed, analyzed, and even included. They have to be. They're too strong to ignore. Besides, Lupe was certainly guilty of making a few of them up herself!

Collectively, this book is the amalgamation of every last detail, the definitive look at the life and career of Hollywood's Mexican Spitfire, Lupe Vélez.

# Introduction

Lupe Vélez — the mere sound of her name and some movie fans will quizzically pause for a few seconds, and then with a snap of their fingers, as if to say, "I've got it!" will flippantly, and quite proudly, respond with, "Oh yeah! She was the one who died with her head in the toilet, right?!"

Wrong!

For years, I've personally experienced this very reaction from many people. But had it not been for Kenneth Anger's graphic *Hollywood Babylon* account of her final few hours, Lupe Vélez may not be remembered today at all.

According to Anger, following a traditional Mexican feast, Lupe took 75 Seconal pills, washed down with her favorite brandy. The combination of spicy food, pills and alcohol made her physically sick and she rushed to the bathroom adjoining her bedroom. Anger wrote that her maid followed a trail of vomit into the bathroom the following morning. There she found Lupe Vélez dead, her head firmly planted in the toilet bowl — drowned.

The truth? Lupe Vélez died in her bed, as she intended.

She was thirty-six years old, unmarried and about to become a mother. She was successful, beautiful, kind, talented, funny, a little bit crazy (even by her own admission), and on December 14, 1944, she was dead by her own hand (a barbiturate overdose). Every ounce of the truth was tragic. No salacious embellishment needed.

Thirty-year police veteran and chief of the Beverly Hills Police Department Clinton H. Anderson was first on the scene. He said Lupe looked so small in her oversized bed that at first sight he thought she was a doll. In his memoirs, published sixteen years after her death, Anderson maintained that she was found in her bed. *If* there was a Hollywood cover-up to protect Lupe's dignity, at the time of his book's publication Anderson had nothing to lose and everything to gain. Further, he would have trumped Kenneth Anger with the "died with her head in the toilet" comment, in turn having his own best seller to boast about. He didn't. Why? Because the truth doesn't change. Anderson's recollections were the same as they were when he was interviewed right after Lupe's death. He wrote:

> I have always felt that Lupe Vélez never really intended to kill herself.... We found her dead in bed in her home, with a suicide note beside her addressed to her lover in which she wrote brokenly of unrequited love and expectant motherhood. I believe Lupe thought her act would bring her faithless lover back, but she miscalculated the amount of sleeping pills [Anderson, *Beverly Hills Is My Beat*].

Unlike many of her foreign peers whose thick vernaculars killed their Hollywood careers once "the talkies" took over, Lupe made the leap from silent to sound films with little effort, *despite* her accent. She was very often typecast as the hotheaded Latin firecracker, but she

made the best of it and got plenty of work because of her personality. Lupe's broken English and mixed-up phrasing were purposefully played up to fit the character she was pigeonholed to play. Her spunky, go-get-'em attitude, flirtatious winks, flickering eyebrows and shoulder shrugs, all made for a unique package, and she knew it. Many of Lupe's lines and actions were improvised, and it shows. There is a refreshing, natural quality to her acting that sets her apart from many of her contemporaries who religiously stuck to the script, and were in danger of turning in wooden performances for fear of stepping outside the box. Both on screen and off, Lupe *always* pushed the limits. Most of the time, she got away with it.

Lupe said what she wanted to say and did what she felt like doing. She refused to censor herself or be censored, and for this realism, she was called wild, uncontrollable, a spitfire. She was feisty, fiery, loud, impulsive, outspoken and always ready to fight for anything and anyone. Ironically, the one fight she did lose was the most important one of all. Her moralistic battle with her own conscience when she discovered she was pregnant with actor Harald Ramond's* love child, and her subsequent suicide because of her "predicament," brought the Hollywood community to its knees.

Being unmarried and pregnant was a shameful situation for any woman living in the 1940s to be in, and despite Lupe's fame, wealth and ability to raise a child as a single woman (if she so inclined), she was a strict Catholic. It was out of the question.

Furthermore, the scandal would surely ruin her career — or would it?

Lupe Vélez was all about shock value. Her frequent outbursts and public dust-ups were legendary. Newspaper reporters loved her because she always gave them something to write about. Lupe made sure of it. No doubt, she eventually played the off-screen role the papers (and the public) wanted her to play. Her mannerisms and phraseologies were played up for publicity purposes, and while she was usually willing to go along with it, it's obvious that toward the end of her career, Lupe was getting tired of the print interviews that simplified her ethnicity a little too much. The shtick was getting old and Lupe was over it. Besides, after all those years in Hollywood, did the public truly believe that her English hadn't improved at all? Following her divorce from Johnny Weissmuller, a reporter asked Lupe why she spoke such poor English. Lupe snapped back, "[Because] I was married to a guy who can only say, 'Me Tarzan, you Jane'" (www.thisdayinquotes.com).

When Lupe was in the room, you could bet something newsworthy would happen eventually! But despite her free-spirited personality, her religious beliefs ran deep. In moments where even *she* thought she'd stepped over the line, she'd voluntarily sink to her knees and pray to the heavens for forgiveness.

Following Lupe's death, one old friend summed her up by saying she was "the most colorful figure who has ever lived in Hollywood. A girl who didn't know what rules and regulations meant. She had nothing restrained about her. No fear, no timidity. She had a terrific confidence in herself, was a complete individualist, and eccentric to the nth degree" (*The Milwaukee Journal*, December 28, 1944).

Lupe's unpredictable temperament was often stereotypically blamed on her nationality. "She's a fiery Mexican!" was a line frequently used to explain away her wild, primitive behavior. In the days before political correctness, this and other racially demeaning expressions like it were commonplace. The reality of the situation was that Lupe's frequent mood swings were most probably the result of undiagnosed, thus untreated, bi-polar disorder. Whatever

---

*Lupe's fiancé Harald Ramond was also known as Harald Maresch. He will be called the former name throughout the following pages.

the reason for her explosive, capricious personality, Lupe was pretty much accepted for who she was, and what she did, simply because she was, well — Lupe! She was a Hollywood curiosity, useful and entertaining to keep around, though not taken seriously enough to transcend the race barrier into meatier roles that she was more than capable of playing.

If anyone was going to get pregnant and raise a child on her own as a single mother in mid–1940s Hollywood, would anyone really have been *that* shocked if it was Lupe Vélez who did it? In hindsight ... probably not! Lupe thought otherwise...

As 1945 approached, Lupe was already four months pregnant. Depressed at the thought of impending motherhood without a husband and father for her baby, she saw no other way out but to end her own life and that of her child.

On December 15, 1944, the day after Lupe's death, close friend (and the last person to see her alive), actress, Estelle Taylor, was quoted in *The Montreal Gazette*, "She [Lupe] said she had plenty of opportunity to get rid of it [the baby]. But she said, 'It's my baby. I couldn't commit murder and still live myself. I would rather kill myself.'" And she did.

December 14, 1944, is the day on history's calendar that marks the untimely end of Lupe Vélez. Sure, it's important to remember her death, but only if it's remembered as *one* day out of a thirty-six-year, short, but very well-lived life. Put simply, her death does not (and should not) define her existence. Yet, for years, it has done just that. There is so much more to Lupe Vélez's life story than the tragic last page.

# 1

# *A Stormy Beginning*

"I had to play with boys, girls found me too rough."[1]— Lupe Vélez

On July 18, 1908, María de Guadalupe Villalobos-Vélez was born in the family home in the Barrio de San Sebastián section of San Luis Potosí, Mexico. On the very day she entered the world, many buildings and homes in the area were devastated by what is known as a "tromba," a strong rainstorm with hurricane-like winds. Lupe's stormy spirit was partly due to genetics (her father was a wild man); however, some were certain that Mother Nature played a part too. Spiritual believers and superstitious gypsies were convinced the storm would infuse the soul of San Luis Potosí's newest arrival. Ironically, during her Hollywood years, one of Lupe's nicknames was "The Mexican Hurricane."

Her birth name María de Guadalupe translates to "María of Guadalupe," in honor of the Virgin of Guadalupe (aka Our Lady of Guadalupe), Mexico's most revered and historically significant Catholic figure. Her surname Villalobos-Vélez follows the Spanish tradition of using the father's name (Villalobos) first, followed by the mother's name (Vélez).

Lupe's father, Jacobo Villalobos (b. 1879), was twenty-two when he married (October 30, 1901, at Iglesia del Sagrado Corazón, Monterrey, Nuevo León, Mexico) his eighteen-year-old bride, Josefina Vélez (b. 1883). Lupe's paternal grandparents were documented on the marriage license: Jacobo Villalobos-Cuadriello and Luisa Reyes. Her maternal grandparents were also named: Silverio M. Vélez and Carmen Gómez.

Contrary to many reports, the Villalobos family wasn't poor; in fact, quite the opposite. They lived in a big house with servants. They were not without cash or comfort for most of Lupe's childhood, but during her early teenage years, the Mexican Revolution changed everything. Their world, as they knew it, was turned upside down. Lupe's second cousin Pedro Quintanilla Gómez-Noriega said:

> The Villalobos family was a very prominent family in San Luis Potosí. They were quite rich and belonged to the upper crust in the state. Lupe's grandfather was a very well-known, highly respected attorney [and politician]. Most, if not all of the male members of that family were university-educated professionals. In those days, few adults could boast a professional degree.

In its March, April, May and June 1929 issues, the short-lived *Screen Secrets* magazine published a four-part interview entitled "Senorita Cyclone," an in-depth account of Lupe's life, in her own words (as told to Ruth Biery), as only she could tell it. Of all the stories published in the fan magazines at that time, this one was the most honest and accurate account of her life to date. In the March 1929 *Screen Secrets*, she recalled the horrors of war, and the bloodshed she witnessed as a child, saying:

**Lupe Vélez at five months old. Photograph courtesy University of Washington Libraries, Special Collections.**

People love Lupe but they do not understand her. Perhaps it is because I am born in the Revolution. When your American kids go to kindergarten, I am riding with my father[2] in the Mexican Army. I see the horse of my brother[3] shot from beneath him. I see many mens try to kill my father. I see my father kill other peoples.

One day four mens stand up before an old wall with holes made by many guns in it. Four other mens stand fifty — a hundred feet — away from them with big guns. They shoot them down like so many ducks when you go hunting. I watch and then I climb upon my pony and go along behind my father and my brother. I am five, maybe six years old. It is my first school, thees Revolution. I do not cry. I do not have goose pimples on my flesh. I do not have fears of the bullets.

**Jacobo Villalobos-Cuadriello, Lupe's paternal grandfather, at age 30. Born some time in 1855 in San Luis Potosí, Mexico, he married Luisa Reyes-Manrique de Lara in 1875. At the time this photograph was taken, four of his eight children had been born, including Jacobo, Lupe's father. Following his wife Luisa's death, he married his daughter's best friend, Luz Mejía. They had one child together, a girl. Jacobo Villalobos-Cuadriello died on February 21, 1911. Photograph courtesy Pedro Quintanilla Gómez-Noriega.**

Lupe's father was definitely the black sheep of the family and his daughter had obviously inherited his fighting spirit and mischievous approach to life. As a young girl of ten or eleven, Lupe would assemble the servants and her family to sit and watch her one-girl show. She'd strip the beds of their sheets and wrap herself in them. Curtain rings became jewelry; flowers and a huge tortoiseshell comb would hold back her unruly hair. In such attire, Lupe would glide around the house "playing theater" and giving herself "old style Spanish lady" airs (*Lupe Vélez: la mexicana que escupia fuego,* Gabriel Ramírez, 1st ed., Cineteca Nacional Mexico, 1986).

Whether she pretended to be a woman of importance or a tough boy (she often dressed in her brother's clothes and tucked her hair under a cap), Lupe would insist on performing on the roof of the house because it felt more like a stage. Her impromptu open air performances drew crowds of local boys who'd watch Lupe from below, cheering and whistling. She'd blow them kisses and bow and twirl in joyful appreciation. Lupe said:

Luisa Reyes-Manrique de Lara, Lupe's paternal grandmother, at age 20, circa 1881. She married Jacobo Villalobos-Cuadriello in 1875 when she was just 16. She died of cancer in 1902, at age 41. Photograph courtesy Pedro Quintanilla Gómez-Noriega.

> My poor family. They never knows what to do with me. When I am older and have to go to school once in a while I will not wear the socks which my mother gives me. I steal the silk stockings of my mother. One day she finds them all gone and she says to Lupe she does not know what to think of it. I say, "Mother, I think the servants must take them," and mother fire some of the servants because of which I say about the silk stockings.
>
> My three sisters — to me, they are different like hell. They are so good. They *like* to go to school. They *like* to wear socks. They *like* to be ladies. They make me nervous, being always so good like a lady. They have no fun. They do not flirt with all the mens like Lupe ["Senorita Cyclone," *Screen Secrets,* No. 48, March 1929].

By age twelve, Lupe was sneaking into local theaters and watching the actresses dress for stage plays and apply their makeup[4] prior to their performances. She would then sit in the wings and study their every move. When she got home, she attired herself in her mother's clothes. She substituted white flour for face powder and she used crushed ripened strawberries or dampened red paper to stain her lips. Lupe was so enamored with her look, she kissed her own reflection in the mirror, then she imitated the actresses of the stage and put on her own show for anyone who cared, or dared, to watch (*The Pittsburgh Press,* March 29, 1929).

Whether she was imitating theater actresses and using whatever she could find to

transform herself into someone else or riding in the Revolution with her father and watching men die in front of her, Lupe's childhood was one big dramatic adventure. She explained:

> I do not always go to fight with my father. I am at home sometimes and sometimes I am with the army. When I am home I go outdoors and the old mens and the old womens and the young mens and the young womens they crowd around me and cry, "Dance for us, Lupe!" I dance in the streets and they clap and yell, "Hurrah for Lupe!"
>
> I do not know when I see my first movie. Five, maybe six. I come home and they say, "Lupe, how do you like it?" I do not tell them. I can say nothing. It hurts here. [*She pressed both hands over her heart so forcibly that the imprint of her fingers remained on her chest, exposed by the low gown she was wearing.*] But from the time I see my first movie, I am an actress ["Senorita Cyclone," *Screen Secrets*, No. 48, March 1929].

Lupe's uncanny ability to impersonate people became a lifelong passion. As an adult, her mimicry would both embarrass and delight her family, friends and enemies. More importantly, audiences the world over would roll in the aisles with uncontrollable laughter as they watched her transform herself into Dolores del Rio, Gloria Swanson, Marlene Dietrich, Shirley Temple, Simone Simon, Katharine Hepburn, even Hitler! As a teenager, Lupe's imitations were her way of retaliating against the catty performers of the Mexican stage. Her public mimicry was a form of humiliation that would set her apart from the rest of the performers and eventually make her a household name.

By Lupe's own admission, she

Jacobo Villalobos-Reyes, Lupe's father. This photograph was taken in Monterrey, Mexico, circa 1900 when he was 21, approximately one year before he married Lupe's mother, Josefina Vélez. Lupe was born about eight years after this photograph was taken. The inscription reads: "For my distinguished and highly esteemed friend Ramona. Your friend who appreciates you, Jacobo Villalobos-Reyes." Jacobo died of natural causes some time between mid–December 1943 and mid–January 1944. Photograph courtesy Pedro Quintanilla Gómez-Noriega.

was a tomboy and a flirt, all rolled into one explosive little package. Despite her family having the means to buy her dolls and pretty things other girls her age would like to own, she preferred to thrust herself into a world of make believe. She said:

> I never like to play with dolls. I like better to play actress with my pillow. I go to my room and grab first one pillow in my arms and then the other and pretend that they are real live people. They are the mens in the plays! I make love to them and say, "Some day I will make love like this to a mans in the theater." Sometimes they are bad mens and I grab up a big knife and kills them. The feathers, they come out. They are white, but to Lupe they are red like the blood of the mens killed by a stiletto. The white blood all over the floor makes my grandmother hate me some more. When I gets tired of the pillows I looks in the looking glass and kisses myself and watches myself make eyes like I make eyes in the theatre. My bed, it has four big sticks; what you call it? Posters! To me these are peoples, and I talks to them and kisses them like I see peoples act in the movie. From the time I am able to walk I want to dance and from the time I see my first movie I want to act for peoples ["Senorita Cyclone," *Screen Secrets*, No. 48, March 1929].

In 1932, long after Lupe had made it in Hollywood, *New Movie* magazine printed a blunt, racially stereotypical story about her budding sexuality as a pre-teen. The article stated, in part:

> ... Even at that tender age [12], Lupe had sex appeal and no race is as quick to recognize this quality as the Mexican. The house was surrounded by boys of all ages.... [S]he discovered, young as she was, that her kisses were marketable. She would bestow a chaste salute on a masculine cheek in exchange for a picture of a [film] star or a colored ribbon to wind in her dark braids....

Perhaps it wasn't so far from the truth. After all, Lupe just couldn't help herself when it came to men and she was the first to admit it. She had two sides. She could fight like a boy, and yet she also knew how to use her femininity to lure a boy. Long before she was a professional actress, she knew what part to play, and perhaps more importantly, *when* to play it. Lupe said:

> My father wants a boy. I am a girl but he make a boy out of me. He take me where I will learn to be afraid of nothings. Perhaps that is where I first learn to be a devil· perhaps it is where I first earn to be a flirt. No! I am a flirt ever since I can remember. I wrinkles my eyes at the mens when I am a baby. Maybe this is why peoples do no always

María Luisa Villalobos-Reyes at age 26, circa 1916. She was Lupe's paternal aunt and mother ot María Josefina Gómez-Noriega Villalobos (Lupe's first cousin); Pedro Quintanilla Gómez-Noriega's mother. She died in Monterrey, Mexico, on February 21, 1974. Photograph courtesy Pedro Quintanilla Gómez-Noriega.

understand Lupe. My father teach me to be hard like a boy. My love of mens make me soft like a woman ["Senorita Cyclone," *Screen Secrets*, No. 48, March 1929].

Lupe confessed to having her first sweetheart at age *seven*. His name was Víctor and he lived in the house next to her. It all started when his dog got into a fight with her dog. They stuck their tongues out at each other, then the dogs made up, and of course Víctor and Lupe made up too. Years later, Víctor later came to Los Angeles to catch up with his first love. Lupe said:

I think there is no friends like the old friends. Then I see [Víctor]. Bah! He has pimples all over his face. "My Lord!" I think. How can I ever like him? Even when I am seven. How can I have for a sweetheart a boy who has pimples? I guess that's how we get different when we grow up. Even if we don't know it — we changes.

I fight like a hellion always. When I am a very little kid the milk boy picks a fight with my little brother. [My brother] is two years younger than Lupe. The milk boy is beating my brother when I see him. I run like the devil. I am maybe seven. I throw myself on him and I scratch and I kick and then I picks up a big stone and crack his nose with it. Then I laugh! A little girl has beat up a sixteen-year-old milk seller! ["Senorita Cyclone," *Screen Secrets*, No. 49, April 1929].

Lupe was a lover and a fighter; history tells us she often combined the two. Many of her relationships were tumultuous, but at the tender age of thirteen, Lupe had truly fallen in love ... with a twenty-one-year-old man.

# 2

## *First Love*

"When I go to church, I go to pray, not to wiggle and yawn. I go when I really want to — not as a duty."[1]— Lupe Vélez

In the April 1929 issue of *Screen Secrets* magazine, Lupe explained her first real love [Mil-a-tone[2]] in great detail:

I fall very much in loves when I am thirteen and a half. I have flirt with everybody. Even my own father and my own brother but I have never been in love up to this minute. I am going to school with some girls; running down the road, swinging my hands; laughing, very happy. A mans on a horse comes very fast on us. He thinks it is funny to skeer us. He rushes his horse close and more close to us. I am not afraid of an army but I am afraid of this one horse rushing down on us. I hit a tree when I jump out of the way and hurt my arm. I scream and I yell bad names at him. He thinks he has hurt me and jumps off his horse to say he his sorry. I will not listen to what he says. I just keep screaming at him. Isn't it terrible?

"Did I hurt such a little beautiful kid like you? I'm so sorry."

That make me look at him. He is twenty-one years old; he is tall and very handsome. I like him. We talk and talk there by the tree. The girls call, "Come on, Lupe!" I say, "I will follow."

"Where are you going?" I say to him.

"To see my sweetheart."

That hurt me on the inside to think he have a sweetheart. I flirts with him until he says he wishes I am a little older.

"I am old enough. I am fourteen and a half," I tell him. I add one year to my age to make me seem bigger.

I do not go to school that day; I play hooky, go into the fields and think about him. I spy on him and sneak up every day and watch him talk to his sweetheart through her window. I take a stitch out of my dress to make it longer. I take my sister's shoes and put on me. They are too big but they have high heels and make me look taller. I go to the roof of my house to watch and watch and see if he come down the road. One day I wait on the corner. I just have to see him. He stop and asks me how I been.

"You going to see your sweetheart?" I ask him.

"Yes," he tell me.

"Do you really love her?"

"Yes, I love her."

"Oh, I see."

"You talk like a child," he tells me.

"But see, I wear high heels now. My mother say I am too old to wear low heels any more."

"Yes, you are *very* old. Do you want to see me tomorrow?"

"Yes! I love to see you," And I wrinkled my eyes hard at him. He grab my hand. That make me very happy. But when he pat me on my head like I am a kid, that make me angry. I tells him only my father do that.

The next day I puts on my best dress. My mother say, "What is the matter with you, Lupe? That dress is for Sunday." I tell her it is a big day at school and we have to dress up for it. Then I paints my cheeks with red paper. It make good rouge when you lick your tongue on it. I burns a match and uses it on my eyelashes. I don't go to school. I just wait four hours on that street corner. My heart is beating, beating!

"You look cute," he say when he see me. "You look sweet enough to kiss. What would you do if I kiss you? Would you scream?"

I say, "No!"

I never forget that kiss. It is the sweetest I ever get in my life. Oh, my Lord, wasn't it wonderful!' [*Lupe paused in her story. Were those tears in the eyes of the girl? Tears in eyes which usually gleam with the dangerous lights of what she calls "a devil"?*]

I see him that night and every day and night. I go out and not come home until eight and ten o'clock at night. That is terrible. My mother raises hell about it. I pay no attention. I tell him he must give up that girl. "But you are just a child," he tell me.

"I will show you if I am a child! I will flirts with every mens in this city if you do not give up that girl for me!"

I did. I have eight — ten — oh, twenty mens in love with Lupe. I am always with them. So he give up the girl and then I gives up the mens and we promise to marry one another. Oh, how I adore him to death. And he adores me to death also. We are very happy. But my mother, she is worried. She think that Lupe is too young to have a mans really love her. She is afraid something bad will happen to Lupe. So she make up her mind to teach Lupe what happen to girls who have lovers. She give Lupe the biggest shock of her life. Something Lupe never forgets. It is what *makes* Lupe forever a good woman.

My mother is a very wise woman. She knows life and she wants her girls to know also so they will not get into trouble. When my sisters is thirteen she taken them to see about life just as she now goes to take Lupe. But it is a death secret. One girl can never tell another.

I know nothing where we are going until she take me by the hand one morning and lead me to a hospital where there are many sick womans. She take me first to a womans beautiful like the Madonna! Her skin is like the snow, and hands, ah, Lupe can never forget the hands of that womans. They lie like two beautiful flowers more white than the covers beneath them. She cannot raise them; this wonderful, beautiful womans. She try to talk. She make no words come from her mouth; only sounds. I stand there and I suffer. I never see anything so beautiful; I never see anything so terrible.

My mother turn to the nurse. "She will live?"

"No." The nurse answers and shakes her head very sad. "She can live only a little longer."

Lupe cry. It does not seem possible that the womans so young — she is not more than twenty — so beautiful, almost like the Virgin, can die!

Lupe turns to go away. She cannot stand it. But her mother, she grabs my arm and makes me stay and watch the womans try again to raise those lovely hands, try to say something. I cry out! My mother takes me away a little and ask me, "Do you know the matter with this womans?"

I do not know.

My mother tell me; tell me about the womans who let mens get ahead of them.

"You want to go straight, Lupe?"

"Yes," I sob as I answer.

"You can do as you wish, Lupe. You can have beautiful jewels, beautiful clothes and be like this womans. Or you can have less and be a good womans. No one can do it for you. Go to hell if you wish, or live a good life. It is your life, and it is up to you to live it!"

I owe everything to this lesson from my mother. I feel sorry for the American boys and girls when I see them on the beach at night, parked in their cars taking drinks of whiskey and petting one another.

In America, I do not think the mothers tell their children. In my country mothers know that life is life and they make their girls understand it. I trust no man ever. I flirt with them

but I do not trust them. I can never forget. It was a shock to a young girl. It took me long time to get over it. It is crude; it is rude; I cannot eat; I cannot sleep. I cannot forget the face of that womans or the faces of the other womans which my mother shows me. But I can never go away with a mans who do not marry Lupe. Never! But I do not stop flirting and I do not stop seeing Mil-a-tone, the man who I wishes to marry ["Senorita Cyclone," *Screen Secrets*, No. 48 and 49, March/April 1929].

Obviously, Lupe's mother attempted to scare her romantically vulnerable daughter straight by giving her a tour of a syphilis ward at a local hospital. While, at the time of her visit, Lupe was obviously affected by the women suffering from the disease, she continued to see her twenty-one-year-old boyfriend and she continued to drive her mother crazy with worry. Ordered not to see him, Lupe rebelled even more. No one forbid Lupe to do anything. There was only one thing left to do: separate them.

Soon after, arrangements were made to send Lupe and her sister Josefina (aka Josephine) away. And so, a seemingly sweet Mexican teenager going by the name of María de Guadalupe Villalobos-Vélez was the newest pupil enrolled at Our Lady of the Lake Convent in San Antonio, Texas. Lupe smiled sweetly as the nun introduced her to her fellow students. When the nun turned her back, Lupe poked out her tongue. When the nun turned around again, Lupe smiled sweetly. She repeated this pattern two more times. She didn't get caught and the pupils snickered at the brave comedic routine the new girl was daring to perform. Lupe quickly learned how good it felt to have an appreciative audience. Maybe the convent wouldn't be so bad after all.

Unbeknownst to the nuns, the devil had just arrived.

# 3

## *"I Must Be Good!"*

"My Lupe is full of pep," said her father.
"My Lupe is full of hell," said her mother.[1]

Lupe was too young to be "with" any man, yet she insisted she was "in love" with Mil-a-tone. Lupe had always been a handful for her parents, but this time she had gone too far. In order to straighten her out, and save her from making a life-long mistake, the convent was the only solution her parents could agree upon. Sixteen-year-old Josephine (aka Josefina) went too, primarily so she could keep an eye on her unpredictable younger sister and report back home about her behavior. Lupe said:

I am out every night and mother can do nothing with me.... I drive her nearly crazy. So she decide to send me to the convent with my sister, Josephine. We start for the [Our] Lady of the Lake in San Antonio, Texas. My mother go to the train with us. She cry and say, "Baby may never see her mother again." I am a devil. I just say, "Hurrah! I'm going away and I don't care if I never come back. I am going to the United States and see a different country!"

I hate the convent then. But I like to remember it now. It is the happiest time of my life. Someday when I get through making money in pictures, I think I go into the convent forever. You know, there is another side to Lupe. Lupe never cry but sometimes she get sad and to be back with the Sisters who seem always to have content and be so quiet and happy.

But all I learn at the convent is to write for one thousand times again and again, "I must be good!" I hate it. Everything I do is bad. We cannot chew gum in school. I love to chew gum. One day a Sister takes the gum out of my mouth and sticks it on my nose. I am so happy! Gee, I am happy! For when she turn her back I take it off my nose and puts it in my mouth and when I see she is beginning to turn around I takes it out of my mouth and puts it back on my nose. That way I always have my gum with me.

I dance the hula and the shimmy. We go to a picture show every Saturday afternoon and I learns it from watching the actresses in the picture. The Sisters see me do it. I have to write again a thousand times, "I must be good!" But the minute the Sisters turn their back I stop writing and do over and over again the hula and the shimmy.

The girls all hate me. I take their boyfriends from them. I do not mean to be bad. I love Mil-a-tone but Lupe just cannot help but flirt no matter how much she love somebody. He writes me. I write him. I love him like mad but I must flirt or I cannot live. I get sick if I do not flirt ever. I flirt with the girls' boyfriends. They come up under my windows and sing, "Who's Sorry Now," "Charlie, My Boy," "Poppa Loves Momma" and "I Wonder What Becomes of Sally." That's the way I learn to sing pieces.

I send messages to the boys by my sister, Josephine. Nobody ever think, she is so good, that she will take them. She never get caught at it. But she better take them. I will scratch her eyes out if she don't take them!

There is a bridge in front of the school. We can go to this bridge when we play but we

18

cannot go over it. One day I decide to run away. I ask Josephine to go with me but she is skeered cat and will not do it. The first time, I get just across the bridge when the Mother Superior drive up in a big car.

"Stop!" she say to the chauffeur. She is very angry.

"Where are you going?"

"I go to buy gum."

"Don't you know you aren't allowed to chew gum? Get into this car this minute."

So I go back and write a thousand times more, "I must be good!"

I wait three days then I try it again. This time I changes my clothes and sneak out and get into the city. I have some money and I buy some clothes like I always been wanting. High heels — way high like this. [*Lupe's fingers indicated that her first French heels must have been at least eight inches.*] I get a little dress which is high also — oh, when I come out of that store! I am so happy. For the first time in my life I looks like a real flapper.

A boy wrinkles his eye at me. I say to myself, "I am making a hit." But before I get a chance to speak to him, three other mens come up to me. Then I know I am making a hit! But I am mistaken. They are three policemans, without uniforms, which the school have sent to find me.

When they take me back they say they are going to put me in the reform school because I am so bad. But I go to the Mother [Superior] and I cry and I cry! I just make the tears, and I say, "Oh, please. I be good. I promise, if you don't do this to me." She cannot stand to see Lupe cry so I just have to write a thousand times more, "I must be good!" The girls all run up and say, "How it feels to run away?" They are too dumb to try it, but they want to know all about it when someone else almost goes to the reform school to do it" ["Senorita Cyclone," *Screen Secrets*, No. 49, April 1929].

The convent ledgers show that the girls were enrolled in January of 1923. Lupe was fourteen. Josephine was sixteen. Their classes began in February and continued through March. There is no record of the girls being at the convent between April and August. Summer vacation would normally begin in June, and the new school year would begin some time in September. The records indicate they *were* both back for the start of the 1923–24 school year in

September. It appears their attendance in February and March of 1923 was to evaluate their level of education to date. They could then be properly placed in the appropriate grade levels to suit their individual ability.

Despite Lupe's age, she was placed in grade *four*, a class that would ordinarily be attended by nine- and ten-year-old children. This is certainly not an indication of her slow development. The language barrier would be the primary reason for this placement. However, one has to also remember society's

**A rare early photograph of Lupe (right), her sister Josephine and an unidentified man. It was taken in San Antonio, Texas, around 1923, while the sisters were being schooled at Our Lady of the Lake convent.**

mindset during this period of time. During the early part of the twentieth century, a girl from a conservative Mexican family was taught basic reading and writing skills, at elementary school standard, along with more domestic-oriented skills (typing, cooking, sewing, etc.), for her expected life's work as a wife and mother. A higher education than sixth grade was not considered necessary.

Despite Lupe's constant shenanigans, the convent ledger shows that, academically, she did very well. She earned a grade average of 87 for the year. Josephine was the good girl, but ironically she did not fare as well academically. Her grade average was a mere 55. If the girls returned to the convent, it was noted that Josephine was required to repeat the year. Lupe was promoted to grade five.

The more rules there were to follow, the more rules there were for Lupe to break. She enjoyed taunting the nuns with her verses about birds and bees and flowers and she wasn't beyond blurting a "razzberry" or two when they turned their backs either. The younger girls would laugh and snicker at Lupe's naughtiness, which only fed into Lupe's desire to perform more.

The nuns eventually relented and knew that no matter what they did to discipline her, Lupe's spirit was unbreakable. She tried her best to learn and improve upon her English, but math, typing, history and writing studies bored her. Her constant curiosity and need for new discoveries made conventional learning a humdrum task; and under the stern control of the nuns, the curriculum was uninspiring and tedious. Lupe had trouble sitting still for too long. She wanted to dance, act, sing and explore, not study. Books and classrooms were a cage. She felt suffocated and restrained. Lupe explained:

> The first I learn to hate is school. I hate it like the devil. I do not see no sense to it. Why should I sit still and listen to an old woman talk about something I cannot understand when there are frogs and snakes and mouses for Lupe to pick up and take home to scare her grandmother? I say to my sisters and my brother, "Why go to school? Come with Lupe and she show you how to be happy." Always, since I was a little baby, I think the most important thing in life is to be happy. If I have one car and I want two, why should I think about money? If two cars make Lupe more happy than money, that is all that matters. If picking up big flat stones and watching the snakes fall out of them makes me more happy than school — why not do it? Sometimes we take home fifty frogs and let them hop from one room to another.
>
> At that time we have my grandmother to keep house for us. Sometimes we have much money, sometimes we have only a little. We are like a middle-class American family. But when I am young we always have servants. My grandmother and the servants, how they hate Lupe! My grandmother, she is like a newspaper. She tells all the town what I do to her. That makes everyone know I am a devil.
>
> Some morning I think what's the use to pretend I go to school. I only start out from the house and then run away and play what you call *hooky*. So when they call me I climb out of my window and up on the roof. I stand on the edge and yell, "If you make me go to school, I jump off." If they say, "Stop that, Lupe. Come down here this minute," I slip to the edge as if I fall and they get skeered and they let me play hooky. They can never do nothing with Lupe" ["Senorita Cyclone," *Screen Secrets*, No. 48, March 1929].

Lupe's early schooling had been a battle and her stint at the convent was no different. She was in trouble more than she wasn't, but shortly after the threat of reform school from Mother Superior, she got an escape clause far more dramatic than she could have imagined.

One morning, Lupe and Josephine got word from their mother that their father was missing. In the midst of the Revolution, naturally, they were afraid that he may have been

killed. Lupe's mother had sent $350 (approximately $4,500 in 2011) to relatives in San Antonio to give to Lupe and her sister for their passage home. Instead, Lupe took all the money and spent it on a dozen pairs of silk stockings, slippers with high heels, and silk dresses like rainbows. She had not a penny left, but she looked beautiful. Yet, she still had to get home. But how?

She went to the Mexican Consul and said there was no money to keep her in school and she had to get home. She told them they *must* help her get home to her family. As usual, Lupe was very convincing. The Consulate paid. Lupe played the ukulele on the train home, buying the instrument with the money her mother had sent for travel. She also danced the hula, the Charleston and the shimmy for the other passengers. She had bought oil paintings for her mother but sold them on the train to get some extra money before reaching Mexico. Lupe said:

> My father is gone for six months. He is missing. They do not know if he is killed or what is happened. Mexico is very bad. We take a train which is shot at all the way to our home. My sister, Josephine, is to take care of me. One day she cannot find me. For three hours she go through the train sobbing and crying, "Has anyone seen my baby sister, Lupe?" No one has seen me; no one can find me. I am up in the front driving the big machine. I crawl up over all the coal and I say to the machine mans, "Can I get in your machine?" He say, "No! Girls cannot come here." Then I act like a little girl and I cry and wrinkles my eyes at him and say, "Why not?" like I am a baby.
>
> He laughs and pulls me in beside him and I help drive the machine for him. I flirts with him like I flirts with all mens and he wants me to stay up there with him. The bullets come all around us but they never hit Lupe. I am not afraid. I live with the bullets since I am a baby. The wind blows and we go fast and I forget I am living. I like that. I like to go fast, especially when I have a nice mans with me. When I get tired I crawls back and finds the whole train hunting for me. I laugh. It is so funny. I am all black with the coal but they cannot see it is funny. It is so hard for some peoples to see what is funny ["Senorita Cyclone," *Screen Secrets*, No. 49, April 1929].

Lupe knew that Mexico was in turmoil, but she didn't actually grasp the reality or seriousness of the times until she got off the train. Her mother was nowhere to be seen. Some people who were on the train gave Lupe and Josephine a ride home. Lupe told reporter Gladys Hall that they were the same people who told her she could sing and dance "very well" on the train. She said they were the first people in her life to tell her that she was good at something. And, without ever knowing their names, she long remembered their faces and the proud feeling that swelled in her by knowing she pleased them with her performance. She publicly thanked them for their compliments many years later.

When Lupe arrived at her home, she said there was a "big, black crepe thing" on the front door. Her grandmother opened the door and, when the old woman set eyes on little Lupe, she began to cry. Fearing the worst, Lupe ran into the living room. There her mother, sisters and brother sat in silence. Everywhere, her mother was "sewing on black things." Lupe stood and scanned the room that once looked so beautiful. The velvet and lace curtains — gone. The piano — gone. Candles were lighting the room. Lupe instantly thought the worst: that her father was dead.

"They sit there like mutes," Lupe said. She screamed at them to say something — anything. They sighed and cried that her father has "gone away" and they didn't know where he was — and that they were broke (Gladys Hall Papers, the Margaret Herrick Library, and "Senorita Cyclone," *Screen Secrets*, No. 49, April 1929).

The other family members never thought of going out to work. Their pride got in the

way of even considering that option. With the few dollars left from the money that Lupe got from selling the paintings on the train, they bought food. Lupe sat down and told everyone that with no money left, they *all* must look for work. Her sisters wailed and moaned at the very thought of work. They told Lupe their engagements would be broken if they "disgraced themselves" by working outside the home for money. Lupe retaliated by saying if their men loved them so much, why don't they bring them something to eat? Her sisters cried again and complained to their mother that Lupe was home less than an hour and already starting trouble. Their mother barely spoke, silently gathering newspapers to cover the windows, Lupe had come to the conclusion that the family would rather hole themselves up and die together than to fight to live. Lupe refused to give up (*Pittsburgh Press,* untitled article, December 1929).

The only member of the family who stood with Lupe and agreed with her positive plan of action was her grandmother. Her father was missing and, despite still not having official confirmation that he was dead, the family had him dead and gone. Even worse, they were all ready to die, too.

# 4

## *Time to Grow Up*

"I made up my mind to earn a living and support my family. Instead of getting a modest job and earn four or six pesos a day, I thought of a theatrical career that would give me more money."[1]— Lupe Vélez

The Revolution had taken its toll on the Villalobos fortune. Until Lupe found success as a Hollywood actress, the family's ease of living was affected dramatically. But Lupe's determination to succeed and her decision to share her financial rewards when she *did* succeed ensured that her family lived in comfort and without financial burden for the rest of their lives.

For years, Lupe knew she could sing and dance. Applying for a job in the theater was the most sensible option to make fast money, but by her own admission, Lupe said that if her father were alive he would chop her head off for the very thought. Looking at her family in disgust as they wallowed and wailed in self-pity, Lupe paced the floor, thinking of what to do next. She had an idea. But before she left the house, she gave her family something to think about. She said if their tears would bring their father back, they should go ahead and cry their heads off, but they won't, so they should stop crying and start thinking about ways to survive.

With a theater career forbidden, at least for the time being, just prior to her sixteenth birthday Lupe got a job as a salesgirl at FAL Outfitters, a department store. Dressed in a pretty dress, she smiled sweetly at the owner and told him the whole story of her family's misfortune. She said she spoke very good Americano and because of this, she could be a big help with the Americano trade. The owner frowned for a moment, and then it suddenly dawned on him as to how he knew Lupe. "My God!" he said. "You are that tiny little brat, but it is not a bad idea you have.... I will do this because of my friendship with your father." She worked in the shoe department, in the perfumery, all over the store. She was the salesgirl, the merchandising assistant, a bit of everything. Lupe dreamed of one day owning the most expensive items that she saw in the store. At that time in her life, she thought pretty things brought ever-lasting happiness. Her starting salary was three pesos a day, then roughly equivalent to one American dollar. Lupe turned most of the money over to her mother for food and utilities (The Gladys Hall Papers, the Margaret Herrick Library).

Thanks to Lupe, the family was getting by, but another blow out of nowhere was about to change everything all over again. At 4 A.M. one morning, Lupe woke to gunfire. There were soldiers outside the family home. The government had confiscated the house. The family went to a hotel and the manager gave them two rooms in the back of the establishment. Lupe continued to work in the department store. One of her sisters got a job in a

music store playing the piano, but she didn't last long. The living quarters were tiny and cramped. They were thrown together into two stuffy rooms, with only Lupe's salary to support them all. One evening, a fed-up Lupe told her sisters to get married and leave — immediately! They were all engaged. It was time for their husbands to support them, *not* their sister. Lupe's young brother stayed in school, with the threat that if he didn't continue his education, she'd personally beat the schoolhouse into him. He knew her threat was real. He stayed in school.

For many years, Lupe's favorite pastime was to go to the local theater to watch the actresses on the stage. There she sat, comparing herself to them, convincing herself that she could do better. She followed the same routine for months. She'd work at the department store, then it was straight to the theater. It was a much-needed mental escape before going home for dinner. When she was younger she snuck backstage, but now that she was older and earning enough money to buy a ticket, she sat down as a paying audience member and watched the show from the front, just as it was meant to be seen.

Lupe knew she needed to do something more than work in a department store to get the family back on their feet. While they were getting by on her small wage, it wasn't enough to live comfortably. Forbidden or not, it was time to get paid for something she'd been doing her whole life — performing! It was the only ticket to a better life — for her — for *everyone*.

At the same time, Lupe and Mil-a-tone had rekindled their forbidden relationship and they had now taken things one step further: They were engaged! Lupe said that when she first met Mil-a-tone, he had no money, but after Lupe's family lost their fortune, both Lupe and Mil-a-tone were equally poor. Regardless, they were blissfully happy in their unified poverty. Lupe said:

> We have such good times when we are poor together. [Mil-a-tone] say to me, "When we get one thousand pesos together, we will marry and have a little home and many children." Then he find oil. He get very rich. Bah! Money does not make people happy. That's why Lupe never care much if she save money....
>
> When I first come back from the convent I have a birthday. We are very poor. I want so much a silk dress, what you call it, the silk that stand up like paper? Taffeta! All the girls in Mexico City wears taffeta with ruffles and little ribbons on it. Mil-a-tone, he go to a store and get the taffeta and take it to a dressmaker. He pay the store one dollar a week and he pay the dressmaker one dollar. I never am so happy. That night I go to bed with my hair turned up in papers. I think I will die because I am so happy and can wear the next day my new dress which Mil-a-tone get me! He steal two roses for me from a man's garden. I put them in my hair, put on my new dress, and go out all day with Mil-a-tone. He think I am beautiful; we think we will always be happy — ah, there will never be another birthday like when I am sixteen for Lupe ... ["Senorita Cyclone," *Screen Secrets*, No. 50, May 1929].

*   *   *

While Lupe had always been a natural-born performer, she had never performed on a stage, in a real theater. She said:

> One night when Mil-a-tone begins to have a little more money he take me to the Principal Theatre to see María Conesa. I look at her and say, "She is an old woman. I can do better than her!"
>
> "You do not know what you say!" Mil-a-tone tell me. "What can you do? When you see all these people you will be skeered to death!"
>
> When anyone have say to Lupe, "You cannot do!" it is like when they wave a red flag before the eyes of a bull to get the bull started ["Senorita Cyclone," *Screen Secrets*, No. 50, May 1929].

Lupe felt ready to apply for a job at the theater. She *had* to be ready. Her family relied on her to be. Her father was still missing; presumed dead.[2] One evening, Lupe told her mother that she had just come from the theater and that she going to be a big star and have diamonds and lots of servants and furs. They argued until 3 A.M., her mother wailing, "God help you, Lupe, you went to the theatre.... [W]hen *my* father died I didn't smile for two years..." (*Pittsburgh Press*, untitled article, December 1929).

Along with her doubting mother, who often told Lupe that she had no talent, Mil-a-tone was skeptical of her ability to take the stage, too. And after hearing Lupe scowl at the so-called talent of the revered María Consea, her sisters said, "[I]f you are so good, why don't you?" Everyone doubted Lupe's ability, except Lupe ... and her grandmother. "[S]he got more guts than we have," the old woman cried. "God help and protect her!" (Gladys Hall Papers, the Margaret Herrick Library).

The following day, Lupe dragged her mother to the theater. Her sisters came too. It was hard to tell if they wanted to witness her success or her failure. Either way, they were excited and anxious to see how the afternoon would play out. Dressed in the clothes that Lupe had bought in San Antonio with the money that was originally sent for her passage home, Lupe carried her little ukulele and everyone carried a card with a black border, for the father they thought dead. (They used this "sympathy card" for as long as they could. After all, they weren't *really* lying; they just didn't know the truth.) As soon as Lupe set eyes on the stage manager, she boldly told him she wanted to be in his show. Looking her up and down, he asked her if she could dance. Lupe nodded positively. "Fine," he said, "I shall put you in the chorus." He turned to walk away. Lupe screamed loud enough to stop him cold in his tracks.

"The chorus—*no*! I won't go in the chorus!" she yelled defiantly. She told him she was as good as anyone on his stage. Better than the stars he had. "I will be a star and sing and dance alone!" she cried. The manager was less than convinced. Lupe then jumped on the stage and sang an American jazz song. It was the first song of its type he had ever heard and he liked it. "You are right," the manager said casually, "the chorus is not for you." She was hired at 15 pesos a day. She would dance and sing a solo number, and, *if* the audience liked her, she could stay. If they didn't, she was done for. Whether her moment in the spotlight lasted for one day, or forever, at that very moment Lupe Vélez had officially become a paid performer. Her dream was realized ("Senorita Cyclone," *Screen Secrets*, No. 49, April 1929).

The manager told Lupe that he would contact her soon. The unconventional audition was over as quickly as it began. In shock, the women hurried out of the theater and headed for home. They all went from not talking at all, to all talking at the same time, then back to stunned silence as they collectively tried to absorb the excitement of what had just happened. Then, all at the same time, they asked the same question of each other. Did Lupe really just get a job — in the *theater*? The answer was *yes*! (*Appleton Post-Crescent*, September, no date, 1930).

Lupe did her best to get her head out of the clouds and on with her daily routine. She went back to working in the department store but, not surprisingly, her anticipation about being on the stage clouded everything that she did. As each day passed without hearing a word from the stage manager, her excitement and confidence waned. Every night Lupe would wash and dry her one pair of silk stockings on the window ledge, just in case she was called to work at the theater the following day. With each wash, they got shorter. Before long, they looked more like socks than stockings.

A week passed, and Lupe's patience was wearing thin. There was still no word from the stage manager. Then one morning Lupe was traveling by bus to the store, despondent

and sleepy, she looked up at the theater as the bus passed by. No matter how tired she was, each and every morning she would instinctively perk up as the bus passed by the theater. And on this particular morning, she could hardly believe her eyes: There on the billboard was *her* name! An announcement of her professional theater debut, it said: **Lupe Vélez, daughter of the unforgettable singer, Josefina Vélez!**

Lupe got off the bus immediately. Trembling, she ran all the way home. Everyone was still sleeping but her screams woke up her entire family. "My name! My name!" she kept shouting. In all the excitement, no one thought to get dressed; they just followed Lupe out the front door in their nightgowns and pajamas. Down the street they ran, three blocks, Lupe leading the whole way, eager for her family to see her name on the theater marquee. "I'm famous!" she beamed. Lupe's mother stood there without a word. Staring at the sign, she finally opened her mouth and said, "I knew some day *my name* would carry on!" (Gladys Hall Papers, the Margaret Herrick Library).

For the first time in a long time, instead of being scolded, Lupe was smiled upon. Her mother's attitude had now turned around completely. Josefina even accompanied Lupe to the theater on the afternoon she was to perform. Despite her initial misgivings about her daughter's theater career, she was no stranger to the world of show business herself. She had left that life years before, but it's been widely reported that she was one of Mexico's most notable opera singers. However, her *other* rumored profession dates back much further than performing on stage: Several biographies claim Lupe's mother's profession was the oldest one in the book — a prostitute!

Again, talk of both "professions" made for a good story. She *did* work in the entertainment field, but only when she was very young, before her marriage to Jacobo. The theater chronology published by *Arte e Historia de México* quotes a note dated January 27, 1901, about the successful tour of the Austri-Palacios theatrical company "whose stars are Columba Quintana, Sofía Haller and Josefina Vélez." At the time, Esperanza Iris was also part of the company (she later became one of the most famous Mexican stage players of all time). While the "notable opera singer" tag was a harmless embellishment of the truth, the prostitution story was a blatant lie.

Lupe's second cousin, Pedro Quintanilla Gómez-Noriega, sets the record straight:

> Prior to her marriage, Josefina Vélez was not a "notable opera singer," much less a prostitute! Josefina belonged to a very good family in San Luis Potosí. She was a die-hard Catholic, so much so that she attended mass daily, as was the custom of many if not most married women of that era. She would be absolutely appalled and disgusted to know that the rumor circulating her is that she was a prostitute. She would die all over! She was devoted to her children and her household, and to putting up with Jacobo, her husband, who indeed was a philanderer and a rebel, and *very* unlike his own father. Lupe's paternal grandfather was a prominent and well-respected attorney.

This prostitution myth came from Budd Schulberg's memoirs *Moving Pictures* (1981). It turns out to be a piece of hearsay that Budd recalls was told to him by his father, pioneer studio mogul, B.P. Schulberg, after talking with someone on a train. He wrote:

> Lupe's mother had been a walker of the streets.... Lupe herself had made her theatrical debut In the raunchy burlesque houses of the city. Stage door Juanitos panted for her favors and Mama Vélez would sell her for the evening to the highest bidder. [Lupe's] prices soared to thousands of pesos....

So according to this source, Lupe's mother was not only a whore, she also pimped out her teenage daughter to the highest bidder. This ridiculous story has taken on a life of its own,

and to this day, it is often quoted as truth. But, there *is* finally an explanation as to where the confusion stems from. Lupe's father Jacobo was married three times. He left Lupe's mother *for* a prostitute. Lupe's mother *wasn't* one.

In early 1937, noted Mexican theater journalist Jorge Loyo[3] published two very informative articles in *El Universal Ilustrado* (January 11, 1937, and January 18, 1937). Loyo stated he decided to write them to tell the truth about Lupe's early artistic career days after he had read several American articles claiming that she started performing at low-end nightclubs. He described the theatrical environment in Mexico in 1925. Back then, the Ba-Ta-Clan Vaudeville of Paris, under a Madame Rasimi, had an extremely successful season in Mexico. Loyo said Mme. Rasimi showed Mexicans that "a woman would look more elegant when she wears a feather fan [to cover essential parts of her anatomy] than when she dons a grapevine leaf." All in all, the Ba-Ta-Clan was a hit, and soon several Mexican vaudeville impresarios and playwrights began to imitate its trends. One of the most successful imitations was a parody called "Rataplán Mexicano," presented at the Teatro Lírico. The scandalous show was also taken to the Teatro de la Paz, where the ambiance was favorable for risqué shows.

On Lupe's first official night at the theater, she was a bundle of nerves. It was one thing to sing and dance on a train, or on the roof of her home in front of family, servants and the local boys who adored her; it was another thing entirely to perform in a professional theater for a paying crowd. This night was much different. It would make or break her. Either way, good or bad, this night would change her life and her family's life forever. Lupe said, "Everybody else in the theatre is mad [that she got a job so easily]. María Conesa, who is the star, make fun at me. She say it is all right to fool the boss but I cannot fool the public..." ("Senorita Cyclone," *Screen Secrets*, No. 49, April 1929).

Prior to Lupe's debut, the other performers schemed to sabotage her. While Lupe's debut had been well planned by the theater, out of nowhere, an official order was issued by the Actors' Guild to ban Lupe from performing. The reason given was that Lupe first had to prove herself a first-rate actress-performer, climbing the steps of the promotional ladder, as all other performers did. Clearly the decision was corrupt. The Guild's sabotage was a malicious attempt to prevent Lupe, who was seen as a serious theatrical threat to the other noted performers (and Guild members), from showcasing her talents on a professional level. Protests by the impresarios and Lupe herself fell on deaf ears; neither the support of journalists nor that of influential writers did any good.

And so, for the time being, Lupe was forbidden to perform. She could not make her debut on the night that was originally planned ... at least not on stage. After all, no one had banned her from the audience, and it was from her seat that she made her "unofficial theatrical debut." Before the show started, Lupe bravely stood up from her seat in the stalls, introduced herself and proceeded to tell the crowded theater why she wasn't on the stage. She then asked the crowd for their support. The applause was thunderous.

On the following day, several newspapers reported that the Actors' Guild was being targeted for random attacks. These threats of violent protests, all in support of Lupe Vélez, a performer who'd never even professionally "performed," caused the Guild's general secretary Eduardo Pastor to capitulate. Much to the dismay of the performers who almost succeeded in banning Lupe from taking the stage, her theater debut was once again announced. Only this time, she was more anticipated than before. Ironically, as a result of the publicity, Lupe's jealous peers had helped her beyond measure. Theater seats were sold out three days before her debut (*Y se levanta el telón: mi vida dentro del teatro,* Pablo Prida Santacilia, México, 1960, 1st edition).

According to Lupe, all theatrical performers were required to bring their own wardrobe.[4] Lupe tried to borrow some money from the show's producer to buy some clothes, but he declined, saying that the theater had already spent far too much on her promotion. The family were still barely getting by, so there wasn't enough spare cash for new day clothes, let alone a stage-worthy theater costume. Rummaging through her mother's clothing, Lupe found a satin, orange evening gown, her mother's wedding nightgown and a beautiful sequined hat with a big ostrich feather. Lupe's mother and sisters stayed up until 4 A.M. making new costumes out of old clothes. They transformed the evening gown into a top and the wedding nightgown into fancy pants with lace. Lupe said her mother was the happiest she had ever seen her. Lupe's sisters even hocked their engagement rings to buy her a new pair of shoes.

As Lupe waited backstage to go on, the long white feather on her hat shook violently, even when she was standing still. It shook because Lupe shook too. "You must not be afraid, Lupe," said her mother. "You are singing American songs. No one knows the words. If you forget, just say 'la de da' and no one will be the wiser" (*Photoplay*, undated 1931). Lupe's mother got her out of her catatonic stupor. She told her that an audience is nothing more than a child that you have to amuse.

Years later, Lupe was still able to feel the butterflies from those early theater days. She remembered those fifteen minutes spent backstage, waiting to go on for the very first time, as the most "living-in-hell" minutes of her life. Because Lupe's stockings were ruined from over-washing, she had no choice but to take the stage barelegged, and without realizing it, she made history. Lupe Vélez was the first woman to appear on the Mexican stage with "nude legs" (The Gladys Hall Papers, the Margaret Herrick Library). She said:

> Every seat in the theatre is sold out on the night I opens. My knees shake when I stand outside waiting to go in but I look at María Conesa and I stick out my tongue at her and I run on the stage and throw out my arms and say, "Hello, everybody!' How is you?" ["Senorita Cyclone," *Screen Secrets*, No. 49, April 1929].

Lupe had begged Mil-a-tone not to show up on opening night. She told him she would see his eyes and lose concentration, but he defied her wishes. There he sat, front row — center. Lupe was furious. Her anger drove her determination. She would *have* to put on a great show, even more so now. She felt sick at the thought of failing, not at the thought of performing.

The music peaked and Lupe was hustled onto the stage. The showgirls wished her luck as she left the safety of the wings. She took the stage holding her trusty ukulele; she wanted to begin by playing a song she was good at. But as soon as she started to play, a string broke. It was time to improvise, so Lupe did the next best thing she was good at. She danced. In fact, she shimmied her heart out. She shook all over, out of fear, out of excitement. Her hands, her arms, her legs, her feet — everything shook. She sang and danced and she *did* forget the words sometimes. But, she "la de da-ed" her way through "Charlie, My Boy," just as her mother had told her to do. When it was all over, she stood and waited (*Photoplay*, February 1929).

A moment of silence turned into screams and whistles, stomping of feet and shouts of approval from the excited audience. Lupe danced and sang again, and again, and again. The audience demanded that she continue. They threw hats and furs and gloves and purses onto the stage in appreciation. The fear of the other stage stars had been realized, Lupe Vélez became Mexico's favorite new entertainer. She said:

Do they like me? They go crazy. They throw their hats on the stage. They yell; they shout; they whistle; they call, "Hurrah for Lupe." But the actresses, they are all-jealous and say many mean things like a cat that I have to get even with them. I put on acts and I imitate all the other actresses in Mexico City. That is the way I get really famous — my imitations! ["Senorita Cyclone," *Screen Secrets*, No. 49, April 1929].

In 1925, the magazine *Revista de Revistas* published an article by Arturo Rigel, and in it he posed the question on everyone's lips:

Do we have the Mexican artist of 1925 in the person of Lupe Vélez? Who is she? A little girl without any theatrical antecedents, who from the moment of her debut revealed an exhilarating temperament and conquered the sympathies and enthusiasms of her audience.

Xavier Sorondo wrote (February 1928) that Lupe would move her hips in such a frenzied way when performing on stage, she "got ill" every three to four months, and had to leave the stage for a week at a time to recuperate. Mexican audiences were mixed in their appreciation of certain entertainers in those days. Times were changing and the battle of tradition vs. transformation was strong. Lupe's feud with María Conesa aside, she also endured a well-publicized professional rivalry with another theater star of that time, Delia Magaña.

Delia was another Mexican beauty who was signed to a Hollywood contract some years down the line. However, in 1925, Lupe and Delia were both darlings of the Mexican stage, and both had shows in the same theater. Delia sang Mexican traditional songs, while Lupe danced and sang to the rhythm of jazz and fox trot. There was intense jealousy and bad blood between them from the very beginning; even the audiences took the side of one girl or the other. The conservatives who loved Mexican traditions and folklore went for Delia. The ones that went for modernity and the U.S. way of life preferred Lupe.

Mil-a-tone did not take kindly to Lupe's newfound success. So much so, he came to the theater one night, furious, and demanded that she give it all up — for *him*. He told her she must walk out with him — now! He told her she must never return to the theater and never give the idea of performing another thought. No girl of his would be seen kicking her legs suggestively for other men. Mil-a-tone now had the money to support Lupe with every luxury and he wanted to marry her. But he also wanted to possess her. As much as she loved Mil-a-tone, Lupe knew she'd miss the adulation and applause of the crowds. She couldn't give it up, not for him — not for anyone! There would be other men, but she knew there'd never be another chance if she gave up her career now. Lupe explained:

Mexican men are different from mens in America. They are more jealous. They want when they love a womans, for no one else to see her. Mil-a-tone is getting more and more money [from the oil]. He knows he can give me things.

"The theatre or me!" is what he say to me.

I must make up my mind. I think there is always a time in the life of a womans when she must make up her mind what is going to make her most happy. Every night all the people clap and yell and cheer Lupe. I love it. I love to hear them. I love to act and sing and make them happy. Every night I look into the eyes of Mil-a-tone. I love him. What am I to do about it?

Then I say, "No! I will not leave my career for anybody" ["Senorita Cyclone," *Screen Secrets*, No. 50, May 1929].

Mil-a-tone was history. He would be the first of many men left in Lupe's wake. There were other fleeting crushes before him, and there were other flirtations and great loves after him, but he was Lupe's first serious romance.

# 5

## Hollywood's Hard Knocks

"Hollywood is like heaven but I do not think Lupe Vélez is big enough for heaven!"[1] — Lupe Vélez (1927)

In his *El Universal Ilustrado* articles (January 11, 1937, and January 18, 1937), Jorge Loyo wrote, "When Lupe sang 'Charlie, My Boy,' the traffic stopped. She would dance, and many a gentleman's blood pressure rose." Loyo said the only song Lupe would sing was "Charlie, My Boy" and she did it seven or eight times a night. Jealous fellow performers began to call her "La Charlie My Boy." She wore a two-piece costume, embroidered with faux pearls and crystals. Her headdress had colored feathers.

Loyo asked Óscar Leblanc (pen name of journalist Demetrio Bolaños Espinosa) what he remembered of Lupe Vélez. He answered, "She was the most attractive woman that walked Madero Avenue." (Madero Avenue [Avenida Madero], located in downtown Mexico City, was like a Mexican Rue de Rivoli.) Leblanc said that Lupe began to confide her little secrets in him. He didn't know why. But she was entertaining to listen to and, like most men in Lupe's company, he couldn't help but listen. She told him about two of her boyfriends. One was called Jorge and she said they broke up, because of a silly quarrel. The other was Benjamín, who made Lupe mend his socks. Surprisingly, there was no mention of Mil-a-tone. Leblanc recalled a conversation he had with Lupe:

LUPE: You do not know how much I have been through....
ÓSCAR: Much?
LUPE: A lot!
ÓSCAR: How old are you?
LUPE: Seventeen.
ÓSCAR: I see.

Leblanc had a talent for writing lyrics, so Lupe invited him to her home to listen to some U.S. music she had bought and to see if he could write lyrics in Spanish for them. She had a Pianola at home. Loyo remembered the three-story house at 105 Sonora Street, where Lupe and her family were living in 1925. It consisted of nine rooms, a bathroom, kitchen and a garage. Lupe's grandmother lived with the family.

Loyo recalled that Lupe's mother Josefina was a woman "of aristocratic beauty and artistic temperament" who made her theatrical debut at age twelve, as a singer with the famous theatrical child company Austri-Palacios. Young Josefina reportedly was "a charming kid, with great temperament and an extremely beautiful voice." Some time later, she was on tour in Monterrey, the third largest city in northeastern Mexico, and there she met Jacobo Villalobos, then a factory employee at the famous Cuauhétmoc Brewery. Jacobo and Josefina fell

in love and she relinquished her theatrical career for him. At that time in Mexico a woman could not have marriage *and* a career in the theater. It was one or the other. Lupe chose her career and left her man behind. Her mother chose her man and left her career behind.

Lupe's parents established themselves in San Luis Potosí, raising their growing family in the region. They opened their own business, an eatery called Café Royal. As a child, Lupe would happily run between unoccupied tables, all laughs and mischief. Her amused father nicknamed her "Polvorilla," meaning "a live wire, of short temper" (http://rinconar. blogspot.com). When the Revolution began, Jacobo joined the movement.

\* \* \*

In Mexico, circa 1925 (and much later), plump women were very much in fashion. They were considered voluptuous and beautiful. Skinny women were looked upon as ugly, scrawny and undernourished. (In fact, various tonics for "gaining weight" were advertised in newspapers and magazines across the country.) Lupe was skinny and small-breasted, but she was still described as having a "good figure." Her slight frame certainly didn't hamper her popularity with male theatergoers but pre-fame, as a gangly teenager, boys weren't interested; in fact, some of them were downright mean. Lupe said in a 1937 *El Universal Ilustrado*:

> One day, I went for a walk with two good-looking classmates. We met some young men, who invited us for a ride out of the city, and I'd rather do not tell what happened! Only they saw me so skinny and ugly that they made me get off the car. I had to walk all the way back to San Antonio.

Within his article, Loyo also remembered Lupe's siblings, though he could not recall the name of the older sister (Mercedes). He said that Luisa (aka Reina) was kind, beautiful, talented and romantic, with an enormous enthusiasm for the stage; however, her sweet character never let her succeed. He wrote that Josefina "was unapproachable and disdainful; on the other side, energetic, versatile, an excellent 'segunda tiple'" (second singer).

In his January 18, 1937, *El Universal Ilustrado* article, Loyo asked fellow journalist Carlos Ortega how he felt when he first saw Lupe perform. He said that she was the siren of those nights when she appeared on stage. He said he felt "dazzled" in seeing her perform eighteen dance numbers in a row, applauded by those who considered her "a siren and a vampire.... Lupe's body, in its frantic dancing, exuded an obscure and perverse sensuality..." Even in her youth, Lupe was hypnotically alluring. And she knew it and used it to her advantage. It was said that Lupe made a "cocktail" of U.S. songs and sexually charged dances that had the same effect as champagne on the spectators.

In contrast, Loyo said that he wished he could have seen Lupe with the innocent eyes of a spectator, *not* as a journalist. His job as a reporter gave him a look behind the scenes and he was privy to information that audiences were oblivious to. He knew Lupe was starving back then. Lupe came onto the stage to show her sex appeal, with nothing in her stomach. He said Lupe would improvise her dance steps, sometimes with extraordinary results. One other occasion, she used her creativity to earn applause. Loyo concluded with a somewhat prophetic statement: "[Lupe] was neurotic and mestiza[2] ... is there a more dangerous cocktail?"

Night after night, Lupe charmed audiences with risqué songs and dance numbers. While she had a limited vocal range, she was not expected to have a great voice. Her naughty ways and attitudes more than made up for her weaknesses. Her opening line to Óscar Leblanc ("You do not know how much I have been through...") was no dramatic embellishment. At seventeen years old, compared to most girls her age, she was right. But, com-

pared to where she was about to go, who she would become and what her fate would ultimately be, realistically, she could have used that same line right up until the night she died and it *still* would have been a relevant quote.

At her peak, Lupe was earning 35 pesos a day. At the time, it was the highest salary of any performer in Mexico. After a year and a half, she felt she deserved a raise. The manager refused. She left the revue. Throughout her career, Lupe always knew her worth. She wasn't afraid to ask for something more and if she didn't get it, she'd walk away.

As much as her feisty attitude helped to get her into the Teatro Principal, it also helped to get her ousted from the Teatro Principal.[3] After three months of non-stop work in front of packed theaters, Lupe was furious about her firing and she threw a fit. Not long after Lupe's departure, the Teatro Principal saw a sharp decline in their box office takings. Audiences demanded her return. However, the Teatro Lírico got to her first. She was offered a higher salary, plus a "beneficio."[4]

Little Lupe was a big problem for her impresario, the orchestra director, the stage director, and so on. The sharp replies she gave to any observation were a pain in the neck for those seasoned theater people. For the first time, the orchestra director was incapable of determining if Lupe was to follow the orchestra or if it should be the other way around. When her show was due to begin, she would not even condescend to take a look at the man with the baton. Both her disobedience and her success brought her many enemies, mainly among the female element, but she felt compensated by the popularity she enjoyed among men. She was known for her mischief, for her lack of fear in any situation, as well as for her ingenuity (Don Alvarado, "Rasgos de Lupe," *La Prensa*, May 12, 1935).

A perfect example was a show in Mexico that she was to do for a producer named Mr. Campillo who offered Lupe a staggering 100 pesos a day. She translated the song "Rose Marie" from English to Spanish and practiced for two weeks. This would be the featured number. Two days before the show was to open, Lupe entered the theater and found Emma Duvall singing *her* songs. Mr. Campillo had a crush on Duvall and gave Lupe's songs to her. Lupe, furious, refused to open the show. Mr. Campillo told her she would most definitely open the show. Lupe stormed off the stage and went into her dressing room where in a fit of rage she punched the window. She walked back out onto the stage, dripping with blood. Campillo was so shocked and so angry, he ran toward her, tripped on his shoelace and gave himself a concussion. The show flopped and the Union got together to blame Lupe for its failure. She was blackballed.

At first, Lupe didn't care. She had money in the bank and for two months, she and her family continued to live richly. And then they were broke again. They took a tiny apartment. The jewelry, the car, the sewing machine — all were hocked. The newspapermen and women all loved Lupe. So much so, that on Saturday nights, their pay day, they would all pitch in and take Lupe downtown to buy chicken and wine for the family. They even bought her a cheap car to ride around in. One night when she was really desperate, she looked to the sky and said, "Why can't I find someone who wants to marry me with millions?!" Not more than a day after, Lupe received delivery of five dozen orchids. The flowers were delivered every day, without so much as a note. The butcher wouldn't give the family any more meat, the grocer was done giving them bread, they were starving, but Lupe was getting orchids from a secret admirer. The moment she got them, she'd run down to the nearest florist and sell them for half price. The family came to rely on the delivery of those anonymously sent flowers.

One day, after the daily flower delivery, the doorbell rang again. Thinking it was a bill

collector, Lupe and her family ran to the corners of the room to hide and to wait for whomever it was to go away. The doorbell rang and rang. Finally Lupe told her mother and Nana Tomasa (the live-in nanny who had stayed with the family despite tough times) to answer it. She cried that she owed so much that it *must* be the police. They were going to take her to jail for being in so much debt. "Ohhh, get it over with!" Lupe sobbed. "Open the door." Three men stood at the front door. They were from "La Esmeralda," a famous jewelry store in Mexico City, commonly referred to as "Tiffany & Co. of the south." Lupe's mother immediately thought Lupe had bought something from the store and they had now come to collect their money. But they had not come to collect, they had come to deliver. Curious, Lupe peeped around the corner but refused to sign for it. She was convinced it was a trick. Her sisters whispered, "We can hock it." So, she nervously signed for the pretty box, opened it within seconds and stared open-mouthed at a spectacular diamond bracelet worth about $3,000 (approximately $35,000 in 2011). The bracelet was hocked within half an hour (unidentified magazine clipping, circa 1933).

Giving up such a beautiful, expensive piece of jewelry was necessary, but heartbreaking. It appears this incident was the catalyst for Lupe's later bracelet obsession. When she had the money to buy as much jewelry as she desired, bracelets were her number one choice and she sometimes wore six to eight of them on one arm at a time.

Lupe called the newspapers to tell them the story. She had found a note with the bracelet; it had come from an American millionaire, a colonel, who wrote that he did not wish to insult her with such a gift, but it was the only way he knew how to express his admiration. He asked Lupe's mother's permission to call on them. Lupe's mother clutched her chest dramatically and told Lupe that her wish had come true. She had prayed for a millionaire and now her daughter had miraculously found him. And he was American. Lupe loved American men and she wondered if he was tall, with blue eyes.

On the day he came to call, Lupe, her mother and her sisters cleaned the house like it had never been cleaned before. The newspaper reporters came over and hid in the closets so they could hear everything that was said. Lupe's mother and grandmother dressed in the only good dresses they had left. They opened the door to receive him, and there he stood: a skinny, 6' 3½", millionaire, with a moustache like a walrus. He had brought his sister and an interpreter with him. He meant business.

He told the interpreter to tell Lupe's mother that he was very much in love with Lupe and wanted to marry her. He handed her papers with proof of his identity and offered to take care of the entire family. Lupe was finding it hard to contain her laughter. He sisters made faces at her, which only made it harder to stifle her amusement.

Directing the conversation toward Lupe's mother, the millionaire's sister made the suggestion that Lupe travel back with them to America. She could stay for six months; if she could then decide that she could love her brother and be married to him, she would then throw a big, beautiful wedding. They offered to leave $50,000 (approximately $600,000 in 2011) in the bank for Lupe's mother, as a sort of bond posted for her. Lupe's mother told the millionaire that it was not up to her to answer. It was Lupe's decision. She did, however, give the smitten gent permission to call upon Lupe between five and six each evening.

Years later, Lupe told reporter Gladys Hall that she developed the most awful hatred for him. He turned pale each time he saw Lupe. Whenever he touched her hands she would run off and wash them. She cried every day. She did not want to go. He kept sending gifts of orchids and jewels and books, but she was not happy. Still, she could not let her family starve. Two days before she was to leave with him, her bags all packed with new clothes

that his sister had bought for her, Lupe got an unexpected telegram from Cuba. She was being asked to perform in a big show and was offered 60 pesos a day. Lupe was thrilled.

Lupe's mother told the millionaire's sister that they would leave for the United States alone, that she would not sell her daughter. Under her breath, Lupe sarcastically snickered, "Not much she wouldn't!" (Gladys Hall Papers, the Margaret Herrick Library).

Following Lupe's Hollywood break and newfound fortune, she willingly shared her wealth and provided for her family in ways she, or they, never thought possible; yet, her mother's materialistic demands were a constant burden. In her 1985 book *Some Day We'll Laugh: An Autobiography*, actress Esther Ralston wrote of Lupe's frustrations with her mother's lavish taste and frequent guilt trips to get what she wanted. She wrote:

> [Lupe] launched into an impassioned recital of the troubles she was having with her mother. "No matter what I do for her," she wailed, "I cannot satisfy her."
>
> "I can't see what your mother can find to complain about, Lupe." I tried to comfort her. "You've given her a house, a mink coat, clothes, diamond bracelets, everything. What in Heaven's name is she fussing about?"
>
> "My mother, she say to me," Lupe explained, "for nine months I carry you in my body. You owe me *rent*!"

*　　*　　*

In a 1925 edition of the *El Universal Ilustrado*, a small note describing Lupe's attributes was published. It said she had "perfect teeth," her weight was 105 lbs and she had bad taste in clothes. It also said she had a natural talent for mimicry and she would imitate the voices and movements of her fellow "tiples" to purposefully annoy them. Soon after, Lupe was labeled as a "loca" (crazy) and her whimsies and jokes were commented on in all circles.

However, her popularity among the poor was the result of the sincere pleasure that Lupe took in sharing their customs and celebrations.[5] Time and again, one could find Lupe with a group of friends, very early in the morning, happily having breakfast at a local market, perhaps after a night of partying. She would willingly take a seat beside a humble worker, enjoying coffee and milk, beans, tacos, and *pan dulce* (Mexican sweet pastries). Despite her success, Lupe remained true to herself, and true to her homeland, too.

In April of 1943, writer Juan Tomás (*Cinema Reporter*) commented on Lupe's unaffected personality: "The long years Lupe has been far from her homeland do not show in her. Her expressions, her tastes, her unassuming manners, her frankness; all in her is Mexican; all in her recalls Mexico."

Lupe always had a smile and a kind phrase for each of her fans; however, her often irrational temperament was apparent from a very young age. An article in the October 2, 1925, edition of the Spanish-language newspaper *La Prensa* reported that 17-year-old Lupe had attempted suicide because she came in second place in a talent contest. There were three articles mentioning this same incident. The first got the story completely wrong, saying,

> Lupe Villalobos, better known as Lupe Vélez, popular "segunda tiple" who has been recently in the news because of her taking part in the contest "Tiple of 1925," attempted suicide today, by means of shooting herself in the temple. The wound has her in the brink of death.

This shocking news had the theater community and the loyal fans of her nightly shows in a state of turmoil. Obviously, Lupe didn't shoot herself in the temple, but she did slash herself, albeit in the company of others, so the claims of a "suicide attempt" are certainly exaggerated.

By October 3, 1925, the dramatic situation was still big news. *El Heraldo de México*, a Spanish-language newspaper published in Los Angeles, reported that Lupe took part in a

**With a strategically placed feather fan to protect her modesty, seventeen-year-old Lupe Vélez poses seductively in this pre–Hollywood photograph (circa 1925).**

talent contest sponsored by the local weekly and according to the vote count, she came in second place, behind her rival Celia Padilla (the article mistakenly calls her Celia Montalván). Lupe had a tantrum that ended in her cutting the veins in her hands at the weekly's office, because of "the injustice committed on her." The note adds that authorities were investigating the matter, to find out if any irregularities existed in the contest. It was suggested that favoritism might have had something to do with Lupe's defeat.

By November 1, 1925, *El Heraldo de México* published a follow-up article that noted that the feud between Celia Padilla and Lupe was far from over. In fact, the situation was worsening. There were accusations of defamation and attacks going both ways. Finally, Lupe reportedly presented a legal demand against Celia Padilla for harassment that appeared valid and of solid grounds. It was known by many that Celia did many spiteful things to sabotage Lupe and her burgeoning career, like paying newspaper boys 50 cents a day to shout insults at her each time they saw her.

Lupe's father (Jacobo survived the war and eventually returned home to his family) was outraged that his daughter had chosen to perform for the masses — so much so that he would not allow her to use the family name Villalobos. So she used her mother's maiden name, Vélez. Lupe's second cousin Pedro Quintanilla Gómez-Noriega said:

It was precisely because they were such a well-known family and the fact that in those days being in entertainment was viewed as appealing to the lower classes that Jacobo, Lupe's father, once he realized it was impossible to talk Lupe out of becoming a singer and actress, demanded from her that she *not* use his last name for such an appalling purpose. The words he used were, "I forbid you from staining our good name now that you are entering that disgusting environment." Those are famous words within our family and they come directly from my grandmother having been told that by Lupe's mother [her sister-in-law], Josefina Vélez. Can you imagine? I would have been proud of it as a father, but one has to understand the morals and mores of the Mexican upper class society in the 1920s.

I have always wondered how on earth Lupe's father was so shocked by Lupe being rebellious when he himself was such, having entered the Mexican army when *that* indeed was viewed upon as being attractive to the lower classes who knew no better and for whom economic options were more limited. Jacobo's family (parents and siblings) were constantly

shocked by him and his rebellious, wild, uncontrollable ways. And even though he did fight in the Mexican Revolution he did *not* die fighting.

In fact, it's clear that Lupe's spirited personality came directly from her father, Lupe's cousin continues:

[Jacobo] would often mortify his six siblings with his unruly behavior, but his mother especially. Sometimes he would play dead or run away from home for days on end, not letting her know where he went or was; then days later he'd just show up with a big smile on his face, laughing when his mortified mother realized he was finally back home and safe.

On such occasions, his well-behaved siblings hated him for doing this to their dear mother. His father sternly scolded him and grounded him, although he still always managed to escape. He was completely uncontrollable and had a very wild spirit. That is perhaps why, to the shock of everyone in his family, he decided to enter the army, an occupation which was certainly not approved by his parents not only because of the danger involved but also because it appealed only to lower classes, not to well-to-do families. Also by that time his parents had completely given up on him. What *is* surprising is the fact that he disapproved of the wild spirit of his own daughter, Lupe, when in all probability she herself inherited that emotional need to be in the spotlight from him. One of the worst things Jacobo did to his mother was at a time in his life when he was old enough to know better.

His mother was quite nearsighted and apparently the use of eyeglasses at that time was either not widespread or she did not use them much because of vanity (she was considered quite a beauty in her time). Some time while he was in his late teens, maybe early twenties, a part of a cemetery was being cleaned up, so skeletons of people who were long forgotten and thus not claimed were habitually sold to medicine schools and medical students for their activities. Since he had some friends in that community, he managed to buy a complete skeleton. He then proceeded to go home, and while no one was watching he took a dress, shoes and hat from his mother's wardrobe, dressed up the skeleton including glasses, sat it in the parlor easy chair, and when his mother was nearby, he rocked the easy chair and went to his mother, telling her a lady was in the parlor and she had asked to see her. Jacobo hid in the dining room nearby, finding a place where he could watch and hear the entire event.

His unsuspecting mother approached the parlor and she, of course, could see a foggy figure sitting on the easy chair, all dressed up, to her, a clear indication it was a lady. "Good morning, ma'am, may I help you?" she asked. The skeleton of course did not answer. She then walked a few more steps and asked again, "Good morning, ma'am, may I be of assistance?" No answer. A few more steps. Same question. No answer. Finally she came before the sitting figure and, bending over, she asked, "May I help you?" She then clearly saw the skeleton's face, gave out a loud, terrifying scream and fainted on the spot! Jacobo came out of his hiding place laughing like a maniac.

Needless to say, everyone else heard her scream and maids and other children came running to her assistance. Barely able to contain his laughter at such a practical joke, Jacobo ran away. The family doctor was summoned immediately and his mother eventually came to after some much-needed medical intervention. That was one of the occasions when Jacobo, knowing what he had done and fearing his father's retribution, stayed away from the family home for many days. Even so, when he returned his mother was in bed still recovering from the shock and Jacobo's father [Lupe's grandfather; Jacobo Villalobos-Cuadriello] grounded him for weeks with no spending money (all of the children were given money each Sunday). Of course, his house arrest made no impact at all. Jacobo always found ways to escape.

As another example, many typical grand mansions in Mexico were normally built in a square form with a patio in the middle. Jacobo used to climb to one of the four corners of the roof where his mother would see him and then he'd jump from one side to the other to make her scream and beg him to stop it, thus avoiding a possible fall. And we are talking a *long, long* way down. So much so that someone falling from that altitude would find certain death. He did that a lot when he was in his early teens.

These are just a couple of the many instances when Jacobo would show a complete lack of empathy or concern for others, including his own parents. His unruly behavior caused strained relationships with all of his siblings from a very young age. These character observations are important because it can clearly be shown that the part of his personality that refers to a free, wild spirit was most probably inherited by Lupe, and may help to explain her own character and her need to be in show business, to be known, to be famous; in short, to find her own place in the sun.

Lupe was preparing to go to Cuba when she got another unexpected wire, this time from Los Angeles. Throughout her life, her vivacious personality attracted all types of people, two of whom were Mr. and Mrs. Frank A. Woodward, an American couple. Mr. Woodward was a theatrical agent and he knew talent when he saw it. While the Woodwards can be given credit for bringing Lupe to the United States, he would later take her to court in a very messy contractual dispute that threatened to stop her from working until he was financially compensated.

Richard Bennett was a close friend of the Woodwards, a veteran of the American stage and the father of film stars Barbara, Constance and Joan Bennett. He was told of Lupe's beauty and promise. Via a telegram, Bennett wrote that he would consider her for a part in the Willard Mack play *The Dove* in which he needed to fill the role of a Mexican cantina singer. He hoped that Lupe would travel to Hollywood so he could meet her in person and discuss the role. Her salary was to be $250 a week (approximately $3,000 in 2011).

Lupe turned down the role in the Cuban revue show; after all, Hollywood was the place to be and she could barely contain her excitement at the prospects of becoming a stage star in America. Lupe did not have enough money to take her mother with her to Hollywood, so she took Mil-a-tone. Not Mil-a-tone the man. Mil-a-tone the dog! A fiesty little Chihuahua she named after the man! Lupe explained:

> That is all I have left from the mans, is the little dog which I name after him. I love that dog more than any person. He is always with me. I would die if anything happen to him. One time he got lost in Hollywood and I cry for three days and cannot work. Maybe it is because Mil-a-tone, the dog, comes to me from Mil-a-tone, the man. But — I have never tell anyone else about him — the man — and I can talk no more about him ... ["Senorita Cyclone," *Screen Secrets*, No. 50, May 1929].

When Lupe announced her intention to leave Mexico, the papers ran headlines "Lupe Vélez Goes to Hollywood!" Her departure from Mexico was a very big deal and there were many celebrations and parties to mark the occasion. The newspaper reporters were so happy for Lupe, they embellished headlines, writing that she was offered a $50,000 contract. They meant well, and the headlines got a lot of attention, but they also forgot that Lupe (and her family) still owed a lot of money — to everyone! The very morning that headline ran, there was a line of people at the house, all waiting to be paid. After all, Lupe was now rich and they'd all come to collect before she skipped the country.

The situation was out of control. There were warrants out for Lupe's arrest and a policeman was waiting for her to exit the house. She was trapped. Then, one of the crafty newspaper boys had an idea. He grabbed a baby carriage and when no one was watching he signaled to Lupe to get in. They exited out the front door, past all the people and right past the vigilant policeman. Lupe was covered with a blanket but she could hear the boy whispering breathless prayers that the wheels on the rickety carriage would hold out until he could get Lupe past the irate crowd (The Gladys Hall Papers, the Margaret Herrick Library).

The celebrations ended at the American border near Laredo, Texas. Upon her arrival at customs and immigration, Lupe wasn't allowed to pass. She was underage and did not have the signature of her mother to travel outside of the country as a minor. Lupe explained:

> The dirty sons of a gun will not let me go over. I am seventeen; I have not what you call of *age*; I have no mother and only one dog with me. I come back to Mexico City like one dog myself! I cry all the way on the train. It is the first time in my life I find something really to cry over ... yet it was my poor Mil-a-tone — Mil-a-tone, the dog, who really suffer. He go in a suitcase with holes poke in it. He is upside down on his nose one moment; on his tail another. He do not cry. So I say to him, "Poor Mil-a-tone! Don't you worry. You did not go through it for nothing. Lupe will bring you across the border so you can see Hollywood and Los Angeles..." ["Senorita Cyclone," *Screen Secrets*, No. 50, May 1929].

Back home, this time the papers announced headlines of a different nature: "Lupe Vélez Sent Back To Mexico!" The locals laughed. The other theatrical stars, the ones Lupe took great fun in imitating, poked fun at *her*. A humiliated Lupe appealed to everyone who'd listen — ministers, politicians, even the Mexican president. *Someone* had to clear her way to the United States. People were waiting for her there, she said. She had a job offer. She had a telegram from Richard Bennett to prove it. Lupe explained the process, saying, "After a lot of letter writing between Mexico City and Washington and what you call 'red tape,' they said I could cross the border" (*How I Broke Into the Movies*, Facsimile Edition, Video Yesteryear, 1984).

Prior to Lupe's departure to Hollywood, she went to the newspapers to prove that this time she would be allowed to enter the United States without a hitch. The reporters laughed at her. The newspapers got stung once by giving her blazing headlines. They also helped to get her out of the house and to the train station without being caught by the people she owed money to. They didn't expect her shameful return and they weren't about to help her again.

It didn't matter. Lupe knew she'd reach Hollywood this time. However, through no fault of her own, she was now very late for the part that Bennett had offered her a few weeks prior. After all, that part was the only reason she was leaving for Hollywood in the first place. Without the role in *The Dove*, there was no job. Lupe was arriving in a new country with no money and very possibly no work. She couldn't return home defeated for a second time. No matter what, Lupe was determined to succeed. As she boarded the train for America, she remained nervously optimistic.

Next stop — Hollywood!

# 6

## *The Train to Tinseltown*

"Her allurement is something which defies description by tongue or on paper."[1]—Reporter Ruth Biery "describes" the indescribable Lupe Vélez (in an unidentified scrapbook clipping).

As the train pulled out, there were no manic goodbyes from the Mexican people. No newspaper headlines announcing her second departure for Hollywood. No return journey with Mil-a-tone to the train station. This time, Lupe left in silence. Her only companion was Mil-a-tone — the dog. No one thought there was a reason for a goodbye because everyone expected her to come back in a few days' time. Little did they know that it would be over ten years before Lupe would return home to Mexico.

Of her second attempt at entering the United States, Lupe said:

I put Mil-a-tone back in the suitcase and start again. My Lord, what a trip! I have no money but I have a berth on the bottom. I sell it to a mans for twenty-five dollars so I can eat. Poor Mil-a-tone. He cannot bark! For then they will take him away from Lupe and put him in the car back of the machine. The night I go to bed on the top I forget to tell the porter that I am no longer on the bottom. I tie Mil-a-tone to my wrist with a handkerchief so he cannot get me into trouble.

Gee, this is a vacation for my poor little Mil-a-tone after all day in the suitcase with holes in it. The porter, he come to wake up the mans at five in the morning and he does not know that he is on the bottom. He push me to make the mans get up and Mil-a-tone bark.

Oh, Baby! I am skeered. The porter, he say, he must take Mil-a-tone. But I make the tears come and I wrinkle my eyes at him and flirt, even though he is black, and he say if Mil-a-tone no bark any more he will keep his mouth shut. Mil-a-tone does not bark again till we get to Los Angeles ["Senorita Cyclone," *Screen Secrets*, No. 50, May 1929].

Several articles have stated that Lupe knew limited English at the time of her arrival. This claim contradicts other reports stating that Lupe spoke better English when she arrived in Hollywood than she did ten years after she moved there! *Photoplay* wrote that some of the words she knew upon her arrival were "chocolate malted milk," "strawberry ice cream soda," and "hell." The latter would be used often, and loudly!

In the 1929 *Screen Secrets* series of interviews, Lupe stated that the only American words she remembered from the convent were:

"...Son of a gun," "son of something else," which they say I must not print, "ice cream soda," "cantaloupe," and a little poem which says:
"Go to hell
"Ring the bell
"And tell your mother

"I am well!"

I tell this to everyone on the train so they know I speak English. I wish I did not know the word "cantaloupe." It is the only thing they have to eat on the train which I can say. For four days, I eat nothing but cantaloupe.

On the last morning I go to the dining room and I make up my mind. I will not eat any more cantaloupe. I will have an egg. So I say egg in Mexican. The waiter, he no understand. Then I scream, "egg, egg, egg," in Mexican at him. Then I get very mad; I am going to have an egg for my breakfast. I roll up my napkin in a little ball; jump out of my chair; go to the corner, put the napkin on the floor and sit on it. Then I cry, "Cockle doodle doo!" I get the egg for my breakfast.

I flirts with one mans on the train. He come and sit with me. We cannot talk but we make eyes at one another. When I get off at Los Angeles and I opens my purse to give the porter something, I have one dollar. That dirty son of a gun who wrinkles his eyes at me have taken my twenty dollars, which I have made by giving up my bottom bed. All I have when I come to this city is just one dollar. The porter starts with my bags but he has a red cap on and I think he is an American policemans. I scream and I yell, "Why you put Lupe in jail?" I say it in Mexican and he no understand. So I scream, "Go to hell," and he put my bags down. I am so happy because the American policeman's no put Lupe in the American jail on her first morning in this country.

I go and sit on a bench and watch all the peoples. It is fun to watch the American peoples. It makes me so happy to see Mil-a-tone running around under the feets of the people. I sit there till six o'clock. Then I smell food and my stomach begin to feel very funny. Also, Mil-a-tone's stomach. I buy one hot dog, one hamburger and one Coca-Cola. I forget to say I can talk "Coca-Cola." I give Mil-a-tone half and I have seventy-five cents left. I do not know what to do with it. I go to the door. I sees a big car with a beautiful womans go by in it. I toss my head and I say, "In one year I will have a car like that. I am in Hollywood; I am going to make good in the theatre and have everything which is nice for Lupe" ["Senorita Cyclone," *Screen Secrets*, No. 50, May 1929].

Before filming on her first feature was over, Lupe had purchased a car. Not just any car, a limousine! And, a driver to go with it. One day, as she was getting into her limousine, the young son of an influential studio financier, showing off in front of his friends, yelled out, "Who gave you that car, Lupe?" Always ready with a quick reply, Lupe calmly purred, "It was that dirty old man, your father, who gave it to me" (www.austinfilm.org).

Upon her arrival from Mexico City, Lupe needed a car and a driver of a different kind. She looked for a taxi, got in and said "'Otel," to the driver. "What hotel?" asked the driver. "'Otel," shouted Lupe. "What hotel?!" the driver shouted back. "Hell! 'Otel!" Lupe shouted louder.

Without another word between them, the driver dropped her at the nearest hotel. He didn't care how good it was, he just wanted this crazy girl out of his cab. It was the Hotel Louise, a hostel in the apartment district of Los Angeles. Lupe got out of the cab, struggled inside with her trunk and her dog, only to be met by a cross-eyed desk clerk. "Oh, my God, I come here with no money and the first person I see has cuckoo eyes." To Lupe, "cuckoo eyes" were bad luck. She ran back to the cab, got in and shouted, "'Otel!"

Before starting the car, the driver asked Lupe how much money she had. Lupe shook her head in the negative, pouted her lips and shrugged her shoulders. Furious, the driver got out of his seat and physically removed her from his vehicle. Lupe stood on the sidewalk, stomping her feet wildly, "Hell! Hell! Hell!" she screamed (*Photoplay*, February 1929).

Embarrassed, and now a little bit sympathetic for her plight, the driver told her to get back in. Upon arrival at the second accommodation, the clerk's eyes were straight and a lovely shade of blue, Lupe was happy and she handed him the wire from Bennett. He called

someone who could speak Spanish and together they deciphered the story of why Lupe was there. They immediately called Bennett at the theater to announce Lupe's arrival. He told them to take care of her. Whatever she needed, he'd cover it. The hotel clerk paid for her taxi and he took the telegram as a guarantee her room would be paid for too. Lupe said, "I go into a beautiful room which had a bath all to itself. I am wild with happiness because now I know everything is to be easy." Bennett arranged to meet with Lupe the following day ("Senorita Cyclone," *Screen Secrets*, No. 50, May 1929).

On Lupe's second day in Hollywood, she was up early and excited and eager to meet with Bennett about her first acting job in America. They traveled to the theater together, but upon arrival, everything fell apart. As soon as the director saw Lupe in person he said she was too young and too skinny, and lacked experience for the part required of her. Bennett asked that she be at least given a chance. He said he had seen her perform in Mexico and he knew what she could do. Also, she had traveled a long, long way; the least they could do was give her a chance.

Lupe *was* tiny; she needed *a lot* of plumping up. The intense transformation included fake hips and breasts being attached to her tiny frame. They aged her by adding lines and dark circles under her eyes. By the time they were done, she was unrecognizable. But she could hardly walk with all the padding she had on under her clothes. As soon as Lupe stepped onto the stage, the director burst out into uncontrollable laughter. Lupe was angry and humiliated. She walked off the stage, tore the stuffing out of her clothing and slumped into a chair. She wanted to cry. She didn't. She was too mad for tears to come.

Bennett realized he was wrong to send for Lupe and he felt terrible that he'd raised her hopes so high. But he knew he had made the right decision in casting twenty-eight-year-old Dorothy Mackaye in *The Dove* instead. For Lupe, it was a double blow. After the devastating rejection, Bennett paid Lupe's hotel bill for the week and wished her well. Unless she found another job, and soon, Lupe had no choice but to return home. But she would never recover from such a major rejection. She had to succeed—somehow.

Discouraged but not broken, Lupe begrudgingly took a job dancing at a benefit for local Los Angeles traffic policeman. It was about as low as she could get, but it beat returning home to Mexico in disgrace. After finding out that she was still in town and still looking for work, Bennett got Lupe a job as an "atmospheric dancer" at a movie theater (www.austinfilm.org). Soon after that, Lupe got a job with the brother-sister theatrical producing team Fanchon and Marco. Again guilt-ridden, Bennett continued to help Lupe find work. He arranged for Miss Fanchon to see Lupe. After Lupe danced, Miss Fanchon was

An early 1927 pose (with bare back and shoulders implying nudity) during Lupe's time with Hal Roach. She was barely nineteen when this photograph was taken.

impressed enough to offer her a one-year contract on the spot. Lupe couldn't believe her luck. But she told Miss Fanchon that she would dance for her without signing the contract, and if the public liked her, only then would she sign on for the full year. Miss Fanchon agreed.

Lupe danced. The public loved her. She signed the contract.

Not long after the contract was signed, Bennett came to the theater to ask Lupe for a favor. Of course she agreed. He had been so good to her, it was the least she could do in return. It was actually a well-orchestrated plan (on his behalf) to show an audience, mostly made up of celebrities, what Lupe could really do. What *he* already knew she could do. Everyone who was anyone in Hollywood was there, including Harry Rapf, Joe Schenck, Mary Pickford, and Norma Talmadge.

Bennett was *Hollywood Music Box Revue*'s master of ceremonies. He had known the show's star, Fanny Brice, for years and he wanted to surprise her with a Mexican valentine during the February 14, 1927, show. Lupe would be wheeled out on stage inside a giant paper heart. Once in position, she'd jump out and sing and dance and have a chat with Brice about this and that. As usual, Lupe stopped the show. It was the first time she had heard such raucous applause since leaving Mexico. She reportedly wore so very little that first night, the audience gasped. Due to the positive reaction, Lupe was asked if she'd like to be a permanent part of the production. It was a major step. Lupe accepted the offer without hesitation (www.austinfilm.org).

However, there was one problem. She had just signed a one-year contract with Fanchon and Marco. Lupe went to Miss Fanchon and begged her to let her out of the contract. This hard-boiled businesswoman of the theater had Lupe secured for one year and she was perfectly within her legal rights to keep Lupe for the duration. If she refused her requested early release, then Lupe would have to turn down her biggest opportunity in America to date. However, Miss Fanchon knew Lupe's big break was looming and she also knew she wouldn't get it by staying in her show. So she let a small gold mine go. It was a selfless act of kindness that Lupe never forgot.

The *Hollywood Music Box Revue* opened on February 2, 1927, at the Music Box Theatre. Lupe's salary was $35 a week (approximately $432 in 2011). Despite being headlined by Fanny Brice, and even with the injection of enthusiasm brought on by Lupe's appearances (she was nicknamed a "tropical hurricane"), reviews were poor and the show closed a couple of months later, on April

**A promotional shot for Hal Roach Studios, circa 1927.**

7, 1927. Many of Brice's rehashed routines were used on audiences who had seen them too many times before. A veteran of the stage, including multiple *Ziegfeld Follies* shows, Brice was someone Lupe looked up to; she went to Brice for advice on all aspects of the acting profession. Lupe said:

> What a good woman she [Brice] is. She is just like a mother to Lupe in this country. I do not know what I would do without Fanny Brice to take care of me. I begin [performing in the *Hollywood Music Box Review*] on Valentine's Day, 1927. I am a valentine brought from Mexico City to Miss Brice. I kick open the heart, a big red heart made of paper, and jump out on the stage to sing and to dance for them [the audience]. I am singing a sentimental song when my little skirt start to go off me. I grab it and keep pulling it up all the time I am supposed to be sentimental. They laugh and they yell; I stop the show for them.
>
>   The American people go crazy just like the Mexican peoples. They keep calling me and I do more and more; I imitate a policemans; I sing "Charlie, My Boy"; I dance and shimmy and the hula; I do everything until there is nothing more I knows to do for them. Fanny takes me out and says, "Speak a few words, Lupe."
>
>   I am not skeered. Lupe has never been skeered of any peoples. So I say, "Meesees and Sirs"–
>
>   In Spanish, that is correct. But Fanny stop me and say, "No, no, Lupe. It is '*Ladies and Gentlemen.*'"
>
>   I stop and look at her and say, "Naughty, naughty, Fanny, eet is not goot to say 'Ladies and Gentlemen!'"
>
>   We stand there on the stage and she says, "Say 'Ladies and Gentlemen,' Lupe." And I will not say it. I will not say it because to me it is bad. I tell her I see it in bad places; I see it on doors which peoples do not talk about in public.
>
>   They [the audience] laugh till they nearly split. Then I say, "Me love; much love; me many kisses; goodbye." I have learn all these words working for Mr. Fanchon and Marco. Fanny says for twenty-two days I stop the show ["Senorita Cyclone," *Screen Secrets*, No. 51, June 1929].

Lupe was a hit the first night she appeared in *Hollywood Music Box Revue*, and she was a hit every night after that. She may have been small in stature, but she more than made up for that with her showy stage presence. She wasn't enough to keep the show open, but that didn't matter. There were much bigger things on the horizon and the show had served its purpose in getting her noticed.

Brice was so impressed with Lupe's musicality, professionalism and enthusiastic personality that she called in a favor. American Broadway impresario Florenz Ziegfeld, upon Brice's recommendation, offered Lupe a sixteen-week, $500-a-week (approximately $6,500 in 2011) contract to perform in *Rio Rita* in New York. It would have been her next big break, but as it happened, the film business had noticed Lupe too. It was time to choose — Broadway or Hollywood?

Shortly thereafter, an elaborate luncheon was given at the Biltmore Hotel in Los Angeles. A number of dancers and singers performed for an audience of big businessmen and motion picture executives, all chewing their cigars and bored out of their minds at the lackluster performances, when all of a sudden, a young girl with boundless energy and a huge smile whirled onto the stage. Everyone sat up and took notice. "Who is *she?*" MGM executive Harry Rapf asked. He'd seen many pretty talented girls in his time, but when Lupe took the stage, he was spellbound. "That was an experience I shall never forget," Rapf said in a 1931 *Los Angeles Record* item. "The girl had so much abandon, such vivacity that the audience was electrified, and when she finished her dance we all got up and cheered. I suggested that we make a screen test of the young Mexican girl, and we did."

That moment was the second time that Rapf had seen Lupe perform on stage. He had also been in the audience for the Valentine's Day performance of *Hollywood Music Box Revue*. It was enough confirmation for him to realize he should sign her before someone else beat him to it.

Harald Bucquet shot Lupe's first screen test. He declared her to be a "ball of fire." In the silent film days when singing and guitar-playing (both of which Lupe could do very well) were no asset, Lupe had to utilize her dancing and personality to impress people. But her movements were almost too quick for the camera. She was like a young colt, and Bucquet said she was "just as hard to tie down." Her MGM test was good enough for Rapf to alert Hal Roach of his new find (*Los Angeles Record*, undated, 1931).

Lupe knew the type of films Roach made and the physicality and comedic timing he'd expect of her if he signed her to a contract. "Comedies?" she said, "Sure I could make comedies," and she did. On October 14, 1927, Roach signed her to a three-year contract. "I worked in several [comedies], darn near broke my neck, but I felt I was getting some place in this town where what you do counts, not what you did before you came" (*How I Broke Into the Movies*, Facsimile Edition, Video Yesteryear, 1984).

Despite constant attention from the opposite sex, Lupe had little faith in her looks; in fact, she thought she was "too ugly" to have any long-term success in the film industry. But, while the ride lasted, Lupe Vélez decided she'd at least have some fun. As it turned out, she'd have seventeen years worth.

# 7

## *The New Girl*

"Any person in the films who gets excited about their career is foolish and conceited. The main thing is to be happy."[1]— Lupe Vélez (1931)

In the Hal Roach two-reeler *What Women Did for Me* (1927), Lupe is prominent as the dean's daughter who saves the star of the short, Charley Chase (playing a girl-fearing teacher, ironically working at an all-girls school) from a group of wild female students.

*Sailors, Beware!* (1927) was next. Yet another Hal Roach two-reeler, this time starring Stan Laurel and Oliver Hardy as individuals, before they became the beloved comedy team. The uncredited Lupe is easily recognizable in her role of Baroness Behr; an intertitle introduces her character as she exits Chester Chaste's (Stan Laurel) cab. Much of the comedic action takes place aboard a luxury passenger liner and surrounds a midget dressed as a baby (Harry Earles) and a con artist, Madame Ritz (Anita Garvin), posing as his mother. Oliver Hardy plays the ship's purser. Lupe's last screen moment in the short sees her poolside with Stan Laurel — and she gets wet!

The common retelling of Lupe's discovery and big Hollywood break into feature films is the all-too-typical tale of being spotted out of nowhere. Yet, by the time she was cast as the female lead in *The Gaucho* (1927), she had already appeared in several shorts at Hal Roach Studios.[2] While neither of the aforementioned two-reelers catapulted her to instant stardom, it's fair to say she had been noticed and was well on her way. Each new job that Lupe did was a promotion to something bigger and better. That said, the following story seems like just that — a good story.

Supposedly, talent scout Ted Reed spotted nineteen-year-old Lupe in the courtyard of the Egyptian Theater in Hollywood and brought her to his boss, Douglas Fairbanks. At the time, he was desperately searching for the right actress to play "The Wild Mountain Girl" opposite him in his new adventure feature *The Gaucho*. Fairbanks liked her. She got the part. And so it goes ... yet another Hollywood fairytale began.

Not quite. The more likely version of events was that Roach Studios story editor–director, F. Richard Jones[3] had noticed Lupe's ability and wasted talent. He himself would soon leave Roach for United Artists, and when he heard Fairbanks expressing his frustration at not being able to find the right leading lady for his new film, Jones threw Lupe's name at him.

Lupe told reporter Gladys Hall (The Gladys Hall Papers, the Margaret Herrick Library) that as a practical joke, actor Eugene Pallette hid her dog Mil-a-tone during the filming of *Sailors, Beware!* Lupe asked everyone, "Where is my dog?" She was getting madder and madder by the second. Finally, the electricians told her that Pallette had taken him. Lupe's

A candid shot of Douglas Fairbanks with Lupe and her little dog, Mil-a-tone (aka Milton). This postcard was issued for publicity purposes before filming began on *The Gaucho* (1927). Photograph courtesy of the Agrasánchez Film Archive.

eyes blazed. As Pallette walked past, she jumped on his back, pulled his hair, scratched at his eyes and screamed, "Give me back my dog!" The electricians who ratted Pallette out used all their strength to pull Lupe off him. Standing in the doorway, watching every second of the action unfold was F. Richard Jones. "She *is* the girl in *The Gaucho*," Jones said to himself.

Upon his recommendation, Fairbanks agreed to see Lupe. Close to two hundred girls had already unsuccessfully tested for the part of the Wild Mountain Girl. Incidentally, Jones got a promotion of his own after leaving Roach; he would go on to direct *The Gaucho*. The right female lead was now just as important to him as it was to Fairbanks. Although Jones had already produced and directed his fair share of films, his role as director on the Fairbanks adventure was a major career boost and he was in high demand following the film's success. Tragically, just three years after *The Gaucho* was released, Jones died of tuberculosis on December 14, 1930. He was only thirty-seven. His wife of less than a year was famed costume designer Irene Lentz. Although her husband was instrumental in getting Lupe the part that launched her career, "Irene" (she was eventually famous enough to be known by her first name only) had another connection to Lupe Vélez — Gary Cooper.

Irene went on to marry screenwriter Eliot Gibbons, brother of MGM art director Cedric Gibbons, but it was not a happy marriage and the couple essentially lived separate lives. Shortly before Irene's death on November 15, 1962, she had confided in her friend, actress Doris Day, that she had been in love with Gary Cooper and he was the only man she had ever loved. (Cooper had succumbed to cancer the year before.) Day recalled that she got the feeling that she was the first person to whom Irene had shared this information. "Thinking about it now," she wrote in *Doris Day Her Own Story*, "I cannot honestly say whether Irene's love was one-sided or whether she and Cooper had actually had or were having an affair."

A few weeks prior to her sixty-second birthday, under an assumed name, Irene checked herself into the Knickerbocker Hotel. She went to her room, slashed her wrists, and then jumped from the bathroom window to her death. She was interred at Forest Lawn Memorial Park in Glendale with first husband, F. Richard Jones.

In her 1988 book *Cooper's Women*, author Jane Ellen Wayne wrote that Cooper and Irene would "become involved in a relationship" that continued over the years. So, it's entirely likely their affair was very real. After all, would a woman commit suicide over a fantasy, a love affair that never happened, and over a man who was now deceased? Not likely.

Cooper had a powerful hold over the women he came to know and love, and even those he left behind. There were many women. And, as it happened, Lupe Vélez would eventually become one of them.

\*   \*   \*

As Lupe stood stone-faced in front of Douglas Fairbanks, he was uncertain of the petite nineteen-year-old's ability to pull off a strong, vivacious role in *The Gaucho*. He gave Lupe the once-over and shook his head. He thought she looked too young and too innocent. He wanted a passionate, fiery, volatile leading lady. On looks alone, Lupe had him fooled.

Jones knew better. He gestured to wardrobe to get her into costume for a try-out on the set. Lupe told reporter Gladys Hall that John Barrymore, Mary Pickford, Gloria Swanson and Corinne Griffith were all there to watch. Fairbanks kept repeating, over and over, "She's not good for this, too young, too sweet, too timid..." Jones knew that Lupe was anything

Following the aforementioned physical spat, Gary confided in his friend that Lupe was really the only woman he truly trusted (and there had been many women) but he still had an awful feeling that she was running around on him (seeds of doubt implanted by his meddling mother). When he confronted Lupe with his suspicions, followed by direct accusations of infidelity, Lupe went into a rage. She threw the first punch. Cooper said he was just trying to calm her down (Conner, *Lupe Vélez and Her Lovers*).

When Cooper physically collapsed from the stress and strain, he was diagnosed with jaundice and depression. Doctors feared he was on the brink of a nervous breakdown; those closer to him were convinced he'd already had one. Doctors ordered him to take a year off.

Paramount gave him five weeks!

While the studio certainly knew how hard they'd worked him (about thirty movies in five years), they'd now convinced themselves that Lupe was the cause of most of his problems. Then again, Lupe blamed the studio for Cooper's ill health and she insisted on nursing her "Garree" back to health. Hearing this news, the studio swiftly arranged for their star to take a five-week trip to Europe, on one condition: no Lupe Vélez! As expected, Lupe was far from happy when she heard about this solo trip to Europe. Knowing the grief he'd get for leaving her behind, Gary did all that he could to avoid seeing Lupe before departing. He *almost* made it. Somehow Lupe found out the day and the time that he was scheduled to leave on the Twentieth Century Limited. And if it killed her (or him), she was going to find out why he was leaving the country without her.

In his 1980 Cooper biography, Hector Arce described the manic scene at the station:

> [Gary] was there talking to a couple of people. [Lupe] sneaked around and saw him. He was standing right outside the train. She shouted, "Gary, you son of a bitch!" Then she took a shot at him, but she missed. By that time, Coop had slammed the door and was inside. The train pulled out but a hell of a lot of people were wise. Some woman had taken a shot at Gary Cooper.

By late July of 1931, Gary returned from his five-week European trip. He had regained some weight and was eager to get back to work. While he had spoken with Lupe by phone during his time away, he wasn't faithful to her. Yet the first question a swarm of American reporters asked when he returned was if he intended to marry Lupe. He responded by saying he'd already asked her and she flatly refused.

Soon after Gary's return to the United States, Lupe made her way back to California following a brief publicity trip east. Upon her arrival, reporters asked her if Gary's words were true. "I don't love Gary Cooper," she said. But she didn't leave her statement there. Lupe proceeded to give the American press a story they couldn't have made up if they tried. She told them she turned down Cooper's marriage proposal because his parents didn't want him to marry her and because his studio thought it would destroy his career. Lupe said: "His mother! I hope she never cries the tears that I have cried. I hope she never knows the suffering I have known.... I don't hate her that much" (Wayne, *Cooper's Women*).

Lupe's unexpected statement began a very ugly, very public feud between Gary Cooper's mother and herself. Mrs. Cooper felt the need to respond to Lupe's accusations, and to her son's horror, she also used the press to do it. Without doubt, the mudslinging prevented any possible reconciliation that may have potentially happened between Lupe and Gary. Gary was well aware of Lupe's "say it as she saw it" approach to life, but this time his beloved mother was on the receiving end. When Gary left for Europe five weeks before, he never believed things could get any worse. Yet somehow the mess had gotten a lot deeper. It was a full-scale war of words and *he* was in the middle of it!

At a November 1937 costume party in Hollywood, two of Gary Cooper's ex-lovers, Clara Bow and Lupe Vélez (left), compare notes on the one that got away.

Mrs. Cooper was stoic in her statements and she calmly stood her ground. She emphatically declared that she had no ill feeling toward Lupe and she wished her continued success. She said she thought of her as a fine "little actress" and she wished her happiness. That said, she then expressed her regret that Lupe had talked openly and "violently" to the media. Mrs. Cooper added that she was shocked by headlines claiming she had invaded Lupe's home to get personal knickknacks belonging to Gary. She said she had not been inside Lupe's house since before the couple broke up.

Mrs. Cooper ended by addressing the rumors of her threat to kill herself if Gary married Lupe, and what she called "preposterous stories" that claimed she suggested to her son that Lupe was unfaithful while he was away (ironically, it was the other way around) and not good enough for him. Mrs. Cooper said that she would never set down any dictates about the type of girl that her son should marry and it was not the duty of her husband or herself to select a wife for their son. She *did* admit that she had not entirely approved of *any* of the women that her son had been romantically involved with (Wayne, *Cooper's Women*).

Gary's father was a successful rancher and Justice of the Montana Supreme Court. After serving on the bench from 1919 to 1924, his staunch exterior was hard to crack, but with Lupe in the room, he acted like a kid in a candy store. Cooper later admitted that his conservative, English-born parents just didn't know what to make of Lupe's exuberant Latin spirit.

Despite his old-fashioned attitude, Gary's father was both charmed and amused by Lupe's impromptu dance routines and impersonations. And if he dared to challenge her with a stern look, the look of a judge giving a disapproving eye to a wayward offender, Lupe would go one step further and do something so outrageously funny that even he couldn't help but to burst into uncontrollable laughter. Lupe would then climb on his lap, grab his ear, and say, "You do love me, judge, don't you?" Lupe had both Cooper men right where she wanted them and it made Alice Cooper furious (Conner, *Lupe Vélez and Her Lovers*).

**The sultry tango between Lupe and Douglas Fairbanks was the highlight of *The Gaucho* (1927). At just nineteen years of age, Lupe matched wits with the older, more experienced Fairbanks and became an overnight sensation.**

but "timid," and he kept insisting she could certainly play the role. The Wild Mountain Girl would go barefoot in the movie so Fairbanks ordered Lupe to take off her shoes. Lupe said, "Oh, no!" She was very sensitive about her feet. She insisted they were ugly and full of corns from years of dancing. Fairbanks responded, "Then you don't get the part!" Lupe told him she didn't care. "I don't take off my shoes for you, or no one.... I go back to Mexico!" (*Los Angeles Post-Record*, June 10, 1933). Jones smirked knowingly as Lupe stood toe to toe with Fairbanks, daring to challenge him. People started to laugh. Lupe didn't know why. She was dead serious. Fairbanks was intrigued.

Next he instructed Lupe to climb up onto some fake rocks. Up she went. He yelled at her to climb down the rocks. Down she went. Then he yelled at her to hit her potential co-star, Eve Southern, in the face. Lupe took his directions — literally! She not only hit Southern, she knocked her out cold! Fairbanks and the onlookers were panic-stricken as aides rushed to Southern's side. Despite the miscommunication and mayhem that followed, Lupe got the part. Southern got a black eye.

Shortly before filming began on *The Gaucho*, Fairbanks visited the set of Mary Pickford's latest feature *My Best Girl* (1927) and witnessed a love scene between Mary and her leading man Charles "Buddy" Rogers. Even if it was "acting," and even if he (of all people) should have understood that, he couldn't bear to watch his wife in the arms of another man.

Steaming mad, he stormed off the set and never forgot it. Some say Fairbanks began an affair with Lupe in retaliation for *that* incident, and while it may have been a short-lived, superficial union, it served to give *The Gaucho* a sexual energy (for example, the tango scene) that was driven by the passionate off-screen relations between Lupe and her leading man (Vance and Maietta, *Douglas Fairbanks*).

Hugh Munro Neely, film historian and curator of the Mary Pickford Institute, offered some interesting insight into the relationship between Fairbanks and Pickford. Regarding the claims that Lupe and Fairbanks had a fling on the set of *The Gaucho* (1927), he said:

> The information I've seen on [Pickford] suggests (and I do mean "suggests," *not* "confirms") that she could be at least a little bit understanding of Doug's flings, so long as they did not become public. *If* she hated 19-year-old Lupe [because of the "supposed" fling with Doug], she doesn't seem to have done anything to blackball her career. Lupe went from *The Gaucho* to a 1928 DeMille Pictures production [*Stand and Deliver*], and Mary was a good friend of Cecil B. DeMille. Further, she had a much closer relationship with D.W. Griffith than Fairbanks did, so presumably she could have had a good shot at nixing Lupe's casting in *Lady of the Pavements,* too. Lupe stayed with the Paramount clique for *Wolf Song*, before she went over to MGM for the Tod Browning production of *Where East is East*. And then *Hell Harbor* was released by United Artists.... Mary was a person full of self-doubt and personal recrimination. She was easily hurt, and was always deciding that she had made a mistake to do *Rosita* (1923) or *Dorothy Vernon of Haddon Hall* (1924) or something like that, and she could be angry at a person, sure ... but she had a lot of power, especially during late '20s and early '30s Hollywood. It doesn't appear to me that, whatever she felt, she tried to hurt Lupe in any way. That doesn't mean she liked her ... but I don't think that any dislike could have run too deep. After all, years later she let "Buddy" make the *Mexican Spitfire* films with Lupe and if you thought that 19-year-old Lupe had stolen your man during a movie shoot, wouldn't you think twice about allowing your next husband to work with her on a film where *she* was the star? I suspect that she either chalked the Lupe-Doug fling up to Doug's advances, not Lupe's, or she was really much more understanding than anyone realizes.

It's clear that Lupe Vélez had a deep respect for Mary Pickford. During filming on *The Gaucho*, Mary helped Lupe with her makeup and also gave her acting advice. It's unlikely that she'd repay her kindness by having a fling with her husband. In fact, Lupe once told reporter Gladys Hall that if anyone said anything against Pickford to her, she'd stab that person with a knife! (Gladys Hall Papers, the Margaret Herrick Library).

After casting Lupe in the role of the Wild Mountain Girl, Fairbanks was forewarned about Lupe's quick-change personality. He'd already had a little taste of it, but he was yet to be around her on a full-time basis. At least a dozen people who had seen Lupe around the studio lot said, "When she puckers up her lips, it is impossible to tell if she is going to kiss you, bite you, or spit on you!" (Austin, *More of Hollywood's Unsolved Mysteries*). Fairbanks enjoyed a challenge and he got one in Lupe Vélez ... and so did the president of United Artists, Joseph M. Schenck.

After filming began, Schenck reprimanded Lupe for swearing too much on set. As previously mentioned, many people thought it was amusing to "teach" Lupe new "American words" but most of them were, of course, curse words. Lupe said:

> I do not know what word means something bad and what word means something good. When I first go on the set in the movies everybody teaches me things I must say. The prop boys, the electricians, the extras — oh, everybody. I do not know I swear. They think it is a little fun to hear me swear. It makes people feel what you are saying. I swear so much that Mr. Schenck send for me. He said, "Lupe, you know why Mary Pickford is America's Sweetheart?"

"No, Mr. Schenck."

"It is because she is so sweet, such a lady. Did you ever hear Miss Pickford swear, Lupe?"

"No, Mr. Schenck."

"Did you ever hear Miss Talmadge swear on the set?"

"No, Mr. Schenck."

"Did you ever hear Gloria Swanson say anything she shouldn't?"

"No Mr. Schenck."

"Well, Lupe, I want you to swear for the last time. I want you to raise your right hand and say, 'I, Lupe Vélez, swear that I will not swear any more.'"

So I do it. I like to do what is right in this country. Then I turn to go out and I trip my foot on the rug by the door. Before I can think a minute, I turn around and stamp my foot and say, "Why in hell you have not this damn rug nailed down?"

Mr. Schenck, he is a good sport. He just throw up his hands and laugh and say, "Lupe, that beats me!"

It's no use. I am not bad but it's no use trying to make me a lady. My mother try; my sisters try; the convent try; Mr. Schenck try, but Lupe still swear when she want to make people to understand just how much she means it ["Senorita Cyclone," *Screen Secrets*, No. 51, June 1929].

Following the release of *The Gaucho*, Lupe was asked about her reaction to the media hype and reports of her "overnight success." Lupe said she was deliriously happy when *The Gaucho* opened because the public loved her. She had always enjoyed the adulation of a crowd, but to be so well received in her biggest film to date, and in America, was overwhelming.

Due to the success of *The Gaucho* and the positive public response to Lupe, Schenck paid $50,000 (approximately $600,000 in 2011) and bought out Lupe's contract. Her new

**Lupe with her mother Josefina, circa 1928.**

Circa 1928 — Lupe (left) with her often-talked-about rival, fellow Mexican actress Dolores del Rio.

salary was $1,000 a week; it then escalated to $1,500, then $2,500 (The Gladys Hall Papers, the Margaret Herrick Library).

Lupe's good Hollywood fortune continued when she was chosen as one of the thirteen WAMPAS Baby Stars of 1928. Sharing the honor with her were Lina Basquette, Flora Bramley, Sue Carol, Ann Christy, June Collyer, Alice Day, Sally Eilers, Audrey Ferris, Dorothy Gulliver, Gwen Lee, Molly O'Day and Ruth Taylor. Lupe was the most successful actress of her WAMPAS peers from that year.

Following her break-out role in *The Gaucho*, it was apparent that Lupe had invaded the film colony and she was there to stay. Her fellow countrywoman, Dolores del Rio, had established herself as a viable Hollywood actress a couple of years before, and suddenly Lupe was compared to her, even hailed as her successor by some. Writer Dan Thomas analyzed the two women in the *Dunkirk Evening Observer* (May 10, 1928): "Lupe Vélez is a star of a different type. Dolores has more of an air of sophistication and finesse. While Lupe possesses a fire and impulsiveness that Dolores will never know. I cannot think of a role that would be suitable to both. And yet they are intensely jealous of each other."

Two talented Mexican actresses who had in no way stepped on each other's toes or vied for each other's roles were thrown into a public catfight that neither one of them had ever started.

In December of 1931, Elizabeth Yeaman of *Hollywood Citizen News* announced that

**A scene from *Stand and Deliver* (1928). Rod La Rocque plays Englishman Roger Norman, who is forced to defend Lupe (playing Jania, a Greek girl) from her own countrymen.**

Lupe was set to play a "heavy vamp role in *Blood and Wine*, which will co-star Dolores del Rio and Richard Cortez." Yeaman played up the rivalry:

> David Selznick is trying very hard to engage the services of the little Mexican actress [Lupe] for the role of the spitfire villainess. This casting combination should be good, provided Lupe and Dolores can't clash too violently. You see they are rivals in the same field and some say that the disparity of social prestige in Mexico has set up a barrier of enmity between them!

*Blood and Wine* was never made. In 1932, del Rio was cast in *The Broken Wing*, but a scheduling conflict caused her to drop out and Lupe replaced her in the lead role of Lolita.

Their Hollywood careers appeared to mirror each other's for a time, but aside from the aforementioned roles, there were parts designed for Lupe Vélez and parts designed for Dolores del Rio. These were two very distinct on- and off-screen personalities, both tailored to specific films, with roles to suit each of them.

Del Rio came from aristocratic Castillian heritage; she was a debutante presented to the Spanish court and she more or less toed the Hollywood line. Married to Cedric Gibbons, one of MGM's leading art directors and production designers, she was thrust into Hollywood's high society circles and acted accordingly.[4] She was also stereotyped into exotic, Latin-type roles, but unlike Lupe, she was *not* stigmatized. In many ways, right or wrong, del Rio transcended her ethnicity. Hollywood accepted her because, in the eyes of the film colony, she acted "white."

The American way of life with its freedom of speech and expression suited Lupe's personality perfectly. That said, it sometimes got her into a lot of trouble. On January 23, 1929, an interview published in *La Opinión* ("I Am Free; Free! Shouts Lupe Vélez") upset the Mexican community so much, the Mexican government wanted to boycott Lupe's films. "I believe that they are lying to the girls in Mexico," she told the interviewer. "But what else can I do? One is not able to laugh, speak, say what you think. All you can say is yes, sir. He can say what he wants. Here I laugh and do what I want, because the American boys understand well."

The following week, *La Opinión* published a letter of apology, with the headline, "Lupe Vélez Says That She Loves Mexico and Mexicans." Lupe blamed the interviewer and said that her answers were misunderstood in English. She wrote:

> I wish to explain that when I spoke about the liberties enjoyed in America, compared with what young women in Mexico enjoy, I only commented on the peculiar customs of our country in general, without referring to them negatively, one or the other, and certainly this is not my personal opinion about this topic.

Lupe now realized she had to think before speaking her mind — which was not something she did well. So, whenever she did happen to speak out of turn, she'd use the language barrier excuse as the reason why she was misinterpreted.

During Lupe's early days as an actress, many of her scripts were automatically written for her in broken English. The first time it happened, Lupe flew into a rage, screaming, "Who is this so-and-so who writes this stuff?" With that, she picked up the script, went to the writer's cubbyhole, threw it on his desk, and said, "What do you think I am? You write this in English!" (*The Milwaukee Journal*, December 28, 1944).

Without doubt, Lupe's take on the English language was manipulated to fit the situation, and almost always to her benefit. She was often offended by stereotypical references to her broken English, and yet she'd often use her lack of understanding to get out of a sticky situation. By the time the "Mexican Spitfire" series was filmed, her "you write this in English!" mindset had changed completely. Lupe wholeheartedly embraced the role of Carmelita. In fact, she even embellished her natural accent to fit the character. Because of Hollywood's interpretation of who she was and who she *should* and *shouldn't* be, Lupe fluctuated between embracing and detesting her Mexican heritage. It helped her, yet it also hindered her.

Lupe was a proud Mexican woman. Without doubt, she loved her country and its people. However, it was Hollywood's narrow-minded, racial overtones that embroiled her in a love-hate relationship with herself and with her own ethnicity. If Lupe *wasn't* Mexican,

**Twenty-one-year-old Lupe poses seductively in a scene from *Lady of the Pavements* (1929).**

would it have been easier for her to exist on a higher professional level in Hollywood? Absolutely. Because she *was* Mexican, and because (unlike del Rio) she was excitable, loud and fiery, was she typecast and pigeonholed into hotheaded, ethnic roles? Absolutely. There was a place for Lupe in Hollywood, and that's why she succeeded. However, Hollywood also kept Lupe in her place.

*   *   *

Next, Lupe took second billing to leading man Rod La Rocque in the silent feature *Stand and Deliver* (1928). *Photoplay* (March, 1928) was impressed with her performance:

> "Lupe Vélez, the girl who finally interests Rod, proves without question that she has a permanent place on the screen. She is a combination of Dolores del Rio and Olive Borden, with something neither of them has."

The D.W. Griffith–directed *Lady of the Pavements* (1929) was Lupe's next feature film. Lupe was given top billing as Nanon del Rayon, a Spanish cabaret singer who is transformed into (and passed off as) a lady by the revenge-seeking Countess Diane des Granges (Jetta Goudal), ex-fiancée of Count Karl Von Arnim (William Boyd). Of course, the countess' evil plotting backfires and Count Karl and Nanon live happily ever after.

On the *Lady of the Pavements* set, the gloves were off between leading ladies Lupe Vélez and Jetta Goudal. In 1929, when Harry Carr wrote a series of articles about his experiences in silent film for *Smart Set* magazine, the subject of working with Lupe on the set of *Lady*

*of the Pavements* came up. "Lupe out-gamed Griffith," said Carr. "This is a little secret. Griffith's method is to acquire complete domination over every actress. If he can't accomplish this complete surrender of will in any other way, he wears them down physically."

Carr said that Griffith started in with Lupe early one morning. From breakfast time on, he put her through difficult close-up scenes. When noon came, Griffith was tired; the cameraman was tuckered out; but Lupe was still frolicking around like a kitten. They went through the whole afternoon, and ended staggering on their feet—all except Lupe. Late that night, long after midnight, Griffith collapsed with fatigue in his chair. During this pause, Lupe leaped up and said to the exhausted orchestra, "Play some jazz; I want to dance!" That was the only time in Griffith's career that his directing method hadn't worked. Lupe could not be broken!

Lupe's stamina, combined with the ongoing feud between Lupe and Jetta Goudal, was too much for Griffith to take. By the time filming was complete, he was worn out. A shadow of his former self, he had lost control of his actresses, his life (he was drinking heavily) and his career.

In post-production, Griffith experimented with the sound and its volume. Author Alexander Walker explained the debacle in his 1979 book *The Shattered Silents: How the Talkies Came to Stay*:

Lupe and real-life lover Gary Cooper share a tender moment in the Victor Fleming–directed romantic Western *Wolf Song* (1929).

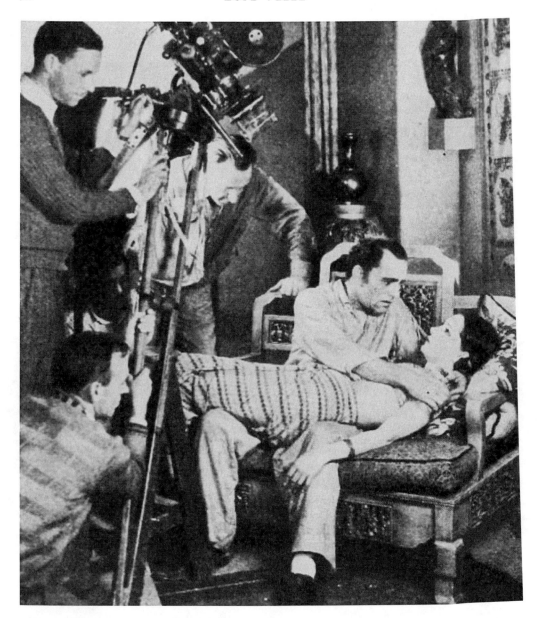

**A rare behind the scenes photograph of Lon Chaney with Lupe in *Where East Is East* (1929). Director Tod Browning is standing behind Chaney with his hand resting on the arm of the chair. This was the final Browning–Chaney collaboration as well as Browning's last silent film.**

The laboratories not only printed the sound sequences in the film so poorly that their imperfections were plainly visible, but also imperfectly recorded the songs to the extent that the only sounds that could be heard were the high notes. It took three days to rush substitute discs out to the cinemas.

Before word spread about how badly the film was received at the premiere, producer Joseph Schenck worked fast to save face. He used the vivacious charm of his leading lady to his advantage and quickly organized a cross-country tour for Lupe. In theaters playing

the film, she would perform a few songs, answer questions from star-struck audience members, and even poke fun at her co-stars and Hollywood peers by impersonating them. In the eyes of the audience she was a huge hit. In the eyes of the studio, she was a much-needed diversion that worked!

Prior to every showing of *Lady of the Pavements* at the Rialto Theater in New York, Lupe took the stage and performed. Audiences and critics were so captivated with her one-woman pre-show, they paid little attention to the flaws of the film. It was still panned by some papers, but not nearly as much as it would have been had Lupe not traveled the country to deflect attention from this mess of a movie. Of Lupe's performance, Doris Denbo of *Hollywood Daily Citizen* (March 1, 1929) wrote, "Here is a little personality [Lupe] that simply radiates appeal, dramatic verve and vivacious winsomeness and walks off with the major honors of the picture..."

In 1931, Griffith retired from an industry that had ironically progressed past the point of one of Hollywood's greatest innovators. Sound ended the career of many silent era stars, but for it to be triumphant over the "father of film" was incomprehensible. Griffith died on July 23, 1948. He was 73 years old.

Next up for Lupe was *Wolf Song* (1929), which marked the beginning of a long, passionate, tumultuous, and exceedingly complicated romance between Lupe and her leading man, Gary Cooper. The heat between them in *Wolf Song* burns up the screen. In fact, their sexual chemistry has been captured with such passionate intensity, at times it feels uncomfortably voyeuristic to be watching at all!

Lupe broke up with the film's director, Victor Fleming, to pursue a romance with Cooper. She had already had her way with newcomer Russ Columbo, a fling that burned out quickly. However, Lupe's relationship with Cooper was starkly different to any previous, or future, relationship with any man. Despite the fact that they never made it to the altar, by Lupe's own admission Gary Cooper remained the love of her life.

In spite of Lupe's break-up with Fleming, he didn't appear to harbor any resentment toward her. "[Lupe] is the best morale doctor imaginable," Fleming declared upon returning from a location trip for *Wolf Song*. "Gloom and that girl simply could not stay in the same vicinity." Whenever she wasn't working, Lupe would happily entertain other members of the company with song-and-dance numbers. Anyone who was not otherwise occupied would gather around her for the energetic one-woman show (*Northern Territory Times*, Darwin, Australia, April 12, 1932).

Many *Wolf Song* reviewers complimented Lupe on her beauty and vivacious personality. Many also noted that she was difficult to understand. Negative comments aside, Lupe took something much more rewarding from the production: the leading man.

It's no secret that studios would frequently fabricate off-screen love affairs between lead actors in order to drum up publicity for a new film. But in Gary and Lupe's case, no fibbing was needed; they were in love (even living together) and Paramount took full advantage of their affair by sending them on a cross-country tour to promote *Wolf Song*. It worked. The film was well received. However, when there was no film to promote, Paramount was less than thrilled with a diversion of the Lupe Vélez kind.

*Where East Is East* (1929), directed by Tod Browning, was her next feature and it allowed her to work with one of Hollywood's silent greats, "The Man of a Thousand Faces," Lon Chaney. Chaney plays Tiger Hanes, a physically (and emotionally) scarred animal trapper living in Southeast Asia. Lupe plays his half-caste daughter Toyo. The unsettling closeness between father and daughter is apparent throughout. *Where East Is East* was Browning's last

silent film (by the end of 1929, talkies had all but taken over the industry); it was also the tenth (and last) collaboration between the director and Chaney.

Because of the macabre nature of the stories and character portrayals, the censors criticized most Chaney-Browning collaborations for being too violent, too graphic, and too grotesque. This production was no different. At the time of its release, the pro-censorship publication *Harrison's Reports* was less than impressed with *Where East Is East*:

> The endeavor of the producers to find suitable material for Mr. Chaney has led them to accept all kinds of gruesome stories. In *Where East Is East*, the main feature is the hero's letting loose of a gorilla on his ex-wife [Estelle Taylor], mother of the heroine, tearing her to pieces. The actual killing is not, of course, shown: it is only implied. But the thought is there. And it is an unpleasant thought.

The movie had a budget of $295,000 (approximately $3.8 million in 2011). Fourteen-hour workdays were commonplace, and even a few eighteen-hour days were thrown in to satisfy the tight 33-day production timetable. The longest day on set started with a 10:05 A.M. call time with work finishing at 4:30 A.M. the following morning (www.tcm.com).

While there was some pre-production speculation that Chaney's down-to-earth approach to his craft would clash with Lupe and Estelle Taylor's emotional outbursts, Chaney told one reporter: "I'm not temperamental and I won't tolerate temperament in other people. I'm always on time; if the leading woman isn't on the set I just walk off and take off my makeup. Lupe and I are getting along all right; she's a great little actress" (Blake, *Lon Chaney: The Man Behind the Thousand Faces*).

Unfortunately, the "gorilla" used in the climax of *Where East Is East* is just a guy in a bad monkey suit. As a result, the shock value of the scene is significantly decreased. That said, the implied mauling of the villainess and the effect Browning was obviously attempting to achieve serves to end the film in a satisfying way. Estelle Taylor is mesmerizing as Toyo's estranged mother, the evil seductress, Madame de Sylva.

*   *   *

Lupe's last film for the decade, *Tiger Rose* (1929), was her first all-talking picture. She was the leading lady, second billed under leading man Monte Blue. One of Hollywood's most beloved canine co-stars, Rin Tin Tin, also starred in the Northwest drama. While Lupe garnered mostly positive reviews for her performance as the French half-caste Rose, the film was certainly her weakest to date.

Lupe's transition from two-reelers, to silent features, to an all-talkie to round out the decade, along with the people she was introduced to and the caliber of talent that she worked with during those first two crucial years in Hollywood is nothing short of astounding. Producers Hal Roach and Joseph M. Schenck, costume designers Adrian and Edith Head, art directors Cedric Gibbons and William Cameron Menzies, cinematographer G. W. Bitzer, etc. It's a wish list of movie-making *legends*. A dream run for any actress ... let alone "the new girl" in town.

# 8

## *"Loop" and "Coop"*

Three years after they met, a reporter asked Gary Cooper, "What's the biggest thrill you've gotten from motion pictures?" Cooper responded with one word — "Lupe."[1]

Gary Cooper and Lupe Vélez met when they were cast as the leads in the 1929 Paramount production *Wolf Song*. It was a mutual, instant attraction and before filming was complete, Gary, a well-known "Mama's Boy," had moved out of his parents' house and in with Lupe. Cooper's straitlaced mother, Alice, was horrified that her son had fallen for "that Mexican thing" and she would not give him up to her without a fight. The feud between Lupe Vélez, lover, and Alice Cooper, mother, was bitter and long-standing. Even worse, it eventually became public when the women spoke to the press about each other!

Lupe and Gary were about as opposite as opposites could be. She was short. He was tall. One writer described Lupe as "usually clinging to Gary, running along beside him, like a toy puppy beside a Newfoundland" (*Modern Screen*, October 1931). Additionally, Lupe talked all the time. Gary was a man of few words. She was loud. He was quiet. But they had two things in common, their acting profession and their love for each other. Their romance was one of the most talked about in Hollywood, the most written about in fan magazines, the most speculated on by reporters.

During the filming of *Morocco* (1930), Lupe kept a watchful eye on her man. Marlene Dietrich was the film's leading lady. Though married, she had a man-eater reputation and Lupe was fiercely protective of Gary and their relationship. In a letter to her husband, Dietrich wrote:

Gary Cooper is pleasant and good-looking. The newspapers have said that Lupe Vélez (his girlfriend) has threatened to scratch my eyes out if I come near him. How can I? She sits on his lap between scenes. I don't go close enough, God knows, to see what they're doing, but it looks like they are doing something that is usually done in private [Riva, *Marlene Dietrich*].

Lupe may well have prevented Dietrich from having a chance with Gary during the filming of *Morocco*, but several years later, Lupe was nowhere to be seen and Dietrich more than made up for lost time during the production of their next film together. And Cooper was a willing participant. Between scenes on the Frank Borzage–directed *Desire* (1936), Cooper would often be seen visiting Dietrich's dressing room, and they weren't running lines (Skaerved, *Dietrich*).

Towards the latter part of 1930, when their relationship was in full swing, Lupe was spotted wearing what looked to be a wedding ring. Rumors swirled that she and Gary had

secretly married. However, Lupe insisted it was her mother's ring. "When and if I'm married to Gary Cooper," she elaborated, "I'll sure tell the world about it" (*Appleton Post-Crescent*, November 29, 1930).

Lupe enjoyed shopping for Gary, and he let her pick out whatever she thought would look good on him. Gary's mother was mortified by her son's sudden "ethnic transformation." He'd often show up at his parent's house wearing brightly colored shirts that he once wouldn't be caught dead wearing. But, if Lupe bought it, he'd wear it.

\* \* \*

Wherever she went, and long before Paris Hilton made it a Hollywood trend, Lupe would carry a couple of Chihuahuas with her. Her constant house companion was a giant white rat that wasn't much bigger than her dogs. She trained it to run around her neck and to lie perfectly still on her shoulder. Her favorite birds were canaries. At one time their number reached 100 and she would often stand in the huge aviary and sing right along with them. Lupe raised the birds in an up-to-the-minute, temperature-controlled aviary that boasted hot and cold running water, two large trees and curtains that were opened and closed to regulate the light (*Los Angeles Evening Herald*, January 10, 1931).

One Sunday evening during the last year of her life (1944), Lupe's beloved dogs Chips and Chops ran away from home. Lupe was in such a state, she had to "take a peel to go to sleep." Chips, a year-old Sealyham, and Chops, an eight-month-old Scottie were, "a combination, like feesh and cheeps," Lupe explained, and so they ran away together. The following day, Arthur J. Fitzgerald found both dogs wandering around in his front garden. He looked at the tags on their collars and contacted Lupe to tell her that he had them. Fitzgerald told the paper that Lupe was so excited they'd been found, she rushed over to pick them up in her nightgown ("Lupe Vélez Gets Back Dogs, Chips and Chops." *Los Angeles Times*, April 18, 1944).

On the morning of their mistresses' death, a photographer snapped a photo of Chips and Chops

Back into the arms of her lover Gary Cooper, Lupe happily returns home after a lengthy publicity tour across the United States, circa 1928. Cooper had spent most of his salary on long distance telephone calls while she was away and on the afternoon of Lupe's return, he reportedly paced the platform of the railway station for two hours before her train was due to arrive.

Circa 1929, Gary Cooper proudly shows off his Alibi Club membership card to girlfriend Lupe. Located in a row house (built in 1869) in Washington D.C., not far from the White House, the private gentlemen's club prided itself on its elite members. From presidents to senators, military personnel to actors and inclusive of many prominent private citizens, the Alibi Club was the exclusive gathering place for all leading men in their fields.

locked outside, behind a wire door. Both dogs quizzically looked inside at the police activity, confused as to why their luxurious, insulated world had so suddenly changed. Given Lupe's attachment to the pair (she named them in one of her suicide notes), it's a heartbreaking photo.

All her life, even when she was in Mexico, any stray furry, feathered or scaly critter that was lucky enough to cross Lupe's path would be instantly adopted and taken back to the Vélez zoo.[2] Lupe gave a loving home to many cats, dogs and birds over the years. There

were many horses, for both leisure and sport, including a stable of polo ponies during her engagement to Guinn "Big Boy" Williams. During one encounter with a horse that dared to take a bite of Lupe's arm, without missing a beat, and in order to teach the horse "a lesson," she bit the horse right back! Not content with the usual array of domesticated animals, she had several monkeys, and even a baby leopard. A few years after her death, Fred Sandman, supervisor of the Central Park Zoo, said. "Lupe Vélez used to come here [all the time]. I'd have the chimps put on a special act for her because she was so fond of them" (*Corpus Christi Times*, May 13, 1948).

One gift that Gary gave to Lupe was a wild eagle that he had reportedly trapped himself. As a surprise, he arranged for the bird to be delivered to her house in a crate. It had a wingspan of nine feet; it took a carpenter three days to build a cage big enough to keep it in. At first, Lupe was enthusiastic about her new pet. She excitedly drove down to the meat market and asked the butcher what she should feed the bird. "Fresh meat and a couple of rabbits daily," said the butcher. So Lupe put two rabbits a day on order. Then she discovered that none of her servants would go near the cage. She had to feed the eagle herself, and she did, but it took an hour a day to get the job done. After ten days, Lupe was frantic. Besides the time and expense involved in taking care of the wild bird, there was the constant commotion with everyone in the house who was scared of it. "I don't know what I am going to do!" she cried, as she took a friend away from the cage after telling her the story. "I can't go away, I..."

A knock at the door stopped their conversation. It was a telegram from Gary Cooper. As soon as she saw the sender's name, she eagerly tore it open. He wrote that he was in the north, on location. He missed her, etc. The last line read: "Am sending you a mate for your eagle."

For the first time in years, or quite possibly her entire life, Lupe was speechless! ("Fowl Play," *Screen Secrets*, No. 49, April 1929). Soon after, the Mexico City Zoo was gifted with two eagles.

\* \* \*

As Gary Cooper's acting career took off, he was working a schedule and juggling a lifestyle that was detrimental to his health. He was churning out five pictures a year, which meant pulling double duty on set. One picture would be filmed during the day and another at night. After a 20-hour workday, what little time he had left to sleep was taken up with Lupe's demand for time and attention. She wanted to go out. He wanted to sleep. For months, Cooper existed on very little sleep.

His usual weight of 180 pounds, an already lean build for his height (he was 6'3"), dropped to a dangerously low 148 pounds. Despite his burgeoning career and the increase in salary that came with it, he was almost broke. Between supporting his parents and constantly buying trinkets of love to keep Lupe happy, he was spending more than he was earning. When Cooper collapsed with emotional and physical exhaustion, Paramount executives realized that working their star player for close to five years without a break had almost killed him. While his romance with Lupe served the studio during the promotion of *Wolf Song*, they had anticipated it to fizzle out soon after. It didn't. Much to the delight of his mother, Paramount was now also concerned that Lupe was no good for Gary Cooper. The naysayers were piling up and the relationship cracks were beginning to show.

While Lupe and Gary's love affair was tumultuous and passionate, it was often extremely violent. Lupe would get mad but Gary wouldn't argue back. His silence made Lupe even

madder and in order to get a reaction, she'd get physical. She'd throw things, or grab the nearest weapon she could. One time that weapon was a kitchen knife. While Cooper was cooking dinner, out of nowhere, Lupe stabbed him in the arm. She admitted it too, saying, "...I got him with a knife once ... in the arm, and he sweat and bled. Boy, he sweat..." (Wayne, *Cooper's Women*).

Hollywood columnist Jimmie Fidler reported that after having an argument over the phone with Cooper, Lupe went about her house gathering all the presents he'd ever given her, piled them on her front porch, and then sent him a telegram to come and pick them up! (*The Chronicle*

Circa 1929, Gary Cooper holds one of the troublesome eagles that he gave Lupe during their romance. Though Lupe loved all animals, the wild birds became too much to handle. The birds lived out their remaining days at the Mexico City Zoo.

*Telegram*, February 27, 1948). This impulsive, extreme love-hate behavior was a regular pattern throughout their three-and-a-half year relationship. Actually, this behavior was a familiar pattern in *all* of Lupe's relationships. *She* was the common factor. Reporter Ruth Biery said:

"I have seen her beat him [Gary Cooper] with her shoe one moment and sob because she has done it the next; I have heard her rail at him in anger so terrible that I feared his life was in danger. But if another person said an unkind word about Gary I have known that his or her life was in danger" (http://web.mit.edu/cms/People/henry3/lupe.html. Jenkins, Henry. "You Don't Say That In English!").

Eventually the quiet, low-key Cooper just couldn't withstand Lupe's moods and impulsive outbursts. He was genuinely concerned for his safety, and rightly so. Apart from being overworked at the studio, his relationship with Lupe was getting increasingly combative, unpredictable and unsafe. Lupe kept a handgun in her dresser drawer — for *her* protection. She also kept a sharpened stiletto in her garter belt — for *her* protection. Of course, Gary was threatened with both weapons on several occasions. One day when Cooper showed up at the studio with scratch marks all over his face, he had no choice but to explain what had happened. He told his friend that he let Lupe "have it."

"You mean you hit her?" said the friend.

"No, kind of slapped her."

"So it's all over between you two?"

"Nope, happens all the time."

Cooper later confessed to feeling horrible about the incident. Yet, according to Lupe, striking a woman was something he had done before. She said he belted former lovers Carole Lombard and Clara Bow, and he belted her too.

As much as Judge Cooper enjoyed Lupe's entertaining qualities, he assured his nervous wife that their son's fascination with her would wane and they'd never have to entertain the thought of Lupe becoming an official member of the Cooper clan. Alice wasn't so sure. So she made it her business to meddle in her son's relationship until she could be absolutely sure her husband's prediction would come true.

Aside from making up stories about Lupe cheating on Gary, on several occasions his mother pretended to be seriously ill for the sole purpose of him breaking a date with Lupe at the last minute. Other times she'd ignore Lupe completely or make wisecracks in her presence, which would in turn cause Lupe to demand that Gary confront his mother about her rudeness (something he'd never do). Alice's manipulation and innuendo caused enough conflict between the pair that eventually she achieved her goal of breaking them up. Not many people were able to take on Lupe and win. Alice Cooper did.

Following her messy split with Gary, Lupe was seen around town with actor John Gilbert. The new romance rumors made for a good story but once again Lupe denied being in love. She always said if she were in love, the whole world would know it. It was true. Whenever Lupe was in love, she announced it to the world. But she announced nothing of the sort when she was seeing Gilbert, which is reason enough to regard the relationship as a brief, casual fling that ended as quickly as it began. Lupe said that Gilbert was a sweet boy, so intelligent, so cheerful, and above all else, he made her laugh like no one before him. However, on her broken romance with Gary Cooper, her mood shifted and with a somber tone she admitted that she would love him always and forever. "Never will I be able to love so much again. I was happy with him. But I'm a little crazy. Marriage is not for me" (*Los Angeles Evening Herald and Express*, undated, 1933). For several years following their split, Lupe freely spoke of her broken relationship with Cooper:

> I stopped loving, Gary, that's all. I mean I stopped loving him *that* way. But always, as long as I live, if Gary were sick or broke or needed me in any way I'd go to him, even if I had to walk a hundred miles. But now he is well, successful, and I am out of love with him [*Syracuse Herald*, January 10, 1932].

Her final few words were less than convincing. She had obviously forgotten about her recent (September 21, 1931) interview with Gladys Hall for *Modern Screen*. During that interview, Lupe was asked why she really broke up with Gary, but before she could answer, Hall came straight out and told her that she knows Lupe had been lying about the "real reasons" in all of her previous interviews. "[It's] because you love him," Hall said.

The room went deathly still. After a moment's thought, Lupe gave a sharp, bitter, burning answer to Hall's question: "*His mother!*" The floodgates opened and Lupe told the whole story. She said she had been faithful to Gary from the first day she loved him. But his mother told Gary that Lupe wanted nothing but fun, money, excitement, parties, etc. When Lupe and Gary were together, they rarely went out. Gary was a loner who didn't like parties so they didn't go. He rarely liked company so in order to stay active in Hollywood's social circles, they'd entertain a handful of close friends in Lupe's home. They frequented quaint neighborhood movie houses where no one would recognize them, they took trips in the car — simple things. "Gary liked to live quiet and so I liked it, too," she said.

Lupe said that Gary's mother would tell him to do exactly what the studio told him to do. He was afraid he'd lose his job if he didn't. His mother told him he must eat at the commissary, or they may not like that either. Lupe said she would beg him to come home and eat good, warm food. When he wasn't eating at the commissary, his mother would tell Gary to come home and eat dinner with her and his father. When he showed up, she'd be off playing

bridge with a friend. She'd come home late and give him a tiny piece of hamburger and canned vegetables, followed by canned fruit for dessert. Meanwhile, Lupe would be at her house, eating alone. She would tell her maid to take Gary's meal to the stove and keep it hot for him. Later in the night he would come by and devour the meal that he should have eaten hours before.

Hinting at another suicidal thought over the broken romance, Lupe said, "I wish I could go out this minute and fall under a trolley car. That is how I feel about it. I love him. Yes, I do.... He believed what his mother said about me. He didn't stop loving me, he stopped trusting me and that's what broke us up."

All throughout the 1931 *Modern Screen* interview, Lupe referred to Gary as

**Lupe Vélez during her early Hollywood years.**

mentally weak. He was a man in every sense of the word, he was a Hollywood movie star, yet in many ways, he was still just a timid child who was *completely* controlled by his overbearing mother.

In the spring of 1931 Gary was on the Italian leg of his "rest and recreation" tour of Europe. There he began a highly publicized relationship with American-born Countess Dorothy di Frasso. Thirteen years his senior (Lupe sarcastically referred to the countess as Gary's grandmother), the forty-three-year-old socialite had snared her title via her second marriage (in 1923) to Italian Count Carlo di Frasso, who was thirty years her senior. The relationship between Gary and the countess ran its course, but not before she taught him everything he needed to know about society life. She bought him expensive clothes and taught him about art, wine, self-confidence and etiquette; she also introduced him into international social circles that otherwise would have been off limits to him. A few weeks away from his mother's clutches and Gary Cooper became the man he should have been with Lupe. However, it was too late for that. Gary got what he needed out of the May–December romance, as did the countess. By 1933, she was dating gangster Bugsy Siegel(!). As for Gary Cooper, he finally cut the apron strings and found himself a respectable wife.

Louella O. Parsons reported in her *Los Angeles Examiner* column (October 3, 1933) that Gary and Sandra Shaw (stage name), otherwise known as Veronica "Rocky" Balfe,

attended the Friday night Hollywood Legion fights. On this particular evening, in a seating snafu, Gary was seated next to Lupe. Just to show Gary how she really felt, Lupe turned her back on him and devoted her entire attention to her soon-to-be husband, Johnny Weissmuller. Gary, greatly embarrassed by the awkward seating arrangement, also turned his back. A quick-witted individual a few seats behind them called, "Two aces back to back." Soon after, Groucho Marx, seated directly behind the ex-lovebirds, leaned over and tapped Lupe on the shoulder. "Pardon me," he said, "but have you met Mr. Cooper?" (*Los Angeles Evening Herald and Express*, October 7, 1933).

On December 15, 1933, thirty-two-year-old Gary Cooper, the eternal bachelor, got married. Twenty-year-old Rocky was his new bride. A countess and a string of Hollywood actresses, all older, wiser, and prettier, had been unable to get him down the aisle, but now Rocky had achieved the impossible. While they remained married right up until Cooper's death, faithfulness wasn't a part of their union. In fact, his wife's nickname Rocky was an omen of how their marriage would play out.

Rocky was the daughter of the governor of the New York Stock Exchange and the niece of Hollywood art director Cedric Gibbons. She attempted a film career under the name Sandra Shaw; however, it was just another short-lived diversion for a bored little rich girl. She appeared in minor roles in three films, most notably as the blonde in *King Kong* (1933) who is dropped to her death by the monster gorilla during his New York rampage. After marrying Cooper, not surprisingly, her plans for a film career were abandoned and Rocky became a dutiful wife and Hollywood socialite.

Once again, Gary had chosen a woman very different in personality and background from Lupe Vélez. Ironically, Gary's mother *still* didn't approve ... and neither did Lupe. Not surprisingly, Lupe and Rocky despised each other. Lupe lost Gary and Rocky had him. Lupe was bitter and Rocky was aggravated because Lupe was a constant reminder of her husband's past. One night at the Trocadero nightclub, Lupe threw a drink in Rocky's face. Gary stepped in and restrained Lupe until she simmered down. Faced with a heated situation between his wife and his ex-lover, Gary didn't grab his wife, he grabbed Lupe! This didn't go unnoticed. That split-second decision of who to restrain, or protect, fed into Rocky's insecurities and her jealously only intensified further (Wayne, *Cooper's Women*).

For many years following their break-up, Lupe openly admitted her undying love for Gary Cooper. According to the Gladys Hall Papers at the Margaret Herrick Library, Lupe said in 1938 that at first it was Joseph Schenck who wouldn't allow them to marry; then, other "older people objected." It was an unusually subtle referral to Gary's parents, specifically his mother. The interferences in their relationship came from all sides — both professional and personal. During the 1938 interview with Hall, Lupe said: "Hearts where love lives are like the nests of birds ... poke at them with human fingers and the birds do not nest there any more, they fly away."

Lupe concluded by saying she could live 100 years and die 100 deaths and there never would be a man so fine as Gary Cooper. She said she was grateful to God for the time they had together and she looked upon their relationship as a gentle gift that she would never stop remembering.

\* \* \*

Gary Cooper became one of America's most-loved, most successful actors. He was nominated for several Academy Awards during his long film career, winning Best Actor Oscars for *Sergeant York* (1941) and *High Noon* (1952). Near the end of his life, for his many

memorable screen performances and the international recognition he had brought to the motion picture industry, he was given an honorary Oscar at 1961's Academy Awards ceremony. While his body of work was certainly worthy of such recognition, the award's timing couldn't be ignored. Too sick to attend, he asked his good friend and fellow actor James Stewart to accept the award on his behalf. Cooper watched the TV broadcast at home with Rocky and their only child Maria.

Up until the Oscar ceremony, Cooper's dire health condition had been a well-kept secret. Rumors circulated as to why he wasn't attending the show, but the media had no solid evidence to explain Stewart stepping in. An emotionally overcome Stewart accidentally hinted at Cooper's grim prognosis during his tearful acceptance speech. The following day, headlines of "How Ill Is Gary Cooper?" were everywhere. The question was soon answered ... and the news wasn't good. Newspaper headlines on April 19, 1961 read:

Circa 1934 — Left to right: Gary Cooper with his new bride, Veronica "Rocky" Cooper (nee: Balfe) and Lupe with her new husband, Johnny Weissmuller.

### Gary Cooper Has Cancer

On May 13, 1961, less than a month after the Oscar ceremony and a little over a year after he was diagnosed with prostate cancer that had spread to his colon, lungs and bones, Gary Cooper died. Six days prior, he had turned sixty. Despite the frequent infidelities, including a three year separation (1951 to 1954), Gary and Rocky remained married until his death. In 1964, Rocky married Dr. John Converse, a plastic surgeon; they had met in 1958 after Gary contacted him to get some facial "tweaking" done. Dr. Converse died in January of 1981, and Rocky died on February 16, 2000, at age eighty-six.

While Gary and Rocky's marriage was plagued with lies and affairs, the biggest, most controversial storm that was weathered was Cooper's relationship with actress Patricia Neal and her subsequent pregnancy. Fearing their careers would be over if they had the baby, Cooper reportedly pressured Neal (a devout Catholic) to abort his child in 1950. (Cooper had starred alongside Neal in 1949's *The Fountainhead*. He was forty-eight, she was twenty-three.) For Neal, the abortion was a scar that would never heal. In the 2006 book *Patricia Neal: An Unquiet Life*, Stephen Michael Shearer quoted Neal:

> For over thirty years, alone, in the night, I cried. For years and years I cried over that baby. And whenever I had too much to drink, I would remember that I had not allowed him to

exist. I admired Ingrid Bergman for having her son [the result of an affair with director Roberto Rossellini]. She had guts. I did not. And I regret it with all my heart. If I had only one thing to do over in my life, I would have that baby.

Neal went on to marry British best-selling children's author Roald Dahl. They had five children together. Their daughter Olivia died at age seven (complications from measles), and their son Theo suffered brain damage when he was four months old after his baby carriage was struck by a New York City taxicab. Neal's life was plagued with personal demons and health problems, including (in 1965) a series of strokes that almost killed her while she was pregnant with her fifth child, Lucy. Miraculously, the baby was born healthy. Following Dahl's affair with family friend Felicity Crosland, they divorced in 1983 after thirty years of marriage (*The Evening Independent*, October 24, 1983). In a 2008 interview, 82-year-old Neal said, "I loved Gary Cooper, for years and years and years. And I still love him..." Neal passed away from lung cancer on August 8, 2010. Even in her old age, she still mourned the loss of her forbidden relationship with Cooper, she still loved him, and she never got over the loss of their aborted love child (www.imdb.com).

Cooper had relationships and casual dalliances with many Hollywood actresses, including Clara Bow, Ingrid Bergman, Carole Lombard, Marlene Dietrich, Evelyn Brent, Grace Kelly and Tallulah Bankhead, just to name a few. Even after the break-ups, somehow Cooper always managed to remain in the good graces of the ladies he'd loved and left behind. No one had a bad word to say about "Coop"—not even a scorned woman. Gary Cooper was the lost love that haunted Lupe Vélez for the rest of her life. She never got over him and she publicly admitted that she'd always love him.

The day after Lupe's death, journalist Harrison Carroll wrote a lengthy tribute article in the *Los Angeles Evening Herald and Express* (December 15, 1944). One of Lupe's friends confided in him, saying: "After the breakup with Cooper, Lupe was always whistling in the dark. She kept saying, 'I don't care, I don't care, I don't care,' and she found other loves, but she never was able to forget Gary."

On screen, via his films, Cooper was looked upon as the quintessential all–American hero.

Lupe wore many traditional Spanish-style costumes throughout her film career. The outfit in this photograph is a Hollywood version of the Manola costume that originated in Seville, Spain.

Off screen he was perceived to be the strong, silent type with a boyish charm, and in many ways he was just that. But underneath that country-boy façade, he was a quintessential "ladies man." Whatever he said (or didn't say) worked to lure the women into his bed.

And perhaps the men too: Rumors of affairs with openly gay actor and Broadway producer Anderson Lawler (whose brother confirmed their relationship) and photographer and designer Sir Cecil Beaton (his diaries revealed their long-standing relationship) circulated for years (Swindell, *Last Hero: A Biography of Gary Cooper*). Lupe knew about Gary's relationship with Lawler. In fact, according to actor William Janney (1908–1992), Lupe even participated in at least one of their bedroom romps. Author Michael Ankerich interviewed Janney for his book *The Sound of Silence*, and wrote:

> It was after a party and a lot of drinking had been going on. After much to drink, they all went to a place to spend the night. There were two beds in the room. Janney slept in one and in the other bed was Cooper (in the middle), Vélez, and Anderson Lawler. During the night, Janney heard a lot of giggling going on. The next morning, he asked Lawler what had gone on in the bed. Lawler said Lupe was "sucking Cooper off while I was fucking him in the ass."

Ankerich went on: "Andy Lawler and Cooper were 'good friends' in those days. Janney might have been more than a witness to this scene, but he never admitted to being under the covers with them. Janney and Cooper shared the same boarding house for a time."

Lawler and Cooper also shared an L.A. house (7511 Franklin Avenue) and, strange as it seems, Lupe was consensual to Gary's sexual liaisons with Lawler, on one strict condition: only when *she* was involved. If she was excluded, she became exceedingly jealous. One time she unzipped Gary's pants (at a very crowded Hollywood party), bent down and sniffed his crotch to see if she could detect Lawler's signature cologne (Conner, *Lupe Vélez and Her Lovers*).

Author William J. Mann was privy to Lawler's personal papers and scrapbooks and did extensive research for his 2001 book *Behind the Screen: How Gays and Lesbians Shaped Hollywood, 1910–1969*. He wrote:

> In letters to his mother.... Lawler wrote of slipping away with Cooper to Catalina Island for the weekend—a break from the studio and Gary's volatile girlfriend, Lupe Vélez.... Andy Lawler was in love with Gary Cooper. That much is obvious from the letters and scrapbooks he left behind, as well as the memories of others. In one scrapbook Lawler pasted pictures of Cooper carefully cut from fan magazines. Beside them is mounted every clipping mentioning the two of them together, along with every photograph and every telegram Gary ever sent him, all carefully pasted and preserved.

Not long after his split with Lupe, Gary said that he regretted letting others determine his life for him. Without naming names (notably his mother), he said, "I shall never be dominated by other people again as I had allowed myself to be..." (Thompson, *Gary Cooper*). It was a strong statement for a man of few words to make at any time, let alone publicly. But his stance was too little, too late. For no good reason, Alice Cooper despised Lupe. For a while Lupe was willing to fight the fight for the sake of keeping her man, but the constant battle became too draining. She got tired of competing for Gary's affections, not only with his mother, but with Anderson Lawler too. Gary may have eventually realized his many mistakes, but by that time, Lupe had moved on.

In 1956, five years before Cooper's death and over a decade after Lupe's death, *The Saturday Evening Post* published a reflective piece written by Cooper. On his relationship with Lupe, he said: "I guess I was in love with Miss Vélez, or as much in love as one could

get with a creature as elusive as quicksilver.... You couldn't help being attracted to Lupe Vélez. She flashed, stormed and sparkled...."

At the conclusion of her September 1931 interview for *Modern Screen*, Lupe said she would go on loving Gary Cooper all her life. Then, with a tearful voice she sang two poignant lines in reference to their lost romance:

> Now that I've lost you — please understand
>  I live forever — at your — command.

When she had him, and even after she lost him, Lupe lived for Gary Cooper. On December 14, 1944, part of her died for him, too.

# 9

# *Misunderstood*

"With Lupe, every night is Saturday night."[1]— Lupe's business manager, Bö Roos

When Ted LeBerthon of the *Los Angeles Record* arrived at Lupe's home for a one-on-one interview, like most reporters, he got more than he bargained for. In the June 17, 1930, article, LeBerthon wrote:

It is a pretty house, something a little American housewife would "just admire." A glorified candy box. It was a fitting setting for Lupe's red silk chorus girl pajamas, but seemed to be to have no relation to Lupe's soul. No more than the pastels of seductive, somewhat naked cuties, reminiscent of La Vie Parisienne, belonged on the walls. The only clues to Lupe, the only signs of her spirit in the house were a stuffed eagle in the drawing room; and two stuffed owls and a stuffed hawk in a den. The taxidermist was an artist. They seemed, wings and talons spread, beaks agape angrily, to be ready to pounce off the walls. They seemed to have flown onto the walls from the desert, to remind Lupe of hot dry winds and high blue skies.

"I have just been in the swimming pool," she laughed, a little cautious to begin with. "I wear these pajamas because they are comfortable — because I want to. People say I am wild. That is not true. But I do as I please. If it does not please others..."

And on and on. She vowed she never went out at night, especially to nightclubs. She defended her right to live as she pleases. Her voice, strong and tense, seemed almost more than her somewhat immature little body could stand. It seemed strange, unreal, listening there to her. For I had not accused her of anything. Evidently some fan magazine writer or newspaper writer has said something about Lupe that has bewildered her, that makes her want to justify something or other. What that is, I don't know.

Such a kid! Transported by sudden movie fame into the opulence that a $2,500 [approximately $32,000 in 2011] a week salary may command; probably at heart quite dubious about her impulses; and having been told–perhaps–that all great actresses, such as Bernhardt and Duse, have considered themselves above "the herd's conventions," she may be confused.

Too, she did not look to me to be well. I never had seen her before, except in her first picture, *The Gaucho*, when I was, like millions of others, bowled over by her madness. But, face-to-face, she seemed as one who had once been strong, but had been sick, and was bearing up through sheer nervous energy, through a fighting spirit.

Had I left her house shortly after entering it, I would have felt extremely sad. Something off-key about Lupe and her big, pretty, sterile house would have nettled me. I would have felt like getting drunk. But things took an unexpected turn. Lupe had been telling me, in a high nervous key, that she hated night clubs, that she never went out, but that she wanted to do as she pleased in her own house. I said:

"What is the difference whether you do as you please in your own house or at a night club? For instance, I think the greatest spot in Los Angeles is the Apex Night Club, with its wonderful Negro entertainers."

She became intensely interested. Soon the ice was broken. She was laughing, and describing animatedly "The Blackbirds," a Negro revue she'd seen in New York City.

"Yes, and I have a treat for you," she said. "We go into the front room. You will hear some jazz. Oh, mama, and wait to you hear that piano player." Lupe, with her Mexican accent, tried to copy the Negro dialect. She shrugged her shoulders, tossed her hair back and sang and shouted and danced.

The fine humanity of this youngster cropped out when she told me, a while later, of her beginnings. "Every peecture I make almost ees wrong," she stormed. "Thee directors they want to make me a leetle gaga girl. You understan,' huh? And I am not thee gaga. They even make me a gaga een *Tiger Rose*. Peecture that!

"I cannot help what I am. That ees what God he makes me. I am thee wild one. I am born in one little place, San Luis Potosi. Eet is a day and one-half from Mexico City.

"They ees 385 churches een that small place. And such a devil like I am come from that place. You know, I raise thee devil everywhere!"

"But, Miss Vélez," I coughed, "I—can't—er—"

"Call me Lupe," she laughed raucously. "And tell me—what ees your first name? What they call you? Oh, Ted. Well, I call you Ted. Now, what you want to know?"

"How could they ever get 385 churches in one small town, Lupe?"

"Oh, they ees five or seez in each block. But maybe I don't count right. First I say to some woan [someone] I meet 'They ees one thousand church een San Luis Potosí!' And he say 'They cannot be room for so many.' So I theenk. 'If there is not one thousand, maybe there is 385. So I steeck to that.'"

Lupe tells me that she started in pictures at $600 a week, and has worked up to $2,500 a week. She says, like a duchess:

"I could not afford to work for less. Een Mexico I were thee beegest of all star in revue. I were thee beegest heet in the coantry. I made feety dollar a day."

There seemed to be some inconsistency between this grand statement and Lupe's recounting of her arrival in Los Angeles. For, she says, she came in with $1.15 in her pocket, unable to speak a word of English, and with Milton [earlier referred to as Mil-a-tone], her Chihuahua puppy, hidden in her one suitcase.

"It was seez o'clock woan evening. I am hungry. I seet een front of the depot, thee Southern Pacific. I buy a hamburg for Meelton, and a hot dog and a Coca-Cola for myself."

Surely not a grandiose debut in Los Angeles for Mexico's "beegest" and highest-salaried star. She had come here, she said, at the behest of Richard Bennett, who had seen her act in Mexico. Lupe, then 17, finally landed with Fanchon and Marco, and later with Hal Roach comedies. 500 girls (I have Lupe's word for the number) were tested by Fairbanks for the feminine lead in *The Gaucho*. And how could one doubt Lupe's word?

"Out of all these, he peek me!" she laughed happily.

Lupe tells me that she answers personally about 500 fan letters a day. Truly a prodigious daily task!

"Thee public geev me my bread, my home, my car, my sweeming pool," she says, fierily, "and I am grateful. I am humble."

Lupe says that her creed is to "love everytheeng, and everywoan." To go to bed happy, to arise saying, "Well, well, I am still leeving, eean't that fine!" To "leeve" and be happy every day, as "eef" it was the last. To leeve "everytheeng up to God."

Lupe is herself a movie fan! She has a scrapbook filled with nothing but photographs of Greta Garbo she has scissored from movie magazines.

"Every day of my life I look at them," she exults. "I love her. I adore her. Yet I have never met weeth her. She ees so beautiful, she make me cry. Maybe eet ees because I am so damn homely. Oh, that beautiful theeng. I see every Garbo peecture four or five time! Een *Anna Christie*, when she first meet her father, you remember how her face go? Like she want to be happy, but she can't?

"Well, I feel so bad for her. I break down. I cry like a goddam leetle fool. She ees a fine

lady, you know, not like me. And she play thee part of that poor bum of a girl like she suffer every-theeng..."

Lupe's best hours at home are spent in the great, reposeful garden. There one finds Eric, the Great Dane; and Coco, the English bull; and Milton, the Chihuahua; and "Skippy," the big gray cat, and "Jolin" (pronounced Ho leen), who is Skippy's offspring. And there is an aviary, full of parrots, parakeets and canaries.

And every evening at twilight, a dove perches on a nearby housetop and calls and calls. And if Lupe is at home, she calls back. "Me and that dove, we ees old friends now," she laughs. She feeds and cares for the birds, puts mother canaries on eggs, cleans the aviary herself, and all alight on her without fear.

"They ees my friend," she smiled seriously. "Can tell always a friend. I am like thee dog. I smell whether people like me. No one can fool me. I know what everybody theenk about me."

Lupe poses by her backyard pool, circa 1934. This photograph was taken during her marriage to Johnny Weissmuller. A five-time Olympic gold medalist (1924–1928), he retired undefeated and swam every day for most of his life. Lupe disliked most recreational water sports *except* swimming.

When I was leaving, it struck me that Lupe spends so much time with her garden, with her birds, with the dogs and cats because "she like them."

The house looks so empty-spirited, so unlived in, because Lupe instinctively and unconsciously, cannot endure to stay inside it. But, of course, she does not realize the truth.

Socially, Lupe's unpredictable nature was called into question numerous times, but professionally, she took her career very seriously. On the job she was proficient in every way, showing up on time, working late if asked, helping fellow actors with their lines, etc. On set, Lupe was as reliable as could be. A December 1930 *Photoplay* article ("Lupe — No Change!") written by Barbara Lawton stated that Lupe came down on herself hard if she flubbed a line; running to the side of the set, out of microphone range, she'd say, "Dam' fool Lupe. Lupe bad girl. Lupe silly idiot. Dam' Lupe. Dam' dam' dam'!" After she vented and scolded herself, she'd return to the job at hand, refreshed and renewed, ready for another take.

Lupe's free-spirited personality allowed her to do whatever popped into her head for

a laugh at a moment's notice, but she learned a lesson when one incident went a little too far. After pulling her skirt up over her head and doing a wild dance at a party, Lupe soon realized that the very people who laughed at her (and with her) were the same people who spread reports about her misbehavior the following day.

During Lupe's much-publicized affair with Gary Cooper, the newspapers reported that he had "gone native," a derogatory reference to his newfound passion for drinking Tequila, eating chile and wearing colorful shirts. Suddenly, two of Hollywood's biggest movie stars were embroiled in a highly publicized inter-racial relationship, and for the most part, the media didn't have a clue how to deal with it. On December 17, 1932, San Antonio's Spanish-language newspaper *La Prensa* wrote that Lupe displayed Gary about L.A.'s Mexican theaters, calling him "su viejo" ("her old boy"). The paper said they made a "bizarre pair," continuing with:

> [Lupe is] as nutty as always, and bold; sometimes foul-mouthed; irresponsible, childish....
> [He] meekly walking his tall figure wherever his girlfriend fancied, being displayed as a rare
> animal at the Mexican cafes, at the theatres, on the street. Lupe was furiously jealous.... [She]
> hogged him, had him under her thumb.... [O]n more than one occasion [Lupe] boasted to
> have him captive.

Whether she was in a relationship or not, Lupe couldn't help but flirt with other men, but when she was committed to one man, flirting was as far as it went. When she was single, she played the field and went on many dates with a variety of men. She was no different to any other actress at the time, and yet Lupe has long been touted as a sex-crazed tramp who slept with any man who crossed her path.

For at least a decade of her Hollywood career, collectively, Lupe was either married or in committed relationships. First, there was her three-and-a-half year affair with Gary Cooper, then a five-year marriage to Johnny Weissmuller. Then Lupe was engaged three more times[2]; Guinn "Big Boy" Williams, Arturo de Córdova, and Harald Ramond were all husbands-to-be that never were. Given the fact that she was faithful in her marriage to Weissmuller, as well as her other long-term relationships, there was little time left for her to bed the laundry list of men that she's long been associated with. Lupe was no saint; in fact, she was a self-confessed "devil." But if you believe history as it's been told to date, then Lupe was the "Grand Whore of Hollywood." In reality, this promiscuous, hyper-sexed image was just another stain on her name, deriving from her "Mexican-ness" and her hot-blooded ancestry.

In many ways, Hollywood wasn't ready for the likes of Lupe Vélez. And in turn, she wasn't ready for the likes of Hollywood. No doubt, the industry, professionally and socially, had trouble fitting her unique, forthright personality into the "Hollywood hypocrisy" mold, mainly because Lupe refused to change who she was in order to fit in. And for that, the race card was used to explain away "Lupe's wild, crazy behavior." Lupe often said she was sorry that people didn't understand her when she acted like herself. "I hate not to be myself. But I learn. I learn that people laugh to your face and say you are terrible behind your back ... but here [clutching her chest] in my heart I will not change" (*The Argus*, December 4, 1937).

Unfortunately, Lupe's unbridled enthusiasm and excitability was habitually mistaken for lack of class. Her willingness to give to others, not just her family, was rarely talked about. Whether it was financial or professional assistance, for someone she knew or didn't know, Lupe was never too busy to help out. She once signed a pair of twelve-year-old girls under a personal contract to herself. The girls were talented tap dancers and she introduced

them to everyone she knew with the hope they'd get a Hollywood break. She opened her home to a guitar player from Mexico and she encouraged and taught him how to sell his talent to the Americans.

Homeless animals that wandered across Lupe's path were taken home and cared for. She would give cash to strangers in need, help a new actor cast in one of her films by rehearsing lines and doing her best to make him/her feel at ease in their new environment. The list of kind-hearted gestures goes on and on. Yet, despite all the good that she did, Lupe soon learned how malicious the Hollywood tongue could be.

Who could she *really* trust?

With that very question circulating in her own head, in certain situations and around certain people, by late 1930, Lupe tried her best to tame her ways and control her enthusiastic outbursts in public places. The operative word was *tried* ... it didn't always work out that way.

# 10

## *The Voice of Vélez*

"Jewels I have to have to live ... they make me sparkle and feel alive."[1]— Lupe Vélez

Along with New Year's Day 1930 came the realization that Lupe Vélez was a bonafide Hollywood star. A popular leading lady, she had a firm grip on the film business and an even firmer grip on the hearts of American theatergoers. She started the talkie era with four new films, including a Spanish-language remake (*Oriente y occidente*) of the English-language production (*East Is West*) that she had just completed.

At the same time, Hollywood was at the crossroads of a revolutionary new medium: the talkies. Prior to the introduction of sound films, silent films were relatively universal. The only additional post-production cost involved for international distribution was the interchangeable intertitles in the language (text) required for the country in question. However, sound changed that too.

Many foreign-language films were shot back to back, or even simultaneously with their English counterparts. Lupe, like many foreign actors with the ability to speak another language other than English, would often star in both versions of the same film. It wasn't uncommon to have a different male or female lead in the foreign version, even a different director and crew.

While most reviewers were favorable in describing Lupe's early dramatic performances, negative comments were usually directed toward her "heaving chest" and "over-acting." Some critics had trouble understanding her accent, but there were many actors (even American-born) who were difficult to decipher during the difficult transition years between the silent and sound era.

In silent film, overt physical and facial expressions were used to help tell the story. When the talkies arrived and voices could be heard for the first time, silent actors took some time to adjust their emoting and pull back their overacting to also allow their dialogue to tell the story. Memorizing lines and delivering them clearly and convincingly made acting with sound a whole new craft to learn. A foreign accent or inaudible voice didn't matter in silent film. It was all about looks. When the talkies arrived, looks were just part of the complete package needed to succeed.

Of course, film crews had hurdles of their own to get over. Sound equipment was heavy, and microphones picked up every little nuance. The camera and cameraman were initially housed in a virtually airless, padded booth, known in the industry as a "sweat box." The cameras were covered with "blimps" (soundproof covers) to prevent the noisy movement of the bulky equipment from being heard on the soundtrack. Microphone and camera immobility often resulted in a stilted film that even the miracle of sound couldn't save from a bad review. Actors were left to their own devices and directors were silenced when shooting

began. Everything changed. The usually bustling, noisy, silent film set was now deathly quiet—and ironically, it was all because of *sound*!

The expected hiccups caused by the introduction of the exciting new medium were eventually ironed out and it was soon apparent that silent films were yesterday's news. While "part-talkies" hovered for a while, they were the apprehensive, experimental stepping stones into the eventual future of productions with "all sound."

Sound killed the careers of many big-name film stars of the silent era. Actors with stage experience had a leg up on their Hollywood counterparts and many Broadway stars moved in to take the place of silent film actors who were unable to make the leap when the talkie era arrived.

More so than ever before, all Hollywood actors who made that shaky silent-to-sound transition (successful or otherwise) learned the new medium in front of the camera with everyone watching, analyzing, "listening" and criticizing his or her every movement (www.filmsite.org).

Unlike many of her foreign contemporaries, Lupe stood her ground and survived during a time when her ethnicity could have sent her back to Mexico as a failed film star. Her films were still popular and she was liked enough by the public to tough out the occasional "heaving chest" and "over-acting" criticism that came her way during the early days of talking pictures. In his "Previews of New Talkies" article (March 15, 1930), published in the *Los Angeles Record*, Jimmie Starr wrote a detailed account of Lupe's first film for the year, *Hell Harbor* (1930), saying:

*Hell Harbor* is one of the most thrilling—in a melodramatic style—talking pictures I have seen. There is considerable hokum, but it is used with a certain rare finesse and I doubt that even the most jaded of critics will mind. I hope not, for the film is beautifully done and abounds with thrills and romance.

Director Henry King is a master at presentation and he is also a firm believer in unusual, but thorough, characterizations. His work with *Hell Harbor* is superb. He tells the story, which is not terribly original, except in locale, with ease and apparent enjoyment in revealing twists.

The story is laid on the Island of Madre—long and green—sprawled carelessly in the Caribbean Sea. Strange characters are the denizens of this mysterious village—a village of derelicts of the world, pearl divers, dishonest traders, murderers, half-castes, a few whites and weird natives.

One of the most fascinating things of the picture is the strange music, supplied, I believe, by a native band. It is the most intriguing music I have ever heard, and it certainly adds much charm to the production.

The story is rather ancient in plot. It is alone saved by King's original direction and by the clever work of Jean Hersholt, Gibson Gowland and Lupe Vélez.

Hersholt gives a magnificent performance as Joseph Horngold, the dishonest trader, while Gibson Gowland wins new fame in a like role. These two, who won many plaudits for their work in *Greed*, are splendid actors. I could watch their work night after night.

Lupe Vélez does her usual amount of over-acting, but it is rather charming in this film. John Holland performs nicely as the leading man. Al St. John and Paul Burns offer rare bits of comedy and little George Book-Asta is excellent in a small role. Harry Allen is outstanding as Peg-Leg. The dialogue by Clarke Silvernail is commendable, while the photography by John Fulson and Mack Hengler is unusually beautiful.

Following the release of *Hell Harbor*, United Artists "released" Lupe of her contractual obligations, due to their plans for her fellow countrywoman, Dolores del Rio. Lupe wasted no time in getting picked up elsewhere. *The Storm* (1930) was Lupe's first film under her new five-year contract with Universal Pictures.

*Film Daily* (August 24, 1930) wrote a brief synopsis of *The Storm* and praised the cast for "very good work":

Lupe sings one song. In evading the mounted police for smuggling, Lupe's father dies of a shot and leaves her with two friends in a cabin in the wilds. William Boyd falls for her. Paul Cavanagh also wants her. When the snowstorm comes up, Boyd almost kills his friend who has gone into Lupe's room against his orders. Later he is saved from an avalanche by Cavanagh, who resigns to leave the lovers to themselves. A fine cast does very good work....

Harry Mines of the *Los Angeles Independent Daily News* (August 15, 1930) was lavish in his praise for the film, and especially complimentary of Lupe's performance:

Besides being a personal triumph for Miss Vélez, who never before appeared so convincing[,] *The Storm* is recommended to fans who like their drama dramatic and it will be especially interesting to the fans of Lupe Vélez, for she is at her finest in this one.

*East Is West* (1930) was next and Lupe played the role of Ming Toy. To better understand her character, she immersed herself in the Chinese language and traditions. The Chinese extras were tireless in their efforts to help her understand their culture. In return, Lupe would entertain them all by reeling off long sentences in jargon talk with the accompanying Chinese-like gestures, whereupon her Oriental audience would burst into fits of laughter. "I would like these Chinese very much," Lupe said. "But what a terrible language. Ooh! My tongue is twisted to speak even a few little werruds" ("Lupe Vélez Learns Chinese for Picture," *The Brownsville Herald Ten-Year Review*, December 28, 1933).

Despite Lupe's Chinese cultural research being a little unconventional, it worked. The *Los Angeles Evening Herald* (November 14, 1930) gave her one of the best reviews of her career:

Lupe Vélez's characterization of Ming Toy marks a highlight in her career.... [H]er Ming Toy role is alive and active. It thrives as fragrant as the lotus blossoms in spring. Her wee Chinese dialect is her finest achievement. Without a doubt, Ming Toy is Lupe's best characterization to date....

Danish actor Jean Hersholt was originally cast in the role of the conceited fifty-fifty Chinaman Charlie Yong, and preview audiences laughed in all the wrong places at the Dutchman's Asian impersonation. The studio cut him from the film and reshot his scenes with Edward G. Robinson in his place. Knowing they were desperate for a replacement, Robinson played hardball and negotiated himself a salary of $10,000 (approximately $130,000 in 2011) for one week's work (Lennig, *The*

**John Holland and Lupe Vélez in a tight embrace in a promotional still for *Hell Harbor* (1930).**

*Immortal Count: The Life and Films of Bela Lugosi*). *East Is West* is a good example of Hollywood's skewed version of a mixed-race relationship in the 1930s, made acceptable only by the revelation in the final scene that Ming Toy is not "yellow" but white after all, thus clearing her for social acceptance and marriage to her American sweetheart, Billy Benson.

*Oriente y Occidente* (1930), the Spanish-language version of *East Is West*, was shot immediately following the English-language version. Lupe again played the lead role of Ming Toy. Manuel Arbó played Edward G. Robinson's role of Charlie Yong and Barry Norton was Billy Benson. George Melford and Enrique Tovar Ávalos directed the foreign alternative for the international market.

By 1931, Lupe was again starring in two versions of the same film, *Resurrection* and *Resurrección*, based on the Leo Tolstoy novel. The plot is based on a story that Tolstoy read in a newspaper. Considered one of the greatest novelists of all time, Tolstoy's major works include *War and Peace* and *Anna Karenina*. Lupe's role as the tragic Katusha holds many dramatic, Garbo-esque moments, and without question, *Resurrection* is one of her finest dramatic performances. The *Los Angeles Record* (February 20, 1931) wrote an in-depth analysis and review of the film:

> John Boles and Lupe Vélez are co-starred in the production, taking the roles that were played by Dolores del Rio and Rod La Rocque in the silent picture. While Edwin Carewe directed both pictures, the silent version was more dynamic and more forceful.
>
> Miss Vélez and Boles both give good performances. Her work at times is splendid, despite the fact that she had to try to talk in the language of the old Russia of 1876. Boles is given little opportunity to do anything but make love.
>
> The story winds around a little servant girl in the home of Prince Dmitri Ivanovitch Nekhludof. The prince and the girl fall in love. He enlists in the Czar's army, and the girl is turned out of the home of his aunts after her love affair is discovered.
>
> Seven years later she is being tried for murder–Dmitri is on the jury that convicts her. She is sentenced to hard labor for life in Siberia but Dmitri follows her.
>
> Miss Vélez wins the sympathy of the entire audience, but her role is an exceptionally sad one, and a difficult one to play, without getting on the nerves of the watchers.

The Spanish version, *Resurrección,* was produced simultaneously

Katusha Maslova (Lupe) cowers in the presence of an overbearing guard (actor unidentified) in the melodramatic courtroom scene from the English-language version of *Resurrection* (1931). Lupe also starred in the Spanish-language version.

baritone into a bloated shadow of his former self. He died as a result of tripping on a rug in his apartment; he hit his head on the corner of a table, causing bone fragments to lodge in his brain. Tibbett died following surgery on July 15, 1960. He was 63 years old ("The Lawrence Tibbett Papers," the New York Public Library for Performing Arts — Music Division, and "Music: Opera's Grand Trouper," *Time*, Monday, July 25, 1960).

*    *    *

On October 10, 1932, Lupe's niece Juana del Valle accompanied her grandmother Josefina to the United States. Too young to understand the lifestyle change she was about to experience, the little girl left her mother (Lupe's sister, Mercedes) in Mexico and was told that "Aunt Lupe" would be her mother from now on. America was her new home. Several newspaper reports suggested the child was four years old; however the manifest of entry into the United States clearly states she was six. American newspapers printed the child's name as "Juanita," a common nickname for "Juana," although the little girl would soon take on a whole new name and a whole new life. Shortly after her arrival in the United States, it was announced that Lupe had adopted her six-year-old niece. Her name was changed to Joan Vélez and there were a flurry of stories in the press to announce the good news.

However, the American media failed to mention a November 6, 1932, *La Prensa* interview with the little girl's mother Mercedes and father Emilio, Lupe's sister and brother-in-law. Within the interview, her biological parents clearly state that they did *not* give Juana up for adoption. They said they only gave permission for the girl to spend "some months" with her Aunt Lupe and her grandmother Josefina in Los Angeles. As usual, Hollywood didn't let the truth get in the way of a good story, and so the stories of Lupe's newest role, that of a real-life mother, continued to spread.

The article "Old Santa Finds New Faces In Hollywood" in the *Oakland Tribune* (Christmas Day 1932) told of Lupe's excitement at having a child to spoil at Christmastime:

> When I was little girl, I am tomboy. Christmas tree to me then is sissy. I have nothing to do with him. But now you

Lupe is pictured with four-year-old Juanita del Valle, the daughter of her sister Mercedes. By late 1932, Lupe had officially adopted Juanita and changed her name to Joan Vélez. However, it seems any chance of motherhood was cursed for the actress. After a series of kidnapping threats, for the little girl's own safety, Lupe sent her back to Mexico — for good.

watch! For my baby, I get the bigges' Christmas tree ... all full of dolls and toys. You know what I do, maybe? I won't give her no toys till Christmas, and then see her blue eyes — big as saucers....

Lupe didn't stick to the "no toys until Christmas" plan. Little Joan hadn't been in town for more than two days before she and Lupe were walking the aisles of the toy department in one of Hollywood's finest stores. She charmed the sales staff with her newly learned greetings of "Hello!" and "Goodbye!" and whatever her little finger pointed at, Lupe said, "We take him, you bet!"

By August of 1933, dramatically scary headlines such as "Lupe Vélez Hides Child from Gang" were featured in newspapers across the country. The *Oakland Tribune* (August 26, 1933) reported that Lupe had become terrified and increasingly nervous about the threats of kidnapping that had come to her in the form of three letters. All three were hand-delivered to her house on the same day and all were threatening abduction and violence toward the child if Lupe didn't comply with the monetary demands. One note demanded $25,000 (over $400,000 in 2011); each of the other two notes demanded $15,000 (over $250,000 in 2011). However, there were no further instructions as to where, or how, the money should be paid or delivered.

A typical studio glamour pose, taken during a rare demure moment at the height of Lupe's Hollywood career.

Heartbroken, Lupe decided to return the little girl to Mexico, but not to her mother. She arranged for her to stay at an unidentified convent for safekeeping. In an interview with *The Southeast Missourian* (August 18, 1933), Lupe explained:

I took this step to protect the child. She is safe now and I don't have to worry about her. I was frantic when I received the letters so I had mother take her back to Mexico where she is safe from harm in the convent. I am going to leave her there indefinitely.

Lupe said she received no further threats or letters since the child left her care. Following the kidnapping threats, Lupe employed three armed guards to patrol her home and she started sleeping with a pistol under her pillow. "I've learned how to shoot pretty good," she said as she brandished her weapon, twirling the cylinder. "I'd like them to come in here some time. I'd show them" ("Lupe Now Sleeps on a Pistol," *The Southeast Missourian*, August 18, 1933).

By August 30, 1933, police were finally advised of the kidnapping threats. It was a notification long overdue. In all likelihood, the police contacted Lupe after reading the papers. However, by that time, Lupe had returned the little girl to Mexico. However, Lupe was still exceedingly nervous. With the girl gone, she now became paranoid about the same thugs going after her widely publicized jewelry collection.

It was no secret that Lupe had one of the biggest and most valuable jewelry collections in Hollywood. So every guest, delivery boy, gas or water company employee, etc., who stepped into her home were all "greeted" by a servant with gun in hand! "My jewels are no more a pleasure to me," Lupe said despondently. "I've locked almost all of them up in a safety deposit vault" ("Lupe Vélez, Actress Constantly Guarded," *The Norwalk Hour,* August 17, 1933). One evening Lupe took matters into her own hands. She heard what she thought was a prowler in the back garden so she grabbed her gun and shot at random through the closed back window. The window was repaired the following morning.

When the doorbell rang after hours, Lupe would burst down the stairs, gun in hand, and shove the muzzle of the revolver right into the caller's faces. "Who the hell is there?!" she'd scream. An example of Lupe's fearless behavior was demonstrated during a trip to New York. A pair of gangsters came up behind her on a busy street and calmly told her to remove her chinchilla coat and she wouldn't be hurt. The men underestimated the pluckiness of the lady. Lupe turned around to face them and let loose with a tongue-lashing (in English and Spanish) that left them open-mouthed. Lupe kept her coat (*The Milwaukee Journal,* December 28, 1944).

Professionally speaking, art was about to imitate life — well, almost. Hollywood colum-nist Jimmie Starr wrote (*Evening Herald Examiner,* June 24, 1932) that Harry Cohn's Colum-bia Pictures had a "hot idea" for Lupe Vélez to play a sort of feminine Tarzan of the Apes. *Fury of the Jungle* was the proposed title of the film. Reportedly, Lupe was close to signing for the role. It never happened. That said, Lupe's relationship with Tarzan would generate years more publicity and have more action and drama than *Fury of the Jungle* ever could have.

Enter Johnny Weissmuller.

# 11

## *Me Tarzan, You Lupe*

"I felt before like saying I wasn't married and now I feel like saying I am married."[1]— Lupe Vélez Weissmuller (1933)

Following the March 25, 1932, New York City premiere of his latest feature *Tarzan the Ape Man* (1932), Johnny Weissmuller was spotted by Lupe Vélez as he walked into an elevator of the Manhattan hotel, where they were both guests. She had just returned from the *Tarzan* premiere (they attended separately) and both on screen and off, Lupe liked what she saw.

Johnny was a former Olympic gold medalist (for swimming) turned movie star. He was tall, broad-shouldered and ruggedly handsome, all attributes that reminded Lupe of Gary Cooper ... the one that got away. (Weissmuller had been married to Bobbe Arnst since early 1931, but the marriage was on the skids.)

Weissmuller was relaxing on the bed in his hotel room. It had been a long and tiring day of talking, smiling, signing autographs and just general promotion for the film. He had intended to stay in for the remainder of the evening. The ringing phone changed everything. Not just then, but from then on.

Picking up the receiver he heard a Latin purr on the other end of the line. The woman claimed to be Lupe Vélez. Weissmuller instantly thought the call was a prank, but before hanging up he sarcastically responded with, "Yeah, sure [you're Lupe Vélez], and I'm John Barrymore. I'm also tired and going to bed" (Weissmuller Jr., Reed and Reed, *Tarzan, My Father*).

Immediately the phone rang a second time. It was Lupe again, and she was mad. And, when Lupe was mad, she'd always express her feelings in her native tongue, just as she did in her films. Weissmuller was the recipient of a Spanish rant like he'd never heard before. She yelled. He listened. Then, *she* hung up on *him*. He may not have understood everything she said, but there was no mistaking her mood.

At that moment, Weissmuller realized he might have made a huge blunder. Did he really just hang up on Lupe Vélez? He called the front desk to find out if she was indeed a guest at the hotel. She was. He immediately asked the clerk to connect him to her room and he swiftly prepared a smooth apology to win her over and, more importantly, calm her down. Following some small talk, he asked if her invitation for a drink was still open. It was. Weissmuller said, "I [then] walked into the most dangerous lion's cage that I have ever entered in my life!" (Weissmuller Jr., Reed and Reed, *Tarzan, My Father*).

About nine months later, just a few days before Christmas of 1932, the *Los Angeles Evening Herald and Express* spotted Lupe dancing at the Club New Yorker. Her partner was

87

Johnny Weissmuller. She still denied anything serious between her and movie land's favorite swimmer: "Johnny is just one of my many friends," she said. "It ees no question of my taking him back. When I sent him away he was a married man and I wouldn't walk to the corner with a married man. Now, he is free, so why I should not see heem?"

The "we're just friends" line was the stock standard answer given to reporters for many months. If nothing else, she was certainly consistent in her denials. And Lupe always told the press if she was in love; she said she'd shout it from the rooftops and name names too. So, if she *was* in love, why wouldn't she say so this time? There was one very good reason why she kept her mouth shut. Johnny was in the process of a sticky divorce. The last thing he needed was to be associated with another woman, especially Lupe Vélez!

Of all the wild animals that Johnny Weissmuller's Tarzan character was associated with, off-screen Lupe was wilder and harder to control than any of them. In fact, the studio makeup people would need additional time to cover and camouflage the scratches, bruises and bite marks that Lupe had given him during their notorious and frequent physical squabbles before they could begin filming his scenes.

In, *Tarzan, My Father*, Weissmuller's son wrote of his father's life and career, including, of course, his tumultuous marriage to Lupe. He admitted that Lupe was good for his father because she was very funny and made him laugh like no one else. On the other hand, she was *bad* for his father because her volatile temper caused them to fight constantly. When their relationship was good, it was really, really good. But when it was bad, it was really, *really* bad. Weissmuller Jr. said, "Dad just couldn't handle her."

Lupe's very public romance with Johnny made 1932 a memorable year for her. But the love affair and the extensive (and often intrusive) media coverage surrounding the relationship showed no signs of distracting her or slowing her down professionally. Lupe made four films in 1932.

The Spanish-language film *Hombres de mi vida* was the first for the year, with Gilbert Roland as her leading man. The aviation romance, *The Broken Wing* with Leo Carrillo and Melvyn Douglas was next, followed by the jungle drama *Kongo* with Walter Huston and Conrad Nagel. The comedic carnival romp *The Half-Naked Truth* with Lee Tracy, Eugene Pallette and Frank Morgan rounded out the year. The overall quality of work for 1932 was weak and disappointing. Personally, Lupe had a much bigger production looming—a wedding!

Lupe and co-star Melvyn Douglas in *The Broken Wing* (1932).

\* \* \*

Lupe and "Johnee," or "Popee" as she affec-

Seven years before his multiple character portrayals in the 1939 classic *The Wizard of Oz*, Frank Morgan shares an olive with Lupe in the sideshow comedy *The Half-Naked Truth* (1932).

tionately called him, were married on October 8, 1933, in Reno, Nevada, just two days after Weissmuller's final divorce decree from Bobbe Arnst. Lupe was filming on location and Weissmuller drove out to be with her. They were married at 4 A.M. by Justice of the Peace Frank M. Ryan. Lupe became the third Mrs. Johnny Weissmuller. Ruth Biery, film magazine writer and friend of the pair, and her husband Edward acted as witnesses. Lupe wore a simple linen and silk frock that she bought on sale for $2.50 (approximately $45 in 2011). Johnny wore a tweed suit (*Los Angeles Examiner*, October 30, 1933).

Ruth Biery, aside from being a witness to the nuptials, got the media scoop on the marriage. She did some subtle, clever planning to keep the story from leaking out to rival reporters. By calling all states adjoining California to learn their marriage laws, she found out that a Nevada wedding doesn't have to be recorded for thirty days. Only the marriage license was recorded. As a result, Ruth got the exclusive, first-hand account (*Hollywood Citizen News*, November 4, 1933).

Following the marriage, Lupe's niece's return to Mexico made a lot more sense. The incident being in such close proximity to the wedding day can't be ignored. The little girl had left the U.S. by the end of August of 1933, just five weeks prior to Lupe's wedding. While the timing certainly *could* be coincidental, in all likelihood, the story of kidnapping threats was a pre-meditated move that doubled as a sympathetic publicity ploy to shuffle the child back home in order to make way for a husband.

It wasn't until after their wedding, when they were both living under the same roof at Lupe's Spanish-style home on North Rodeo Drive, that Weissmuller realized how truly opposite their personalities were. He got up early and went to bed early. She got up late and went to bed late. She wanted to party, he wanted to stay home. She drank and smoked cigarettes. Neither vice ever appealed to him. He was a fitness fanatic.

The cracks in their relationship began appearing within a matter of weeks, and the so-called honeymoon period was a harsh reality check that neither one of them expected. As early as February of 1934, Lupe openly admitted that she and Johnny "will probably go on quarreling forever." Lupe often went to bed as her sports-loving husband got up. She said:

I don't like the daytime. Johnny, he gets up at 6 A.M. to play golf. Then he plays handball and some other game — I don't know what kind of a game it must be to make him so tired.

**Throughout their marriage, Lupe and Johnny enjoyed horseback riding together. It was one of the few recreational activities they could agree upon.**

But he doesn't want to take me out. We argue about that and everything else ... ["'Night Owl' Lupe Wins Tiff with 'Early Bird' Weissmuller," *Rochester Evening Journal*, February 5, 1934].

Elizabeth Yeaman of the *Hollywood Citizen News* (August 5, 1932) wrote that Columbia Pictures was "turning somersaults trying to get Lupe for the feminine lead in the Wheeler and Woolsey comedy, *In the Jungle*." The film was released in 1933 (now titled *So This Is Africa*), and due to scheduling conflicts, without Lupe as the female lead. Instead, the film starred another Mexican actress, Raquel Torres, alongside the popular comedy duo. She played "The Leader of Amazon Women." Just previous to Columbia's desperate bid to snare Lupe for one of their films, RKO had reportedly already signed her as the female lead, alongside Lee Tracy, in the mystery *The Phantom of Crestwood* (1932). Both were bumped from the cast. The film stars Ricardo Cortez, with Karen Morley, Anita Louise and Pauline Frederick as the top three leading ladies.

Career-wise, things were not going well for Lupe. Marriage was a much bigger job than anticipated and it appeared that Lupe's roller-coaster personal life had finally caught up with her. Something had to give, and it did. The musical comedy *Hot Pepper* was her only release for 1933. Not since *Stand and Deliver* (1928) had audiences been relegated to a solo Lupe Vélez film for an entire year. Next came the boxing-themed comedy *Palooka*, starring Jimmy Durante as Lupe's male lead, Knobby Walsh.

Less than four months after Lupe and Johnny's marriage, *The Courier Mail* (Queensland, Australia) announced news of the couple's "first" separation. The paper quoted

James Cagney's lookalike brother, William Cagney, alongside Lupe in a scene from the boxing-themed comedy *Palooka* (1934).

Lupe as saying, "We fight all the time, Johnny and I. I guess it is Hollywood. I don't blame him. It is fifty-fifty." When asked about the possibility of them reconciling, Lupe said, "I do not think we will go back."

But, they did get back together ... for a little while, anyway. Breaking up and making up would be a constant pattern in the Weissmuller marriage. Lupe's business manager Bö Roos said, "[Lupe] was always locking [Johnny] out of the house." And, since Johnny would then knock down the doors, their biggest household expense was Yale locks (Olsen and Hudson, *Hollywood's Man Who Worried for the Stars: The Story of Bö Roos*).

By February 15, 1934 the Weissmullers were back at it again, and this time fighting over food. *The Courier Mail* (Queensland, Australia) reported that at meal times, whenever Lupe got up to answer the telephone, Johnny continued to eat, and if she took too long, he'd eat hers too! "Nobody should have an appetite as big as that," said Lupe. "I tell Johnny he must be more refined; that starts a fight," she said.

According to *The Meridien Daily Journal* (February 17, 1934), a nightly bone of contention was that Johnny didn't want Lupe to sit up in bed reading murder stories when he wanted to go to sleep. "Maybe he's afraid it will give her ideas," the article stated.

One night at Ciro's, Lupe was dancing so wildly that her dress flew up, revealing that she wasn't wearing any panties. This crude public display happened on more than one occasion. But on this particular night, Johnny got so mad and embarrassed, he hustled Lupe back to their table, where they got into yet another public spat. It ended with him dumping his meal right into Lupe's lap. (Jacobson, *Dishing Hollywood: The Real Scoop on Tinseltown's Most Notorious Scandals*).

Lupe's unpredictable behavior frequently required Johnny to try and make his impulsive wife see reason. However, his level-headedness clashed with Lupe's madcap spontaneity. It didn't take long for things to get out of control. He'd talk. She'd scream. He'd scream. She'd throw something. He'd throw something. She'd file for divorce.

That was the pattern of their relationship. The imbalance of personalities almost always guaranteed a fight and the newspapers would have a field day reporting on the latest war of the Weissmullers.

Ramon Novarro plays the lead Navaho role of Laughing Boy in the 1934 film of the same name. Lupe plays his Indian wife Slim Girl, who's been corrupted by white men and finds conflict in resorting to the ways of a traditional tribal past. The film was based on the 1929 Pulitzer Prize-winning novel by Oliver La Farge.

Louella O. Parsons wrote about one incident in her January 26, 1934, *Los Angeles Examiner* column. The couple were attending a screening of *Eskimo* (1933) at the Four Star Theater in Hollywood, as were comedians Harold Lloyd and Charlie Chaplin. All of a sudden, Lupe and Johnny got into a very loud argument outside the theater. Lupe insisted on buying one of the penguins that were on exhibition to promote the film. Johnny wouldn't let her.

Another incident was big enough to cause a brief split (Weissmuller moved into the Chateau Marmont for a few days to cool off): Lupe and Johnny had gone to see *Flying Down to Rio* (1933). Lupe commented that it was too improbable to have chorus girls dancing on top of airplanes. "[Johnny] said I was dumb," said Lupe, "and I told him he was stupid, too" (*Los Angeles Evening Herald and Express*, February 8, 1934). After their hurt feelings healed, Johnny moved back into their Rodeo Drive home a few days later. As usual, life went on as if nothing had ever happened ... at least until the next argument.

A July 11, 1934, headline ("Lupe Vélez, Still in Love Sues 'Tarzan' for Divorce") in *The Pittsburgh Press* reported that the couple had again split up. And this time it was for good. Lupe had filed for divorce based on mental cruelty and violent physical outbursts that included Johnny throwing furniture and other objects within their home. Lupe claimed she was struck during some of these moments. She admitted that the stark differences in their temperaments had caused the breakdown of their relationship. "We simply couldn't make a go of it," she explained sadly. "We still love each other, but we also get on each other's nerves ... so I tell Johnny everybody else in Hollywood gets divorced, so why shouldn't we?"

Lupe cooled down and eventually took Johnny back. But soon after their latest reconciliation, the Weissmullers had another fight on their hands, only this time it wasn't with each other. The *Brownsville Herald* (Sunday, August 19, 1934) ran an explosive front-page headline: "Four Stars Named as Alleged Financial Supporters of Communism." Dolores del Rio, Ramon Novarro, James Cagney and Lupe Vélez were the four named in the scandal, and pictures of the stars accompanied the accusatory article. If the allegations were proven true, all four were in danger of being blacklisted. District Attorney Neil McCallister announced he would seek an injunction against Cagney for advocating or giving financial aid to communist causes and he would take the same action against the others if evidence suggested they had any such connec-

Lupe as Jane with a *faux* hairy-chested Jimmy Durante as Schnarzan from *Hollywood Party* (1934). Lupe had married the real Tarzan, Johnny Weissmuller, the year before, which made the spoof even funnier.

tion with radicalism. Detective Ray Kunz, a member of the so-called "red squad"—intelligence units with city police departments, gathering information against labor unions and communism. Kunz said the names of the two actresses, along with Novarro, were simply found written on a slip of paper among the effects of Caroline Decker, secretary of the Cannery and Agricultural Workers Union, a communist organization. The scandalous claims were eventually quashed, but not before Weissmuller stepped in to publicly defend his wife by saying the accusations were "silly and ridiculous." He continued:

> Lupe doesn't even know what the word communism means. I can safely say that for her, and I know she's never given money to any such cause.... We give money to needy people—crippled people on the streets who ask us for a quarter or something to eat. But we have never given money to any communist organization.

Not one to remain quiet for long, Lupe eventually responded.

> Me a Communist? Ho, I don't even know what the blazes a Communist is! ... What is the matter with this Sacramento man [McAllister], anyway? I think maybe they should put him in the lockup tight? [Ellenberger, *Ramon Novarro: A Biography of the Silent Film Idol, 1899–1968*].

**Without her makeup, Lupe Vélez is almost unrecognizable alongside husband Johnny Weiss-muller in this shot taken in London in 1934.**

With the communism controversy behind her, Lupe's was back to her prolific self with four film releases for 1934. The aforementioned boxing-themed, comedy-romance *Palooka* was the first of three comedies alongside her equally excitable male co-star, Jimmy Durante, for that year. The Native-American-themed *Laughing Boy* with Ramon Novarro was her only drama, followed by *Strictly Dynamite,* a musical comedy, again with Durante in the lead role.

Last came *Hollywood Party,* an MGM "all-star production," yet again co-starring Durante. The ensemble cast including Laurel and Hardy, Charles Butterworth, Polly Moran and even Mickey Mouse; they did little to save what became a sorry mess of a film. The two most memorable scenes in *Hollywood Party* both involved Lupe. The hilarious tit-for-tat egg-breaking routine with Stan and Ollie is a highlight, as well as the Tarzan parody with Durante playing "Schnarzan" to Lupe's "Jane." The latter is funnier still because of the obvious real-life nod to Lupe's relationship with Johnny Weissmuller.

With *Hollywood Party,* MGM set out to mirror the success of *Hollywood Revue of 1929.* The studio intended to film almost everyone on the MGM payroll to ensure that it equaled, or even topped, their earlier hit. This installment would be a sequel of sorts, aptly titled *Hollywood Revue of 1933,* and some big names were set to appear. But most didn't. By late September of 1933, newspapers announced that Jean Harlow (the original story was supposed to focus on her), Joan Crawford, Marie Dressler, Marion Davies and even Lupe's other half,

Johnny Weissmuller in character as Tarzan. MGM billed him as "the only man in Hollywood who's natural in the flesh and can act without clothes." He was Lupe's only husband. They divorced in 1939.

Johnny Weissmuller, were some of the stars slated to film sequences for the lavish production (*Hollywood Citizen News,* September 28, 1933).

Just prior to filming, Harlow was assigned to another production and the script was altered to focus on Durante instead. It was the beginning of the end; Durante was no Harlow! While scheduling was arranged for the bigger-named stars to film their bits, MGM boss Louis B. Mayer previewed some of the footage that had already been shot, Lupe's aforementioned scenes with Laurel and Hardy and Durante included. Though Lupe's skits were the eventual highlights of the finished film, Mayer wasn't impressed. In fact, he was so furious at what he saw that he immediately ordered production to be shut down — permanently! Mayer told producer Harry Rapf to "patch up the existing footage" and "let it go" (Hemming, *The Melody Lingers On: The Great Songwriters and Their Movie Musicals*).

The studio proceeded to try to wrap up an unfinished production into a comprehensible story. The new "it was all a dream" ending was a wretched attempt at explaining away some of the silliness. It didn't work. Hal Erickson of *All Movie Guide,* said:

> Director Allan Dwan, brought into the project at the last minute, took a look at the existing footage and declared, "It's a nightmare!" In an attempt to save the film, he directed a closing sequence that suggested the whole plot had been dreamed up by Jimmy Durante; [after] his wife, played by Mrs. Jimmy Durante, wakens Durante from his slumber. Even with Dwan's intervention, *Hollywood Party* makes no sense at all, but it's a must for comedy lovers and 1930s film buffs.

*   *   *

With his own movie career as Tarzan in "full swing," and his make-ups and break-ups with Lupe making headlines everywhere, it seemed as though Johnny Weissmuller had literally "gone Hollywood." He went from a champion of the pool, to modeling bathing suits, to beating out 150 Tarzan wannabes for the role of a lifetime. With not an ounce of acting experience, his screen test consisted of climbing a tree and running past a camera with a girl under his arm. Weissmuller's portrayal of Tarzan (for sixteen years, in a dozen films) made him a star of the screen, but he was a star of the pool long before he ever stepped in

front of a movie camera. Aside from winning five Olympic gold medals (1924 and 1928), Weissmuller also broke the record in each race. In fact, he repeatedly broke his own world records as well as national freestyle records (over multiple distances) and he was the first man in the world to swim the 100-meter freestyle in under a minute.

Like any sport, swimming has progressed with time, and with that progression, faster swimming times are now commonplace. However, in Weissmuller's day, lane markers, starting blocks, slick swim costumes, flip turns and full body shaves to eliminate drag were methods and procedures that were unheard of. The simplistic nature of the sport during Weissmuller's reign made his swim times all the more astounding, reason enough for the Associated Press to vote him the greatest swimmer of the half-century in a 1950 poll (*Palm Beach Post-Times*, August 16, 1970).

Miraculously, Weissmuller retired from his amateur swimming career — undefeated. He had 52 U.S. national championships (thirty-six individual and sixteen relay team), and an extraordinary 67 world championships under his belt. He set 51 individual world records in his ten years as an amateur, but he reportedly broke many more records and just never bothered to turn in the record applications to make them official. He was a member of 13 American record-setting relay teams from 1921 to 1928. Additionally, he won a bronze medal as a member of the U.S. Olympic water polo team at the 1924 Summer Olympics. All of Weissmuller's swim records have long been broken, but in the eyes of many, he's still considered the greatest swimmer of all time. Moreover, he's often touted as the greatest Tarzan of all time. Between his swimming career and his screen career, Weissmuller became the quintessential American hero.

Lupe certainly had her own laundry list of nicknames to boast about during her Hollywood career, but during Johnny's swimming career, he earned several fitting nicknames of his own. The "Human Hydroplane," "Prince of the Waves," "Flying Fish," "King of Swimmers" and the "Aquatic Wonder" were monikers used to describe him at one time or another.

In the summer of 1927, he added "Hero" to the list when he and his brother, Pete saved at least twenty people from a sunken double-decker excursion boat on Lake Michigan after a freak storm squall caused it to capsize. Of the estimated seventy or eighty people on board, at least twenty-seven people died in the tragedy; the victims were mostly women and children (*The Morning Leader*, July 29, 1927).

In 1962, decades after the tragic accident, Johnny got an unexpected letter from a mother of seven children. She told him that she was one of the children he saved. All those years later, she wrote to thank him for saving her from certain death, thus allowing her to marry and have children of her own. She told him her children said a prayer of thanks on his behalf every night. He kept that letter in a special box until the day he died. All his life, Weissmuller was eternally grateful to the sport that made him an international champion and eventual screen star. He once said, "I owe everything to swimming ... without swimming, I'd be a nobody" (www.ishof.org).

Whether he was swimming in it or sailing on it, Weissmuller and water was a daily combination. In an attempt to involve Lupe in his passion of boating, Johnny bought a thirty-four-foot schooner. He even renamed the boat (originally called *Chula*) *Santa Guadalupe* in honor of his wife. While Johnny attempted to get Lupe involved in his love of boating by teaching her all the ropes, her first attempt at captaining the vessel didn't go well. She said:

> On the very first day I bump the ship three times very hard, tear a balloon spinnaker (anyway, that's what Johnny said it was) and pitch the first mate overboard during sharp tack into the

wind. After that, Johnny say the control cabin and steering wheel are "out of bounds" for me [*Los Angeles Examiner*, May 20, 1937].

Lupe involved herself in ways that kept her busy and out of Johnny's hair while still very much involving her in his passion for a secondary life at sea. In an attempt to turn the boat into a real home, Lupe made lace curtains and pretty cushions; she even painted it. Their first big trip to Catalina Island (about 20 miles from Los Angeles) had been planned for weeks. Lupe was hoping to please Johnny by at least pretending to enjoy herself. But Lupe got so violently seasick, they had to turn back. A year later, Johnny sold *Santa Guadalupe* and bought a sixty-foot sailing vessel named *Allure*. The good sport that she was, Lupe attempted another trip. The bigger boat was easier on her weak stomach, and she sailed many times, but she found any excuse she could to stay on dry land. In the end, Johnny would sail with his friends, *sans* Lupe. She liked it that way. So did he. As often as he could, Johnny would race *Allure* to Catalina Island against Humphrey Bogart onboard his *Santana* and Errol Flynn onboard his *Sirocco*.

One of the Weissmullers' most amusing well-publicized spats occurred after disembarking from a plane at Newark Airport. The *Los Angeles Independent Daily News* (September 28, 1934) wrote that Lupe walked over to a Yellow cab and deposited her belongings. Johnny walked over to a Red cab with *his* things. Then the battle started. "Get in this cab!" shouted Johnny. "No!" said Lupe, stamping her foot. "You come to these one." "I said get — in — this — cab!" countered Johnny. "You go to hell!" shouted Lupe.

Johnny turned and entered the Red cab. Lupe hesitated. She started to get in the Yellow cab. Then she reached in, removed her things, and walked fuming to her husband's cab. They sat staring straight ahead as the car pulled out for Manhattan.

When Lupe and Johnny were together, they were usually at war. They were often seen arguing in the middle of a nightclub or restaurant and one, or both, would have to be physically restrained by patrons. The newspapers had a field day because the Weissmullers made good copy. As the years progressed, the volatile nature of their relationship escalated. Eventually, Lupe's denials of trouble stopped, and her public confessions of a relationship in trouble began.

A permanent split was inevitable ... it was just a matter of *when*.

# 12

## *Stage, Screen ... and Splitting Up!*

"We may kill each other some day, but we will not get a divorce."[1]— Lupe Vélez
on her marriage to Johnny Weissmuller (1934)

The UK production *The Morals of Marcus* was Lupe's only film release for 1935 and her first time making a film in England. Although she received decent reviews for her own performance, the production was a cheap throwaway that did little to advance her career. Director Miles Mander (1888–1946) praised Lupe as an actress and her professionalism on set. In an interview with *Film Weekly* (December 21, 1934) he said:

> I found Lupe to be the most natural screen actress I have ever met.... I can honestly say that she is the finest film artist I have ever worked with.... [W]hat struck me particularly was the quick way in which she grasped my meaning when I told her how I wanted a scene done ... you explain your object, and [*he flicked his finger*] she's got it....

Mander spoke of Lupe's intuition and enthusiasm for her craft, saying she would listen to his instructions on how he wanted a particular scene played, and if she didn't agree, she would tell him how *she* saw it. He admitted that on nearly every occasion that she challenged him, she was right. That said, if he still maintained that *his* way was best, she would bow to his decision and do her job as instructed.

Mander was also impressed with Lupe's ability to work herself into an emotional mood. She would merely stand in a corner alone, silent, taking no more than a minute or two, and then she would return to shoot her scene and she'd be worked up enough so the tears or the rage would flow. Furthermore, she even had the ability to switch ill health on and off at will. Calling her a "trouper," Mander recalled a day when she was looking haggard, tired and worn out. She felt awful and she looked awful. But, she insisted she would be fit enough to work as required.

When it was time to shoot a scene, a miraculous transformation took place. Listless Lupe disappeared and she became the character. Her appearance, her lethargy, her ailment — all of it vanished. Then the moment "cut" was called, like a withered flower, she'd droop again. Together with her ability to switch emotions at a moment's notice, Mander gushed, "That, I consider, is screen artistry" ("Handle Lupe Vélez with Care," *Film Weekly,* December 21, 1934).

The English-made *Gypsy Melody* was her only film release for 1936. Lupe's Hollywood career was beginning to take a nosedive. Yet, despite her U.K. work jaunt, a Native American "fan" had not forgotten Lupe; in fact, he turned up at her house to "claim her"!

In early December 1936, a Red Indian Chief was arrested for creating a disturbance outside Lupe's Hollywood home. When police arrived, he explained that Lupe had been

awarded to him as his squaw at a tribal council meeting (*Tyrone Daily Herald*, December 11, 1936). Frank Joseph Wittman, age 31, of Milwaukee, was arrested for disturbing the peace as he shouted, "Hi-yi-yi! Hi-yi-yi! I'm a chief of the Creek Tribe and Lupe's my squaw. Where is she, you palefaces?" He later told police that Lupe was a Chickasaw princess and he came to Hollywood to claim her as his own. "I've sent word to Johnny Weissmuller, who's been looking after her for me, that I'm going to exercise my tribal right as soon as I've found her tepee" ("Indian Claims Lupe His Squaw, Warns Johnny," *Oakland Tribune*, September 11, 1936).

* * *

With film work sparse, Lupe utilized her time across the pond to get back to her first love: the theater. During the latter part of 1936, she was in London for *Transatlantic Rhythm*, a stage show she had agreed to do to give herself and Johnny a much-needed marital break. Despite the rocky nature of their relationship at that time, Johnny knew Lupe was missing him. Deciding it might be a good idea to inject a little spontaneous romance into their marriage, he cleared his schedule and made arrangements to fly to the U.K. to surprise his lonely wife.

Lupe greeted Johnny with open arms and the impromptu meeting induced some wild lovemaking. But hours later, as Johnny drifted off to a satisfied sleep, out of nowhere and without warning he was hit in the head with a shoe. Lupe was a good shot and she often threw anything she could find — hard! In order to survive, Johnny learned to throw things back, but he did his homework and knew exactly which items were disposable. Even during a moment of rage, he would purposefully bypass the irreplaceable objects and reach for something of lesser value. He said, "The only way I could quiet her down was to smash one of her antiques. That used to break her spirit. But I had to learn to be a collector before I knew what vases were worth smashing" (Olsen and Hudson, *Hollywood's Man Who Worried for the Stars: The Story of Bö Roos*).

Following the unexpected shoe to the head to get Johnny's attention, Lupe began to lecture him, in Spanish and English, about his rumored social outings in New York. While she was working in London and crying over Johnny not being with her, she had read in the papers that he was out nightclubbing and enjoying himself. If she was miserable, she wanted Johnny to be miserable too!

Johnny attempted to defuse the situation by approaching Lupe to explain himself, but as he came closer, she threw more things to keep him away. Lupe ran out into the hallway. Johnny followed. The problem was, Johnny never wore pants to bed. Wearing his pajama top and naked from the waist down, he chased Lupe down the hall. Lights from other rooms turned on as they passed by each door. Lupe screamed, "Help! Murder!" Johnny screamed, "Shhhhh!" And just like that, unsuspecting hotel guests awoke to yet another Weissmuller war. Johnny and Lupe were guests at London's Claridge's, the most exclusive hotel accommodation that England had to offer. Claridge's was the place of choice for royalty from all over the world. It was highly unlikely that any guests previous to Johnny and Lupe had ever chased each other through the halls, let alone half-naked! During their second lap, a matronly lady in her late-fifties, dressed in a long frilly nightgown and matching nightcap, opened the door to her room to see what all the fuss and noise was about. "Go a little faster, Johnny!" she encouragingly cheered as he went by. "You'll catch her the next time around!" (*Los Angeles Evening Herald and Express*, February 21, 1937).

The spectator was right: He caught Lupe on the next lap. They went back to their

Right from the start, Lupe and Johnny's relationship was full of confusion and contradiction. When they were together, they wanted to be apart, and vice versa. In the early stages of their relationship, during separations because of scheduling conflicts, they'd often pine for one another and end up flying to be by each other's side. One night of passion and calm could just as quickly turn into an explosive showdown the following morning. One or the other would leave in a fit of rage, this time swearing they were done for good. Certainly, Lupe's 1937 interview claim of only having "three big fights" during their entire marriage was a *major* understatement. She once told journalist Harrison Carroll:

> Johnny is so beautiful. Sometimes I sit up in bed at night, when he is sleeping, and just admire him. He is like a piece of sculpture.... [T]hen for no reason, I punch him right in the nose. He rears up and says: "Mama, you hit me." I say: "Darling, I am sorry, hit me back, hit me in the face." And he says: "Never mind, honey, you couldn't help it, you did it in your sleep" ["Life and Loves of Lupe Vélez," *Los Angeles Evening Herald and Express*, December 15, 1944].

Apparently, Lupe learned her physical moves from the professionals. A fixture at the Friday night fights at Hollywood Legion Stadium, she had her seat reserved, front and center, and she was as much a part of the experience of going to the fights as watching the boxers on the bill. Lupe would ritualistically enter the stadium *after* the fight had begun (usually mid-way through round two, she'd make her grand entrance). The lights were low but as soon as Lupe appeared in the doorway and began her strut down the center aisle, the houselights would go up and loud cheers of "Tarzan and Lupe are coming!" would stop the boxers in mid-punch. The fight would break while Lupe took her bows, blew kisses to her adoring crowd and settled herself into her seat for the remainder of the match. There she'd shout and scream orders at her favorite fighter and shout and scream obscenities at his opponent. One time she climbed into the ring and hit the referee with her handbag because she believed *her* fighter got a bad decision! (Onyx, *Water, World & Weissmuller: A Biography*).

On another occasion, Lupe caused a near riot at the stadium. There was a match between a Mexican and a North American. While it was clear that the former had won, the referee declared the latter the winner. The controversial decision drove Lupe into such a rage that she entered the ring and attacked the referee and the boxer, this time using her umbrella as a weapon. Al Jolson, who felt the same way about the fight results, followed Lupe, and soon the arena was like an asylum, as everyone was engaged in fistfighting. The following morning, Lupe appeared in court and the judge sentenced her to a $1,000 fine (*La Prensa*, San Antonio, Texas, June 29, 1941).

During an interview with *La Prensa* journalist Mark Barrón (September 25, 1938), Lupe told another story that took place at Hollywood Legion Stadium: As she and Johnny were leaving a Friday night fight, a short guy approached them. Obviously looking for trouble, he boldly said he wanted to have a fistfight with Weissmuller. "Johnny is very big," Lupe said. "And so he told that shortie he would not fight." But the short guy insisted, so Johnny looked to Lupe and said, "Well, Lupe, this guy is about your size." Lupe understood what Johnny meant and she gave the guy a punch on his chin. "Zas!" she said. "He was knocked out." Barrón described Lupe's animated gestures as she told her story in the middle of a fancy Broadway restaurant, clad in pink pajamas (a Hollywood fashion fad at the time) that she had been wearing for rehearsals of the play *You Never Know*. She stood up to do a replay of the punch that took down "shortie" and once the demonstration was over, she sat down and resumed eating, unaware that the restaurant patrons were staring at her in astonishment, as was the journalist.

Another evening, Lupe was on her way to the prizefights with actor Bruce Cabot, her frequent fight companion. She decided to first stop off at the Brown Derby, the favorite film colony café; just as they sat down, there was a mass strike by the staff. Thirty waiters, cooks and bus boys walked out. Lupe was hungry and she had a fight to get to, and there was no time to go elsewhere. So without missing a beat, she rolled up her sleeves, stomped into the kitchen and came back balancing plates with two servings of prime rib beef, salad, string beans, peas and cheesecake for dessert (*Abilene Reporter-News*, August 7, 1937).

Many papers speculated that Bruce Cabot had been the third wheel in Lupe and Weissmuller's marriage. He *was* a regular dinner guest, but Johnny was present at all times.

> At dinner Johnee and Bruce would have duels with their table knives, and we would all laugh [about the supposed affair]. Bruce is one of only three men that Johnee will let me go to the boxing matches with when he is away. The others are our business manager and Eddie Mannix [*The Spartanburg Herald-Journal*, October 17, 1937].

In the aforementioned interview with Paul Harrison of *The Spartanburg Herald Journal*, Lupe once again discussed her marriage (over a game of badminton, with Harrison as her playing partner). Attempting to explain her complicated relationship with Johnny, she was perfectly frank about its imperfections. Unlike most stars who were programmed to "deny, deny, deny," Lupe was the first to admit that both she and Johnny had bad tempers and short fuses. As an example, she brought up a big fight that came about when they started talking about which actress first wore pants, Dietrich or Garbo. Each had their opinion on the matter and the fight was on! Lupe also proudly declared to Harrison that on October 8, 1937, she and "Johnee" would be celebrating their fifth wedding anniversary. She told Harrison that a star (whom she would not name) once gave a party and somebody asked if Lupe and Johnny were invited. The hostess said she didn't dare invite them together; as solo guests they were fine people, but their fighting was beyond embarrassing and she didn't want her party to be the scene of their latest divorce headlines. Lupe went on:

> Since this time, this "certain star" has been twice divorced, and I send word to her last party that I do not weesh to come because I do not like to get mixed up in other people's divorces. Mee-o-oww!

Around the same time as the Weissmullers' anniversary celebrations, Lupe returned to her native Mexico for the Spanish-language production *La zandunga* (1938). Lupe hadn't been south of the border in over a decade and her return to shoot the romantic drama nearly caused riots. She and Johnny sailed their yacht *Guadalupe* as far as Acapulco, and from there they proceeded to Mexico City. After building a successful film career in Hollywood, this was Lupe's first starring role back home. Upon her arrival by train, she was mobbed by over ten thousand screaming fans. Windows were broken, doors were torn off hinges and children were jostled in the hysteria. To keep Lupe from harm, local police vigorously cleared a path for her as she stepped off the train. They whisked her off to her hotel in the sidecar of a patrolman's motorcycle. Lupe later admitted that she was "enchanted" by the reception but at the same time she was "scared to death" by the over-exuberant crowds. However, Lupe did not escape unscathed. Before police could rescue her, her clothes were almost torn off, her ankle was sprained and she suffered scratches and bruises during the excitement ("Lupe Vélez Gets Noisy Welcome." *Herald-Journal*, November 12, 1937).

Alistair Tremps, producer of *Perdida*, a 2009 Spanish language documentary focusing

on the pioneering efforts of the Calderón family in the Mexican film industry as well as a study of the rise and fall of Mexican cinema throughout the twentieth century, said:

"Pedro A. Calderón was the producer of *La zandunga*, but his father and uncle, Jose U. Calderón and Rafael Calderón, were pioneers in the business and helped to set up the first film that Pedro produced, when still in his early 20s. The family business included a string of theaters in northern Mexico and south Texas — Circuito Alcazar. Distribution in Mexico and the United States — Azteca Films and studios in Mexico City — Estudios Azteca.

"Although the Calderón family had been producing indirectly for years, with advances on distribution payments and guidance for budding producers (in order to ensure a steady supply of Mexican films for their distribution business and theaters), as soon as Jose U. Calderón's eldest son Pedro was old enough to begin producing in his own right, his father and uncle Rafael used all of their know-how and contacts to make sure that his first film would be a hit. This included hiring Lupe Vélez to star in *La zandunga*."

Mexican journalist Hortensia Elizondo,[2] reported in *La Prensa* (April 4, 1938) on the rousing reception that Lupe and Johnny received at the premiere of *La zandunga*:

[The crowd] frantically applauded the Mexican star [Lupe Vélez] in her debut on the national silver screen. The first applause went to Johnny Weissmuller.... "Tarzan" told the audience that he loved Mexico very much, because it has given him his beloved, "Lupe Vélez." The applause was loud, and became roaring when Lupe appeared onscreen....

On November 11, 1937, a large crowd anxiously awaited Lupe's arrival at the Buenavista Railroad Station in Mexico City. Lupe was returning home for the first time in years for the filming of *La zandunga* (1938). A cameraman can be seen at the bottom right. The men wearing the metal helmets are policemen. Photograph courtesy of the Agrasánchez Film Archive.

Usually, when Lupe was on location, Johnny's own work commitments would require him to stay in California. He'd put in his day's work at the studio, and then he'd begrudgingly go home to take care of Lupe's menagerie of pets. During their marriage, Mr. Kelly and Mrs. Murphy were Lupe's beloved Chihuahuas. Johnny hated them. Additionally, Lupe owned a parrot that she had bought when she was living with Gary Cooper. The parrot was a constant talker and he let Johnny know who his previous master was by incessantly squawking his name.

Fed up with Lupe's aggravating animals, Johnny went to the pound and picked out a big dog for himself. He named him Otto. Johnny purposefully chose a mutt that was the complete opposite of Lupe's two Chihuahuas. In fact, Otto was as tall as Weissmuller (6'3") when he stood on his hind legs. Johnny loved him. Lupe, of course, hated him. But, as big as he was, Otto was a gentle giant. Lupe would often find him sleeping soundly with Mr. Kelly and Mrs. Murphy lying on top of him. Still, this was Johnny's dog, not Lupe's, and as with most aspects of their relationship, if Johnny loved something, Lupe hated it, and vice versa. Even Otto couldn't change that.

While Lupe may have frequently fought *with* Johnny, she also fought *for* him. *Los Angeles Examiner* reporter Reine Davies wrote (September 23, 1937) that Johnny had just returned from a three-month stint at the Billy Rose Aquacade in Cleveland. Aside from his career in Hollywood, his past swimming career was still a present part of his life and he was still in demand. In between films, he often made personal appearances at swimming events and expositions across the country. Upon his return to Hollywood and Lupe, he commented that he was exhausted and glad to be home. After three months of unremitting work as the star attraction at the Aquacade, which included dodging traffic, salesmen and wide-eyed souvenir and autograph hunters, he was quite prepared to retire permanently into the character of Tarzan and move to the jungle where nothing happened outside of the occasional bump and scratch from an irate lion, tiger, elephant ... or Lupe!

During his three months away in so-called "civilization," Johnny got hit by a car, knocked down by a miniature Ferris wheel, and bruised in a collision with a motorboat while surfboard riding. He also caught the flu and ended up with a mild case of pneumonia from too much nightly exposure in the swimming pool. Lupe came to visit and, "because she thought I hadn't been getting the proper attention, she hit one of the physicians over the head with a vase!"

Lupe's love of jewelry was well known. She'd often be photographed out and about, bracelets halfway up her arm, thousands and thousands of dollars of gems adorning her flesh. Johnny was forced to live behind barred windows and steel doors, servants carried guns, all because Lupe insisted on keeping her jewelry collection in their home. Before the door was opened to any caller, that person was submitted to intense scrutiny by at least two people. The person opening the door held a revolver and, from a side window, another employee would wait as back up, just in case the caller forced his or her way inside.

If Lupe kept her jewels in bank vaults, none of these stringent security measures would have been needed, but she didn't believe in owning such beautiful things if they had to be hidden away. That's precisely why she bought jewelry instead of stocks and bonds. They were an investment in beauty.

Although Lupe's fear of burglars was always on her mind, she admitted to *Screen Book Magazine* (February 1934) that danger came with keeping potential burglars out of her home. "If there should be a fire," she said, "all of us would probably be burned alive if we could not find one of the keys to the steel doors." She was right. The barred windows elim-

inated them as a means of escape, and every door had to be opened from the inside with a key. Lupe was a prisoner to her jewels, and Johnny hated it.

One night when the doorbell rang, Lupe answered it. Before opening the door, naturally, she enquired who was calling and received no response to her question. She asked again. Still no response was given. So, Lupe took matters into her own hands. Without uttering another word, she fired her gun through a small opening in the door. The next morning, she spotted blood on the front lawn and along the walkway running out to the street. Lupe had most certainly hit her silent target. She never heard a word from her victim but she convinced herself that she was well within her rights to shoot. "If it was someone with legitimate business they would have replied when I asked who it was," she said (*Screen Book Magazine*, February 1934).

Lupe's security measures extended to her car too. She had a tear gas container installed and at the press of a button, the gas would be activated and the potential jewel thief would be thwarted. It was never used on a potential thief ... only on Johnny! Just after the device was installed, Lupe forgot which button activated the gas. Much to Johnny's dismay she started randomly pressing buttons in order to find out. Of course, Lupe found the button and Johnny got a face full of gas. Once again, an argument ensued...

Additionally, within the car[4] they traveled in, Lupe would cradle a pearl-handled .38 revolver in her lap; Johnny carried a specially constructed .44 inside his jacket. Another pistol sat in the side pocket of the door and the chauffeur was armed with two guns. Just to be sure, there was a bodyguard in a car behind them, also armed to the teeth! Further, so that no one got to know his identity, Lupe would use a different bodyguard each time she went out. The guard would follow Lupe and Johnny into their nightclub of choice and mingle amongst the crowd, all the time watching for a potential jewel heist.

When the Beverly Hills Police Department got wind of Lupe's collection of guns, they paid a visit to her home and told her it was against the law for her to have so many. She told them if she wasn't allowed to carry the guns, they should know that if she was ever robbed, she'd sue them and cost them plenty. "Everybody know I will not go out and stick up somebody; I carry guns only for [my] protection," she said (*Screen Book Magazine*, February 1934). The police were convinced of Lupe's motive for ownership and were thus relieved of any responsibility in the matter.

Lupe wasn't bluffing when she said she'd do whatever it took in order to protect herself and her property. She was never afraid to use her weapon, even if it wasn't always on the right person. Following a night at the Legion fights, Lupe almost shot actor Jack La Rue! As she was leaving, he decided to play a little joke. He approached her car window and said, "Stick 'em up!" Lupe reached for her gun and a pale-faced Jack screamed, "Lupe! It's me, Jack. Don't shoot" (*Screen Book Magazine*, February 1934).

Lupe's fear of being robbed got a lot worse following the delivery of the ransom notes in relation to her niece. She became paranoid about people breaking into her house, she constantly heard noises, she was weary of suspicious-looking deliverymen and she hated being home alone. Under ordinary circumstances, Lupe's jewelry collection, had it ever been stolen, would have been covered by insurance. However, Lupe didn't have insurance! In 1934, the yearly premium to insure her collection had been estimated at $40,000 (approximately $650,000 in 2011), and unless she agreed to keep her most expensive piece, a necklace worth $75,000 (approximately $1.2 million in 2011), in a bank vault, no company would assume the risk of covering it anyway. Lupe was so publicly outspoken about the security measures she had taken to protect her collection, no thief in their right mind would have risked certain death to go anywhere near her — or it! The strategy worked perfectly.

\* \* \*

In his *Los Angeles Evening Herald and Express* column (February 16, 1938), Jimmie Starr reported that Mexico City's ace producing company, Filmos Selectos, was trying to negotiate a deal whereby Johnny and Lupe would star in a series of Spanish films based on Tarzan. Since Weissmuller was already under contract to MGM, the Mexican film firm planned to borrow him and purchase the Spanish rights to the Tarzan series. While the concept was enthusiastically received, it never eventuated. Incidentally, Lupe was able to belt out the infamous Tarzan call better than Weissmuller ever could. There are several versions of how the actual call was recorded; Weissmuller maintained that the sound was mostly his doing, heightened by audio effects to give it more oomph. The Tarzan yell received its own trademark registration on August 1, 1995, and was renewed on December 28, 2005 (www.trademarkia.com). At Weissmuller's request, the Tarzan yell was played three times as his coffin was lowered into the ground.

\* \* \*

In the 1930s, Lupe intertwined her film career with her stage career. She began with the Flo Ziegfeld production *Hot-Cha!* in 1932 (119 performances); *Strike Me Pink* followed in 1933 (122 performances), and then the aforementioned London-based production *Transatlantic Rhythm*. Aside from various cross-country vaudeville tours and countless personal appearances, Lupe's last big theatrical production was the seemingly cursed Shubert musical comedy *You Never Know* (78 performances) in 1938. No matter what state the show was in, the troubles continued, not just with the feuding between Lupe and co-star Libby Holman, but with the show—period. Scores were changed, new songs were included, other songs were cut, chorus girls were added, dialogue was altered, pay cuts ensued, and surprisingly, most of the changes were all done behind the director's back! The show was a mess, and the Shubert brothers were blamed for the shoddy production value. In order to cut costs and not pay overtime, they ordered stagehands to pack up props while the actors were still performing onstage. During one performance in Philadelphia, Holman made her entrance late in the second act and, upon discovering that all of the pictures and some of the furniture were missing from the set, she casually looked around and ad libbed to her co-star, Rex O'Malley, "I'm terribly sorry you lost your inheritance and had to sell all your pictures." Thinking the line was a part of the play, that night's audience was oblivious to the joke but the muffled laughter of O'Malley and the actors and the stagehands in the wings gave it away. It seems the writing was on the wall from the very beginning. Cole Porter refused to attend the opening night party and later said that *You Never Know* was the worst show that he had ever been associated with (Bradshaw, *Dreams That Money Can Buy: The Tragic Life of Libby Holman*).

With so much discord going on behind the scenes, reviews were lukewarm. Male lead Clifton Webb was a nervous wreck from the non-relenting off-stage drama (despite getting along with Lupe and Holman individually, he was often the mediator between them). Because of the constant conflict and cat fights, he flatly refused to take the play on tour (www.imdb.com). Holman told Webb that she never disliked a person as much as she disliked Lupe Vélez. Believing herself to be a witch (and many people believed she was), Holman told Webb she'd put a hex on Lupe (Conner, *Lupe Vélez and Her Lovers*).

Lupe once showed Webb a huge diamond ring, saying, "Thees is the ring I'm going to murder that Jewish beech [Holman] with." As was the customary procedure with any of Lupe's hateful outbursts, she then knelt down in the wings, crossed herself and prayed for

forgiveness. In turn, Holman would imitate Lupe's accent and caustic behavior. On one occasion, she showed up to rehearsals wearing a large, gawdy-looking rhinestone ring, which she claimed resembled Lupe's nose! (Bradshaw, *Dreams That Money Can Buy: The Tragic Life of Libby Holman*).

David L. Smith, author and documentarian of Clifton Webb's life and career, has done extensive research regarding the production of the troubled play. He said:

> In New Haven, on March 5, 1938, *You Never Know* opened to a sold-out audience. Webb was teamed with his old friend, Libby Holman, and Lupe Vélez, who was known as "The Mexican Spitfire." Also in this show were the dance team that appeared with Webb in *Flying Colors* in 1932 ... Buddy and Vilma Ebsen. It was soon apparent that Webb and Holman were working with mediocre material. Just as bad was the fact that Lupe Vélez was stealing the show from them. After New Haven, the show moved to Boston, then to Washington, D.C. All the while changes were being made in the book and the score. To top it off, Vélez began to hate Libby Holman. She even threatened to kill her. Webb gave her a straight talking-to. "Lupe, you must not say such things. One day you'll turn them all against yourself." These were prophetic words since Vélez did eventually commit suicide.
>
> When the show reached Philadelphia, Webb thought it might be salvageable but still needed some doctoring. Webb persuaded J.J. Shubert to call in George Abbott to try to fix the problems. The show went to Pittsburgh, Detroit, and then Chicago. The notices were mixed. The final date of the road show was in Porter's and Webb's home state. *You Never Know* opened on May 23, 1938, for a three-day engagement at the English Theater in Indianapolis.
>
> The show finally got to the Winter Garden in New York. The critical reviews were mild. The night before it closed, J.J. Shubert came to Webb's dressing room.
>
> "Clifton, if we put things back the way they were, don't you think we could get a run out of it?"
>
> "Not with me," Webb replied.
>
> The play was a genuine bomb even though Porter had written a fine selection of songs for it. Despite its poor reputation, it has been revived frequently in summer stock and even had a Broadway revival in 1973. Webb and Porter remained close friends throughout their lives.

Lupe's threat against Holman was taken so seriously, the stage manager escorted Holman to and from her dressing room and the stage. Holman was awfully near-sighted,

Circa 1938 — A rare shot of Lupe on stage with co-star Clifton Webb in the trouble-plagued play *You Never Know.*

but she was far too vain to wear glasses. She felt her way around, usually unsuccessfully, often tripping over props and scenery. Lupe stood by, watching, and suddenly she had an idea. Urinating in the wings, Lupe hoped that her pee-puddle would cause Libby to "accidentally" slip and fall! For several nights she watched and waited as Libby was safely escorted past her. Much to Lupe's dismay, Libby remained upright. In New Haven, however, Libby wasn't so lucky. Lupe was done with waiting for revenge and she took her down with her own hands. At the completion of the show, during the curtain call, the two women came to blows. The following night, extra makeup was needed to cover Libby's black eye. Lupe may have been smaller, but she was a much better fighter (Conner, *Lupe Vélez and Her Lovers*).

*   *   *

Given Weissmuller's "Tarzan — King of the Jungle" association, it was ironic that animals, of all things, would split Johnny and Lupe up — permanently.

Weissmuller made *Tarzan Finds a Son!* (1939) on location and was excited to return to California — not so much to see Lupe, since their relationship was now hanging by a thread, but because he really missed his dog Otto. Whenever Johnny walked in the front door, Otto would run to him and put his paws on Johnny's shoulders and greet him with a giant lick on his cheek. This time, as Johnny opened the door, there was no Otto. Johnny looked around and repeatedly called his name. Still no Otto. As Lupe came walking down the stairs, Johnny was already sick with dread before he asked the burning question, "Where's Otto?"

"He's dead," said Lupe bluntly.

She claimed a stranger had entered the house and poisoned him. Johnny knew Lupe's story was bogus and he called her a "lying bitch," obviously devastated that Otto had probably been murdered by his own wife. Mr. Kelly and Mrs. Murphy were yapping and nipping at Johnny's feet and that obstinate parrot was repetitively screeching, "Gary, Gary, Gary!"

Infuriated, Johnny walked over to the parrot, grabbed him in his huge fist, broke his neck and threw his limp body at Lupe's feet. "Goodbye, Gary," he muttered as he stormed upstairs to pack his bags. He left the house that night. He never returned. Years later, Weissmuller told his son that he loved Otto more than he loved Lupe — at least at *that* point in their relationship (Weissmuller Jr., Reed and Reed, *Tarzan, My Father*). Ironically, Weissmuller once described his Tarzan films as being, "an idealistic, down-to-earth story about a man's love for animals and the care of his family" (www.imdb.com). Yet, by 1938, his beloved dog had been poisoned by his soon-to-be ex-wife and he just choked a parrot with his bare hands. (In previous divorce filings, Lupe accused Johnny of "cruelty and physical and mental violence.")

During the 1938 divorce trial, Lupe told the judge, "He didn't like the way I did everything. He was always telling me to get a divorce." She testified in the superior court that Weissmuller was "very insulting," went into rages in front of her guests, broke a lamp and threw dishes at her, called her "dirty names," and even threatened to kill her beloved dogs. "Your honor," said Lupe to Judge Charles S. Burnell. "I didn't want a divorce. I tried so hard, but it got so I couldn't stand it" ("Weissmuller 'Couldn't Forget He Was Tarzan,' So Lupe Gets Divorce," *Lincoln State Journal*, August 16, 1938).

Lupe complained that Johnny didn't want her to go places, not even the beauty parlor. Judge Burnell offered her an unexpected compliment that broke the seriousness of the situation: "He probably thought you didn't need beauty treatments." Lupe giggled. Continuing

**Lupe and Johnny in happier times.**

with her testimony, she said her husband would often stay out all night, and be away four times a week. Yet if she went out, he threatened to break her neck if he found her at a place he didn't approve of. "He just couldn't forget he was playing Tarzan, could he?" asked the court. Lupe giggled again ("Weissmuller 'Couldn't Forget He Was Tarzan,' So Lupe Gets Divorce." *Lincoln State Journal*, August 16, 1938). Judge Burnell continued with his humorous dialogue, interrupting Lupe when she explained about Weissmuller's dish-throwing. He commented that it must have been hard for her to keep a complete set of china in the house and asked why she didn't buy paper plates to prevent the breakages. Lupe didn't giggle that time.

When all was said and done, an out-of-court settlement required Johnny to pay Lupe $200 a week for 156 weeks, *except* when she was working. She also got the Beverly Hills home, including all furniture. None of the eight Beverly Hills apartment houses they owned and rented for $800 per month (approximately $13,000 in 2011) were mentioned in the settlement. Naturally, Johnny kept their two boats, a schooner and a speedster. Lupe had no use for them.

Some time in 1938, Lupe gave reporter Gladys Hall a detailed account of her marriage

to Weissmuller. Lupe admitted she went into the marriage thinking that she would not be lonely any more. She kept working because she was still supporting her extended family and she did not feel it right that the responsibility of her family's welfare be the sole responsibility of her new husband.

She questioned whether her continued working hurt her marriage. She admitted that much of her touring, be it stage work or personal appearances, was to separate herself from the unhappiness of a destructive relationship. During their marriage, Lupe left Hollywood and film opportunities behind, to simply get away.

In saying that, she still knew in her heart that she had put every part of herself into her marriage. "I can close my eyes and say, honestly, that I gave Johnny everything," she claimed. She said she cooked every meal that he ate in their house. She fixed his socks and his shirts. She bought his clothes because he liked her taste in fashion. She gave up all her friends for his friends because he was jealous of them. She said she was servant and slave to him, and still, it wasn't good enough.

The scenes of humiliation and the "things" she claims were "not repeatable" got so bad, even their servants left. Her friends left too. If she had no respect for herself, they told her, then they had no respect for her. For five and a half years, she claimed she tried everything she could to be happy, and to make *him* happy, yet she was, for the most part, the unhappiest she had ever been in her entire life. As a result of the relationship, Lupe said she bore the bruises and the marks that could be seen as well as the bruises and the marks that couldn't be seen. "I love him and he loves me," she said sadly. "But we are both much happier apart" (The Gladys Hall Papers, the Margaret Herrick Library, and *Los Angeles Examiner*, July 18, 1938).

As Lupe testified, Johnny played golf. He wasn't contesting the divorce. There was no need. After all, he had already found his next wife, twenty-one year Beryl Scott, a Canadian-born San Francisco socialite. (Legal papers show that her first name was originally spelled Beryel.) As far as temperament was concerned, she was Lupe's polar opposite. Prior to his next marriage, Lupe ran into Johnny at a restaurant. She had read in the papers that he intended to marry Beryl but she wouldn't believe it until she heard it from him. In the book *Water, World & Weissmuller*, author Narda Onyx retold an eerily prophetic part of that conversation.

> LUPE: "I read in the papers you have met a nice society girl. You will marry her, no?"
> JOHNNY: "I will marry her, yes!"
> LUPE: "But she ees not an actress! She will be no fun for you, Popee!"
> JOHNNY: "I've had fun!" Johnny said. "I want peace!"

"Poor Johnee," Lupe said as she walked away. "You do not know that peace only comes in the grave."

Lupe was granted a divorce (without contest) on August 16, 1938, and never remarried. Johnny remarried as soon as he was legally able (on August 20, 1939). Beryl would go on to have his only three children: John Scott, Jr. (aka Johnny Weissmuller Jr.), Wendy Anne and Heidi Elizabeth. Johnny Jr. died of liver cancer in 2006. In November 1962, Heidi died in a car accident. She was married, reportedly pregnant, and only nineteen years old. Surprisingly, despite their personality differences, the ex–Mrs. Weissmuller and the current Mrs. Weissmuller would grow close. They'd often schedule beauty parlor appointments to chat about the children, Johnny, and just general "girl talk." During the final few weeks of Lupe's life, Lupe desperately attempted to confide in Beryl about her pregnancy. First at

the beauty parlor, before disappearing under a dryer, Lupe told Beryl that she must speak with her privately. They never did. Not long after, Lupe invited Beryl and Johnny to a cocktail party at her house. Lupe pulled Beryl aside and, according to the latter, there was clearly something important that Lupe wanted to tell her. But there were so many guests in the house and so much noise, Lupe only enquired about the children and asked Beryl to please come by the following day. Author Narda Onyx said, "Beryl detected a note of urgency in her voice. It sounded almost like a plea."

But Beryl was behind schedule all day the next day. She finally found time to drive over to Lupe's house in the evening, but she did not go in. There were several cars parked outside, none she recognized. Not wanting to start any unwanted rumors, she turned the car around and drove home. Given the tragedy to follow, it's unlikely that Beryl had the chance to tell Lupe that she had been and gone, and more importantly, *why* she chose not to go inside that night. Two days later, Lupe was dead.

"Not Lupe!" Johnny repeated over and over again upon hearing news of her death. "She could not have killed herself because of a man!" As Johnny and Beryl paid their respects by Lupe's casket, her suicide note had been revealed in the papers and her pregnancy secret was divulged to the world. The secret Lupe had so desperately tried to share with Beryl for weeks prior to her death, was now eerily revealed from beyond the grave. For both Johnny and Beryl, there was now a lot of soul-searching, a lot of "what ifs?" (Onyx, *Water, World & Weissmuller: A Biography*).

Now in his mid-forties, with his loincloth days coming to an end, Johnny was far from washed up. When Columbia Pictures developed the popular comic strip *Jungle Jim* into a low-budget multi-film adventure series, Weissmuller was their choice. Despite his advancing age, he was still fitter than many of his younger contemporaries, and the production made sure of it with regular weigh-ins. For every pound he was overweight, he was fined $5,000. It was reason enough for Johnny to keep his waistline in check (www.imdb.com). But his relationship with Beryl dissolved beyond repair and they divorced in 1949.

Though he fathered no more children,[4] Johnny was in no way done with marriage. Golfer Allene Gates[5] was the next Mrs. Weissmuller, then Irene Bouvier, and finally (his last and longest marriage) Maria Brock Mandell Bauman. She was widowed by his 1984 death (pulmonary edema).

# 13

## *The Girl from Mexico (1939)*

"Oh, you don't say that in English."—Carmelita (Lupe Vélez) in *Mexican Spitfire* (1940)

Following the completion of *La zandunga* (1938), Lupe was offered a very tempting and lucrative long-term contract to stay in Mexico. A four-picture deal at $4,500 per week (approximately $70,000 in 2011) was a generous offer, but she graciously declined and returned to the United States. It was a smart move. Her next American film, *The Girl from Mexico* (1939), would take her Hollywood career in a whole new direction.

American journalist H. Allen Smith interviewed Lupe at the Hotel Elysee in 1938. At the time, Lupe was still married (barely) to Johnny Weissmuller. Smith recalled that the stock standard opener to most stories regarding the pair started with, "My Johneeeeeeee! I keeeeeeeel heeeeeeeem!" Then a few "Carambas" scattered here and there and some hysterical shrieking of, "I die! My God, I die." Smith described Lupe's voice as husky, and whenever she got emotional, her Mexican accent became more prominent.

Lupe sat down with Smith, and in all seriousness she told him a story of a girl from an unnamed Los Angeles newspaper who had arranged to interview her. She wasn't a stranger; Lupe had known the girl for years. Lupe trusted her to stick to the topics they had spoken about during the interview (Mexican moviemaking vs. British moviemaking, etc.). When Lupe saw the article, the opening line was the usual "I keeeeeeeel heeeeeeeem! I keeeeeeeel my Johneeeeeeee!" Lupe felt horribly betrayed and told Smith that she had only granted one interview since that time. *That* interviewer was a young man from California. Before they started, Lupe told him that she had three witnesses for the interview and one person transcribing her words in shorthand to prove exactly what was said. The young man scoped the room, looked everyone over, and said, "I am sorry, Miss Vélez, but this is not the kind of interview I have in mind." He walked out.

By 1938, Lupe had been typecast as the hotheaded, erratic Mexican Spitfire. Almost every newspaper article printed her words in exaggerated form and broken English. Lupe was obviously frustrated and Smith promised that his print article would stick faithfully to their conversation. Lupe explained that scripts were always written backward for her, with an accent. "They make me say, 'Is you goin' the street down?' and 'The horse you ride in the saddle sidesaddle.' I do not talk that way. But I have to do it because they write it like that."

Smith left the hotel room and, unlike his predecessors, he stuck to his promise and transcribed exactly what Lupe told him. The press associations picked up his story and it was sent around the country. But while the interview was most certainly different, many readers didn't believe a word of it!

Lupe and Donald Woods in *The Girl from Mexico* (1939). The success of this film was a springboard for the popular "Mexican Spitfire" series.

In *The Girl from Mexico* (1939), Lupe appears as fiery Mexican songstress Carmelita Fuentes. A dashingly handsome advertising executive, Dennis Lindsay (Donald Woods), brings her from Mexico to New York with the promise that he'll take care of her and show her the sights of the big city if she'll appear on a radio broadcast to appease his boss, who's looking for a first-rate Mexican entertainer.

In New York, Dennis gets distracted by his work and upcoming wedding to snooty fiancée Linda (Elizabeth Price), so a bored Carmelita and the always-willing mischief-maker "Uncle Matt" (Leon Errol) strike up a friendship and sneak out to party the night away. Carmelita parties a little too hard and she loses the one thing she desperately needs to keep — her voice! When Dennis realizes his neglect was the reason Carmelita ran amok, he pays more attention to her, at the expense of his seething fiancée, who calls off their wedding. Dennis isn't too upset by his broken engagement because now he realizes that he's really in love with Carmelita anyway. They get married in the final scene, but not without a hilarious climax between new bride Carmelita and the scorned Linda.

*The Girl from Mexico* played to sell-out crowds for its entire three-week run at the Rialto in New York. Critics in Mexico said it was a "great comedy" and "an hour of non stop laughter." According to *Film Daily* (May 17, 1939), "This picture is indeed a pleasant surprise. Although a slapstick comedy, it has plenty of action and Lupe Vélez comes through a swell performance as a first-class comedienne."

The success of the low-budget film was unexpected. RKO was quick to act on its popularity and Lupe was offered a contract of $1,500 per week (approximately $24,000 in 2011) to reprise her role of Carmelita indefinitely. *The Girl from Mexico* was quickly followed up with seven more installments, all directed by London-born Leslie Goodwins (1899–1969). From 1940 to 1943, the "Mexican Spitfire" series scored at the box office time and time again. Goodwin's solid background as a gag writer and director of two-reel comedies made him the right man for this type of good-natured family entertainment. Throughout the course of the series, Carmelita's husband Dennis Lindsay was played by three different actors: Donald Woods, Charles "Buddy" Rogers and Walter Reed.

Australian-born comedian, Leon Errol (1881–1951) went on to play two key roles in the series: first the mischievous Uncle Matt, then, beginning with the first film in the "Mexican Spitfire" series, the befuddled Lord Basil Epping. Errol's two characters were the foundation of the storylines and the springboard for the "mistaken identity" gags.

During Carmelita's Spanish-language tirades, she was given free reign to say whatever she felt was appropriate for the occasion. For instance, in *The Girl from Mexico* she says "estupidote" (big stupid), "animalón" (big animal) and "cara de perro" (dog face). What's of particular interest when viewing *The Girl from Mexico* is Lupe's accent. There's no hiding a noticeable "English accent" within her Spanish speaking — further proof that Lupe spoke much better English in private than she ever let on.

Errol was no slouch in the ad-lib department. He'd match Lupe's off-the-cuff comments with his own impromptu vocal and physical outbursts. The on-screen chemistry between the pair was unmatched and Lupe would break up when Errol did something crazy and unexpected, which was often. If you look carefully, many of the takes of Lupe's unanticipated reactions were left in the "Mexican Spitfire" films. It was a masterful plan by director Goodwins to not over-direct the cast. The series has a fresh, unrehearsed spontaneity that many comparable Hollywood comedies lack.

The "Mexican Spitfire" series utilized Lupe's ethnic

**Uncle Matthew Lindsay (Leon Errol) does his best to cheer up a forlorn Carmelita (Lupe) in *The Girl From Mexico* (1939).**

background for all its worth. Many of Lupe's English phrases were purposefully mixed up enough for audiences to realize what she meant to say, while at the same time, her scripted innocence and "how you say?" Mexican interpretation of any given situation served to give audiences a laugh. With another new decade beginning (the 1940s), Lupe found herself with a solid acting gig in a popular series of films that the public loved.

*   *   *

In December of 1939, a shrewd Gypsy woman robbed Lupe of $2,500 (approximately $40,000 in 2011). Out for justice, Lupe went to the Beverly Hills jail to view a dozen women in a lineup but the thief was not there. A month earlier, Lupe's maid had introduced her to a "dark young woman" who said she was a Gypsy with mystic powers. The Gypsy told Lupe she had many enemies and they had cursed her. In order to break the curse, the mysterious woman paid daily visits to Lupe's home on Rodeo Drive to pray for the overthrow of her enemies and their curses. This ritual lasted for two weeks. Then came the con: The Gypsy told Lupe she would have much better success if there were some money to pray over. Lupe gave her $150. Two days later, the Gypsy brought the money back. She told Lupe she needed more money to pray over — at least $10,000. Lupe negotiated her down to $2,500, telling her, "Give me a fourth of what I want and I'll be happy."

A week prior to Christmas, the Gypsy shuffled Lupe's two $1,000 bills and the remaining $500 and "supposedly" wrapped the money in a piece of red silk that had been torn from one of Lupe's party dresses. She handed the neat package to Lupe and instructed her to go to bed and clutch the silk and concentrate. The Gypsy left and Lupe did precisely as she was instructed. The following morning, Lupe awoke and opened the package. Inside, she found a neatly clipped bundle of blank paper. Lupe told police, "The money — eet ees nothing. But just wait unteel I get my hands on that woman" ("All Lupe Wants Is to See the Gypsy Again." *The Palm Beach Post*, December 29, 1939).

The police rounded up twenty-three Gypsy women, all of whom were eyed at the Central Jail by Lupe and other victims of the same scam. Everyone except Lupe studied the women's faces. Lupe looked at their legs! "Thees woman, she [also] take seex pair of my $15 [approximately $235 in 2011] seamless stockings. Eet ees a clue, you bet!" Lupe dashed from one side of the room to the other, ordering the women to hike up their long skirts so she could check their legs for her silk stockings.

The Gypsy woman who duped Lupe was not among them; however, two other women were held after victims identified them as the Gypsies who stole *their* cash in the old "money blessing game." The others were let go and police promised to round up a new batch for Lupe to inspect at a later date ("Lupe Vélez Fails to Identify Gypsy Legs." *Los Angeles Evening Herald and Express*, January 5, 1940).

By August of 1940, several newspapers reported that Lupe was informed that the Gypsy who conned her was apprehended in Chicago. Just one day after Lupe's death in December 1944, Judge Charles Griffin of Beverly Hills Justice Court discovered the suit and dismissed it. The *Los Angeles Independent Daily News* (January 10, 1945) wrote that the defendant (court documents provide her name, Nancy Miller) was never found, the victim (Lupe) was now deceased and the statute of limitations had since expired. While fortunetelling and Gypsies were commonplace in Mexico, Lupe came to realize that her beliefs were easily exploited for profit by Hollywood con artists. She learned her lesson and concentrated on her work ... but not before meeting and making "an arrangement" with a man who would go on to become one of America's greatest TV heroes: *The Lone Ranger*!

# 14

## Lupe and "The Lone Ranger"

"The truth never has much to do with what people in Hollywood believe, as I found out when I struck up a very close relationship with Lupe Vélez."[1]—Clayton Moore

By 1940, Lupe was divorced from Johnny Weissmuller and her career had taken on a whole new life thanks to the popularity of the "Mexican Spitfire" series. But, according to Clayton Moore, Lupe still wasn't completely content. Out of the blue, via a mutual friend, she invited him to a party she was having at her Beverly Hills home. Curious, he arrived at her front door as a complete stranger. By the time he left, their newly formed relationship was much more involved than he'd ever imagined it would be.

Moore was still years away from his most famous role as "The Lone Ranger"; in fact, at the time, he had only about eighteen film roles (mostly small and uncredited) under his belt. But he had something she desperately needed: the right look. Moore was tall, muscular, handsome, charming, and most importantly, he was single. He was the perfect catch and Lupe was about to throw out a line of bait that would fool the press.

According to Moore's 1998 autobiography *I Was That Masked Man*, he enjoyed a wonderful Sunday afternoon at Lupe's home and as the party was breaking up, Lupe took him aside to ask if he would like to stay for dinner. He noticed that she looked like she needed to talk. He liked her, and besides, he was interested in what she had to say. He accepted her invitation and said that even though it was a private dinner, he never really got the impression that she was making any romantic moves on him. By all means, she wanted him and needed him. Just not in *that* way.

Over dinner, Lupe was very serious. Confiding in Moore that she was worried about her career in Hollywood, she said she needed some positive publicity and her plan involved *him*. He was puzzled as to why he would be the proverbial flame to ignite her flagging career. He didn't have to wonder for long. Lupe had it all worked out.

Lupe told Moore he was a very handsome man and that she needed to be seen at all the right places around town. No longer married, she couldn't go out alone and Moore was the perfect "date" to be photographed with—no strings attached. Lupe reeled off all the names of the "places to be," or the "places *she* wanted to be": the Macombo, Ciro's, the Trocadero, etc. Moore was a beginner at the time and those nightclubs were for the Hollywood big shots. He felt way out of his league. At twenty-six, he was still almost a decade away from donning the white hat and black mask of the Lone Ranger. (*The Lone Ranger* TV series premiered on September 15, 1949, and lasted until 1957.)

In 1940, Moore could barely afford to feed himself at a diner let alone the most expensive

with the English version and supplemented by writers, translators and actors who were native speakers. Gilbert Roland (billed as Luis Alonso) played the male lead, Prince Dmitri Nekhludov (www.dimitritiomkin.com).

Next, Lupe was cast as the female lead in Cecil B. DeMille's third directorial attempt at the same film, *The Squaw Man* (1931). The 1914 version gave DeMille his very first taste of filmmaking as a director and is available on DVD. The 1914 film grossed a staggering $244,000 (approximately $5.5 million in 2011) and since it only cost $20,000 (approximately $450,000 in 2011) to make, it was an unheard-of profit for its time. Not content with his success the first time around, DeMille took a second stab at the story four years later and directed a 1918 version, of which only the final reel survives. Lupe's 1931 sound version was his third attempt at the same story. (DeMille holds the record as the only Hollywood filmmaker to make the same film three times.)

It takes twenty-seven minutes for Lupe to make her appearance in *The Squaw Man*. As the Indian Squaw Naturich, she's seen (in a long shot) driving a wagon into town with her father. Uttering few words throughout, her performance is understated and primitive. That said, she manages to stay perfectly controlled, exuding every emotion needed with her facial expressions and gestures alone. Her character's death (suicide by gun-shot) over the loss of her young son Hal (Dickie Moore) and her impending arrest over a shooting that saved her husband's life seven years before makes for an incredibly heartrending and dramatic final scene.

Now in his mid-eighties, Dickie Moore (aka Dick Moore) was just a week shy of his sixth birthday when *The Squaw Man* was released. In a letter to the author (December 22, 2010), he said, "I have pleasant memories of working with Lupe in *The Squaw Man*. She was a lovely woman, extremely outgoing and a joy to work with. She displayed no 'temperament' at all.... I can't say the same for Mr. DeMille."

For years, Moore has recounted his negative memories of working with DeMille on the film, saying:

> [He was] a complete and total egotist who didn't give a damn about anyone but himself. He hit me. I was a five-year-old kid and he hit me! [www.imdb.com].

Prior to directing the 1931 *Squaw Man*, DeMille suffered three major personal setbacks: one financial, one medical, one matrimonial. Over a million dollars of his money was lost in the stock market crash of 1929, and he was still very much carrying the finan-

Lupe with Warner Baxter in a scene from director Cecil B. DeMille's *The Squaw Man* (1931), his third attempt at the same story.

**Lupe approaches her male lead (and soon to be on-screen lover) Lawrence Tibbett in a scene from *The Cuban Love Song* (1931).**

cial and emotional burden of the loss. As a result, he was over $100,000 (approximately $1.5 million in 2011) in debt. Additionally, he had recently undergone a painful foot operation due to a yachting mishap that had splintered his heel. Lastly, when his wife Constance visited the set, she discovered that her husband's long-standing mistress, Julia Faye had accompanied him on location. Naturally, there was a massive argument.

As author Scott Eyman suggested in his 2010 book *Empire of Dreams: The Epic Life of Cecil B. DeMille,* "[The argument ensued because] Cecil may have promised to keep his affairs away from the film sets." So, while DeMille's violent on-set mood swings can certainly be explained, they can't be excused, especially when it comes to his vile treatment of a five-year-old child.

*Photoplay* (undated 1931) praised Lupe's performance in *The Squaw Man*: "With scarcely a dozen words of dialogue she holds our sympathy every second...." And, in Eyman's aforementioned biography on DeMille, he quotes the director as praising Lupe for giving "the best of the three performances as the squaw."

Lupe's last film of 1931 teamed her with one of the first noted opera stars to break into the picture business, Lawrence Tibbett. After earning an Oscar nomination for Best Actor in his first role in MGM's *The Rogue Song* (1930), his film *The Cuban Love Song* (1931) turned out to be a box office bomb. It was a surprising result, since most of its reviews were favorable. Marquis Busby of the *Los Angeles Examiner* (November 12, 1931) wrote, "Unfortunately there is a slightly metallic quality to Lupe Vélez's voice — a quality which does not exist off the screen. The little Mexican actress contributes a vivid performance as the Cuban girl, scoring particularly in the scene where her lover leaves her. It is one of her best performances..."

While *The Cuban Love Song* wasn't a box office success, two of the film's songs were big hits: "The Cuban Love Song" and "El Manisero" (aka "The Peanut Vendor Song").

It would be four years before Tibbett's Hollywood "comeback," but after starring in a couple of mediocre musicals, *Metropolitan* (1935) and *Under Your Spell* (1936), he'd had his chance. Despite a dream start, his Hollywood days were over. He continued with the Metropolitan Opera until the 1949–1950 season; years of heavy drinking combined with several acute health problems (vocal problems and crippling arthritis) had turned the once handsome

room. All was forgiven — at least between husband and wife. Not surprisingly, the hotel people weren't so forgiving! Morning came and hotel management delivered a note to the Weissmullers' room. Slipped under the door, it advised them of their immediate eviction. They laughed hysterically as they started to gather their things. Not more than fifteen minutes had passed when they were interrupted by a knock on the door. The hotel manager had come to personally deliver a second note that negated the first. Handing it to Johnny, he didn't stick around for it to be read. Shutting the door behind him, Lupe listened as Johnny read aloud a profuse apology with a plea for them to remain guests of the hotel for as long as they wished. They were still very much amused by the wacky situation, and although confused by the hotel's change of heart, they continued their stay — and without further incident.

Later, Johnny asked a hotel butler to explain the reversal. The butler told him it was by the queen's order. Johnny asked, "What queen?" The butler explained that the woman in the frilly nightgown and matching nightcap was the queen of Denmark. Her Royal Highness firmly stated to the hotel management that if Johnny was evicted, she would move out too. Thinking back, Johnny remembered the voice and the face from the night before. She did seem familiar, and she *did* speak as if she knew him. It was Queen Wilhelmina, who presented him with his Olympic gold medals in 1928! (Onyx, *Water, World & Weissmuller: A Biography*).

During 1937, Lupe had two films on the marquee. Her last U.K.-based production was the forgettable *Star Dust* (aka *Mad About Money*), followed by the wacky Wheeler and Woolsey comedy, *High Flyers*. *Monthly Film Bulletin* (December 1938) commented that *Star Dust* consisted of "a confused plot ... lack of continuity and bad cutting..." Despite the mayhem and silly wisecracks throughout the latter film (*de rigueur* in any Wheeler and Woolsey feature), *High Flyers* has its funny moments. More importantly, it was Lupe's first Hollywood film production in two years. With praiseful reviews for her role as Maria the maid, Lupe was on her way back from a career slump.

**Lupe gets her hair touched up on the set of the 1937 Wheeler and Woolsey comedy *High Flyers*.**

*   *   *

Just prior to Lupe and Johnny's fifth wedding anniversary, Maxine Garrison of the *Pittsburgh Press* (September 8, 1937) interviewed Lupe about her marriage and the ups and downs of their very public rela-

One year prior to their 1939 divorce, Lupe and Johnny publicly celebrate their last wedding anniversary together. Given their rocky romance and constant break-ups and make-ups, it was miraculous that they made it this far.

tionship. After several years as husband and wife, Lupe told Garrison, she and Weissmuller had only had three *big* fights (there were countless little ones). Two of the big fights, she explained, were about silly things; for example, "A man does not like beets, and his wife cooks beets, and they fight...." She said the third fight, their last one (at least at the time the article was printed), was a lulu. Lupe explained that she just wanted to try a separation to see what would happen, but there was never any talk of divorce. She said, "Johnee did not leave this house, and I should not have told the papers...."

Lupe was well aware of the public interest in her marriage; there were times when a reporter would call and Lupe just wasn't in the mood to discuss her private affairs. With that said, she'd still manage to give them something to talk about. Lupe added, "The newspapers telephone and say, 'Are you and Johnee quarreling again?' and I say, 'Sure, we hate each other! Just a minute ago I keel him! Upstairs he is lying in a pool of his own blood!'" (*Pittsburgh Press,* September 8, 1937).

If any newspaper writer attempted to spin a fictional tale about their marriage, Lupe went after them with fire in her eye. An unsigned (and untrue) gossip-type story relating to her marriage appeared in a local paper and had Lupe fuming for weeks, so much so that she publicly offered $50 (approximately $800 in 2011) to anyone who could flush out the anonymous author. She said, "It's hard enough to make a marriage last in Hollywood without having lies told about you" (*Los Angeles Evening Herald and Express,* April 16, 1934).

Hollywood nightclubs. "I'm sorry, Miss Vélez. I don't think I can help you," he said. "I'd love to ... but I can't afford it." Lupe shook her head and waved her finger to indicate that he'd misinterpreted what she was trying to say. "Don't worry about that," she said. "These won't be dates. It's strictly business. I'll take care of everything."

Moore took a few moments to absorb Lupe's proposal. It almost seemed too good to be true. Here was a stunningly beautiful Hollywood actress offering him all-expenses-paid nights out on the town, to all the best places, just so she could get herself back into the papers. She told him the hardest part of the job would be smiling for the cameras. Given the state of *his* own career at the time, he knew it couldn't hurt to be seen (and photographed) with Lupe Vélez either. The arrangement seemed fun, foolproof and, more importantly, mutually beneficial. He agreed. Lupe squealed with delight. And so it began....

Moore said that despite the original pact being a business arrangement, they truly enjoyed each other's company and became very good friends. But that's as far as it ever went. In his autobiography, he called Lupe a "lovely lady." He admitted she *was* a "Mexican Spitfire" when she was out in public, but in her home she was "genteel and intelligent." They'd often attend the Friday night fights; she would never arrive before the first round because she liked to make the grand entrance. By round two, Lupe would arrive in her beloved Dusenberg automobile, dressed as if she were going to a grand ball. Moore said he stood in total astonishment as she'd flippantly tip men $10 or $15 (approximately $150–$225 in 2011) just to park her car. He said he didn't know where her money came from but "there always seemed to be plenty of it."

By round three, Lupe had taken her ringside seat. There she would methodically take off her rings and shove them down into Moore's coat pocket, a handkerchief over the top of them for safe keeping. Lupe put on her own show at the fights and people would come to see her as much as they would the fight. Moore said he'll never forget the sight of Lupe, covered in expensive furs, sitting there yelling at the top of her lungs, "Kill the bum! Kill him!"

Lupe's "business plan" worked: The photographers took their picture at the nightclubs, the fights, even at Lupe's home, by the pool, with her dogs, etc. Buying into the relationship hype, the press even talked of impending wedding bells.

**Adorned in diamonds and fur: This was exactly how Lupe liked to be seen.**

**Clayton Moore as the Lone Ranger, atop his equally famous horse Silver. Lupe had seen the star potential in Moore years before he found fame as the masked man on TV and they became close friends. She didn't live to see his small screen success.**

Throughout the years, the press linked Lupe to many men in Hollywood and beyond, and that fabricated reporting (beginning as early as 1929) gave her a "love 'em and leave 'em" reputation that Lupe was quick to dismiss. She said:

In Hollywood, if you walk a city block with a man they have you engaged to marry him. When I wake up in the morning and look at the newspapers, I find myself engaged to some man.... [T]hey engage me to people I never heard of before. And then they disengage me just as fast [*The Pittsburgh Press*, September 23, 1929].

For the film *Kit Carson* (1940), Moore had grown his hair longer than he normally would, just for the part. Columnist, Louella O. Parsons wrote that he was trying to emulate Lupe's ex-husband, Johnny Weissmuller. Moore knew Weissmuller and took it as a compliment. Lupe didn't. Moore said he never once brought up Weissmuller's name in Lupe's company, and Lupe didn't mention him either. When Parsons reported in her column that Lupe was about to marry Moore, Lupe called her immediately to set her straight. "I remember how infuriated she was," he said. "And you didn't want to get on Lupe's bad side."

Lupe was known for her bubbly, fiery personality, but Moore said he often saw a sadder side to her too. Behind closed doors, and with those she trusted, she was the real Lupe and *that* Lupe was often up and down like a rollercoaster. Perhaps her highs and lows were a form of undiagnosed manic depression. Perhaps it was because she lost her one great love and she just never recovered. In his memoirs, Moore recalled a moment he'd never forget, saying, "She once pointed to a picture of Gary Cooper and said quietly, 'There is the only man I ever loved.'"

Moore ended his recollections of his friendship with Lupe by saying, "I admired her very much and I hoped someday she would meet someone who would make her truly happy." On August 19, 1940, Moore did marry, but Lupe wasn't his bride. His new wife was dancer-actress Mary Francis. Moore said when he called Lupe to tell her the news, she congratulated him and added, "It couldn't happen to a nicer person."

Moore succumbed to a heart attack on December 28, 1999, at 85. For many, when *he* died, so did the Lone Ranger. He had become so synonymous with the character, he's the only person to have both his real name and his character name on a star on Hollywood's Walk of Fame. It reads: "Clayton Moore, The Lone Ranger."

Lupe didn't live to see his success, but she certainly spotted his potential, years before anyone else did.

# 15

## *Little Girl, "Beeg Boy"*

"The first time you buy a house you think how pretty it is and sign the check. The second time you look to see if the basement has termites. It's the same with men."[1] — Lupe Vélez

In 1919, Guinn Williams traveled to Hollywood from his hometown of Decatur, Texas. Like so many others, he planned to make it in the movies. His screen debut was in the 1919 comedy *Almost a Husband* opposite Will Rogers. In fact, it was Rogers who saddled him with the "Big Boy" nickname, because of his tall, muscular physique. The pair would become firm friends and frequent co-stars. Williams was a permanent fixture in the Will Rogers rodeo shows that successfully toured throughout the United States. The like-minded duo also shared a lifelong love of horses and the game of polo.

"Big Boy" went on to become a western star and character actor in over 200 films, including *The Glass Key* (1935), *A Star Is Born* (1937), *Dodge City* (1939), *Santa Fe Trail* (1940), *The Alamo* (1960) and *The Comancheros* (1961). His friends ranged from crew members to $5-a-day cowboy bit players, to Errol Flynn, George Brent and John Wayne. Lupe would call him "Beeg Boy."

By November of 1940, Lupe and "Big Boy" were well on their way to becoming husband and wife. Lupe's Beverly Hills home was up for sale at the same time that, out at the Williams ranch, the hustle and bustle of remodeling was underway; "Big Boy" was preparing for the upcoming arrival of his new bride. The home was western-themed, complete with Navajo rugs and the like. The remodeling included a new bedroom that was 40 feet x 16 feet, topping the already massive master bedroom in Lupe's Beverly Hills home (32 feet x 16 feet). In between filming, Lupe traveled to the ranch where she'd take joy in caring for the numerous horses, cows, pigs, sheep, dogs and Shetland ponies.

Raised on a ranch, Williams was a real cowboy before he was a "reel" cowboy. He reportedly was the best horseman in Hollywood and few argued the fact. He was even dubbed the "Babe Ruth" of polo because he was such a strong long-hitter. Following high school, and prior to his break in Hollywood, Williams attempted a career in professional baseball. However, he soon realized he was much better at hitting a ball sitting atop a horse rather than standing on his own two feet. Polo became a lifelong passion and he had a constant rotation of over 100 polo ponies on his property. Lupe enjoyed riding too and she took a particular liking to a black thoroughbred that "Big Boy" brought back to the ranch. The horse's name was "Boogeyman."

"Big Boy" told reporter Paul Harrison (*Dunkirk Evening Observer*, November 14, 1940) that one day he brought home 100 baby chickens and a brooder as a surprise for Lupe. She

Lupe and fiancé Guinn "Big Boy" Williams in the midst of a serious conversation on December 8, 1940. Lupe's usual stack of diamond and bejeweled bracelets are clearly on view here.

was thrilled. A few days later, he walked into the house and there were all 100 baby chickens in the house, running around and freely pooping on the Navajo rugs. He said he had an awful time getting Lupe to put them back in the brooder. When asked if they'd had any fights yet, he said, "A couple." Then he added, "She won 'em both" (*Kentucky New Era*, November 15, 1944).

"Big Boy" Williams was a tall (6' 2"), lanky, easy-going Texan (former U.S. President George W. Bush significantly resembles him). Lupe was a tiny (5'), petite (she fluctuated between 105 and 108 pounds), hotheaded Mexican. As usual, Lupe had chosen a mate about as opposite as could be. But this time she outwardly transformed herself into a cowgirl in order to suit the lifestyle of her man, dressing in western gear, complete with cowboy outfit and boots, even a bandana, knife and lariat in her belt. With her dyed-red hair pulled back in tight pigtails, she looked more like Annie Oakley. Even funnier, if she left the house, she wouldn't bother changing out of her cowgirl get-up, she'd just wear one of her fur coats right over the top!

Lupe said she would likely choose a November wedding date because: "I married Weissmuller in October. That was a lousy marriage for me and brought bad luck. I don't want to risk it again." She hinted they would probably be married in Reno. As for their honeymoon plans: "I'm not sure," she said. "But I think we go either on a hunting or a fishing trip" ("Lupe Vélez Is Superstitious," *Hammond Times*, October 23, 1940).

The expected November nuptials never happened. The original caption on the photo (see previous page) showing the couple out on the town on December 8, 1940, stated the pair weren't married, but "likely would be before Christmas."

In late 1940, Lupe and "Big Boy" attended a film preview; however, this time they stood on the other side of the ropes. They wore their oldest clothes and joined the gawkers and autograph hounds. They took delight in heckling the stars in raucous voices. Nobody recognized the couple, which made the lark even funnier. Journalist Paul Harrison of the *Kentucky New Era* (October 22, 1940) wrote, "I hope nobody understood some of the remarks Lupe screamed in Spanish..." Lupe had been known to pull this same prank on other occasions, with other accomplices.[2]

By January of 1941, Lupe and "Big Boy" did a joint interview with Gladys Hall for *Modern Screen* magazine. When asked yet again *when* they would marry, Lupe was purposefully vague, saying, "We may marry in five hours, in six months, in a year and a half, maybe soon, maybe never. I do not say things now unless I am sure."

Though she was now "Big Boy's" fiancée, Lupe explained that before he met her, "Big Boy" had pre-conceived a perception of her values via the media's skewed representation of her rowdy personality and wild behavior. When they were introduced, he said she was altogether different from what he had imagined. "I met her," he said, "and I never did a more complete mental and emotional somersault. Because I found a domestic person, a girl who loves her home and takes pride in it and works in it."

Despite their collective wealth as a Hollywood couple, "Big Boy" appreciated Lupe's domestic resourcefulness. Likewise, she enjoyed the simplicity of ranch life — at least while it lasted. Lupe would remind the gardener to save the grass cuttings for the pigs to eat. She'd make extra mashed potatoes at dinner with the forethought of turning the remainder into potato soup the following night ("The best soup I have ever tasted," said "Big Boy"). If something needed fixing, she'd try, and usually succeed, in fixing it. If the house needed painting, she painted it. If the toilet needed fixing, she'd fix that, too. When the gas heater broke, "Big Boy" immediately reached for the telephone number of the plumber. Surprisingly, Lupe got down on her tummy and fixed it before he even finished dialing! "That is the day he propose' to me..." said Lupe, "... a day I look frightful ugly" (*Kentucky New Era,* November 15, 1940).

Lupe's wardrobe was designed and sewn by her own dressmaker, but Lupe had some input. Despite her wealth, her proudest achievement was making a beautiful dress out of a bargain piece of material: "For furs and jewels I pay," she said. "They last and I get only the best — sable, ermine, chinchilla. But the dresses — no! Why should I pay two-honderd feefty dollar for a dress, then find I look like ever-bodee else? So I design my clothes for me..." ("Thees Lupe! She Ees No Slave To Ze Dressmakairs!" *San Antonio Express*, March 2, 1940).

If the cut of a dress pleased her and fit well, she'd have it made in several colors. Most of her outfits had matching hoods or turbans, and her pillbox hats were covered with the same wool to match her collection of sweaters, usually in pastel shades. Her jackets were mostly hip length, nipped in to accentuate her tiny waist, with wide, padded shoulders that deflected attention from her small breasts. That said, size didn't seem to matter; Lupe, and her breasts, could put on quite the show!

In his bestselling autobiography *My Wicked, Wicked Ways* (1959), Errol Flynn wrote of Lupe and her performing "left breast": "Lupe had a unique ability to rotate her left breast. Not only that, she counter-rotated it, a feat so supple and beautiful to observe that you

couldn't believe your eyes." He then paid her a compliment that, coming from a man who had seen his fair share of boobs in his day, held a lot of weight. He said, "[Lupe's] breasts were probably the most beautiful that even Hollywood had ever seen."

Evelyn Keyes, best known for her role as Scarlett O'Hara's sister in the classic epic *Gone With the Wind* (1939), witnessed Lupe's breast trick for herself. Recalling a party that Flynn insisted she attend, Keyes arrived at "Big Boy" Williams' house, and Lupe was there too. Keyes noted that Lupe didn't appear to be living up to her nickname of the "Mexican Spitfire"; she was quiet and subdued. That is, until Flynn started to encourage her to do a party trick that Keyes in no way expected: "Come on, Lupe, show us how you do it," Flynn said.

Lupe tossed her head, "Oh, Errol, *siempre la misma cosa*" [always the same thing].

"Oh, come on, Chiquita, you know you like to do it."

She grinned, "*Para ti*" [For you].

All of a sudden, with her eyes on Flynn, Lupe's breasts began to move beneath the pale blue soft material of her blouse. In circles, faster and faster, round and round. Flynn whooped, "Did you ever see anything like that? Isn't it the damnedest thing?" Keyes admitted she hadn't *ever* seen anything like it (McNulty, *Errol Flynn: The Life and Career*).

Even as a young girl in Mexico, Lupe was the proverbial good time girl. Her Hollywood success most certainly changed her circle of friends and her financial situation, but she worked hard and she enjoyed and indulged in all the luxuries that money could buy. However, unlike many of her peers, she stayed true to herself. The fame and fortune did nothing to change her core personality. Rich or poor, famous or not, Lupe was *always* the same person. Only now, with her celebrity status and net worth, she had the power to help many people in many ways, and she usually did. Paul Harrison wrote an article about Lupe's generosity in his "Harrison in Hollywood" column (*Dunkirk Evening Observer*, October 28, 1941).

Several years prior, Lupe was reading the morning papers over breakfast. After reading the show business reviews, she noticed a touching story about a jobless Polish immigrant who was arrested for stealing food for his children. "I am not mooch of a one for geeving beeg checks to charity," said Lupe. "I like better to see where my money goes and what it does." Feeling the need to help, Lupe telephoned the police and asked them to send the poor man around to the theater where she was starring in the stage production *You Never Know*.

However, the police had allowed the man to go free on compassionate grounds; he wasn't charged for his crime and he was no longer in custody. But, after Lupe's phone call, the police picked him up again. Terrified and confused, the man believed that he was being rearrested. The policeman tried to explain the situation. With trepidation, the poor man's tearful wife went to the theater with him.

When the show was over, Lupe met with the couple and gave them a $100 bill (approximately $1,500 in 2011). Fearful they were being set up, they refused to accept it. After some small talk, Lupe and the policeman managed to convince the couple that the offer was genuine and they accepted the money with deep gratitude.

Several months later, Lupe received a letter in the mail from the man she had helped. Lupe's generous gift allowed the family to pay bills and buy food. Soon after the man got a job. A little ring was enclosed which he had made for her and told her she must always wear because it "represented the prayers and gratitude of seven people and should be luckier than any mere diamond." It was a horseshoe nail twisted to the size of her finger, the ends

cut off and soldered, without polish or adornment — and it became one of her most cherished pieces of jewelry.

Despite having a jewelry collection rivaling many of her Hollywood peers, Lupe cherished that simple homemade ring most of all. A 20-carat diamond on one hand and a bent nail on the other: that was Lupe. She was all about extremes and those two rings were about as extreme as it could ever get! In fact, Lupe was so taken with the simplicity of the ring (and its meaning) that she never took it off. She was wearing the ring when her body was found and she was buried with it on her finger.

Lupe may have had a big personality, but she had a big heart to go along with it. Her stories of good deeds are innumerable. A blind man standing outside a film studio, selling bits and pieces to make enough money to buy a seeing-eye-dog, was offered enough money by Lupe to buy one outright. Too proud to take a handout, he thanked her but insisted on making his own money. So Lupe took him into the studio and encouraged everyone to buy at least one thing from him. Not just on *that* day, but every day until he had enough money to purchase his guide dog.

Another time, Lupe discovered that an office boy at the studio had a cataract on one eye. When she asked him why he didn't have it removed, he blushed and confessed that he was saving his paychecks to afford a visit to a doctor. A few days later, Lupe told the boy that she had arranged for him to see a doctor and she would pay for the visit. He was too proud to accept her charity, so she convinced the doctor to call the boy and tell him that he was particularly interested in cataracts and he would like to perform an operation on him to fix the problem. The boy bought the story. Lupe paid for the operation.

Whether it was a stranger on the street, her servants or her cast and crew, rich or poor, Lupe treated everyone as equals. One crew member said, "She had a gift for making people feel free, themselves, and that she was one of them. There never was that 'queen' atmosphere about her." Lupe was one of the few Hollywood stars whose telephone number was publicly listed. Crestview 5–6161 was called by strangers, friends and friends of friends, and they all usually asked for Lupe's help in some way. If it was advice they needed, she'd give it. If it was money they needed, she'd give that too. "Okay, just come over and get the check," she'd say (*The Milwaukee Journal*, December 27, 1944).

During her relationship with "Big Boy" Williams, Lupe was genuinely happy playing the role of the "cowgirl rancher," at least for a little while. But their relationship ran its course and she left the ranch and went back to her own home on North Rodeo Drive. Once again, Lupe was alone.

"Big Boy" went on to marry three times — all actresses. His first two marriages (to Kathleen Collins and Barbara Weeks) were short-lived unions. Then in 1943, he married Dorothy Peterson. She was widowed by his death (uremic poisoning) on June 6, 1962. He was 63 years old.

# 16

## *The "Mexican Spitfire" Series*

"I am very happy with my present life and intend to stay that way."[1]—Lupe Vélez (1938)

In *Mexican Spitfire*, the first official film of RKO's new "Mexican Spitfire" series, newlyweds Carmelita Lindsay (Lupe Vélez) and Dennis Lindsay (Donald Woods) return from their Mexican honeymoon, only to find the groom's ex-fiancée Elizabeth (Linda Hayes) awaiting their arrival and still determined to win back her man and break up his marriage. When Carmelita and Dennis arrive at the airport with a new addition to the family, a Chihuahua, Carmelita enthusiastically delivers the first insult to her love rival, smugly introducing the dog as — *Elizabeth*!

In retaliation, a scheming Elizabeth convinces a naive Carmelita that it'd be a wonderful surprise for Dennis if she were to show up at his office unannounced pretending to be his secretary. Only problem is, Dennis's prize client, the absent-minded, exceedingly wealthy distiller "Lord Epping" (Leon Errol), is there too. Carmelita is unaware of Lord Epping's invitation to dinner at their apartment that evening. After Lord Epping sees (and believes) Carmelita as Dennis's secretary, in order to keep the story straight, Elizabeth gladly steps in to play the role of Dennis's wife for the occasion.

Prior to the dinner, Carmelita and Uncle Matt look for Lord Epping to explain the identity mix-up. But, when they find him, without listening to a word of Carmelita's explanation, Lord Epping tells her that he won't be able to make dinner that evening after all. In order to get revenge of her own, Carmelita comes up with a plan and convinces Uncle Matt to disguise himself as Lord Epping and goes ahead with the dinner anyway.

As the evening begins, Uncle Matt's impersonation of his Lordship is flawless. To the delight of Carmelita, Uncle Matt flings countless insults at the snooty Elizabeth and his equally snooty wife Aunt Della (Elisabeth Risdon). With the knowledge that a retaliatory response would ruin Dennis's chances of getting his contract signed, the two women sit open-mouthed and take the verbal barrage on the chin. Thrilled that their vengeful plan is working, Carmelita and Uncle Matt revel in their deceptive game ... until the *real* Lord Epping unexpectedly arrives.

The identity confusion reaches grand proportions at the dinner table. After both contracts are sabotaged and destroyed, the *real* Lord Epping gets fed up and storms out. Feeling responsible, and thinking he'll be arrested for impersonation (after his moustache falls off and his cover is blown), Uncle Matt and Carmelita flee to Mexico to escape the wrath of their family (and the law).

Back in her home country and on the run, Carmelita and Uncle Matt obtain quickie

Hot on the heels of the success of **The Girl From Mexico** (1939), RKO began the "Mexican Spitfire" series that showcased Lupe's manic, high-spirited comedic talents (in an albeit stereotypical way) to perfection. The first official film of the series was aptly titled **Mexican Spitfire** (1940).

divorces from their respective spouses; unbeknownst to them, the divorces are invalid in America. Thinking Carmelita has returned to her native Mexico for good, and upon news of the surprise divorce, Dennis is easy prey. His weakened state of emotions leaves him wide open for Elizabeth to pounce—and she does. Elizabeth manages to convince Dennis that Carmelita has left him for good and that she'd be the perfect wife. Despite still being in love with Carmelita, he half-heartedly agrees to make Elizabeth his wife. Feeling victorious, Elizabeth and the always-meddling Aunt Della go about planning a lavish ceremony. As the *Lima News* (November 9, 1940) put it, "What happens when the volatile wife and the blundering uncle return home on the eve of the husband's second marriage leads to a hilarious climax and whirlwind finish."

Despite her tiny frame, Lupe had an appetite fit for a large man! Thirty cream pies were placed on tables that were set up for the massive food fight planned for the hilarious final scene of *Mexican Spitfire*. Prior to filming, the horrified assistant director spotted Lupe happily indulging in her *fourth* pie! Unbeknownst to her,

they'd all been sprayed with fly spray to keep the bugs away. "They're not for eating," he screamed. "You'll die!" (Conner, *Lupe Vélez and Her Lovers*).

In the second installment, and second release for 1940, *Mexican Spitfire Out West*, Lord Epping (Leon Errol) arrives in New York by boat and Dennis Lindsay (Donald Woods) and his ruthless advertising rivals Skinner (Eddie Dunn) and Brown (Vinton Haworth) show up at the docks to greet him. With a lucrative advertising account at stake, Lord Epping's signature on their respective contracts is the grand prize, and they'll stop at nothing to get it. Dennis wins round one when he tips off detective Jim (Fred Kelsey) about overhearing his rivals plotting to kidnap Lord Epping. As they're hauled away for questioning, Dennis drives Lord Epping to the safety of his office.

Meanwhile, Carmelita (Lupe) is at home, dressed to party and pacing the floor. Con-

vinced that Dennis has forgotten about their first wedding anniversary, she can't reach him by telephone and she's getting angrier by the minute. When he finally calls her, she's initially happy to hear from him, but then suspects he's lying about his whereabouts and angrily hangs up the phone. She then threatens to pack her bags and go back to Mexico to teach him a lesson; however, Carmelita assures Uncle Matt (Leon Errol) that she's only bluffing in order to scare Dennis into an apology.

Aunt Della (Elisabeth Risdon) and Elizabeth (Linda Hayes) are still scheming to break Dennis and Carmelita apart. When Elizabeth sneakily plants her lipstick print on Dennis's handkerchief, Carmelita's worst fears are confirmed. After a Spanish tirade, she storms out of the apartment, bags in hand.

As Carmelita gets into the elevator, Lord Epping steps out. A bumbling Dennis is torn between going after his angry wife or keeping the always confused Lord Epping in his apartment (and away from his scheming rivals) until his associate Chumley (Cecil Kellaway) arrives from England with Lady Epping (Lydia Bilbrook). In the meantime, Carmelita makes her way to Reno to get a quickie divorce.

Skinner and Brown track down Lord Epping and telephone to arrange for a meeting. Overhearing the conversation, Dennis, Uncle Matt and the butler (Charles Coleman) hatch a plan to hide Lord Epping's clothes. By keeping him housebound in his bathrobe, the get-together with Dennis's rivals is prevented, at least for the time being.

One week passes, and an anxious Skinner and Brown persistently call to ask Lord Epping about the hold-up. Tired of the harassment, and in a desperate attempt to buy more time, Uncle Matt intercepts the call. Holding a letter from Carmelita in one hand, and the phone in the other, Uncle Matt impersonates Lord Epping and tells Skinner and Brown to stop harassing him. Looking at the Reno postmark on Carmelita's envelope, he spontaneously tells them that he'll talk to them when he gets back from Reno. He hangs up the phone. Believing the *real* Lord Epping was on the phone, Skinner makes plans to travel to Reno to find him. Uncle Matt really does plan to travel to Reno, but for the sole purpose of bringing Carmelita home to New York. He instructs Dennis to stay put and hold watch over Lord Epping until Chumley arrives.

In Reno, Skinner can find no sign of Lord Epping. He feels he's been "had" and announces he'll immediately be returning to New York. Uncle Matt overhears the conversation and within Skinner's earshot he springs into action and announces to the hotel clerk that his name is Higgins, manservant to Lord Epping. Skinner asks about Lord Epping's whereabouts and Higgins tells him he'll be arriving in Reno soon. Though Skinner takes the bait, he's still skeptical and tells Higgins that he'll be trailing him closely until Lord Epping arrives. Unaware that the *real* Lord Epping will soon be arriving in Reno, Uncle Matt is again forced into impersonating Lord Epping to keep Skinner from returning to New York. With Carmelita's help, Uncle Matt puts on his trusty "goat face" disguise and flawlessly transforms himself into his bumbling Lordship.

Back in New York, the *real* Lord Epping is upstairs in his room, still in his bathrobe with only his Scotch to keep him company. He spots a thirsty window cleaner (Frank Orth) outside and invites him in for a nip ... or two. In one of his most lucid moments on film, Lord Epping sees his new friend as a way out of the apartment: After getting him drunk, he steals his uniform, runs downstairs and leaves the Lindsays' residence. Ignoring the protests of the butler, he sets out for his long-overdue appointment at the offices of Skinner and Brown. Upon arrival, the wisecracking secretary (Jan Buckingham) tells Lord Epping that her boss isn't in, he's in Reno. So Lord Epping decides to follow him.

After finding out that Lord Epping is on the loose, Dennis and Aunt Della set out for Reno to find him. Lady Epping and Chumley next arrive at the Lindsays' apartment, both clueless about the harebrained shenanigans of the past week. Upon hearing the news that Lord Epping (and everyone else) is in Reno, naturally they head west too.

Upon arrival in Reno, Dennis makes up with Carmelita, and all is well. With everyone now in the same place, including the *real* Lord Epping, and Uncle Matt still pretending to be Lord Epping, poor Uncle Matt finds himself in over his head as the mistaken identity games go into overdrive.

*Film Daily* (October 9, 1940):

> This latest picture of the Lupe Vélez-Leon Errol series is sure-fire for laughs. The duo run through a continuous sequence of comic situations until a crescendo of laughter is attained. Lupe delivers with her usual fire and verse. Errol is strikingly funny. His characterization of the droll Lord Epping is classic.

In 1941, Universal capitalized on the success of the RKO gold mine by individually signing Lupe and her "Spitfire" co-star Leon Errol for the comedy-musical *Six Lessons from Madame La Zonga* (1941). Lupe played Madame La Zonga. The film also starred Lupe's new beau, and then fiancé, Guinn "Big Boy" Williams. Universal based their script on the popular song of the same name, but the script was weak. Even with Lupe and Leon Errol on board, the film was just okay. *Film Daily* (February 2, 1941) opined, "Story is formula stuff, but there are plenty of gags, amusing situations, lots of music and good laugh lines to keep it moving along at a brisk pace which will hold attention."

In *The Mexican Spitfire's Baby* (1941), third film in the official "Spitfire" series, Charles "Buddy" Rogers took over the role of Dennis Lindsay and veteran comedienne ZaSu Pitts made her first appearance as the hotel snoop Miss Emily Pepper. She reprised her role in yet another "Spitfire" installment, *Mexican Spitfire at Sea* (1942). Lloyd Corrigan replaced Cecil Kellaway as Mr. Chumley, the stalwart business associate to Lord Epping (Leon Errol).

While the title *The Mexican Spitfire's Baby*, certainly implies that Dennis and Carmelita are about to become parents, the only "baby" associated with the film is the word in the title. The opening scene shows the couple fighting on the night of their "first" wedding anniversary (a mistake since it was an occasion they'd already celebrated in the previous film, *Mexican Spitfire Out West*). The night after their rocky celebratory dinner (that ends with Carmelita pushing her husband's head into their anniversary cake), Uncle Matt comes up with a perfect solution for the couple's marital woes by explaining to Carmelita that a mutual interest would eliminate their constant bickering—a baby.

Despite Carmelita's obvious misgivings, Uncle Matt puts his parenting plan into motion and writes to Lord Epping to advise him of the Lindsays' desire to adopt. He asks him to arrange for a French war orphan to accompany him on his trip to New York the following week. However, when Fifi (Marion Martin) arrives, she's not the size, shape or age that Uncle Matt had in mind ... a tall, busty, ditzy blonde. Fifi *is* a French war orphan, all right ... but she's not from the current war, she's an orphan from World War I! Dennis is unaware of the adoption plan and after meeting his newly adopted "daughter," he hits the roof.

Dennis tells Uncle Matt to get Fifi out of town immediately. Uncle Matt smuggles her to Lake Cherokee and they both check into the Bide A While Inn. After signing the hotel register as Fifi Lindsay, she and Uncle Matt are naturally mistaken for newlyweds. While Uncle Matt assures the hotel clerk (Vinton Haworth) that they're most certainly *not* married, Miss Pepper (ZaSu Pitts), the gossipy hotel manager, suspects something fishy is going on and makes it her business to find out exactly what it is. Meanwhile, Fifi's fiancé Pierre (Fritz

Feld) comes looking for her at the Lindsays' apartment. Unaware of Fifi's existence, Carmelita agrees to help Pierre find her.

After Aunt Della hears on the radio that her husband Uncle Matt was seen dancing the Conga with a "gorgeous blonde," everyone travels to Lake Cherokee to confront him. Before long, Uncle Matt, Dennis and even Lord Epping are all romantically linked to Fifi. When Pierre shows up to stake *his* claim on her, he overhears Miss Pepper telling the hotel clerk that Lord Epping intends on divorcing his wife to marry Fifi. Furious, Pierre challenges him to a duel. Carmelita accepts the duel at dawn, saying, "Okay, we fight you with knives!" On the morning of the duel, the crossed wires of confusion instigate the biggest laughs of the picture.

In its review of *The Mexican Spitfire's Baby*, *Film Daily* (September 4, 1941) said: "[The] film has one of those complicated plots with much confusion and lot of laughs.... [A]lthough gag situations at times are drawn thin, Leslie Goodwins' direction keeps proceedings moving at a swift pace.... Burden of film is carried by Errol who contributes a dual performance geared for guffaws. His portrayal of Lord Epping is a splendid piece of comedy work.

\* \* \*

Despite their now-divorced situation, Johnny Weissmuller was still using his ex-wife as a weapon, at least while he was out in public. Journalist Sidney Skolsky of *Hollywood Citizen News* (November 10, 1941) told an amusing story:

> Johnny Weissmuller was at a party, and a girl, who had a couple of drinks too many, started to bawl him out. She said: "I don't like you. I don't like your face. You've got a bad mouth. You've got a mean chin. I don't like anything about you." The girl continued. Finally, Weissmuller, who had been silent, couldn't take it any longer. He said to the girl. "You're lucky I'm not married to Lupe Vélez now, or she'd kick the stuffings out of you."

By the end of the year, Lupe had another non–Spitfire-release in theaters with *Honolulu Lu* (1941). When journalist Paul Harrison of the *San Jose News* wrote (October 23, 1941) from the set of *Honolulu Lu*, he said he was unsure if Lupe's sensuous honky-tonk dance (she strips off her sailor pants to reveal a cellophane hula skirt) would get past the Hays office. A paid audience of 100 extras, all dressed in naval uniforms, were so enthralled with Lupe's South Seas hip-slinging, many of them felt guilty about being paid to watch.

Keeping with the consistency of Lupe's down-to-earth attitude, Harrison said, "Lupe is a star, but she consistently refuses to behave like one." He said that when he arrived on set, he found her in the midst of a heated argument with director Charles Barton over whether she should work late that particular evening. He had some extra scenes that needed doing, but it was fight night at the Legion Stadium and Lupe *always* went. Funnily enough, Barton was trying to convince Lupe that she had been working too hard and ought to go, and *she* was insisting that she should stay on and finish the scenes. Harrison wrote:

> Her un-star-like behavior on the sets is equally remarkable. When the assistant director goes to look for her to tell her they're ready for a scene, he may find her outside the stage, in the middle of a delighted group of technicians and extras, giving forth with her original story about the three polar bears, or the one about the little owl.

He also wrote that whenever Lupe messed up one of her scenes on the film, she'd reproach herself with an acrobatic kick in the ass. No matter what she was wearing, an evening gown or a sailor suit —*wham*! She'd kick herself and yell, "Lupe, you are terr-r-rible! Lupe, you steee-e-e-enk!"

*Playmates*, Lupe's second film release for December 1941, was her fourth and last film for the year. It starred John Barrymore[2] (in his final screen appearance), Kay Kyser, Ginny Simms, May Robson and Patsy Kelly; the ensemble cast made this offbeat (and often odd) comedy-musical something special.

Barrymore plays a hilarious parody of himself, while Lupe plays his feisty female bull-fighter love interest. Lupe doesn't appear until the thirty-nine-minute mark, but when she does, she's noticed. Storming into the room, she threatens to cut off Barrymore's famous "profile"! The pair get into a hilarious physical altercation that ends up being one of the funniest moments in the film.

On August 8, 1941, the *Jefferson City Post-Tribune* reported on that very scene. As Barrymore relaxes on a divan, Lupe bursts into the room, a scorned woman on a steadfast mission. As she wildly shakes him, she also subjects him to nose and hair pulling, all the while screaming, "You double crosser, you louse, you theenk you can leave mee standeeeng at the church? Eet ees too moch. I weel cut off your beeyouteeful profile and shove eet down your throat!"

The scene was physically exhausting the first time, but Lupe kept muffing her lines. By the time the paper interviewed Barrymore, they were up to take five and he was plum out of breath: "I suspect a conspiracy," he boomed, adding a few adjectives. "But they won't get me down. No sir. I've been training for this sort of thing for years." The paper asked him to recall a similar incident in his life. "Let's see," he mused, "married four times. Yes, the routine's familiar. Very familiar" ("Great Profile Takes Beating in New Picture," *Jefferson City Post-Tribune*, August 8, 1941).

Following her two-film break from the "Spitfire" series, Lupe returned in the New Year with *Mexican Spitfire at Sea* (1942). For the second and last time in the series, ZaSu Pitts and Marion Martin appeared as Emily Pepper and the busty blonde Fifi Russell, respectively. This time the Lindsays' are sea-bound to Hawaii on their long-overdue second honeymoon. However, their romantic getaway looks to be getting a little crowded when Dennis (Charles "Buddy" Rogers) runs into a flirtatious Fifi at check-in. Then Miss Pepper (ZaSu Pitts) shows up to collect her cabin keys and begins to promote her amateurish acting and writing talents to the ship's uninterested purser (Marten Lamont).

Carmelita (Lupe Vélez) is under the impression that the cruise is completely work-free, unaware that Dennis is after a lucrative contract from Mr. and Mrs. Baldwin (Florence Bates and Harry Holman). She's also unaware that Uncle Matt (Leon Errol), Aunt Della (Elisabeth Risdon) and Lord and Lady Epping (Leon Errol and Lydia Bilbrook) are all along for the ride. With a promise of an introduction to Lord and Lady Epping, Dennis has cleverly concocted the idea to lure the socially conscious Baldwins out to sea so he can get the contract signed and prevent his rival, Skinner (Eddie Dunn), from snaring the deal out from under him. However, Dennis is unaware that Skinner is also on board.

Carmelita finds out that her "two-time honeymoon" is ruined by her husband's work plans and she's furious. She threatens to leave the ship before it sails, so Dennis picks her up and carries her to their cabin. Carmelita tells him she's fed up with his workaholic ways and she's leaving. Uncle Matt takes Dennis aside and tells him that in order to get her to stay, he has to use "negative psychology" and pretend he doesn't care that she's leaving. The plan works ... well, kind of.

When Carmelita sees that Dennis is acting carefree at the thought of her leaving, she changes her mind and tells him she's staying. She then tells him that *he's* going! Carmelita physically throws Dennis out of their cabin, and in doing so, he falls straight through the

door of the cabin on the opposite side of the hall ... Fifi's cabin. When Mr. Baldwin walks past and sees Fifi tending to a dazed Dennis, he mistakes the scene for a romantic situation and naturally assumes that Fifi is his wife.

A contrite Carmelita asks Uncle Matt to briefly impersonate Lord Epping, so he can convince Dennis to make up with her. Uncle Matt is reluctant because the *real* Lord Epping is on board the ship. He thinks it's too risky, but Carmelita doesn't think so. As usual, she drags him off to don his usual "goat face" disguise.

Back in Fifi's cabin, the Carmelita-hating Aunt Della thinks Fifi posing as Dennis's wife is a sensible idea and convinces her nephew to keep up the charade until the business deal is closed. Skinner is doing his best to keep the *real* Lord Epping in his cabin and away from Dennis and the Baldwins.

Dennis ends up taking Uncle Matt, who's dressed as Lord Epping, to meet the Baldwins in their cabin. They fawn over him and insist on meeting Lady Epping at dinner that evening. He thwarts their attempt to call her by telling them that his wife is horribly deaf. With the false promise that the Baldwins have the money and influence to get her unpublished play *Love and Lavender* produced, naive Miss Pepper is talked into playing the part of Lady Epping by Uncle Matt and Carmelita.

So the *real* Lady Epping can have a peaceful trip, she's traveling incognito and has registered herself and her husband under assumed names. Part of the confusion surrounds the fact that a forgetful Lord Epping can't remember the name his wife has used. Not realizing the *real* Lord Epping *is* on board, Carmelita tells a nervous Uncle Matt that he can go to the dinner as Lord Epping, and without risk of being caught, since she's already checked with the ship's purser and Lord and Lady Epping *aren't* on board after all. Skinner and Agnes, the maid (Mary Field) are the only people on board who know the assumed names that Lord and Lady Epping are traveling under.

Uncle Matt breaks the news to Carmelita that Dennis is taking Fifi to the dinner as his *wife*. She explodes and wants instant revenge. When Carmelita runs into Skinner, he takes advantage of her anger and asks her to accompany him to the dinner as payback to Dennis. Carmelita happily agrees to participate, but tells him they must pretend they're engaged to be married. He agrees.

When Uncle Matt shows up at the dinner party dressed as Lord Epping, he has Miss Pepper on his arm and she's eagerly playing the part of Lady Epping. Thinking she's stone deaf, the other members of the party shout their words of welcome. After taking a drink, Uncle Matt loses his Lord Epping moustache, so without anyone realizing it, he hurriedly leaves the gathering to get a new one, making way for the *real* Lord Epping to appear and take his place.

Carmelita and Skinner arrive and introduce themselves as a newly engaged couple, infuriating Dennis. When the *real* Lady Epping appears, the Baldwins eject her from the party (they believe Miss Pepper is the real Lady Epping).

The Baldwins decide that a wedding would reverse their run of bad luck, and they look to Carmelita and Skinner to marry in their presence — immediately! When Mr. Baldwin offers a reluctant Carmelita his signature on the elusive contract as a wedding present, she takes it, pretends to go ahead with the ceremony (with Dennis as best man) and asks Uncle Matt to do something — quickly — to keep her from illegally marrying her husband's business rival. Rushing out of the room, Uncle Matt goes to the deck, puts a life jacket in a coat and hat and tosses it overboard. "Man overboard!" is yelled and whistles are blown, and everyone races around in a panic to get their life jackets. Aunt Della once again gets her husband and

the *real* Lord Epping confused. After realizing her mistake, she faints in the hallway. The Lindsays happily reunite and Carmelita shows Dennis that she has the signed contract.

The next installment within the same year, *Mexican Spitfire Sees a Ghost* (1942) is the weak link in the series. Had the story featured an "authentic" haunted house, as the title implies, the potential was there for it to be the best film in the series. That said, it still has its funny moments.

*Mexican Spitfire Sees a Ghost* opens with Lord Epping (Leon Errol) being advised by telegram that his former girlfriend Edith Fitzbadden (Minna Gombell) will be arriving in New York with her frazzled brother Percy (Donald MacBride), who's in need of a rest. Initially, Dennis (Charles "Buddy" Rogers) is thrilled about the visit and has hopes that Percy will invest in their business ventures. However, when Lord Epping realizes the visit clashes with his Canadian moose-hunting trip, he gathers his guns and tells Dennis to entertain his guests at his country house until he returns.

When snobbish Aunt Della (Elisabeth Risdon) tells Dennis that it would be best if the Fitzbaddens were kept from meeting the unpredictable Carmelita (Lupe Vélez), he secretly confesses to Uncle Matt (Leon Errol) that he agrees with her. Uncle Matt tells Dennis not to worry and that he'll keep Carmelita busy by taking her to a prizefight.

Aunt Della and Dennis drive to the country house together and meet Bascombe (Harry Tyler), the realtor. Letting them inside the dusty, deserted residence, he informs them that no servants have been present for a year. Horrified at the thought, Aunt Della asks about employing more, but Bascombe tells her that no one is interested in working there because the place has acquired a "bad name." Leaving on that mysterious note, Bascombe is next seen entering the basement from the outside of the home. He's revealed as the leader of a group of crooks who have set up home in Lord Epping's basement so they can make batches of nitroglycerin.

Aunt Della has no choice but to clean the house herself. She calls Uncle Matt to ask if he could bring the Fitzbaddens up from the city. While he agrees to help out, he informs her that he won't be coming out there as her husband. "I still have a little pride left, you know," he says.

When the Fitzbaddens arrive at the estate, they initially mistake a busy Aunt Della for a maid; when Dennis introduces himself and Aunt Della, they apologize for their mistake. When Uncle Matt and Carmelita appear in the doorway, they're introduced as Maria and Hubble, the lady's maid and manservant. Confused, Dennis and Aunt Della pull their respective spouses aside and demand to know what's going on.

Outraged that Lord Epping has put a hunting trip ahead of their visit, the insulted Fitzbaddens announce they're leaving immediately. Uncle Matt as Hubble steps in and prevents a disaster by announcing that Lord Epping will be arriving soon. This scenario once again leads Uncle Matt into impersonating Lord Epping in order to stall the Fitzbaddens until the *real* Lord Epping appears.

With the Lord Epping transformation complete, Edith is thrilled to see who she *thinks* is Lord Epping and she peppers him with kisses and giddy memories of their past. Meanwhile, the dog whose fur created the wig and moustache (the infamous "goat face") for Uncle Matt's clever disguise follows him wherever he goes, whining for his lost fur.

Following Uncle Matt's arrival as Lord Epping, Hubble is called to retrieve his Lordship's bags. Not wanting to arouse suspicion, Uncle Matt is forced into yet another quick change. Meanwhile, the *real* Lord Epping returns early from his hunting trip and makes his way to the country house.

A poker game between Percy and Lord Epping (played by Uncle Matt) gets richer than Uncle Matt anticipated so, impersonating Lord Epping, he borrows a stash of cash from Aunt Della to keep himself in the game. Shortly after, when the *real* Lord Epping shows up and joins the card game, the usual switcheroos and mix-ups occur. When $2,000 of Percy's money gets swiped by one of the basement gangsters, the hunt is on for the thief. Of course, Hubble is the lead suspect and he's summoned for questioning, again forcing Uncle Matt into a quick change. With Carmelita's help, the Lord Epping hair and moustache pieces are hidden in the hall clock; Uncle Matt reenters the room as Hubble. Meanwhile, the dog spies the hiding spot for the Lord Epping goat face disguise and takes back what's rightfully his!

When Hubble is cleared of thievery, Lord Epping is once again called upon. Rushing out of the room, Carmelita goes back to the clock to find the disguise, only to discover it's gone. Uncle Matt and Carmelita race into another room to figure out what to do. There, with the wig and moustache in his mouth, is the dog. Uncle Matt and Carmelita get down on all fours to impersonate cats so they can lure the dog out from under the furniture. While they eventually succeed in getting back the disguise, it's a little worse for wear.

Through an open door, Aunt Della spies Uncle Matt and Carmelita reattaching the wig. Without letting on that she knows what's going on, she tiptoes away. When the *real* Lord Epping appears, thinking he's her cleverly disguised husband, she proceeds to insult and assault him.

An accomplice of the basement thief orders him to return the stolen cash. With money disappearing and reappearing, everyone's nerves are frayed, there's fighting and accusations flying back and forth and everyone demands to know what's going on. Bascombe reappears and confesses that the house has a reputation for being haunted. Following a heated altercation with the *real* Lord Epping, the Fitzbaddens want to leave right away. However, the last train of the night leaves before they can catch it and everyone is forced to stay in the "haunted" house for the evening.

The basement thief takes matters into his own hands and dons the hall-

A one-sheet with spectacular graphics showcasing *Mexican Spitfire Sees a Ghost* (1942). Unfortunately, the film was far from the comedic spook-fest it could have been.

way armor to scare them. As night falls, the thief clanks his way through the upstairs hallway and releases a balloon with a ghost face drawn on it. Terrified, the rest of the house responds to the screams of Aunt Della and the Fitzbaddens. Chaos ensues and mistaken identities are revealed. Dressed as Lord Epping for one last time, Uncle Matt manages to get Percy to sign Dennis's contract. Naturally, it all ends with a bang when the bumbling basement crooks blow themselves up while trying to leave the house with their illegal concoction.

*Film Daily* (May 6, 1942): "Sanity and intelligence give up the ghost in this latest in the Lupe Vélez–Leon Errol series of comedies. This is simple-minded hokum with humor of the most elementary brand.... [A]udiences that are easily amused will find loads of entertainment in *Mexican Spitfire Sees a Ghost*..."

*Mexican Spitfire's Elephant* (1942) was the third "Spitfire" release within the same year. Walter Reed made his first appearance as Carmelita's husband Dennis Lindsay and he stuck around for the final installment in the series, *Mexican Spitfire's Blessed Event* (1943), the following year. "Lupe was the most tragic of Hollywood's glamourous stars," Reed remembered. "She was unbalanced and neurotic, she craved attention.... She was wild, like an untamed cat" (www.independent.co.uk). Marion Martin returned for a third time, though not as Fifi; this time she played a seductive jewel thief, Diana De Corro.

The opening scene shows a cruise ship sailing toward New York with Lord Epping (Leon Errol) on board. Using him to smuggle their precious gem past customs (hidden inside an ornamental onyx elephant figurine) are fellow passengers, and jewel thieves, Diana De Corro (Marion Martin) and Reddy Madison (Lyle Talbot).

Diana "accidentally" bumps into Lord Epping and takes advantage of his absentmindedness by pretending to have previously met him one New Year's Eve. She then makes him a present of the elephant figurine, the idea being that Lord Epping is above suspicion and will unwittingly smuggle the gem past customs agents without incident. The plan works; however, getting the elephant back is far from easy.

Lord and Lady Epping (the latter played by Lydia Bilbrook) are welcomed at the dock by Dennis (Walter Reed) and Aunt Della (Elisabeth Risdon). The always-interfering Aunt Della is still doing her best to keep hotheaded Carmelita (Lupe Vélez) away from any public function that will embarrass the family; and this time it's the Women's War Relief Drive, the very reason the Eppings have traveled to America.

Diana accosts Lord Epping at the dock and asks for her elephant back, but he tells her that he's put it in his trunk for safekeeping. She asks where he's staying and follows him to the Hotel Regal. At the hotel bar, Diana asks Dennis if he's seen the elephant she gave to Lord Epping. He says he hasn't, but offers to buy her a drink. Aunt Della and Lady Epping arrive and are introduced to Diana.

Uncle Matt and Carmelita show up at the Hotel Regal where Carmelita unexpectedly bumps into Luigi (Luis Alberni), owner of Villa Luigi. When he offers her a job as a singer-dancer at his café, she graciously declines, telling him that Dennis wouldn't approve of his wife working. Her attitude changes when Carmelita sees Dennis getting into an elevator with Diana. Carmelita assumes Dennis is cheating on her and she goes after him. Causing the scene that Aunt Della knew she would, Carmelita races into the crowded dining room, kicks Diana in the behind and tips a large bowl of food over Dennis's head. Carmelita then goes to Villa Luigi to accept Luigi's offer of a job. She's paired with a dashing male dancer, Jose Alvarez (Arnold Kent).

Diana meets Lord Epping at the café. In a desperate attempt to get him to return the hidden jewel, she turns on the tears. Blubbering and dabbing her eyes, she tells Lord Epping

that she's in a lot of trouble because she mistakenly gave him someone else's present. Of course, the whole thing's a set-up and Reddy is waiting in the wings, ready to burst in and pretend to play the jealous boyfriend who wants back what's rightfully his. Playing the heavy, he tells Lord Epping that he wants his gift and he won't leave until he returns with it. A confused Lord Epping goes to the bar for a drink or two, all the while trying to work out what it was that Diana gave him in the first place.

Carmelita has witnessed the situation unfold and she once again convinces Uncle Matt to impersonate Lord Epping so they can find out exactly what Diana and Reddy want from him. Returning to the table as Lord Epping, an empty-handed Uncle Matt riles up a now furious Reddy, who gives him a deadline of two hours to return the onyx elephant *or else*. The *real* Lord Epping returns to the table and confesses that he has no idea what they want from him.

Carmelita convinces a worried Uncle Matt that she can make things right and leaves to find an elephant of her own. After making contact with her "elephant connection," she calls the *real* Lord Epping to ask exactly what color elephant is needed. "Pink with green spots" is the answer he gives her.

Returning to the hotel, an increasingly nervous Uncle Matt asks Carmelita where the elephant is. "Outside," says Carmelita. Not realizing she's brought back a *real* elephant, Uncle Matt instructs her to bring it *inside* the café. Confused as to why he would want her to do that, she shrugs it off and follows orders. In the next scene, a spotted elephant walks into the café and causes mayhem. The customary "Spitfire" chaos ensues, right to the very end.

*Film Daily* (October 5, 1942):

> Lupe Vélez is better as the Spitfire in this film than she has been in its predecessors in the series. She is at her most entertaining in a brace of song and dance numbers....

Following, *Mexican Spitfire's Elephant*, Lupe took another hiatus from the series. *Ladies' Day*, her first film release for 1943, was a baseball-themed comedy that teamed her up with "Spitfire" director Leslie Goodwins. While it's an enjoyable farce, it doesn't quite hit a homerun. *Film Daily* (March 24, 1943) agreed, writing: "Exhibitors will have to play up the baseball atmosphere to get satisfactory returns on *Ladies' Day*, a frail comedy padded out beyond all reasonableness. The humor is no great shakes..."

In *Ladies' Day*, Pepita Zorita (Lupe Vélez) is a Hollywood actress who visits a baseball game to sell kisses for war bonds. After falling in love and marrying champion baseball pitcher Wacky Waters (Eddie Albert), the lovestruck ballplayer suddenly can't pitch straight. The furious wives of the other players hatch a plan to kidnap Pepita. They hold her hostage in a Kansas hotel room until the World Series can be won without distraction; the rest of the film surrounds the pandemonium that comes with keeping the newlyweds apart. The catfights between the determined ladies make for some comical scenes. It all ends when Pepita disguises herself as a bellboy and escapes the clutches of the baseball wives. Much to their dismay, Pepita makes it to the stadium just in time to see Wacky pitch the last part of the final game in the series. Her jinx is lifted when she cheers her husband's losing team to victory.

*Ladies' Day* has a solid ensemble cast, with especially fine performances by the players' wives Hazel (Patsy Kelly), Kitty (Iris Adrian) and Joan (Joan Barclay). Together with Lupe's Pepita, these women save this male-dominated theme of a story.

In *Redhead from Manhattan* (1943) Lupe plays the dual role of lookalike cousins Rita

and Maria aka Elaine Manners. Rita is a stowaway on the run from the police (due to mistaken identity, a common plot point in this story) and her cousin Maria aka Elaine (the latter being her stage name) is a Broadway star with a predicament or two of her own. *Redhead from Manhattan* marked the first instance where audiences heard the closest version of Lupe's actual real-life speaking voice — "fluid English" with a noticeable Mexican accent. Her role of Maria (aka Elaine) was a far more subdued character, and in stark contrast to her role of Rita, the usual

In the comedic baseball-themed RKO production *Ladies' Day* (1943), Lupe and Eddie Albert play Pepita Zorita and Wacky Waters, respectively. Photograph courtesy of the Agrasánchez Film Archive.

manic Mexican fireball that she so often played. The dual roles and their diverse nature went a long way in proving Lupe's versatility as an actress.

The *Los Angeles Independent Daily News* (January 14, 1943) wrote of Lupe's wicked sense of humor in rehearsals for the film:

> At Columbia the main point of interest is the stage where Lupe Vélez is learning her eight song numbers for *Redhead from Manhattan*. Lupe's spicy comments, when lyrics come to mind, keep her audience in an uproar. Too bad they can't be used in the completed musical.

*Mexican Spitfire's Blessed Event* (1943) was the last film in the popular series. Actually, it marked the end in more ways than one. *Mexican Spitfire's Blessed Event* would conclude Lupe and Leon Errol's longstanding working relationship. Between 1939 and 1943, they starred in nine comedies together. Aside from their roles of Carmelita and Uncle Matt/Lord Epping in the "Mexican Spitfire" series, they were co-stars in the comedy-musical *Six Lessons from Madame La Zonga* (1941). Further, it was Lupe's final Hollywood production.

Dennis (Walter Reed) is now serving in the Merchant Marines and Carmelita is upset that he's missed the birth of her baby ocelot. With only her maid Verbena (Marietta Canty) at home (they're now living in Arizona) to share her excitement, she sends a telegram to Uncle Matt (Leon Errol), whose hunting moose in Canada with Lord Epping (also Errol) to announce the good news. The telegram reads: Congratulations. Your little kitten is a momma. Blessed event is very cute and fuzzy. Carmelita.

Dennis, on leave for two weeks, has made a quick stop at Lord Epping's Canadian cabin in an attempt to get his latest advertising contract signed. Intercepting the telegram, Dennis assumes that Carmelita has given birth to *his* child. The core of the story surrounds

the crossed wires and ongoing confusion surrounding the identity of the latest addition to the family.

In an attempt to make him confess to being Uncle Matt, the *real* Lord Epping is repeatedly dunked in a well. Undoubtedly, it's one of the funniest conclusions of the eight-film series, certainly on a par with the hilarious *Mexican Spitfire* (1940) food-fight climax. And lastly, after all the familiar "Spitfire" mix-ups and make-ups, a doctor confirms that Carmelita really *is* pregnant.

# 17

## *Nana (1944)*

"My fans down there [Mexico] want me in drama, not comedy. And what a drama *Nana* is!"[1] — Lupe Vélez

In May of 1943, Lupe traveled back to Mexico with the intention of signing a contract for the Shakespearean parody *Romeo y Julieta* (1943). The film was to be told in rhyming verse with the use of Mexican slang predominant throughout. Lupe was slated for the female lead, Julieta, opposite wacky Mexican comedian Cantinflas in the role of Romeo. As good as it sounded, it wasn't to be.

Soon after her arrival home, Lupe withdrew herself from the film. She explained her decision by saying it was a good slapstick role but she did not want to reappear in Mexican cinema with a slapstick comedy. Her replacement was María Elena Marqués, a young Mexican actress with a budding career. At the time of filming *Romeo y Julieta*, María had not yet turned eighteen. Lupe was about to turn thirty-five, and although she was more than capable of the comedic requirements, in reality she was just too old to pull off the role of Julieta with any believability. By June 6, 1943, Louella O. Parsons reported (*Los Angeles Evening Herald and Express*) that Lupe was back from Mexico City after rejecting the script for the Shakespearean satire, deciding it was "not for her."

Away from the cameras, a few years earlier Lupe had appeared in a *Gone with the Wind* (1939) parody at the popular San Fernando Valley nightclub, Grace Hayes' Lodge. Grace Hayes would run a nightly *Gone with the Wind* spoof and with many of Hollywood's most popular stars attending the club it was anyone's guess who'd volunteer to perform the lead roles on any given night. In April of 1939, months before the iconic film premiered in the United States, Lupe played Scarlett O'Hara to Jack Benny's Rhett Butler, and as if those legendary lead roles weren't screwball enough, Groucho Marx stepped in to play the family patriarch, Gerald O'Hara. In the audience, enjoying the riotous show were Gracie Allen and George Burns, Mary Livingstone, the Phil Harrises, the Ed Sullivans, Annette and Al Ritz, Norman Krasna, and Dolores (Mrs. Bob) Hope. One could only dream of such a hilarious skit existing somewhere on film, or even in still photographs, though in all likelihood, this one-time moment of comic brilliance escaped immortality (*Los Angeles Examiner*, April 23, 1939).

Next, Lupe was approached with the dramatic script *Nana*. Originally, *Nana* was part of a three-film deal along with *Anna Karenina* and *La dama de las camelias* (*The Lady of the Camellias*) and some powerful people were behind the project. In those days, film distributors backed most Mexican producers. The distributor gave the producer an advanced payment, estimated accordingly to the profits that the film "should" make at the box office. The backers in this case were the Calderóns and Salas Porras (partners in Azteca Films, main

distributors of Spanish-language films in the U.S.) and quite possibly the infamous Jenkins family, a clan that had secured a strong film exhibition monopoly in Mexico.

Aside from a promising new film prospect, Lupe had a new love interest, too. In Louella O. Parsons' September 5, 1943, article "Lupe Plans to Quit Career For Marriage," she wrote that she had known Lupe from the first day she came to Hollywood. Parsons knew that Lupe's career was extremely important to her, if not *the* most important aspect of her life.

So when Lupe called Parsons and said, "When Arturo [actor Arturo de Córdova] and I marry, I'll cook for him, keep house and forget my own career," Parsons knew she had to meet the man who had seemingly domesticated her fiery friend. Lupe agreed to bring her fiancé to Parsons' house for cocktails. Describing him as "dark eyed, with an agreeable personality and a very winning manner," Parsons was noticeably impressed with the Mexican star.

When Parsons commented on how well he spoke English, with scarcely a trace of an accent, he said, "I was educated in New York and learned to speak English as a child. My family left Mexico during the revolution and I went to a public school..."

Lupe never took her eyes off de Córdova when he spoke. Later, she said: "... When Arturo finishes his picture, he will go to Mexico and get his divorce."

"And then you'll cook happily ever after," Parsons stated.

"And raise chickens and vegetables and have a farm," Lupe laughed.

While the whole "home sweet home" charade certainly appeared genuine, Lupe's relationship with Arturo de Córdova was brief and its origins sketchy. In all likelihood, their relationship was fabricated for publicity purposes in order to boost his Hollywood career.[2] A

In the early 1940s, Lupe nuzzles the ear of one-time co-star (*La zandunga*) and then fiancé Arturo De Córdova at the Clover nightclub.

A promotional photograph of Lupe in full costume for *Nana* (1944), her final film. *Nana*'s costumes and set design were extravagantly detailed throughout. No expense was spared. Photograph courtesy of the Agrasánchez Film Archive.

common publicity ploy employed by studios in order to bolster the career of a new or flailing star was to "create" a love affair with a more popular star. In reality, de Córdova had been married to Enna Arana, an Argentinean-born Mexican actress, since 1933. They never divorced.

After his film success in Mexico, de Córdova was coaxed to Hollywood, not only by Paramount Pictures, but with Lupe's encouragement too. In an attempt to turn him into the screen's newest Latin lover, the studio signed him to a contract in 1943. Soon after, very conveniently, his love affair and "engagement" to Lupe was big news. Probably no one was more surprised than his wife!

By mid–January of 1944, Lupe had returned from Mexico City (where *Nana* was

From left to right: Director Celestino Gorostiza, unknown lady, unknown man, Lupe, *Cinema Reporter* magazine editor Roberto Cantú Robert and actor Miguel Ángel Ferriz, circa 1944. Photograph courtesy of the Agrasánchez Film Archive.

filmed) and she publicly announced (*Los Angeles Evening Herald and Express*, January 14, 1944) that it was de Córdova's intense jealousy that broke them up. She said:

> When I was in Mexico City, [Arturo de Córdova] would call me at two o'clock in the morning and I had to get up at five to go to work. He accused me of playing around with a Mexican leading man. And all this time I was staying with Arturo's mother.... [H]e spied on me day and night....

Despite the well-orchestrated studio hype, de Córdova's appeal was lost on American audiences. After several film roles in Hollywood, including *For Whom the Bell Tolls* (1943), *Frenchman's Creek* (1944) and *Incendiary Blonde* (1945), he returned to Mexico to pick up his south-of-the-border career where he left off. Upon returning to his homeland, de Córdova was as popular as ever, if not more than before he left for Hollywood. He went on to become a major star in South America and Spain.

Between 1946 and 1958, de Córdova won and was nominated for several Ariel Awards for Best Actor. To this day, the Ariel Award is still the most prestigious award given for excellence in all aspects of the Mexican film industry.

This still from *Nana* (1944) shows Lupe scantily clad in her boudoir. Risqué scenes such as the one shown here were part of the reason the New York State Film Board banned the film from distribution in that state. Photograph courtesy of the Agrasánchez Film Archive.

Beginning in 1946, despite never divorcing his wife (she refused to grant him one), de Córdova lived openly with the much-younger Argentinean-born Mexican film actress Marga López. A few years after they began their relationship, he had a stroke and suffered serious health issues from that point onward. He died on November 3, 1973. He was 65 years old.

Before and during the production of *Nana*, Lupe's conversations with the press in Mexico City and with Hollywood columnist Louella O. Parsons remained consistent. Her desire to retire from the film industry was strong. But Lupe had a history of making impulsive statements to the papers so her retirement announcement was taken with a grain of salt. Tomorrow it would be something else, a new film, a new love, and any talk of retirement would be a distant memory. That was Lupe.

Despite Lupe's outstanding performance in *Nana*, at the time of its release it received mixed reviews and unfavorable public reaction. Audiences just weren't ready to see Lupe Vélez switch gears and take on such a heavy role. Despite the fact that she had received high praise for dramatic performances earlier in her career, by the early 1940s, mostly due to the "Mexican Spitfire" series, Lupe was primarily typecast as a comedic actress. There are several amusing scenes in *Nana*, but the majority of the role is weighty and melodramatic. The ending is tragic.

Following her young son's death, Nana is seen walking the dimly lit streets in rags, with bags under her eyes and tear-stained cheeks. Unrecognized by the very men who once flocked to her feet, she begs for loose change. Without doubt, it's a fitting end for an unfeeling character who ruthlessly used the power of sex and seduction to destroy the lives of every man who crossed her path.

However, there is more to it than that; *Nana* was Lupe's final film. The overwhelming sorrow of an unwanted woman, lost and alone, crying and confused, is eerily parallel to Lupe's last days. And because that final scene is the last piece of acting that Lupe ever did, the ending of *Nana* is hard to watch without sentiment stirring for Lupe Vélez, *not* necessarily for "the character" who most certainly deserved her bitter end as payback for the lives she ruined throughout the film. Right or wrong, the reality of Lupe Vélez's imminent death heightens one's emotions and greatly affects the viewer's opinion of the final scenes of *Nana*. Further, upon viewing the film today, *Nana* is arguably one of the greatest achievements of Lupe Vélez's career.

Not surprisingly, the mixed reviews and tame public response to the film greatly affected its financial return, and together with Lupe's reluctance to see out her contract, producers decided to release her of her obligations (without penalty) for the other two films. Undoubtedly, Lupe's disillusionment with the three-film contract (and the industry in general) occurred because of the betrayal from the studio and backers of *La dama de las camelias* (1944), the same studio and backers of *Nana*.

In April of 1943, Lupe spoke to reporter Juan Tomás (*Cinema Reporter*) about her upcoming role of Margarita Gautier in *La dama de las camelias*. She showed a good understanding of the complex characters and explained the differences between Margarita and Nana, saying:

> Margarita Gautier is more attractive to me than Nana, you see.... The lady of the camellias was a sad woman in her last days, but formerly she was a woman with lots of pep; vibrant, joyful, temperamental. I would play the role like that.... Margarita Gautier was a kindhearted woman, quite opposite to Nana. [Emile] Zola's heroine is a bad woman, perhaps more selfish than evil....

*La dama de las camelias* went into production about two months prior to *Nana*, with Lina Montes in the role of Marguerite Gautier. It was a part that Lupe had been promised and a part that she desperately wanted to play. However, when production started early (August 1943) and the female lead was given to the much younger Lina Montes, Lupe felt horribly betrayed. She was already obligated to do *Nana*, and *La dama de las camelias* was now off the table. *Anna Karenina* was left to be determined and it was anyone's guess what third role would be thrown at her to make up for *La dama de las camelias*. The situation was a mess and Lupe wanted out. She was let go.

After she was released from her contractual obligations, Lupe was free to return to the United States and she retreated to her Beverly Hills sanctuary for a much-needed rest. As it happened, Lupe would only go home to Mexico one more time ... for her burial.

# 18

## Broken Promises ... Fatal Consequences

"I have enough jewelry. I just want a marriage that will last."[1]— Lupe Vélez on why she insisted on a plain wedding ring from Harald Ramond

The *El Paso Herald Post* (December 15, 1944) reported in detail about the morning Lupe Vélez was found dead by her secretary-companion of ten years, Beulah Kinder. Following her usual morning routine, Mrs. Kinder went into Lupe's sumptuous silver and white upstairs bedroom to draw the curtains and wake her for breakfast. As she let in the morning light, Mrs. Kinder said something about Lupe's face arrested her attention: "I thought she was asleep, she looked so peaceful. But when I laid my hand on her to see if she wanted some breakfast 1 knew something was wrong. She was dead."

Clothed in blue silk pajamas, her body was lying in the silk-sheeted bed, her long hair (now dyed a much lighter shade) tumbling across a satin pillowslip. One hand was stretched toward a night table on which there was a phial that had contained sleeping tablets. Additional sleeping tablets were found scattered across the bed. "Her features were composed and she appeared as though in a deep sleep," wrote the *Mason City Globe Gazette* ("Lupe Vélez, Found Dead, Is Believed Sleep Pill Victim," December 14, 1944).

The first policeman to arrive on the scene described his first impression of Lupe's lifeless body: "She looked so small in that outsize bed that we thought at first she was a doll" (*Time*, December 25, 1944).

\* \* \*

In late November 1944, Lupe announced her engagement to actor Harald Ramond, saying, "He is the only man who is able to control Lupe, so naturally I am going to marry him" (*San Antonio Light*, November 25, 1945).

Lupe and Ramond had known each other for more than a year and were steadily together for at least six months before her death. After splitting with Arturo de Córdova, Lupe announced her engagement to Ramond. Then (a week before she died) she backpedaled and just as swiftly announced that their romance was off. She said she preferred her dogs Chips and Chops and that she was going on to New York to "forget about romance" ("Lively Lupe Vélez Kills Self and Unborn Child," *The Abilene Reporter-News*, December 15, 1944).

Ramond had come to Hollywood after two years of medical study at the Sorbonne in Paris. Prior to his arrival in the United States he had lived a gypsy life, bouncing all over Europe. After leaving Paris, he returned to his native Austria and acted briefly on the stage. After the Nazis overran the country, he fled, and ended up in Czechoslovakia, then Switzerland and Marseilles. He reportedly served in the French army with the rank of sergeant,

145

but following the fall of France he found his way to America as a refugee. He entered the U.S. as a German national, but classified himself as an Austrian in the registration of aliens by the Justice Department in 1942. Residents of Austria, prior to the German occupation of that country on March 12, 1938, were not required to register as enemy aliens (*The Pittsburgh Press*, December 21, 1944).

Aside from bit parts as an actor, Ramond's main job at Warner Brothers was dubbing French dialogue. In comparison to most jobs at the time[2], his $600-per-week (approximately $7,300 in 2011) salary was exceptionally generous, especially for the lowly jobs he was doing ("Lupe, Who Defied Life, Seeks Peace in Death." *Pittsburgh Post-Gazette*, December 15, 1944).

Around this time, following a two-year hiatus, Lupe's business managers Bö Roos and Charles Trezona had resumed representation of her affairs. The men revealed they had met with Ramond at Lupe's home and gave him the news of his impending fatherhood. Ramond told them he'd been advised by an attorney to go through with a fake marriage, but "for reasons he couldn't divulge," he couldn't go through with a "real marriage." Roos and Trezona told him there was only one acceptable reason why he couldn't marry Lupe immediately, and that was if he was already married. He refused to discuss the matter further. Naturally, this led to speculation that Ramond may have left a wife behind in Europe (*Los Angeles Examiner*, December 15, 1944).

On December 16, 1944 (*San Antonio Light*), Ramond confessed that the first time he knew of Lupe's pregnancy was in early December. A doctor at her home said, "Congratu-

The empty bedroom of Lupe Vélez. She was found unresponsive in her king-size bed on the morning of December 14, 1944. Her cause of death was "Seconal poisoning." A graphic story of her being found dead with her head in the toilet has circulated for decades and become Hollywood folklore.

**Lupe plays with her dogs Chips and Chops in this shot from the early '40s. Both dogs were specifically mentioned by name in her suicide note.**

lations, you are a father." He claimed he immediately renewed his offer of marriage to Lupe, which he had previously made weeks before, "because she was the first real love in my life," he said. Then, all of a sudden Ramond said that Lupe called him to say she was not going to have a child and asked him for her ring back (she had given him a ring to measure for a wedding ring). "I loved her very much and wanted to marry her. We just couldn't agree on a date," said Ramond.

There were conflicting reports about Ramond's marital intentions, but the one consistency throughout was that he *did* love Lupe and he *did* intend to marry her — not immediately, but eventually. Other reports suggested their mutual unfamiliarity with the English language caused such confusion that Lupe misunderstood his intentions and she took her life for fear of being an unwed mother. Ramond said that a mutual friend suggested they publicly

Seated next to Lupe at the Mocambo nightclub is Harald Ramond, her current lover. Ramond's Hollywood career was less than stellar. Prior to Lupe's death, the bit player was the lead contender for a biopic that was being developed on the life and career of Rudolph Valentino; however, after being named as the father of Lupe's unborn child (and the reason for her suicide, just months after this photograph was snapped), his name was mud and his imminent big screen break was history. Ramond most certainly made his mark in Hollywood and he'll be forever remembered ... just never in the way he imagined.

announce they had been married for three months, then they'd really be married as soon as Ramond's affairs were settled. While his evasiveness certainly looked suspicious at the time, it appears those "affairs" were strictly work-related.

Put simply, Ramond did not want to be married until he was able to support his wife on *his* income. He said he told Lupe that, but with *his* poor English, he made the mistake of calling it a "fake" marriage. She misunderstood him. "I really loved her," Ramond said. "I have known many women but Lupe I really loved." He said he planned to attend her funeral services because, "I want to say goodbye before she's gone" ("Lupe Chose Suicide for Love Finale." *The Vidette Messenger*, December 15, 1944).

Actress, Estelle Taylor, and former wife of Jack Dempsey, told police that she had been with Lupe from 9:30 P.M. Wednesday night until 3:30 A.M. the next morning. She was the last person to see her alive. She said that a mutual acquaintance told her that she had never seen Lupe so distressed and she thought something terrible must be wrong. Taylor, one of her closest friends, immediately drove to her house to check on her. The *Los Angeles Examiner* (December 15, 1944) interviewed Taylor the day after Lupe's death. The article titled, "Estelle Taylor Tells of Visit," quoted her as saying:

> She paced the floor the whole night, "I'm just weary of this whole world," she kept repeating. "People think that I fight. I have to fight–for everything."
> "I'm so tired of it all, I don't know what I'll do with myself. Ever since I was a baby I've been fighting. I've never met a man with whom I didn't have to fight to exist."

It got very late and Estelle was afraid to go to her car alone, so Lupe walked with her. Her last words were, "I don't know what you could be afraid of. I'm getting to the point where the only thing I'm afraid of is life itself." She waited until her friend drove away, and when she couldn't see the lights of her car any more, she went back inside and washed down 75 Seconal pills with a glass of her favorite brandy. Beulah Kinder told authorities that Lupe had started using Seconal to sleep in 1934.

In his 1998 book *The Sound of Silence*, Michael Ankerich wrote about a conversation he had with Mexican actress Lupita Tovar:

> I remember one evening when Lupe Vélez was here. We were sitting just about where we are now. I remember her exact words. She said, "Lupita, I envy you, because you have everything, a wonderful husband and two beautiful children." "Lupe," I said, "you have nothing to envy me for. You've had a wonderful career." It wasn't long after that she killed herself. I was so sorry for her."

Circa 1930s — Estelle Taylor, actress and one-time wife of heavyweight boxing champ Jack Dempsey. She was the best friend of Lupe Vélez. Just a couple of hours before Lupe overdosed, Taylor left Lupe's home and waved her goodbye for the last time.

On the afternoon of December 14, 1944, autopsy surgeon Victor Cefalu said his preliminary autopsy findings showed that Lupe was about four months pregnant. He said he found no natural cause of death and the "chemical analysis of stomach contents will soon be made" (*The Montreal Gazette*, December 15, 1944). The Los Angeles County Coroner's Register determined the cause of death to be "Suicide, due to ingestion of Seconal tablets." The probable cause of suicide was listed as "Love affair."

A few days after Lupe's death, a *Miami News* article ("Pose As Child's Mother," Lupe Vélez Begged Sister," December 19, 1944) stated that Lupe had pleaded with her older sister Josefina Anderson to pretend to be the mother of her child. It was during a birthday party for her husband, Army Pvt. Gordon Anderson, at Lupe's home on November 6, 1944, that Lupe pulled her older sister aside and said she "needed help."

During the party, Ramond arrived. He pounded on the front door for a long time before the maid let him in. He yelled upstairs, "Lupe, I am here!" to which Lupe responded, "I am busy with my sister. I want to be let alone." Offended, he left at once, slamming the front door behind him. Josephine's husband corroborated the story. He said he was sitting downstairs with another man at the time of Ramond's hasty entrance and departure (Tom Caton, "Court Contest in Prospect Over Lupe Vélez's Will," *Los Angeles Times*, December 19, 1944).

According to Mrs. Anderson, Lupe's part of the conversation went as follows: "Josie, I'm going to have a child. You're the only one I can trust—my favorite sister. I want you to pretend to have the baby. You're married. It can't hurt you. We'll go away together to a

little town in Mexico.... Then, when the baby is born, you can pretend it's yours and later I'll adopt it."

Mrs. Anderson said she agreed to her sister's desperate plan. But she told Lupe that first, before they do anything further, she must return to her home in San Antonio, Texas, with her husband, to see about a house they were planning there. At the thought of her sister (and savior) leaving, Lupe cried and begged for her to write her soon. Then she said, "Josie, you come right back and we will have another long talk and then go away" ("Sister Declares Lupe Asked Aid," *The Deseret News,* December 19, 1944). Josephine never returned ... at least not while her sister was alive.

When a star of Lupe's caliber dies, especially under such tragic circumstances, the families of the deceased sometimes have to mourn their loss in a very public way. Lupe's closely guarded pregnancy secret was revealed to everyone in her suicide note. Her family (along with Beulah Kinder and Harald Ramond) were the only ones left who could answer the barrage of questions that came with the shocking revelation. According to *The Fresno Bee* (December 15, 1944): "The public, long accustomed to Miss Vélez's violent outbursts, little suspected the pious side of her nature which led to her suicide rather than shame for an infant. She was reared in a convent and throughout her stormy life found refuge in prayer and relief in her frenzied fights across the nation's front pages."

In light of Lupe's decision to end her life rather than face the dishonor she'd bring to her strictly religious family with her bastard child, Lupe's second cousin, Pedro Quintanilla Gómez-Noriega, was asked (by the author) what his family's feelings were at the time of Lupe's death. Her suicide note revealed her pregnancy secret to the world. Were Lupe's feelings of hopelessness realized? He said:

A rare shot of Lupe's sister Josephine (aka Josefina) during her brief Hollywood "career." She is pictured here in her screen debut as the cigarette girl in *Her Man* (1931). Her handful of Hollywood film roles were of little note.

> Aside from her death being a major event and a huge shock to her fans and the American and Mexican movie industry, it was equally shocking to her family, especially her mother Josefina Vélez and Lupe's sister Reina, who of course still did not know that she wasn't mentioned in her will until later on.

Her pregnancy, which was viewed as the irrational cause of her decision to commit suicide, brought into her

family thoughts of empathy, not anger at all, and a lot of "what-ifs." *If* only she had sought help. *If* only she had confided in someone [other than her sister Josephine], maybe then she would have carried the pregnancy to term and then placed the child for adoption. *If* only....

Lupe's death was very hard on her mother and she never fully recovered from her loss. I remember my grandmother saying that Josefina's concern was that (following the Roman Catholic tradition) having taken her own life, Lupe's soul was thrown into eternal damnation and that she *should* have carried her pregnancy to full term. No one in her family ever condemned her or spoke ill of her. On the contrary, they were deeply saddened that she took such drastic measures. As for that awful Kenneth Anger version of her death, that was a gruesome lie; my family never, *ever* heard that. We always knew she had died in her bed, as she had lain down.

\* \* \*

Tucked into the satin pillowcase of Lupe's bed were two manically scrawled notes that had several whole words, and letters from other words, scribbled out. Police investigators came to the conclusion that the angular handwriting and appearance of the suicide notes proved this tragic event was no cry for help, no attention-seeking episode and certainly no accident. Lupe *meant* to kill herself. Her suicide note to Harald read:

To Harald:

May God forgive you, and forgive me too but I prefer to take my life away and our babys before I bring him with shame or killing him.
Lupe

The other side of the note had the following afterthought:

How could you Harald, fake such great love for me and our baby when all the time you didn't want us, I see no other way out for me, so goodby and good luck to you.
love, Lupe

Lupe's note to her secretary and companion Beulah Kinder read:

My Dear, Mrs. Kinder:

My faithful friend, you and only you know the facts for the reason I am taking my life. May God forgive me and don't think bad of me. I love you many. Take care of my mother, so goodby and try to forgive me. Say goodby to all my friends and the American press that were always so nice to me.
Lupe

On the other side, Lupe wrote Mrs. Kinder a reminder about her beloved dogs: "Take care of Chips and Chops."

\* \* \*

The San Antonio, Texas, newspaper *La Prensa* (December 28, 1944) published comments from Mexican actress Susana Cora; within the article, she stated that Lupe's suicide was an end that she (Lupe) contemplated previously that same month (December). Cora said that Lupe was terribly afraid of solitude, and that she was in a deep state of melancholy in the days prior to her death. Her most shocking revelation was that she (Cora) destroyed two suicide notes that Lupe had written to secretary Beulah Kinder several days before the actual event of her death. According to Cora, the notes were written on separate occasions and prior to two planned suicide attempts that were averted by her. Cora stated that on both occasions, she was the only one at the house to prevent Lupe from going through with it. (According to Cora, she was then living there.) Cora also said that Lupe constantly complained to her about "having everything and having nothing."

A few weeks before her death, Lupe visited Hispanic troupe dancer José Greco backstage after a Los Angeles performance. After chatting with him in Spanish for a while, Lupe noticed a huge bottle of vitamin pills on the dancer's dressing table. The sight amused her: "A beeg, healthy boy like you," she laughed. "What for you need vitamin pills?"

"They're for energy, " Greco told her. "Dancing takes a lot out of me and I have to safeguard my health."

"Health, ha!" scoffed Lupe. "Look at me. I betcha ten dollars, even without vitamin pills, I live twice as long as you!" (*The Lowell Sun*, January 19, 1945).

They laughed, shook hands, kissed cheeks and agreed on the good-natured wager before saying goodbye. Soon after, Lupe lost the bet. Greco died on December 31, 2000, at 82 years old.

Lupe's death certificate was filed on January 22, 1945. Her full name was given as Lupe Vélez [*sic*] Weismuller, aka Lupe Vélez. Her address and place of death was 732 North Rodeo Drive, Beverly Hills, California. Her time of death was noted as 8 A.M. on the morning of December 14, 1944. The immediate cause of death was "Seconal poisoning" due to "Ingestion of Seconal tablets." The death certificate erroneously states that her birth date was July 18, *1910*, making her thirty-four years old at the time of her death, not thirty-six, as commonly reported. However, Lupe Vélez was *definitely* born in 1908; she was *thirty-six* years old when she died.

Chief of Police C.H. Anderson said the two phials of pills originated in Mexico and an investigation would be started into the possible smuggling of the drugs into the United States. During the 1940s, Seconal was routinely prescribed for sleep — and was also routinely used to commit suicide. On July 7, 1945, the *Los Angeles Examiner* reported that actress Carole Landis commented to an unnamed friend after Lupe's suicide:

> I know just how Lupe felt. You go just so far, and then what have you got to face...? There's always the fear of being washed up ... you begin to worry. You get bitter and disillusioned. You fear the future because there's only one way to go and that is down.

By July 5, 1948, twenty-nine-year-old Carole Landis was also dead. The reason (at least part of it) and the method to end it all were the same as Lupe's. Cause of death: Seconal overdose. The reason: her affair with actor Rex Harrison and his refusal to divorce his wife, actress, Lilli Palmer, for her.

Commonly nicknamed "reds" or "red-devils," because the capsules were originally scarlet-colored, Seconal is a fast-acting barbiturate that was developed to treat insomnia, anxiety and convulsions. It was also the drug of choice for many high-profile Hollywood suicides. Author E.J. Fleming wrote about the side effects of Sec-

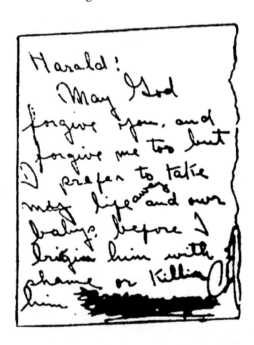

The front page of a two-sided suicide note that Lupe Vélez wrote to the father of her unborn child, Harald Ramond. While it is legible, several words have been amended, and words at the bottom have been scribbled out entirely.

onal in his *Carole Landis: A Tragic Life in Hollywood* (McFarland, 2005):

> [Seconal] is extremely fast-acting, even in small doses.... [L]arge doses produce blurred vision, slurred speech, impaired reflexes and perception of time and space, slowed breathing and sometimes a reduced sensitivity to pain. An overdose will produce a quick and profound impairment followed by unconsciousness, coma and death.

Carole Landis collapsed and died after reportedly taking between 30 and 50 Seconal pills; however, she was almost six inches taller and approximately twenty pounds heavier than Lupe Vélez. As previously stated, Lupe took 75 pills with a brandy chaser. She went to her bed and waited to die.

For the amount of pills that Lupe took, and taking into account her petite frame, *any* mobility, like getting down from

The back of the suicide note that Lupe wrote to Ramond. It reads, "...how could you Harald, fake such great love for me and our baby when all the time you didn't want us, I see no other way out for me, so goodby and good luck to you love Lupe."

her king-sized bed and walking or even crawling to her bathroom to vomit (the all-too-common re-telling of her last moments) would have been virtually impossible. *If* she did vomit (and there's no documentation that states her bed was soiled), she would have vomited in her bed, most likely choking on it there. While the "died with her head in the toilet" myth has overridden these facts for decades, the evidence doesn't lie. Clearly, Lupe died an almost instantaneous death — in her bed.

\* \* \*

Newspapermen who went to Ramond's home to inform him of Lupe's passing were given the following statement: "I am so confused. I never expected this to happen. The last time I talked to Lupe I told her I was going to marry her anyway she wanted. She said then she wasn't going to have a baby. So we parted." He admitted he had once asked Lupe to sign an agreement saying he was only marrying her to give the baby a name. "But I didn't mean that," he said. "We'd just had a fight and I was in a terrible temper" (*The Montreal Gazette*, December 15, 1944).

On December 5, 1944, Louella O. Parsons confirmed Ramond's story in her column (*Fresno Bee*):

> The Lupe Vélez-Harald Ramond marriage will not take place for two weeks. Lupe said, "I cannot talk — he'll tell you." Ramond says he is leaving Warners December 16 and his agent has two offers for him. He doesn't want to marry until he knows something about his business plans and he expects to have his job settled soon....

On the same day (December 5), the *Modesto Bee* reported that Lupe and Ramond had just taken the legally required blood tests before marriage and that they would marry in two weeks, as soon as Ramond signed his new film contract. The media stories about the impending marriage remained consistent.

Lupe's business manager Bö Roos said he had an appointment to meet her at 10 o'clock

on the day she died. He knew of her pregnancy and their meeting that very morning was about how to handle "the situation." He had reportedly made arrangements for her to travel to Mexico. She would stay at his Los Flamingos Hotel until the baby was born, then return to Hollywood and "adopt" the child after a year had passed. Lupe killed herself before Roos could tell her about the arrangements. "We who loved her can be grateful for one thing," said Roos, "the way she chose to die. She just went to sleep" ("Lupe Chose Suicide for Love Finale," *The Vidette Messenger*, December 15, 1944).

According to Roos, he called Ramond (numerous times) to ask what he intended to do about Lupe's pregnancy. Roos claimed Ramond told him he needed a little time to think it over, and then he proposed a "mock ceremony." Finally, Roos said that Ramond stated he'd only marry Lupe if she'd sign a document agreeing that he was only marrying her to give her baby a name. Lupe's response to that proposal was to call gossip columnist Louella O. Parsons and announce the split. "We had one big battle," said Lupe. "I told him to get out of my house." When Parsons asked Lupe how Ramond spelled his name (for the article), Lupe snapped, "I don't know. I never did know. Who cares?" Before hanging up she added, "I like my dogs, Chips and Chops, better." To Parsons, it was just another Lupe Vélez broken engagement story to report. She got the failed-romance exclusive, but she had no idea that Lupe was pregnant (Carr, *Hollywood Tragedy*).

While Ramond said the misunderstanding between Lupe and himself was due to their "mutual" faulty knowledge of English, it has already been established that Lupe understood English very well. A few days after Lupe's death, a press conference was held. Ramond said:

> I went to Lupe and told her we could announce a "fake" marriage, but it was not wise for me to use that word, and I feel she misunderstood me. She apparently did not understand that we could go ahead with a fully legal ceremony at a later date [*San Antonio Light,* December 18, 1944].

Following Lupe's death, Ramond's career in the United States was ruined. As quickly as he was welcomed into Hollywood circles, because of his association with Lupe Vélez, he was just as quickly shunned, because of his association with Lupe Vélez. The film community aside, the American and Mexican public blamed him for her suicide. After several small TV roles and an uncredited role as a German lieutenant in *Stalag 17* (1953), he returned to Germany where he worked sporadically in TV and film until 1968.

In 1949, columnist Louella O. Parsons tracked down Ramond. In an attempt to live down Lupe's suicide, he was now going by his "other" lesser-known name, Harald Maresch. At the time he was married to the ex–Mrs. Hans Hollander, whose first husband was a wealthy whisky distributer. They were expecting a baby in November 1949 (*Los Angeles Examiner,* July 4, 1949). Ramond died in Los Angeles on December 7, 1986. He was 70 years old.

* * *

In a revealing 1938 interview with reporter Gladys Hall, Lupe admitted to an earlier suicide attempt. There were no great details provided, no explanation as to *why* she wanted to end her life at that particular time, but she said that she walked out of her home one night, into the pool in the moonlight. She said, "I tried to drown myself and my mother jumped in to save me and I had to save her life!" (The Gladys Hall Papers, the Margaret Herrick Library). It's conclusive proof that Lupe's reckless, seemingly bipolar personality led her to extreme bouts of hopelessness, depression and suicidal tendencies, on more than one occasion.

Valerie Yaros, Screen Actors Guild historian and biographer of actor-brothers Frank and Ralph Morgan, has done extensive research on the Wuppermann (their birth name) family, including another actor-brother Carlos (who died under mysterious circumstances in 1919, age thirty-one), for over a decade. She had a close relationship with Frank's only child, George Morgan, and during one of their many conversations he mentioned a random "encounter" that he had with Lupe, the very week of her death. Yaros said:

> I don't recall how the subject of Lupe came up, but George was evidently quite "popular" with the young ladies of Hollywood. He was six feet tall with light green eyes. Lupe had co-starred with Frank in *The Half-Naked Truth* a dozen years before, and George said that he was driving on Sunset Boulevard in Beverly Hills when Lupe spotted him (he was 28 years old at the time) and pulled up beside him in her car, winked and gestured for him to follow her. So they went back to her home (he did not provide any details, but the inference of some degree of "intimacy" was there...). Before George left, he said Lupe asked if he wanted to go to the next Friday night fights at the Hollywood Legion Stadium with her ... but she never phoned ... because she was dead before then.
>
> On December 10, 1944, just days before her death, the *Los Angeles Times* published the information that she'd broken up with Harald [Ramond], so Lupe's behavior was certainly extreme in this case, particularly as she was pregnant! George never mentioned anything to me about learning she was pregnant, after the news broke. Not a word. I can't imagine that he knew, that she would have revealed something that personal. But, after he heard the news of Lupe's death, he confessed his first thought was, "I *hope* it didn't have anything to do with *me!*" but then dismissed it immediately as obviously ridiculous.

The day after Lupe's death, December 15, 1944, reporter Inga Arvard of *The Milwaukee Journal* (December 26, 1944) visited Lupe's house. Hollywood had been rocked by news of her death, yet Arvard remarked that her house on 732 North Rodeo Drive looked "calm and placid." The police had left the scene hours before and the only person in the sprawling Spanish-style home was Beulah Kinder. Lupe would often refer to Mrs. Kinder as "my balance" (*Los Angeles Times*, 1942).

Mrs. Kinder had yet to come to terms with her friend's death: The reporter noted that she would talk about Lupe in present tense, and then stop and correct herself before pausing to compose herself. A decade before, when Lupe was going on a trip to South America, Mrs. Kinder had been sketching some dresses for her. Lupe liked her sketches and she liked her, so she asked Mrs. Kinder if she would like to come along on the trip and take care of her for its duration. Mrs. Kinder agreed. Upon returning home, Lupe was scheduled to go to London and Mrs. Kinder traveled along once again. In the present tense, Mrs. Kinder said:

> She is such a good little soul and has so much heart. I just love her like one of my children. She's either high up or low down. Somehow she's never been able to find the way of being happy and contented on a middle register of emotions....

Mrs. Kinder gave some insight into Lupe's upside-down schedule. Her day would usually begin at four or five in the afternoon. She hated going to bed at night and whenever she came home from a party, she'd very often knock on Mrs. Kinder's door and ask if she would like to play a game of "Russian Bank" with her. Lupe usually won, but if she didn't she'd pretend to be angry about it, and then laugh it off with a wink as one big joke.

Mrs. Kinder explained Lupe's love affair with jewelry in more detail than ever before. She shifted in her seat to prepare herself for another memory, her voice got thicker and her eyes glistened with tears. She began by saying that if an unknown guest came to Lupe's house, and it was a pretty girl, she would call her aside and excitedly ask her if she would

like to go upstairs and look at her jewels. No one ever refused. Lupe and the girl would sneak away and once upstairs, Lupe would spread every piece of jewelry out on the large white rug in her bedroom. Then she got down on the floor and told a story about each piece. One particular piece that she enjoyed showing off was a $75,000 necklace (approximately $1.2 million in 2011) made of diamonds, carved rubies, emeralds and gold. It could be broken up and worn as four bracelets, a pin and a clip. Lupe thought this piece was particularly clever and she enjoyed demonstrating the interchangeability of the pieces and its various combinations.

Soon after seeing the collection, the wide-eyed guest would be weighed down with almost all of the jewelry pieces at once. "I want to see how you look in all this," Lupe would say smilingly. Mrs. Kinder said that Lupe always believed that jewelry was the best investment she could make. It went up in value and she could also wear and enjoy it. Of her collection, Lupe said, "I just can't live without jewelry. Their sparkle and glitter make me feel alive." Her favorite gems were rubies. Her collection consisted mostly of bracelets, with a few pendants too. There were very few rings. She always wore a large square cut diamond which she had bought for herself and the handmade horseshoe nail ring that the Pittsburgh man she befriended had sent her. Monetarily it was worth nothing, but to Lupe, it was priceless.

As it happened, Lupe's theory about jewelry being a good investment was correct. When the big crash came in 1929, many of Lupe's friends lost their fortunes, but she still had her jewelry and it cemented her thoughts about it being a safe investment. She continued to buy it, right up until her death.

Secondary to jewelry were shoes. She had close to 100 pairs. Her dresses were simple yet colorful, a necessity to keep her modesty, but more importantly, they were a mere backdrop to showcase her jewelry. It was not unusual for Lupe to go out wearing a $30 dress with $150,000 in fur and jewels to adorn it. She wore her dresses again and again. She was practical in many ways. She'd either have her dresses made for her after finding cheap material that she liked, or she'd buy them on sale, at small shops. Despite her wealth, she still very much enjoyed getting a bargain and she'd often come bursting in the front door of her house, eager to show Mrs. Kinder what she'd found and excitedly tell her the whole story of how much it originally cost and how much she bought it for ("Lupe's Estate to Go on the Block." *The Miami News,* June 20, 1945).

Mrs. Kinder said that it was not unusual for Lupe to go to bed at six or seven in the morning. She would never make an appointment before lunch, not even for cocktails, except for late in the day. When she'd get up she'd always ask for breakfast, even though most people were preparing for dinner. If it was Lupe's first meal of the day, no matter what time it was, it was *still* breakfast! She'd often ask Mrs. Kinder to prepare her a feast of wieners, calf's liver, or bacon and eggs. She'd read the papers as she ate and then get dressed around six or seven in the evening. Whenever she worked on a film, her entire schedule would have to change to meet the production.

Food was a passion for Lupe. Mrs. Kinder said that Lupe never had to worry about putting on an ounce because she was so energized all the time and worked off everything she ate. Whenever she'd get a craving for a particular dish or fruit that was out of season, she would get in her car and drive all around town to find exactly what she wanted. She wouldn't be satisfied until she found it and would be as happy as a child when she did.

Mrs. Kinder said that Lupe was an excellent cook and that she preferred traditional Mexican dishes. A leg of lamb with tomato sauce and chili peppers was a frequent favorite; she described the recipe as "out of this world." Her voice low to control her emotions, she

continued, "The very last meal we had together, Lupe cooked. It was squab stuffed with wild rice." She rarely had a craving for sweets and she drank very little, mostly wine and sherry. The minimal drinking during the last few years of her life wasn't out of choice, it was a medical necessity because of a kidney ailment that she had suffered from periodically.

She hated traveling. Mrs. Kinder said whenever they went abroad, Lupe would sit in her hotel room and tell her to go out and see all the sights. "I'll stay here in comfort and listen to you when you get home..." she'd say. For superstitious reasons, she refused to travel on the thirteenth of the month. But Mrs. Kinder said they recently flew home on *that* date and she chided Lupe about it. In hindsight, Lupe's depressed state of mind showed in her response. She looked at Mrs. Kinder and seriously replied, "I don't think those things matter any more" (*Los Angeles Evening Herald and Express,* December 17, 1944).

One pastime that Lupe never missed were the Friday night fights. Her shrill cry of "Keel the bum!" was a well-known catchphrase. Fight promoters would try and get Lupe to cheer for their guy, because the crowd usually went her way. There'd she'd be, front row, yelling instructions at *her* fighter and yelling obscenities at the opponent. Whenever she put her hard-earned money on the outcome, she was louder still. It wasn't unusual for Lupe to place $1,000 (approximately $15,000 in 2011) on one match.

The *Reno Evening Gazette* (December 7, 1932) reported on a heavyweight bout between the Rumson, New Jersey, Bulldog, otherwise known as Mickey Walker, the giant killer, and Arthur De Kuh. Walker stopped the New York Italian in the first round, after just one minute twenty-four seconds of fighting at the legendary Olympic stadium. De Kuh took a right to the head and was down for a nine count; a few seconds later he was down yet again for another nine count, then a seven count and a ten count to end it all. The last three blows took him down despite being delivered with little force, so the crowd of 6,000 fans knew they'd been had. No one shouted disapproval louder than Lupe: She yelled to De Kuh, "You should wear a bathing suit with that sort of diving!"

If a Mexican fighter was on the bill, leave it to Lupe to yell the loudest of anyone in the entire stadium. The boxers would look to her for advice and she'd often leave without a voice. Yelling herself hoarse was deemed a good night by Lupe's standards. *The Owosso Argus-Press* (July 28, 1950) recalled the crowd reaction as Lupe would make her usual mid-bout trip to the powder room. Her entrance was one thing, but her customary between-bout parade to the powder room always hit the peak of hilarity. As soon as Lupe rose from her seat and started up the aisle, the gallery matched each step with a handclap and a stomp of their feet. That clamp-and-stomp routine went on until she disappeared from view. When she reappeared, the same thunderous theme ushered her all the way back to her seat. Lupe acknowledged the tribute by throwing kisses. The fight audiences lost a friend when she died, and there was hardly a dry eye in the place the night they tolled off ten soft taps on the bell for their beloved Lupe Vélez.

Further, the empty seat that Lupe had regularly occupied at Hollywood Legion Stadium was spotlighted on December 15, 1944, the night after her death. Spectators stood in silence to mark their respect as a bugler sounded taps (*Lima News,* December 15, 1944).

One of Lupe's closest female friends was actress Carole Lombard. Lupe was devastated when she died in a plane crash on January 16, 1942, en route home from selling war bonds in her home state of Indiana. "It's too awful," she cried. "The film world will never forget her" ("Filmland, Shocked, Mourns Death of Carole Lombard." *The Sun,* Baltimore, Maryland, January 18, 1942). Estelle Taylor was another close friend, but mostly Lupe's friends were male. They considered Lupe a "good pal," just like one of the boys, and because she

was often in the company of men, many of her male friends were identified by the press as her lovers. Errol Flynn recounts at least one sexual encounter with Lupe in his 1959 auto-biography *My Wicked, Wicked Ways*, but Flynn's storytelling and embellishment of the truth was legendary. Earl Conrad wrote the book based on Flynn's notes and it was released shortly after Flynn's death. Lupe was long dead, too. Without doubt, they *did* know each other. Without doubt, they *did* mix in the same circles. However, a liaison, based only on Flynn's word, can certainly be called into question.

Mrs. Kinder said it was not unusual for Bruce Cabot or Errol Flynn to come by the house in the early hours of the morning. If Lupe still had the upstairs lights on, they knew she was up and she would be more than willing to play a hand of cards with them before she went to bed. She played endless practical jokes and often initiated them too. One time, when her latest victim retaliated by sending her a dead rat, she howled with laughter, placed a lily on the stiff rodent's chest, and sent it right back again (*Time*, December 25, 1944).

Another time, in the midst of a New York play, Lupe asked to see her Broadway representative. When he arrived, he found Lupe lying on the sofa in her suite, moaning in pain. As he bent down to assist her, she opened her mouth and a cavernous blackness stared him in the face. *The Toledo News-Bee* (December 3, 1936) reported that "there was not a shapely tooth beyond her delectable lips." The agent reeled back in horror, then the joke was revealed. She and husband Johnny Weissmuller had collaborated together to blacken out her perfectly white teeth with blackjack gum, a makeup preparation that was used in the theater.

\* \* \*

As reporter Inga Arvad entered Lupe's bedroom on the afternoon after her death, Mrs. Kinder stood back. She was far too distraught to re-enter the room where she'd unexpectedly found her friend — dead — the morning before. Arvard wrote that the room had a strange sensation about it. Standing on the white rug that had been the showcase for Lupe's joyful jewelry picnics on many occasions, she stared at the ten-foot bed with the black, silver and gold headboard, the shiny white silk bedspread, the open perfume bar with dozens of bottles of expensive fragrances, a porcelain zebra, two sets of playing cards, huge mirrors, love seats, two big pictures of Lupe and the watch on the dressing table that had stopped at 2:22. An eerie silence blanketed the house; it was as though *it* had also died. Throughout most of her thirty-six years, Lupe Vélez was commonly described as a "whirlwind," a "tornado," a "cyclone."

In the early hours of the morning on December 14, 1944, the storm passed.

# 19

## *The Aftermath*

"My poor little Lupe, what madness made you take your life? May God forgive you."1 — Mrs. Josefina Vélez, Lupe's mother

Aside from the fact that Lupe Vélez was pregnant and despondent about her broken relationship with the baby's father Harald Ramond, rumors have swirled for years about additional problems that collectively helped tip her over the edge. Lupe's second cousin, Pedro Quintanilla Gómez-Noriega, said:

> I had read somewhere that Lupe's "failing" career also had something to do with her decision to take her own life. Her career was not fading, in Hollywood or Mexico. Even if she had left Hollywood, she had a burgeoning film career in Mexico, where she was very much loved and admired. She would have had a long and successful film career in her homeland, just as Dolores del Rio had when she left Hollywood [circa 1940], following her divorce from Cedric Gibbons and her well-publicized affair with Orson Welles. Lupe's career prospects were fine. So there should go another myth.

Lupe's career and finances went hand in hand, and both were solid. Her career and popularity were showing no signs of slowing down. Furthermore, she fully owned her Beverly Hills home, and her jewelry and fur collection were worth a small fortune. Two days before Christmas 1944, Lupe was scheduled to make a radio appearance and on December 28, 1944, she was to have started a three-month, $4,000-per-week (approximately $50,000 per week in 2011) personal appearance tour that ran until March. Aside from making future work plans, just days before her suicide she was packing for imminent travel. "We spent Wednesday packing for the trip and trying on dresses," Mrs. Kinder said. "Last night Estelle Taylor came over and visited, and Lupe talked on the telephone with several persons" (Keylin, *Hollywood Album 2: Lives and Deaths of Hollywood Stars from the Pages of the New York Times*).

Mrs. Kinder had stated to police that she said goodnight to Lupe after Estelle Taylor and another guest, Mrs. Jack Oakie, left the house. "She always stayed up late and I didn't think there was anything unusual. I had no idea what was in her mind" ("Lupe Chose Suicide for Love Finale," *The Vidette Messenger*, December 15, 1944). Mrs. Kinder said she placed a call to the police as soon as she found Lupe unresponsive in her bed. Despite a quick response, an hour's work with a pulmotor failed to revive her.

The previous evening, Lupe's gynecologist, Dr. Nestor A. Michelina, made a house call. He examined her, determined that she was healthy and estimated her to be about four months along in her pregnancy. Even after her death and the knowledge of her obvious emotional struggle with the pregnancy, upon reflection, Dr. Michelina said that Lupe didn't seem to be at all upset during his visit (*Los Angeles Examiner*, December 15, 1944). Aside

from Dr. Michelina, Lupe was treated by another doctor. A creditor's claim on Lupe's estate by Dr. Alejandro Wallace showed a bill of $456.66 (approximately $5,600 in 2011) for "medical services, examinations, treatments, medicines, house calls, etc., from August 30 to December 13, 1944." The dates fall between the months of Lupe's pregnancy.

* * *

During a 1929 *Screen Secrets* interview, Lupe said something eerily prophetic:

> If the kind public loves me I don't care if the mans love me. Mens mean a lot to me but no man on earth is worth all the thousands of mens and womens who adore me. If the public stop loving Lupe, she will die; if one mans stop loving her she can find another ["Senorita Cyclone," *Screen Secrets*, No. 50, May 1929].

"If the public stop loving Lupe, she will die..." Fifteen and a half years following that interview, Lupe was still clearly loved by the public, yet her suicide note stated that she believed Harald Ramond had stopped loving her, or had *never* loved her. In the early hours of December 14, 1944, Lupe did think a lost love *was* worth dying over. However, Ramond may not have been the only man, the only lost love ... or the only reason.

Following Lupe's death, her hairdresser (who also styled her hair for her funeral) said that Lupe told him, "[T]he baby was Cooper's..." (Weissmuller Jr., Reed and Reed, *Tarzan, My Father*). And Johnny Weissmuller's wife, Beryl, had suspected the same. The daughter of Lupe's business manager, Carolyn Roos Olsen said, "The rumor in Hollywood was that Gary Cooper was the father, not the Lothario [Ramond]" (Olsen and Hudson, *Hollywood's Man Who Worried for the Stars: The Story of Bö Roos*).

Additionally, Robert Slatzer, an Ohio newspaperman who was just starting out, had interviewed Lupe at her house a few weeks before her death. He commented that Lupe was "very sweet" and that she had personally made several pitchers of Margueritas for them. While he was there, Lupe got a phone call from her mother. Lupe spoke Spanish, unaware that Slatzer knew the language well enough to understand her side of the conversation. According to Slatzer, Lupe said, "I have to have the baby. It's too late now." Then she pleaded with her mother not to call Cooper. She admitted to her mother that it might be his baby, but she ended the call by telling her mother that she wasn't going to tell him. Ironically, Slatzer hadn't been able to get a decent piece of info out of her all afternoon, and now, all of a sudden, he had the biggest scoop of all!

When Slatzer asked about the baby, Lupe knew her secret was out and that he had understood every word she'd just spoken. She told him that Cooper knew about the baby but *he* insisted it must be Ramond's. Maybe it was, maybe it wasn't. But, if the doubts were there, it proves they had certainly slept together as recently as several months beforehand. Slatzer gave Lupe his word that he'd print nothing about the pregnancy, and he didn't.

Following Lupe's death, Slatzer struck up a relationship with Gary Cooper. One day, he brought up the subject of Lupe's baby. After swallowing hard, Cooper tentatively asked Slatzer what Lupe had told him. Slatzer described the aforementioned incident at Lupe's house. Cooper listened. He then claimed that he didn't know if Lupe was carrying his child. "Coulda been," he said. Slatzer let it go. Lastly, he asked if he went to her funeral. "No," Cooper said, "but I sent a nice display of roses." While Cooper downplayed his reaction to Lupe's pregnancy and death, Cooper's ex-lover Clara Bow told Slatzer an entirely different tale. Cooper frantically called Bow as news of Lupe's death spread throughout the Hollywood community. According to her, he was in complete shock, crying and screaming that he was going to kill Ramond for getting her pregnant. However, Bow said she never believed the

baby was fathered by Ramond because he meant very little to Lupe. Bow was convinced that Lupe named Ramond in order to protect Cooper.

Years later, while filming the western classic *High Noon* (1952), Cooper reminisced to Slatzer about the area (the location was very near to where he and Lupe had filmed *Wolf Song* in 1929). Smiling, he began to show Slatzer some scars on his arms and body, reminders of Lupe, all inflicted by her in moments of rage. While the physical scars may have healed long ago, Cooper's reflective demeanor implied that his emotional wounds, and moments of regret, ran deeper than anyone had ever suspected (Wayne, *Cooper's Women*).

According to Pedro Quintanilla Gómez-Noriega:

> My grandmother always suspected [that Cooper was the baby's father], but since the press always blamed that Harald loser, she had no proof. We just thought it was her instinct. On the other hand, it is highly likely that Lupe herself told some members of the family (her sister and mother for sure) and that's where my grandmother got the information. Maybe then, it was *not* a suspicion, it was a *fact*!

Doubts aside, Ramond was solely blamed for the death of Lupe Vélez. Considered by many to be a gigolo who was feeding off Lupe's fame to step up the Hollywood ladder while using her money at will, following her death his punishment was harsh; virtually run out of town, Ramond was shunned by society and blacklisted by the entire Hollywood community. In hindsight, he may have been an innocent victim who unwittingly took the blame for the death of a beloved movie star and a child that wasn't even his!

Cooper might have been married (to Veronica Balfe), but he was known for his wandering eye and, in real life, he was a long way off playing the role of the faithful husband. If Lupe *was* pregnant by Cooper, in all likelihood, he would have pressured her to get an abortion, just as he did with a pregnant Patricia Neal a few years later. Alternatively, he would have likely shunned his paternal responsibilities by shutting her out of his life completely. But for Lupe, the situation would have been much different. The love of her life was yet again that little bit closer because she was carrying his child. At the same time, he was also heartbreakingly distant because he clearly didn't want either one of them.

Suddenly, the senseless tragedy makes a lot more sense. Being unmarried and pregnant may not have been the sole reason why Lupe Vélez killed herself. However, being pregnant with Gary Cooper's child (and the rejection that came with it) could be the key secondary factor that sent her over the edge. She couldn't live with herself if she had an abortion. And, if she *was* pregnant with Gary's baby, their love child, raising the child alone would be a daily reminder of Cooper's heartbreaking rejection of her and the child. Further, with Ramond's less than enthusiastic reaction to Lupe's pregnancy news (his own paternity doubts may have been creeping in), Lupe had no one. While Lupe's suicide notes confessed to her pregnancy, it was a secret she *could* have easily taken to the grave. Overwrought, confused and angry, she confessed her sin.

The "Gary Cooper scenario" aside, there's no way of knowing if society would have accepted Lupe's plight or turned their backs forever. After all, two lovers (Ramond and Cooper) and her sister Josephine had already let her down. The risk of further rejection was far too great. Rather than find out if her beloved public were next to condemn her for her sins, Lupe Vélez chose death.

\* \* \*

The December 16, 1944, edition of the *Fresno Bee* reported that funeral services would be held on Tuesday, December 19, at 11 A.M. in Hollywood at the Cunningham & O'Connor

Funeral Parlor. Several of Lupe's celebrity friends, including her ex-husband Johnny Weissmuller, had volunteered to be pallbearers. The announcement was made that Lupe would not be buried by the Catholic Church with formal Catholic rites, despite the efforts of several friends to obtain a dispensation. Her body was moved from the non-denominational Forest Lawn Cemetery on the afternoon of December 16 to a Catholic mortuary, where rosary services would be said the night before the funeral. A dispensation for formal last rites was denied.

The article went on to say that immigration officials planned *not* to investigate Ramond because his entry into the United States in 1941 was completely legal. Despite initial comments from coroner Frank Nance about his dissatisfaction with the way the case was handled by the Beverly Hills police department (he complained the suicide notes were delayed five hours in reaching his office), he announced there would be no further inquest into her death. The police held the notes for a handwriting analysis before releasing them. The coroner also viewed the two notes (one to Ramond and the other to Beulah Kinder). After a thorough examination it was confirmed that the notes were conclusive proof that Lupe Vélez took her own life.

Ramond was photographed paying his respects to Lupe as she lay in repose. His visit was no more than a minute, enough for the frenzied photographers to capture the moment; he then made the sign of the cross and hurriedly walked away.

Several hundred people, mostly of Mexican descent, attended the brief service. Lupe's mother Josefina Vélez, her sister Josefina (Josephine) Anderson and her husband, Pvt. Gordon Anderson sat in an anteroom. Lupe's mother's sobbing was heard throughout the chapel. She collapsed as she was leaving the mortuary and had to be carried to a waiting car ("Final Services for Lupe Vélez," *Daytona Beach Morning Journal*, December 23, 1944).

The Rev. Patrick Concannon led the recitation of five Our Fathers and Hail Marys. In Latin he blessed the body and then in English he read from the Roman Catholic burial service. Though Gary Cooper had previously been announced as a pallbearer, not surprisingly he failed to show up at all. Weissmuller attended with his wife Beryl Scott; actor Gilbert Roland served as a pallbearer along with Weissmuller and Lupe's two business managers. The largest of the fifty floral arrangements sent was from Red and Edna Skelton ("Mother Collapses at Last Rites for Lupe Vélez," *Ottawa Citizen,* December 23, 1944).

Dressed in a white crepe gown, Lupe wore gold slippers and a diamond bracelet with gold links. Her head rested on a pillow of white gardenias. The chain of a gold crucifix was entwined in her tiny fingers; finally she was at peace. Ramond had sent an arrangement of gardenias that was placed next to the casket. Additional gardenias and chrysanthemums encircled the casket; it was topped by a cross that was made up of white carnations. Two red roses from an anonymous Mexico City admirer lay on the floor. The roses were bought with a tattered dollar bill that was sent to the funeral home with the words, "Send Lupe two red roses — for me." The instructions were written on the currency itself, according to the *Sarasota Herald-Tribune* of December 22, 1944.

When questioned about Lupe's death, her mother wept but managed to say that she forgave Ramond "wholeheartedly." Beulah Kinder revealed that Lupe would be buried in a gleaming ermine cape, a favorite that was taken from her large collection. Lupe did lay in state wearing the ermine cape; however, her sister Josephine refused to allow her to be buried in it ("Ermine Clad Body of Vélez to Lie in State Thursday," *News-Palladium*, December 20, 1944).

Lupe's relatives did not request a funeral mass before the corpse in Mexico City. Father

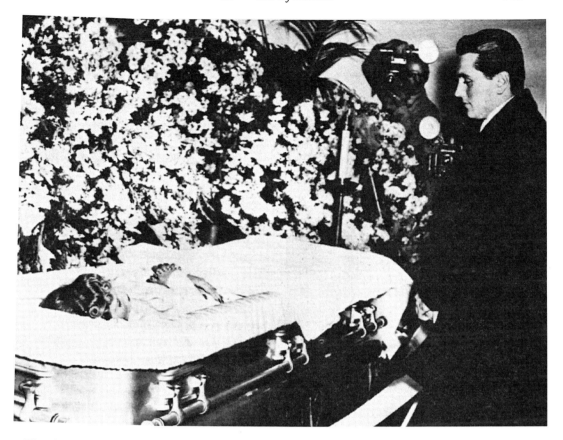

The death of "Mexican Spitfire" Lupe Vélez was one of Hollywood's great tragedies. Here she lies in an open casket as Harald Ramond pays his respects to the woman whose suicide note accused him of "faking his love" for her and their unborn baby.

Avila conducted a responsory service for her at the funeral home and rites were conducted over the grave, but the ceremony before the corpse, necessary for full Catholic funeral rites, was not held. Had the family requested the ceremony, it would have been denied, for it is never accorded in Mexico for persons who have committed suicide ("Mass Before Corpse Denies Lupe Vélez," *San Antonio Light*, January 2, 1945).

A writer for the *Ellensburg Daily Record* (December 16, 1944) a couple of weeks prior had reportedly consulted an authority in the archdiocese in America who said that Lupe's suicide did *not* enter into the church's consideration for a dispensation since it is thought that a person who takes his or her own life is not responsible for this action. Lupe was born Catholic and educated in Catholic schools; however, it was decided that she lost her rights and privileges of a full Catholic burial when she obtained a divorce from Johnny Weissmuller in 1938. It is a little hard to believe that Lupe's "suicide" and "pregnancy before marriage" *didn't* weigh heavily into their final decision, but of course, the archdiocese consulted by the newspaper at the time denounced that suggestion.

\* \* \*

Following the funeral service in California, Lupe's body was sent back to her homeland by train. As she was laid to rest in the Panteón Civil de Dolores (Graveyard of Sorrows or

Civil Cemetery of Sorrows) at dusk, disorder and stampedes reminiscent of the funeral of Rudolph Valentino almost two decades before were repeated at Lupe's burial in Mexico City. The plot, owned by the National Actors Association (Asociación Nacional de Actores aka A.N.D.A.), an Actors' Guild similar to the Screen Actors Guild in the United States, contains the remains of nearly two hundred Mexican stage and screen figures. All graves within this section are securely guarded behind a locked iron gate.

Fifty thousand people filed past Lupe's body at the mortuary. Crowds lined the route of the cortege, there were near-riots at the funeral home as cars were blocked and tempers were fueled by heightened emotions. Lupe's sister Reina fainted and fell into the crushing crowd after her sister's casket was lowered into the grave. Trampled on by grieving mourners, Reina was rescued and revived by her sister Mercedes ("Stampedes Mark Rites of Actress Lupe Vélez," *The Deseret News*, December 28, 1944).

The *San Jose News* (December 27, 1944) reported that religious rites, denied Lupe by the Catholic Church in Los Angeles, were performed in Mexico. At the funeral home, three Catholic priests conducted a responsory service, attended by members of the family and close friends. Father Aurelio Casas sprinkled holy water over the coffin and recited a blessing at the graveside. Jorge Negrete (1911–1953), a popular screen tenor, spoke for ten minutes over the grave, ending with, "Lupe, our friend, you are being lowered into the ground of your homeland ... until we meet again." He was barely heard. His sympathetic words were muffled by a milling crowd of close to 15,000 fans, all jostling to pay their final respects. Police were unable to control the flow of people; in their mad race for vantage points, monuments were knocked over and many injuries occurred. Women with babies struggled through the crowd, shielding their infants from the frenzied, uncontrolled masses ("Many Injured in Stampede at Lupe Rites in Mexico," *The Miami News*, December 29, 1944).

Desperate to view the ceremony, and with no intended disrespect, hundreds scrambled to stand atop existing crypts, and others climbed sycamore trees that grew amongst the tombs. Despite the mayhem, the intentions of the mourners were nothing but good. After all, a little Mexican actress with a big heart and an even bigger personality beat the odds and made it in America as an international movie star. She had now returned to her beloved homeland, albeit prematurely, for eternal rest. The people of Mexico had come to say farewell. They had come to say thank you.

*Their* beloved Lupe was home again ... only this time it was for all eternity.

# 20

## *The Will*

"Imagine having all that to live for—and not wanting to live."[1]—an unknown starlet attending the Lupe Vélez estate auction in June 1945

On December 15, 1944, Lupe's attorney Louis B. Stanton filed her will for probate. Her secretary Beulah Kinder was named executrix of her estate, which had an estimated worth in excess of $200,000 (approximately $2.5 million in 2011). The will, dated May 4, 1942, bequeathed one third of the estate to Mrs. Kinder and provided a trust fund (government bonds) for Lupe's mother Josefina, along with other monetary amounts to selected relatives. She also directed that in the event of her mother and father's death, sums would be made available "for masses for the souls of my mother and father."

Lupe's father, Col. Jacobo Villalobos, lived a wild, adventurous life. Much like his famous daughter, he defied society's rules and didn't care what others thought of him. Lupe was most certainly her father's daughter, in every sense of the word. As previously stated, a thorough investigation of marital records within Mexico showed that Jacobo Villalobos was married *three* times. He married another Josefina in a civil ceremony on February 8, 1936. An article in the San Antonio, Texas, newspaper *La Prensa* (February 10, 1936) announced the marriage (his third) of Col. Villalobos at the Salón Juárez in Sabinas Hidalgo, Nuevo León, to a Josefina Santos Garza, daughter of Mr. Jesús Santos and Mrs. Josefina Garza de Santos. Jacobo's stepmother and the bride's parents were involved in organizing the wedding.

It's common knowledge that the Catholic religion does not recognize divorce, but Jacobo was no bigamist when he "remarried." In Mexico, Church and State have separate laws. One does *not* recognize the other. While Jacobo *was* married to Josefina, they were married by religious rites *only*. Their marriage was recognized by the Church, but *not* by the law. When Jacobo remarried, his second marriage would have been a civil service and the law would note him as a "single" man. He was legally free to marry and went against his religious beliefs to do so, thus making him and his new wife sinners in the eyes of the Church. Jacobo didn't care. But, in order to marry a third time, since the civil ceremony *was* legal, he would need to divorce wife number two. Again, this marriage would be a civil ceremony. As for Lupe's mother, society would have labeled her an "abandoned wife," and despite no wrongdoing on her part she'd carry the shame of this title for the rest of her life.

Jacobo died (between mid–December 1943 and mid–January 1944) of natural causes in Monterrey, Mexico, but he lived decades longer than media reports gave him credit for. Following his recovery from the injuries he sustained in the Revolution, Jacobo remained in the Army and became an accomplished Army official. He was sent out to do relevant work

on several occasions. In 1932, he was head of a commission that traveled to Laredo, Texas, to celebrate U.S. Independence Day; the local military authorities personally invited him.

Until May of 1933, Jacobo was assigned in Nuevo Laredo, Tamaulipas, as Mayor de Órdenes. He was not in charge of the military unit, but was second to the chief. He went on to become the chief for the forces at Camarón, Nuevo León, and he stayed there until 1936 at least. In early 1937, a communist Irrigation Workers Union called for Col. Villalobos' immediate dismissal following military officers (and their families) violent attacks while they were protesting. It seems, as with most incidents in Jacobo's life, once again, he went too far. By January of 1941, the *Laredo Times* reported that he was the officer in charge at the Ciudad Anáhuac (Nuevo León) military station.

In the latter part of his life, Jacobo went back to where it all began finishing his working life at Monterrey's famous Cuauhétmoc Brewery. So, while Lupe's father had abandoned her mother years before her 1942 will was drafted, she apparently held no grudge against him and included him as a one-third beneficiary. He didn't live long enough to benefit from her generosity.

Josephine Anderson,[2] Lupe's sister, fought probate of the will after being left without a portion of her sister's estate. One third of Lupe's assets went to Beulah Kinder while the remaining two-thirds was directed to be divided into two trust funds, one for Lupe's mother with a payment to her of $150 per month (approximately $1,800 per month in 2011) until the fund was exhausted, and the other provided for Lupe's father in a similar way. Upon his death, all remaining funds were directed to go to the four children of Lupe's brother Emigdio Villalobos-Vélez. Since Lupe's father pre-deceased her, as per her will, his portion of the estate was split equally between her brother's children.

Lupe's second cousin, Pedro Quintanilla Gómez-Noriega, said:

I was always under the impression that Lupe's father died sometime in 1945, but the messy probate proceedings following Lupe's death prove otherwise. Newspaper accounts, along with court documents, conclusively prove that Jacobo died *prior* to his daughter. His death must have occurred sometime in mid–December of 1943 or at the very latest, mid–January of 1944. I know this because my mother married in 1943.

Following her wedding, she left Mexico City to live her married life in Monterrey. My grandmother, her mother, came to visit from Mexico City every Christmas; like clockwork, she would arrive in mid–December and leave in mid–January. By that time, for many reasons, she was not on speaking terms with her brother [Lupe's father], Jacobo. Being the black sheep of the family, he was never on good terms with any of his siblings. In fact, Jacobo had once said that when my grandmother [his sister, Lupe's aunt] died, he would wear red! The irony is, when Jacobo died, my grandmother *was* in Monterrey, learned of his death, and she was the *only* member of his family who attended his funeral. She wore black.

On December 21, 1945, Lupe's brother Emigdio asked the probate court for a partial allocation of funds. He requested $2,000 (approximately $25,000 in 2011) to educate his four children. His sister Josephine had already held up the distribution of funds for a year with her attempt to invalidate Lupe's will (as well as her creditor's claims on the estate), hence Emigdio's plea to the court. It was also stated that if Lupe's mother died prior to the trust being exhausted, the remainder of her share would be divided between the daughters of her sister Mercedes Villalobos del Valle of Mexico City. On July 25, 1945, Mercedes asked the Superior Court to aid in protecting the contingent bequest that Lupe made in her will for her four daughters, Lupe's nieces. Beulah Kinder claimed that relations between Lupe and her sister Josephine had been strained for some time, yet her sister countered that claim, telling papers she had engaged a lawyer to represent "my whole family" in probate

court proceedings. Despite Josephine's earlier statement that she was acting to represent everyone, a year after Lupe's death, none of Lupe's bequeaths had been carried out and her nieces and nephews were suffering because of Josephine's legal proceedings. Emigdio and Mercedes were forced to step in and take actions of their own in order to protect the money that Lupe wanted to leave them.

Despite the wealth of the Villalobos family when Lupe was a child, the Mexican Revolution severely depleted their fortune. However, as Lupe's career took off, she spread her riches throughout her family and the life they were once accustomed to was somewhat restored by Lupe's generosity. Aside from financial help, Lupe's mother and sisters lived with her from time to time, she'd send money to family members in Mexico, and generally help out her extended family whenever and wherever she could. This explains why there was such a desperate bid by Josephine to obtain a share of Lupe's estate. When Lupe died, the gravy train came to a screeching halt.

Pedro Quintanilla Gómez-Noriega explained further:

When the Mexican revolution erupted in 1910, many great fortunes in the country, including San Luis Potosí, were lost or heavily diminished. It was a very convoluted era in Mexico, and sometimes revolutions caused a sibling to go against his or her own sibling. My grandmother María Luisa (Lupe's aunt), for instance, married my grandfather (Miguel Gómez-Noriega) who was an established attorney. He became involved in politics and was, in fact, governor of the Federal District and the state of Hidalgo. However, for reasons I do not clearly remember, and wish I did, during the revolution it turned out he was on the "wrong side" so to speak, so he and many other prominent men (including the famous General Pablo Gonzalez) had to leave the country and go into exile "for a few months" in a rush, lest they be executed.

One of those chasing my grandfather was Jacobo himself (in other words, his own brother-in law, or his wife's brother!). You can imagine my grandmother's shock and disappointment, that her own brother was pushing them towards exile. But that's what revolutions beget. In any event, my grandfather and grandmother, carrying my three-year-old mother and my one-year-old uncle, left in 1920 for Los Angeles (and then settled in San Antonio, Texas) allegedly for just three months (my grandmother closed her house and locked it as if just going to the drugstore), but those three months became *twenty years!*

They finally returned in 1940 to Mexico City, to re-start their lives. The point is that my grandparents, as with many other prominent well-to-do personalities of the time, suffered greatly and lost most of, if not all, their fortunes. The same happened to my grandmother's siblings, including Jacobo, who ended up working for a brewery, in (I am sure) menial jobs, after having belonged to such a prominent family. So yes, in the case of Lupe's immediate family, all of them eventually depended on her own fortunes and earnings, as can be deduced from her will and what followed. Lupe was always well off, first when she was a child and a youngster, thanks to the family fortunes; then later thanks to her own earnings, which she willingly shared.

Regarding the will, Mrs. Anderson said, "Lupe loved her family and helped financially many times. It is entirely unlike her to just think of one or two. That is what we want to find out about" ("Sister May Contest Will of Lupe Vélez," *Lewiston Evening Journal,* December 19, 1944).

Ironically, of all of Lupe's remaining family members, it was Josephine who was more than financially capable of standing on her own two feet. Yet she was the one fighting the estate for whatever she could get out of it. Her husband was the son of a wealthy Winnipeg grain merchant so she was not without money but she used plenty of her own funds to fight for a share of her sister's estate, to the detriment of her siblings whose families genuinely needed the money that Lupe bequeathed to them.

Prior to Lupe's burial, Josephine made sure Lupe did not get her final wishes, she filed a creditor's claim stating that she saved the estate $41,800 (approximately half a million dollars in 2011) by removing:

- a 16-karat diamond ring of the value of $16,000 that would have otherwise been buried with the decedent.
- an ermine cape of the value of $15,000 that would have otherwise been buried with the decedent.
- she also arranged for Lupe to be buried in a casket costing $1,200 instead of a bronze casket costing $12,000 as planned, resulting in a saving to the estate of $10,800. Josephine claimed half of the $41,800, but the courts rejected her bill of $20,900.

In a second creditor's claim, perhaps even more jaw dropping than her first, Josephine filed for the $25,000 (approximately $300,000 in 2011) promised her under the agreement that she and Lupe had verbally made to care for her unborn child for a year. Anderson requested the money with this explanation:

The agreement of November 1944 between Lupe Vélez, deceased, and Josephine Anderson, claimant, whereby Josephine Anderson, at the special instance and request of Lupe Vélez, promised and agreed to take and to care for the unborn child of Lupe Vélez for a period of one year, and in consideration of said promise and agreement Lupe Vélez promised and agreed to pay to Josephine Anderson the sum of $20,000 for the purpose of a home in San Francisco Valley and to pay to her the further sum of $5,000 for her maintenance and all other expenses for the said period of one year.

HOME OF LUPE VELEZ, BEVERLY HILLS

A photograph postcard of Lupe's beloved Spanish-inspired home in Beverly Hills in the early 1940s.

Her claim for money based on a promise that *she* failed to keep was rejected by the courts. By April of 1946, all the fighting back and forth came to an end. After all the conflict and money spent to fight her sister's estate, Josephine Anderson received just $3,870 (approximately $45,000 in 2011) in settlement of her claims. It took until June 9, 1949, for the remaining $2,696.77 of Lupe's estate to be distributed to the remaining heirs. Previous court orders had distributed portions of money to benefactors, most of which came from the proceeds gathered from the estate auction ("Last of Vélez Estate Ordered Given to Heirs," *Los Angeles Times*, June 10, 1949).

*   *   *

Lupe's personal property was appraised at $99,702.46. The most expensive items were her assorted jewelry, collectively valued at $49,226.50, assorted furniture pieces and two oil paintings (a woman in prayer by Florentine artist Lorenzo de Bicci and a portrait by T. Corbell) valued at $27,350.55, and a collection of furs, collectively valued at almost $10,000. Her clothing was valued at a little over $2,000. Her savings account at the Security First National Bank of Los Angeles (Beverly Hills Branch) contained $5,065 and she also had a refund claim of over $5,000 pending with the U.S. Treasury for 1942 taxes. Following the sale of the house and personal items, the total value of the estate was $160,000 (a total of approximately $2 million in 2011).

The *Port Arthur News* ("Jewels and Furs of Lupe Vélez to Be Auctioned," June 22, 1945) reported on the upcoming sale of Lupe's most cherished possessions; her collection of jewelry and furs. The auctioneer set the values much higher than the conservative "inventory and appraisement" of assets document that was filed with the Superior Court in September of 1945. This time, the furs were valued at $75,000 and the jewelry was valued at $100,000.[3] The white ermine cape that Lupe had wanted buried with her was one of the thirteen exotic pieces to go under the hammer.

Unlike many lavish movie star homes that existed during Hollywood's silent and classic era, Lupe's house avoided the dreaded bulldozer and is in fine condition to this day. Photograph courtesy of Gor Megaera.

The jewelry collection contained 18 pieces, with the most impressive piece being a carved ruby and diamond ensemble (the aforementioned necklace) containing 95 carved rubies, 42 ruby beads, 66 baguette diamonds and 505 round diamonds. On auction day, at least 500 people attended, three-quarters of them women, all gathered on the lawn behind Lupe's house awaiting the start of the auction. A $20 admission price was set in order to keep away curiosity seekers.

After thirty minutes of active bidding, the house that Lupe proudly called her "Casa Felicitas" (Happy House) sold for $41,750 (it was appraised at $60,000 for tax purposes). The new owner, Virginia Kuppinger, wife of a Navy lieutenant, said she bought it as an investment and would rent it. She attended the auction with no intent to bid on anything at all. She said she was surprised the house sold for her bid of $41,750, since its estimate was $60,000. As of 2011, the house still carries the Spanish influence on the exterior structure. Its value on today's market is $4.2 million (www.zillow.com).

Following the sale of the house, the interior furnishings were auctioned. Furniture, antiques, silverware, ashtrays, cigarette boxes, autographed photos (including one from Gary Cooper autographed to Lupe in Spanish)—the entire contents of the house was liquidated. A carved Italian renaissance style dining set, which Cooper is said to have had made for Lupe, sold for $500. A large Sheffield silver tray sold for $220 and a 66-piece set of cut blue crystal goblets and champagne glasses for $127.50. Mrs. Buck Jones, widow of the cowboy movie star, bought two diamond bracelets for $15,400 and opera singer Ezio Pinza made a winning bid of $5,950 for a 16-carat square cut diamond ring of grand proportions. (All totaled, Lupe owned 2,900 diamonds.) She owned one of the biggest jewelry collections of any Hollywood star at that time, though everything sold at auction for prices well below their original cost. Two pictures of Gary Cooper in wooden frames sold for $1.50 each and one of Arturo de Córdova sold for $2.50. There were no pictures of Johnny Weissmuller or Harald Ramond.

Reporter Florabel Muir of the *Hollywood Citizen News* (June 23, 1945) attended the auction. She commented that she was most saddened when a little scarlet evening dress went up for bid because it was the gown that Lupe was wearing the last time she saw her. Covered with sequins, the dress had no back at all and very little front, a bare midriff, and a long flowing skirt. A young woman modeled the dress for the auctioneer and prospective bidders. She wore one of Lupe's chinchilla capes over it to retain her modesty; however, the crowd yelled for her to "take it off" and finally she did take off the cape. The male members of the crowd let out whistles and wolf cries to show their appreciation. Though the reporter said it was all in "good, clean fun," it seemed a moment of poor taste, given the circumstances. The gown sold for $35.

Muir said she fondly remembered Lupe as she stood and watched her treasured belongings sold to the highest bidders. Their first meeting was in 1928, just as Lupe's career had taken off. Muir said she was "a great-hearted girl, with a talent that grew strong and lusty and violent." It was Muir who christened her "the Baby Popocatelpet," Popocatelpet being an active volcano near Mexico City. Lupe supposedly adored the term.

The auction had something to suit everybody's budget, including pancake turners, potato mashers, even used dust mops. A pair of mottled dog bookends sold for just $1.50, a pair of Italian candlesticks sold for $11, an ironing board for $5, a glass washboard for $1, 250 coat hangers for $2, a soiled clothes hanger for $2 and a broken glass coffee maker for 25 cents. Considering Lupe's wide circle of celebrity friends there was a striking absence of movie stars at the auction, but some of them sent representatives to buy keepsakes. The *Port Arthur News* (June 22, 1945) said:

One surprising appearance came from Mary Pickford, who showed up with her husband, Charles "Buddy" Rogers.... [W]hen she was asked to pose for photographs, she left in haste, saying, "I loved Lupe very much — too much to pose for a picture under these circumstances."

Along with the low jewelry prices, most of the items sold far below their actual worth, a little surprising considering their famous owner and the tragic and highly publicized circumstances surrounding her death. Some items were almost given away. For example, the sale of Lupe's favorite red brocade draperies for just $1 brought tears to the eyes of Beulah Kinder. And when the mattress that she died on was offered for bid, a hush fell over the crowd. No one bid. One of the auctioneer's assistants put in a bid for $70, but it went no higher. The silver, gold and ebony headboard sold for $45 (*The Pittsburgh Press*, June 22, 1945).

And there it ended ... the bidders, most of them strangers to Lupe during her lifetime, all took a little piece of Hollywood's "Mexican Spitfire" home with them.

# Filmography (1927–1944)

"Cinema is an art that calls for constant renovation, a never-ending transformation. Each film is a new beginning...."*—Lupe Vélez (1935)

In the spring of 1932, while Lupe was taking a Hollywood hiatus and appearing on Broadway in the Ziegfeld show *Hot-Cha!*, Katherine Albert of *Photoplay* magazine asked her how she was getting on in New York. Lupe said, "I am fine. I am great. I stop the show every night. I maybe do not sing so good, but I sing loud; I maybe do not dance so good, but I move a lot.... I can stop the show. I am Lupe Vélez. And they all love Lupe...."

Lupe described herself perfectly. Not just then, but for all time. She *was* loud. She *did* move a lot. She *did* stop the show. And for her vivacity, tenacity and honesty, they all certainly loved Lupe. Put simply: In a land of make-believe known as Hollywood, Lupe Vélez was *real*!

In 1940, it was estimated that 60 million Americans would flock to the movies each and every week, almost *half* of the entire country's population at that time (www.pictureshowman.com). The Great Depression and World War II made this an incredibly bleak and frightening period of time the world over and for the price of a movie ticket, Lupe Vélez was a much-needed, much-loved, affordable diversion. While Lupe's comedic romps were, more often than not, bottom-billed on double bills, these B-movies proved so financially successful that they sometimes spawned an entire series. In movies churned out cheaply and quickly, the star and/or ensemble cast would play the same characters, in different situations, such as Lupe's role of Carmelita in the "Mexican Spitfire" series (1939–1943). Those inexpensive fillers featured the lightweight stories and rollicking, nonsensical good fun that the public desperately needed in order to escape the uncertainty of what tomorrow would bring. As a result, many B-movies were as successful, if not *more* successful than their bigger budgeted counterparts.

Watching Lupe's films (both silent and sound), a natural warmth and charm leaps off the screen. It's easy to see why she resonated so well with audiences. Her appeal is timeless.

Prior to her successful leap into the talkies, Lupe managed to be the "loudest" silent actress Hollywood ever knew. Watch any of her silent features and there she is, talking a mile-a-minute. She may have been inaudible, but that didn't stop her from talking—a lot!

"Couldn't you be a little less noisy, Lupe?" barked one studio executive. "Garbo is silent: so Vélez is loud," she barked back [*The Milwaukee Journal*, December 28, 1944].

As previously stated, Lupe's career was far from over at the time of her death. She was still very much in demand. In fact, the $4000-a-week fee for her upcoming personal

*Quote: Don Alvarado. "Rasgos de Lupe," *La Prensa,* San Antonio, Texas, May 12, 1935.

appearance tour was a salary as good, if not better, than she had ever made previously.[1] There were no signs of a career fade-out or a wane in public opinion.

Had Lupe Vélez lived to see the early 1950s television boom, her career might have taken a whole new turn. She had the comedic timing and facial expressions of Lucille Ball and the ethnicity and musicality of Desi Arnaz. Lupe *was* Lucy and Desi, all rolled into one package. It's not too difficult to see the similarities between Lupe's "Mexican Spitfire" series and the much-loved, iconic American sitcom *I Love Lucy* (1951–1957).

Despite Lupe's obvious Hollywood success, towards the end of her career, she openly confessed to her dissatisfaction with the overall quality of her films, "I have had very nice parts, and have known success, but never got what we may call a good film. Many of the films I have taken part in, have been — artistically speaking — quite frivolous" (*Cinema Reporter*, April 1943).

It was a serious statement to make, and printed in perfect English, not peppered with the usual "Lupe-isms" that one had come to expect of her. It certainly proved that Lupe's frustration with the film industry and the overall quality of her films was at the forefront of her thinking.

Hollywood reporter Louella O. Parsons, was a supporter of Lupe and her career, but in many ways she (like most reporters) also served to stereotype her. For instance, in a *Los Angeles Examiner* review (March 27, 1930) for *Hell Harbor* (1930), Parsons begins by saying, "The tempestuous Lupe Vélez, a bundle of concentrated energy and unrestrained fireworks...." Lupe couldn't be praised, or ridiculed, without some sort of colorful description about her wild, unbridled persona working its way into the article. That said, Parsons was genuinely broken-hearted over Lupe's death. More often than not, she would describe Lupe in a loving, protective fashion, similar to the way a mother would talk about her over-exuberant child. Never mean-spirited, usually praising and mostly sympathetic — no matter what.

Following Lupe's death, Parsons wrote a lengthy tribute piece for the *Los Angeles Examiner* (December 15, 1944). In it, she admitted that (in hindsight) Lupe had "acted a little strangely" during their last phone conversation. It was only after Lupe's death, and her pregnancy revelation in her suicide note, that the pieces fit together and Parsons fully understood why. She wrote: "It tears at the heartstrings to think of [Lupe's] anguish and what she must have suffered.... [W]e'll all miss the vibrant, active Lupe, whose love of life makes her death all the more tragic."

Yes, Lupe Vélez was a complex individual, full of contradictions, yet so full of life. She was constantly torn between her sexually liberated views, the power and the privilege her Hollywood career granted her, the stark differences and misunderstandings (at that time) between Mexican and American culture, and lastly, the oppressions that came from her strict Catholic upbringing that went against everything that made her Lupe Vélez. Ironically, after years of loudly justifying *who* she was, and *why* she was that way, it was a culmination of guilt, morality and self-doubt that killed her.

The epitaph on Lupe Vélez's grave neglects to mention her career as an actress and entertainer. It reads:

LUPE VÉLEZ
Lupita[2] (*Little Lupe*)
Descansa en Paz (*Rest in Peace*)
Viviras en el Corazon (*You Will Live in the Heart*)
de Todos (*of Everyone*)
Recordandote (*Remembering You*)
Con Carino, tu Madre, (*with Love, Your Mother*)
Hermanos y Sobrinos (*Siblings and Nieces and Nephews*)
December 14, 1944

The final resting place of Lupe Vélez. Her date of death (December 14, 1944) appears at the foot of the grave. Photograph courtesy of Pedro Quintanilla Gómez-Noriega.

**What Women Did for Me** (1927) Director: James Parrott (as Paul Parrott). Producer: Hal Roach. Production Company: Hal Roach Studios. Distributor: Pathé Exchange. Production Dates: May 14–29, 1927. Release Date: August 14, 1927. Genre: Comedy Short. Running Time: 20 minutes. Black and White. Silent. Language: English. Cast: Charley Chase (Charley). Rest of cast listed alphabetically: Bob Gray, Al Hallett, Gale Henry, Caryl Lincoln, Eric Mayne, Broderick O'Farrell, Viola Richard, **Lupe Vélez (Bit Part)**, May Wallace, Frank Whiteen. This has been shown at various film festivals. Prints are housed at the BFI/National Film and Television Archive (London) and Lobster Films (Paris).

Cast in a minor role in this two-reeler, Lupe plays the dean's daughter and rescues the shy, girl-fearing teacher (Charley Chase) from a group of wild female students. After a series of events, the girls leave poor ol' Charley outdoors clad in only a sheet — in the snow! Lupe comes to the rescue and cures him of his coy demeanor. Then, wasting no time, she makes him her husband!

**Sailors, Beware!** (1927) Directors: Fred Guiol, Hal Roach (uncredited) and Hal Yates (director of retakes). Producer: Hal Roach. Writers: Hal Roach, Frank Butler (uncredited), Lige Conley (uncredited), and H. M. Walker (titles). Production Company: Hal Roach Studios. Distributor: Pathé Exchange. Genre: Comedy Short. Black and White. Silent. Language: English. Filming Location: Hal Roach Studios. Production Dates: April 4–18, 1927. Release Date: September 25, 1927. Running Time: 20 minutes. Alternate Titles: *Ship's Hero*. Cast: Stan Laurel (Chester Chaste), Oliver Hardy (Purser Cryder), Anita Garvin (Madame Ritz). Rest of cast listed alphabetically: Ed Brandenburg (Other Cab Driver), Frank Brownlee (Captain Bull), Dorothy Coburn (Lady in Easy Chair), Harry Earles (Roger/The Baby), Connie Evans, Barbara Pierce, Viola Richard (Society Ladies), Tiny Sandford (Man in Robe), Will Stanton (Baron Behr), May Wallace (Society Lady), Charley Young (Man Boarding Boat), **Lupe Vélez (Baroness Behr)**. Availability: VHS and DVD. Also at Cinemateca de Arte Moderna (Rio de Janeiro, Brazil), Filmoteca Española (Madrid, Spain), George Eastman House (New York), BFI/National Film and Television Archive (London), UCLA Film and Television Archive (Los Angeles),

Filmarchiv (Austria), Lobster Films (Paris), Danish Film Institute (København).

This short features both Laurel and Hardy, as individuals, before they were considered a "comedy team." Stan is the star here, but his character is far more brash than usual. The familiar crying jags appear from time to time, giving us a glimpse of the Stan Laurel that he would eventually evolve into.

**The Gaucho** (1927) Directors: F. Richard Jones. Assistant Directors: William J. Cowen, Lewis R. Foster. Producer: Douglas Fairbanks. Writer — Douglas Fairbanks (under the *nom de screen* Elton Thomas). Original Music: Arthur Kay. Cinematographer: Tony Gaudio. Costumes: Paul Burns. Stunts: Richard Talmadge (uncredited). Filming Locations: Iverson Ranch, Chatsworth, California. Production Company: Elton Corporation. Distributor: United Artists. Production Dates: June–September 1927. Production Cost: $700,000. Gross Receipts: $1.4 million. Release Dates: November 4, 1927 (premiere at Grauman's Chinese Theatre, Hollywood), November 21, 1927 (Liberty Theatre, New York City), January 1, 1928 (general U.S. release). Genre: Adventure-Romance. Running Time: 115 minutes. Black and White with two-strip Technicolor sequences. Silent. Language: English. Cast: Douglas Fairbanks (The Gaucho), **Lupe Vélez (The Wild Mountain Girl)**, Joan Barclay (The Girl of the Shrine — younger), Eve Southern (The Girl of the Shrine), Gustav von Seyffertitz (Ruiz, the Usurper), Michael Vavitch (The Usurper's First Lieutenant), Charles Stevens (The Gaucho's First Lieutenant), Nigel De Brulier (The Padre), Albert MacQuarrie (Victim of the Black Doom), Mary Pickford (The Virgin Mary aka Our Lady of the Shrine [uncredited]). Availability: VHS and DVD. Also at Museum of Modern Art (New York), UCLA Film and Television Archive (Los Angeles), George Eastman House (New York) and Lobster Films (Paris).

The story of *The Gaucho* came to Fairbanks as he visited Lourdes, France, where many afflicted people seek a cure to their various maladies at the cathedral altar. He witnessed apparent miracles of faith healing, the experience was unforgettable. Back home, Fairbanks realized that this religious theme combined with his usual adventurous dramatics would have universal appeal. He transferred the idea into his latest feature production; thus,

*The Gaucho* was born (*The Rock Hill Herald*, February 25, 1928).

On the *Gaucho* set, Lupe matched wits with Fairbanks like no other leading lady before her. On screen, she *was* his equal. Rave reviews for her funny, fiery performance as the Wild Mountain Girl rolled in. She achieved instantaneous star status, becoming the proverbial "overnight sensation."

Lupe made many personal appearances prior to screenings of the film. The June 4, 1928, *Los Angeles Examiner* reported she would appear on stage that day as at the United Artists Theater in a prologue to the film. The article said she would distribute "1000 of her photographs to as many women guests."

George Eastman House has preserved six minutes of two-color Technicolor outtakes of Mary Pickford as the Virgin Mary. In 2009, the process of creating a glow around the Virgin Mary was explained during the introductory remarks at the opening night of the 14th Annual San Francisco Silent Film Festival and later transcribed by Michael Guillen (http://twitchfilm.com/):

> Pickford stood on a pedestal backed against a plank trailing her silhouette. Two bands of leather bristling with a multitude of thin sticks of pliable metal were then rotated behind her and hit with intense floodlights such that — when the metal sticks passed at a rapid pace around her silhouette — they produced a celestial glow...

Throughout his career, Douglas Fairbanks insisted on doing all his own stunts, and he did, except in *The Gaucho*, where certain scenes (for example, swinging between palm trees) were deemed too risky. Surviving outtakes and test footage reveal that Chuck Lewis was used in his place. Upon closer inspection of these scenes in the film, even at a distance it's clear that it's not Fairbanks doing the heroic leaps from tree to tree. Based on votes from 295 journalists, 326 newspapers and 29 film magazines, *The Gaucho* was placed among the top 15 films of 1927–1928 (www.austinfilm.org).

A six-minute Disney parody, *The Gallopin' Gaucho* (1928), starred Mickey and Minnie Mouse and was set in the Pampas of Argentina. Mickey rides a rhea (a large flightless ostrich-like bird, native to South America) instead of a horse and Minnie plays a barmaid and dancer in the local watering hole, "Cantino Argentino." The alluring Minnie captures the attention of Mickey (who smokes and drinks beer in this short) and his soon-to-be rival, Black Pete (a wanted outlaw). Mickey and Minnie flirt and tango together (as Lupe did with Doug in *The Gaucho*). When Black Pete kidnaps a terrified Minnie on his horse, Mickey gives chase on his now *drunk* rhea. In a desperate attempt to stiffen up and straighten out the intoxicated bird for the big chase, Mickey dips him in starch along the way. When he eventually catches up with Black Pete, the much smaller Mickey successfully wins a swashbuckling sword fight, thus rescuing Minnie and winning the girl from the bad guy. The final scene shows the lovebirds kissing and riding happily away on the rhea. It's interesting to note the early personalities of Mickey and Minnie: As seen in *The Gallopin' Gaucho*, they're far more risqué and manic than the innocent characters they eventually evolved into, and still are to this day.

Fairbanks deliberately chose two very different leading ladies (Lupe Vélez and Eve Southern) for the film. In an interview with the *Syracuse Herald* (June 19, 1927), he explained his reasoning:

> My story really is one of contrast between good and bad. Naturally, I must have two girls — one good and one not so good.... [F]rom the feminine aspect, this film is different from anything I ever made before. In my previous pictures, all my leading ladies had to do was sit on a pedestal and let me rescue them in the last reel. Why, Lupe Vélez's role is even better than mine in *The Gaucho*.

After surviving a horrific car accident that broke her back, Eve Southern (1898–1972) retired from the film industry in 1936. *The Gaucho* marked the first time that husband and wife, Fairbanks and Pickford, appeared in the same film together. Fairbanks in the title role and Pickford in a cameo.

Whether or not Fairbanks and Lupe had an affair during the production has been debated for many years. In the Fairbanks-Pickford marriage, the jealousy, the cheating, the accusations back and forth added up to the beginning of the end for the couple dubbed "Hollywood Royalty"; the possibility of a Fairbanks-Lupe fling certainly wasn't the catalyst that split them apart. Fairbanks and Pickford officially separated in 1933 (six years after the release of *The Gaucho*). Their divorce was finalized on January 10, 1936. Pickford and Charles "Buddy" Rogers were married on June 26, 1937, their marriage lasting until Mary's death (cerebral hemorrhage) on May 29, 1979. She was 87 years

old. Rogers died on April 21, 1999, aged 94, of natural causes. Fairbanks married an English model-actress-socialite, Lady Sylvia Ashley, in Paris on March 7, 1936. Their marriage lasted until his death (heart attack) on December 12, 1939. He was 56 years old.

Many years on, Charles "Buddy" Rogers appeared in three installments of the "Mexican Spitfire" series. He played Dennis Lindsay, husband of Lupe's character, Carmelita.

Taglines for *The Gaucho*:

Saints and cutthroats! Shrines and robbers' lairs! A madcap mountain lass and a bandit chieftain — the Gaucho! A fiery tale of the most picturesque adventure beyond the Andes!

Laugh and the world laughs with you! Leap and you leap alone. Doug does both in his most sumptuous production — the greatest of all Fairbanks films!

Reviews:

Mordaunt Hall of the *New York Times* (November 22, 1927):

Whether [Lupe] is in rags or laces she gives blow for blow to the men who get in her way or incur her anger.... She flies at the Gaucho because of his jests, and you perceive a slapping and biting scene, which suddenly ends in the Mountain Girl and the Gaucho sharing an apple....

*Film Daily* (November 27, 1927):

Lupe Vélez, a newcomer, makes a definite dent in a vivid, peppy role. Watch her....

The *Berkeley Daily Gazette* (March 19, 1928):

Lupe Vélez as the wild "girl of the mountains" appears in fascinating contrast to the "girl of the miracle," played by Eve Southern, whose spiritual power over the Gaucho leader evokes the jealousy of the other....

The *Morning Herald* (May 8, 1928):

From beginning to end, Douglas Fairbanks as "The Gaucho" holds its audience. The mystery of the shrine, the towering peaks, the battles of the Gauchos, the grim odds which face the hero and the lure of gold and fair women are powerful elements for screen success.

*The Sunday Morning Star* (June 17, 1928):

Lupe Vélez is introduced to the screen as the fiery sweetheart by Fairbanks and her work is so outstandingly good even in comparison with Fairbanks' impeccable work, that she has come to the screen to stay....

Gabriel Navarro of *La Prensa* (February 8, 1931):

The Lupe Vélez we saw in *The Gaucho*, the starting point of her undeniably successful career, was not the "blondie" in love with the bandit [as the character was] in the screenplay. She was, instead, simply Lupe Vélez herself, taken to the screen with her own mannerisms, her own relentless personality.... [T]his has been the secret to her initial success.

***Stand and Deliver*** (1928) Director: Donald Crisp. Assistant Director: Emile de Ruelle. Producer: Ralph Block. Writers: Sada Cowen (writer) and John W. Krafft (titles). Cinematographer: David Abel. Costumes: Adrian. Production Company: DeMille Pictures Corporation. Distributor: Pathé Exchange. Release Date: February 19, 1928. Genre: Drama-Action-Romance. Running Time: 58 minutes. Black and White. Silent with sound effects. Language: English. Cast: Rod La Rocque (Roger Norman), **Lupe Vélez (Jania)**, Warner Oland (Chika), Louis Natheaux (Captain Dargis), James Dime (Patch Eye), Alexander Palasthy (Juja), Frank Lanning (Pietro), Bernard Siegel (Blind Operator), Clarence Burton (Commanding Officer), Charles Stevens (Krim), Donald Crisp (London Club Member [uncredited]). A 16mm print is located at the George Eastman House Motion Picture Collection in Rochester, New York. There are also copies at the New Zealand Film Archive (Wellington) and the UCLA Film and Television Archive (Los Angeles).

Lupe Vélez plays Jania, a peasant girl. *Stand and Deliver* was her only film for the year.

Reviews:

Mordaunt Hall of the *New York Times* (April 2, 1928):

The exaggerated panting of Miss Vélez during the supposedly agonizing moments may be excused by the nature of the story.

The *Sheboygan Press* (October 20, 1928):

Lupe Vélez, [is] a young Mexican player of rare promise.

Taglines:

SAVED! The man she loved, captured by bandits, faces death, until she avows herself his wife, then ... you'll regret missing this drama of love and banditry

Dashing, colorful, dramatic screen story of modern Greece, brimming with romance, love, war and banditry — a picture packed with thrills, laughs and incidents that will make your nerves tingle with excitement. There's swift-

moving drama in every scene and its beauty will charm every spectator.

### Lady of the Pavements (1929)

*Lady of the Pavements* (1929) Director: D. W. Griffith. Producer: Joseph M. Schenck. Writers: Gerrit J. Lloyd, Sam Taylor (writers), Karl Gustav Vollmöller (short story "La Paiva"). Original Music: Hugo Riesenfeld (uncredited). Cinematographers: G. W. Bitzer and Karl Struss. Costumes: Alice O'Neill. Art Director: William Cameron Menzies. Production Company: Joseph M. Schenck Productions for Art Cinema Corporation. Distributor: United Artists. Release Dates: January 22, 1929 (premiere at United Artists Theatre, Los Angeles), February 16, 1929 (general U.S. release). Genre: Drama. Black and White. Sound Mix: Mono (Movie Tone) with talking and singing sequences and sound effects. Language: English. Alternate Title: *Lady of the Night* (UK). Cast: **Lupe Vélez (Nanon del Rayon)**, William Boyd (Count Karl von Arnim), Jetta Goudal (Countess Diane des Granges), Albert Conti (Baron Finot), George Fawcett (Baron Haussmann), Henry Armetta (Papa Pierre), William Bakewell (A Pianist), Franklin Pangborn (M'sieu Dubrey, Dance Master). Soundtrack: "Where Is the Song of Songs for Me?" Words and Music by Irving Berlin; performed by Lupe Vélez; "Ae Que Ver" sung by Vélez (at the dance); "Nena," sung by Vélez. Availability: Sound discs 6 and 8 are housed and preserved at the UCLA Film and Television Archives. Three of the five double-sided sound discs, including sound for single reels, 1, 3, 5, 6, 7 and 9, are housed at the George Eastman House Motion Picture Collection in Rochester, New York. Prints exist in the Mary Pickford Institute for Film Education film collection and at the Museum of Modern Art in New York.

Harry Carr, an associate editor of the *Los Angeles Times*, also worked for several film studios during the 1920s. In 1929 he wrote a series of articles for *Smart Set* magazine reflecting on his career in silent film, and recalled some behind-the-scenes stories from the making of *Lady of the Pavements*.

Lupe wasn't an entire stranger to him; he had been in Mexico a good deal and knew of her reputation on the West Coast where she had been a belle of the cafes. He knew he was fully prepared for surprises ... and he got them!

Both Lupe and Jetta Goudal were cast in *Lady of the Pavements*. The two women ended up having a long-standing feud and Carr used a tiger analogy to describe the tension between the women on set. He explained that two tigers, on being put into one cage, will advance upon each other but will never fight. One will stare the other down, and the vanquished one will slink back into his corner, thereafter to surrender the best piece of horsemeat to the victor. After witnessing Lupe and Jetta's battles, he changed his mind, saying, "I am now in a position to announce that this is an error. What tigers say to each other is something fierce. And neither one ever gives in."

Carr said that Lupe eventually won the fight when she appeared on the program of a public preview of one of the Warner Brothers pictures. She gave a perfect imitation of Jetta's stuck-up attitude, for the edification of the packed house. It was the ultimate humiliation.

According to the papers, the feud between Lupe and Jetta was deliberately ignited. One fine example of Goudal's diva-like behavior occurred because of a simple handkerchief. The script called for Goudal to drop it in a long shot, but knowing her temperament, they bought a lush square of imported linen that cost $5. But that wasn't good enough for her; she wanted the $100 handkerchief that she had seen in an exclusive Los Angeles store and she refused to work until she got it. She held the company up for an entire day while insisting on the more expensive version. Finally she was told to use the $5 hanky or leave the studio. She gave in.

Following this incident, and various other temper tantrums and meltdowns, the moviemakers decided to teach Jetta a lesson, and they used Lupe to do it. Knowing it didn't take much to set Lupe's fuse alight, they played the women against each other on purpose. After several weeks, the situation came to a head and resulted in a knockdown, drag-out fight, with plenty of screaming and hairpulling. Lupe was stronger and could pull harder. She won. After the brawl, Jetta toed the line, at least until filming finished (*San Francisco Chronicle*, December 29, 1935).

Despite completing the film without further incident, the war between Lupe and Jetta continued for years. In his September 27, 1937, "In Hollywood" column (*Brownsville Herald*), Jimmie Fidler reported that Lupe hired a taxi driver to "rev his engine" outside Jetta's windows at 3 A.M.!

Hugh Munro Neely, film historian and curator of the Mary Pickford Institute, said:

> *Lady of the Pavements* suffers only from being somewhat predictable, but it's a charming film, beautiful to look at, and Lupe is good in it. Personally, I think that people who worship D.W. Griffith tend to give the film [the] short shrift because it's a lightweight film for him ... and it was something of an assignment, not a property that he had personally picked or developed. The first run release of the film had a few sound reels (a la *The Jazz Singer*) with music and some dialogue. Lupe sings an Irving Berlin song, "Where Is the Song of Songs for Me?" as well as two other numbers. At least two of the discs survive, but unfortunately they don't sync up with the silent version of the film (which is 830 feet shorter than the sound version) and is the only film element that we have. Lupe is seen singing in the cut-down song sequences in the silent version. It's kind of maddening to see her sing and not be able to hear her voice.

Lupe's "Where Is the Song of Songs For Me?" was released on 78 RPM disc (Label/Issue No: Victor 21932) in conjunction with the premiere of the film. It is also available on LP disc (Label/Issue No: RCA Victor LPV-538), Album Title — *Stars of the Silver Screen, 1929–1930* ("Hurray for Hollywood," Reissues). LP disc (Unnamed label 9029/3), Album Title — *Stars of Hollywood* ("Hurray for Hollywood," Reissues). LP disc (Label/Issue No: New World 238), Album Title — *The Vintage Irving Berlin* (Reissues of the 78s). Compact Disc (Label/Issue No: Flapper [England] PAST — CD-9735), Album Title — *Why Ever Did They?* (Reissues, 1923–36).

By 1935, Lupe's male lead William Boyd would begin a whole new career in the Western genre as the lovable "Hopalong Cassidy." *Lady of the Pavements* is often touted as Griffith's last silent feature, but this is only partially true. While the film is essentially a silent and was run as such in many of the theaters that were still yet to make the costly conversion to sound, the slightly longer version has some dialogue sequences inserted and a couple of musical numbers too. The silent version has eight reels; the part-talkie musical version has nine reels.

An original press release from John P. Miles of D.W. Griffith Corp. (August 1928) stated that *Lady of the Pavements* was Griffith's 431st production since his Biograph days. Miles wrote that advance bookings in talking picture theaters indicated the

film would easily gross $1,250,000 (approximately $15.5 million in 2011).

Reviews:

*Sheboygan Press* (April 9, 1929):

> [Lupe] appears as a girl of the cabarets and she does a solo dance which is one of the most captivating sights this reviewer has seen on the screen....

Mordaunt Hall of the *New York Times* (March 11, 1929):

> Miss Vélez is appearing in person before the picture four times a day. She is a fascinating, vivacious and resourceful little person who was not in the least dismayed yesterday afternoon by a few thousand persons in the audience.... [H]er songs and chatter were far more entertaining than all but a few of the Hollywood luminaries who have taken the stage before their films were offered....

***Wolf Song*** (**1929**) Director: Victor Fleming. Assistant Director: Henry Hathaway. Producer: B. P. Fineman. Writers: John Farrow, Keene Thompson (writers), Harvey Ferguson (novel), Julian Johnson (titles). Gowns for Lupe Vélez: Edith Head. Original Music: Richard A. Whiting, Leo Robin. Music Director: Irvin Talbot. Cinematographer: Allen G. Siegler. Production Company and Distributor: Paramount Pictures. Release Date: March 30, 1929. Genre: Romance-Western-Musical-Drama. Black and White. There is a silent version and a sound version (Mono with singing sequences, musical score and sound effects). Language: English. Cast: Gary Cooper (Sam Lash), **Lupe Vélez (Lola Salazar)**, Louis Wolheim (Gullion), Constantine Romanoff (Rube Thatcher), Michael Vavitch (Don Solomon Salazar), Ann Brody (Duenna), Russ Columbo (Ambrosio Guiterrez), Augustina López (Louisa), George Regas (Black Wolf), Leone Lane (Dance Hall girl). Availability: The lone print is housed at the Library of Congress. The soundtrack has been lost, along with twenty minutes of the original 80-minute length. While there is some nitrate decomposition (flickering, corrosion, burns, etc., especially in the intertitles), the story is still comprehensible. There are no title or end credits on the LoC print.

Llewellyn Miller of the *Los Angeles Record* (March 29, 1929) wrote an in-depth description and review of the film:

> Lupe Vélez is such an enchanting little star, with such brilliant charm, and such a vivid flair

for pantomime, that she almost triumphs over what is, possibly, the slowest picture released this year, *Wolf Song*....

Into a little Mexican village ride the three [men], to where Lupe, radiant in a white mantilla, is waiting to further the plot. She slips off to a dance, under the influence of a somewhat incredible love at first sight. Incredible, because the permanent wave that they gave Cooper is not becoming, and because he is aggressively untidy after two years in the "mountin's." This untidiness is not necessary, as Lupe herself proves later by living for weeks in the same dress, and looking as immaculate at the end as when she started.

After the dance her father threatens to shoot Gary on sight, so he rides up under her window, says he "has got to be travelin'" and off they go.

Some time later Lupe is seen happy in a little cottage, while Gary glooms with lanky uncertainty over the departure of his equally unwashed pals. "What's calling him is stronger than he is," so he rides glumly away, leaving Lupe without a goodbye, or visible means of support.

As you might guess, Lupe follows him in a double exposure, and he has to go back to her. An Indian shoots him, and he has to stagger the last hundreds of miles to her father's house. Once there, he crawls in and out of a series of close-ups, with the love light shining through the whiskers, and a really unnecessary amount of grease paint to Lupe's feet to tell her that "after all love is stronger than anything else."

That is the end of the picture, and a lot more exciting in print than on the screen. Louis Wolheim and Constantine Romanoff are Cooper's pals, and not once did they try to get the gal. A villainous pair of rogues they looked too. The Indians didn't try to get the gal. Nobody did. And if ever there was a heroine who merited a chase Lupe Vélez is the girl.

Victor Fleming directed what, undoubtedly is supposed to be a poignantly simple tale. Lupe sings a number of songs, and Cooper sings one. It was the first sound in the film, and that is usually startling until the ears become accustomed to the device, so it was doubly hard on him.

There are some rather nice picturesque bits of photography in *Wolf Song*. Incidentally that is what "mountin' men" sing around the campfire, and what pulls Gary back to his life of trapping rabbits and what not.

The film was based on the short story "Wolf Song" by Harvey Ferguson, published in *Red Book* (July–August 1927).

Composer Richard A. Whiting died on February 10, 1938, at the height of his career. A heart attack claimed his life when he was just 46 years old. Whiting's collaborator on *Wolf Song*, Leo Robin, also died of a heart attack, although his death came much later. He died on December 29, 1984. He was 84 years old. Whiting and Robin were inducted into the Songwriter's Hall of Fame, in 1970 and 1972, respectively.

"Mi Amado," sung by Lupe Vélez was released on 78-rpm disc (Label/Issue No: Victor 21932). Also released on CD (Label/Issue No: Flapper [England] PAST — CD — 9735), Album Title — *Why Ever Did They?* (Reissues, 1923–36).

This was Russ Columbo's film debut. Unfortunately, he's not featured in the surviving footage. His singing sequences (he also dubbed Gary Cooper's singing voice) and on-screen time is believed to be part of the missing twenty minutes. In the 2002 book *Russ Columbo and the Crooner Mystique*, authors Joseph Lanza and Dennis Penna wrote:

> Many believe footage exists of Columbo singing off-camera while Cooper mouths the words. But according to sheet music found among his possessions, Russ was slated to serenade Vélez's character Lola Salazar with "To Lola," a ballad that Leo Robin, Richard A. Whiting and Harvey Ferguson wrote, "to be sung slowly and sweetly." But as he [Columbo] later told the *Philadelphia Bulletin*: "After working six weeks (and thinking all the time I had a great break) along came cutters, and when they got through with their scissors, I found myself mostly on the cutting-room floor."

Columbo was a popular crooner and romantic idol with Valentino-like looks. He passed away on September 2, 1934, the result of an accidental shooting. He was only 26 years old. The news of his death was kept from his ailing mother Julia Columbo for *ten years*. Columbo's siblings (he was the twelfth child of Italian immigrant parents) feared their mother's weak heart would give out upon news of his death so they hatched a plan to give her the impression that he was still alive and had eloped with Carole Lombard. Telling the mother that he was on an extended European tour with his new bride, they wrote fake letters, sent gifts and flowers, staged "live" radio programs from previously recorded material, and even sent her a monthly check (drawn from his life insurance).

When newspapers reported the 1939 marriage

of Carole Lombard to Clark Gable and Lombard's own tragic death in 1942, the family edited the headlines (some of which stated, "Russ Columbo's Mother Still Doesn't Know!") to protect her from the heartbreaking truth. In doing so, they successfully kept their brother's untimely death from their frail mother for the remainder of her life. (Read more about it in Max Pierce's "Hollywood's Tragic Crooner" in the April 1999 *Classic Images*.)

Gary Cooper's much talked-about "full frontal" nude scene isn't in the existing print. His bare back is seen as he bathes and shaves by a stream; the camera then modestly moves away before his behind is revealed. Some theaters edited out the controversial bathing scene. The lone copy to survive is one of those unedited versions. It is tame by today's standards.

Lupe's gowns were designed by then-newcomer, Edith Head. Lupe's salary was more than three times higher than Coopers.

Taglines:

> LOVERS! Caught in the grip of a yearning that leaps mountains and class lines! A Love sensation you will never forget! Hear Bewitching Lupe Vélez sing, "Yo Te Amo (I Love You)" in the *Wolf Song*.

> Lupe Vélez — "The girl one never forgets" — Captures all hearts!

> You've never seen love until you've seen Lupe Vélez in the *Wolf Song*.

> Primitive, unrepressed love! The lure of a pair of flashing eyes — the spell of a dazzling smile!

> Romance at its wildest in *Wolf Song*.

Reviews:

Jerry Hoffman of the *Los Angeles Examiner* (March 29, 1929):

> Lupe is glorious to look at in some scenes. By the same token, she is pretty awful to hear in others. Her high nasal notes force a yearning in the auditor to rush down to the screen and tender a 'kerchief to Lupe. However, this be the talkie age, and they must sing. Words that undoubtedly would have sounded beautiful had Lupe sung them in Spanish were so much gibberish in English....

*The Brownsville Herald* (Sunday, April 14, 1929):

> Lupe Velez indulges in a flock of respiratory acrobatics whenever she has a love scene with Gary [Cooper]. Lupe's voice is pleasing enough but she is difficult to understand. Gary is far from being a lady killer in his makeup in this offering and it is difficult to visualize this picture

aiding his lists of conquests among the fair fans....

*The Frederick Post* (July 15, 1929):

> With the brilliant dazzling role of a beautiful dance-mad daughter of old Mexico to occupy her versatile talents, the scintillating Lupe Vélez never had a better opportunity in any production to be "just herself," than she has in the Paramount part-talking thriller, *Wolf Song*.

**Where East Is East** (1929) Director: Tod Browning. Assistant Director: William Ryan. Producers: Hunt Stromberg and Irving Thalberg (uncredited). Writers: Tod Browning (story), Harry Sinclair Drago (story), Joseph Farnham (titles), Waldemar Young (adaptation). Cinematographer: Henry Sharp. Art Director: Cedric Gibbons. Wardrobe: David Cox. Original Music: William Axt (uncredited). Production Company and Distributor: MGM. Production Dates: January 5–February 13, 1929. Release Date: May 4, 1929. Budget: $295,000. Genre: Drama-Action-Jungle-themed. Running Time: 66 minutes. Black and White. Silent. Language: English. Cast: Lon Chaney (Tiger Haynes), **Lupe Vélez (Toyo Haynes)**, Estelle Taylor (Mme. De Sylva), Lloyd Hughes (Bobby Bailey), Louis Stern (Padré), Mrs. Wong Wing (Ming). Availability: An accessible 35mm print is located at the George Eastman House Motion Picture Collection in Rochester, New York.

United Artists loaned Lupe out to MGM for her role as Lon Chaney's half-caste daughter, "Toyo Haynes." Chaney would only make two more films before his death, *Thunder* (1929) and *The Unholy Three* (1930). He died on August 26, 1930, 47 years old. Lupe and her co-star, Estelle Taylor, became life-long friends. Taylor was the last person to see Lupe alive. The costly waterfront village constructed for this film was reused in the Lionel Barrymore drama *Madame X* (1929) the following year (www.tcm.com).

*Photoplay* criticized Lupe's performance, writing, "As compared to Estelle Taylor, Lupe Vélez's work is like a candle beside a 1000-watt light." After reading the remark, Estelle called the writer and said, "I wouldn't say things like that if I were in your place. You know, Lupe might come down and show you just how hot a candle can be."

Taglines:

> Where ... thrills ... are ... thrills! ... Where Chaney is Chaney at his superb best! Where ro-

mance, drama, action surprise follow each other at bewildering speed! Where wise picture fans are headed for!

Reviews:

*Exhibitors Herald-World* (undated, 1930):

I suppose *Where East Is East* is all right ... it packs a lot of atmosphere, elephants, and things like that, and it is supposed to have happened in Shanghai or some such place ... but I went to sleep three times while Chaney, Lupe Vélez, Lloyd Hughes and Estelle Taylor were grappling for strangle-holds upon each other's emotions and I wasn't particularly sleepy either.

**Tiger Rose** (1929) Director: George Fitzmaurice. Writers: De Leon Anthony (titles), Willard Mack (play), Gordon Rigby, Harvey F. Thew (writers). Cinematographer: Tony Gaudio. Production Company and Distributor: Warner Bros. Filming Locations: Lake Arrowhead, San Bernardino, National Forest, California. Release Date: December 21, 1929. Genre: Drama. Running Time: 63 minutes. Black and White. Language: English. Cast: Monte Blue (Devlin), **Lupe Vélez (Rose)**, H.B. Warner (Dr. Cusick), Tully Marshall (Hector Collins), Grant Withers (Bruce), Gaston Glass (Pierre), Bull Montana (Joe), Rin Tin Tin (Scotty, the Dog), Slim Summerville (Heine), Louis Mercier (Frenchie), Gordon Magee (Hainey), Heinie Conklin (Gus), Leslie Sketchley (Mounted Police Officer), Fred MacMurray (Rancher [uncredited]). Availability: University of Wisconsin at Madison has a 16mm copy.

In Lupe's first all-talking film, canine star Rin Tin Tin plays Scotty, the faithful dog of Lupe's character, Rose. The Beacon Theater in New York City premiered *Tiger Rose* as their inaugural film on Christmas Eve 1929. It played to a capacity crowd of 2,600 people (*New York Times*, undated, 1930).

The film was based on the play *Tiger Rose: A Melodrama of the Great Northwest in 3 Acts* by Willard Mack. In a 1923 filmization, Lenore Ulric played Rose.

Taglines:

Untutored in the ways of civilization — yet wise with the age-old instinct of a woman fighting for her man — this unspoiled daughter of the wilderness balks the hand of the law in a series of breath-taking situations, packed with drama and thrills. ALL TALKING!

Reared in the isolation of the Canadian wilds, untamed, unspoiled, she was swept into a vortex

of love, hate and jealousy that brought her world crashing about her.

Reviews:

*Film Daily* (December 29, 1929):

Miss Vélez, as the French half-caste who is designed by several men but remains a "tiger" to all except one, is unintelligible in almost everything she says, though her vivacity sparkles through the play....

The *Sheboygan Press* (February 3, 1930):

This tale holds up from start to finish, with bright, interesting dialogue, powerful dramatic episodes and outdoor scenes that are spellbinding ... and where could one find an actress better fitted to play the wild, untamed Rose, than Lupe Vélez. Here is a girl worth watching. Every glance, every motion, every word is vivid and delightful....

*Photoplay* (1930):

Madcap Lupe Vélez[,] around whom the story revolves, contributes the best moments — and that's not saying so much....

**Hell Harbor** (1930) Producer-Director: Henry King. Writers: Rida Johnson Young (1925 novel *Out of the Night*), Fred De Gresac (adaptation), Brewster Morse (scenario), Clarke Silvernail (dialogue and screenplay). Original Music: Harvey Allen, Gene Berten, Sexteto Habanero, Ernesto Lecvona. Cinematographers: John P. Fulton, Mack Stengler. Art Director: Robert M. Haas. Production Company: Inspiration Pictures. Distributor: United Artists. Filming Location: Rocky Point, near Tampa, Florida. Release Date: March 15, 1930. Genre: Drama-Romance. Running Time: 90 minutes. Black and White. Language: English. Cast: **Lupe Vélez (Anita Morgan)**, Jean Hersholt (Joseph Horngold), John Holland (Bob Wade), Gibson Gowland (Henry Morgan), Harry Allen (Peg Leg), Al St. John (Bunion), Paul E. Burns (Blinky), George Bookasta (Spotty), Ulysses Williams (Nemo). Availability: DVD. (Two versions of *Hell Harbor* are featured on the 2011 VCI Entertainment DVD, one 84 minutes, one 64 minutes.)

Residents of Tampa were used as extras in the film. Rondo Hatton, working as a Tampa newspaper reporter at the time, caught the eye of director Henry King. Hatton had acromegaly, a progressive disease of the pituitary gland (caused by his exposure to poison gas during World War I)

that caused the bones in his hands, feet and face to swell. Hatton was covering the film for his newspaper, the *Tampa Tribune,* when King convinced him to be a part of the production. He reluctantly agreed and King deliberately placed him in full view during the cantina scenes. His cameo did not go unnoticed. In 1936 Hatton relocated to Hollywood (with his second wife) and, using his "looks" to his advantage, he had a decade-long career and starred in a string of horror films until his death (heart attack) on February 2, 1946. He was 51 years old (www.thehumanmarvels.com).

Director King was adamant about shooting the entire film on location. He instructed art director Robert M. Haas to construct the fictional Hell Harbor village securely; he wanted complete interiors and exteriors, no false fronts. The sets were put to the test during the last week of September 1929 when the cast and crew were informed of an approaching hurricane. Everyone was evacuated while Haas and his crew packed sandbags around the sets in an attempt to protect them from the fierce tropical storm heading their way. Despite rising tidewaters and strong winds, the sets designed by Haas and built by local carpenters survived a Florida hurricane! ("*Hell Harbor:* A Forgotten Film from an Overlooked Director." www.moviemorlocks.com, June 8, 2009)

The fifteen minutes of screen time on board Wade's boat took seventeen days to shoot. It takes 16½ minutes for Lupe to make her first appearance in the film.

Reviews:

*Film Daily* (February 23, 1930):

> Rugged drama of the Caribbean with Lupe Vélez excellent and her support likewise....

Doris Denbo of *Hollywood Daily Citizen* (February 28, 1930):

> [King] has used every medium at his command to add power to his story. All the sinister hopelessness of life in this little harbor of derelicts is brought out in characterization and sound. Lupe Vélez ... shows marvelous improvement in her acting....

Dorothy Herzog of the *Los Angeles Evening Herald* (March 3, 1930):

> The photography is beautiful. The story, however, is reminiscent of days gone by, particularly the extravaganza finale. Lupe gives a fine performance of a role that flashes spitfire action but little subtlety, which, of course, is not her fault....

Mordaunt Hall of the *New York Times* (March 28, 1930):

> Lupe Vélez is vivacious and believable as Anita....

*The Brisbane Courier* (Queensland, Australia, August 6, 1930):

> Lupe Vélez plays the leading role with her accustomed charm and vivacity....

**The Storm** (1930) Director: William Wyler. Producer: Carl Laemmle. Writers: John Huston, Tom Reed (dialogue), Charles A. Logue (adaptation), Langdon McCormick (play *Men Without Skirts*), Wells Root (writer). Cinematographer: Alvin Wyckoff. Production Company and Distributor: Universal Pictures. Production Dates: February–March 1930. Filming Locations: Action sequences filmed in Truckee, California. Release Dates: August 14, 1930 (Los Angeles), August 18, 1930 (New York), August 22, 1930 (general U.S. release). Genre: Drama-Western-Adventure. Running Time: 80 minutes. Black and White. Language: English. Cast: **Lupe Vélez (Manette Fachard)**, Paul Cavanagh (Dave Stewart), William "Stage" Boyd (Burr Winton), Alphonse Ethier (Jacques Fachard), Ernie Adams (Johnny Behind the 8-Ball). Availability: The film has been publicly screened at retrospectives worldwide.

John Huston's first job in the film industry was as a writer on this production. Universal had made a silent version in 1922 with Virginia Valli playing Manette.

In the 1930 version, Laura LaPlante was originally cast as the feminine lead; however, she was stricken with such a serious case of the flu that Lupe stepped in as her replacement shortly before filming began.

On July 8, 1930, a month prior to the release of *The Storm*, Louella O. Parsons reported in her *Los Angeles Examiner* column that Lupe had signed a new agreement with Universal that gave her $20,000 per picture (approximately $260,000 in 2011) instead of a straight $3,500 per week. This arrangement also allowed her to make films for other studios.

Reviews:

The *Los Angeles Times* (August 15, 1930):

> The picture provides Lupe Vélez with an excellent role. As the French Canadian to whom tragedy comes by the wholesale after a gay and capricious girlhood, Lupe sheers from mischievous humor to compelling emotion. Her voice, however, is often indistinct. One judges it not

the fault of the actress but rather of the mechanics, as William Boyd suffers in the same capacity....

The *New York Times* (August 23, 1930):

The film has particular merit in the natural performances of all three players, William Boyd, as Burr; Lupe Vélez, as Manette, and Paul Cavanagh in the role of Dave, who finally discovers that the girl doesn't love him and then leaves the other two. Miss Vélez here possesses a vivacity typical of the roles in which she has previously appeared, but it is somehow curbed by the restraint shown by the other players.

According to Elizabeth Yeaman of the *Hollywood Daily Citizen* (September 3, 1930), a Spanish-language version of *The Storm* was planned. It was never made.

**East Is West** (1930) Director: Monta Bell. Producers: E. M. Asher, Monta Bell, Carl Laemmle Jr. Writers: John B. Hymer, Samuel Shipman (play), Tom Reed (screenplay), Winifred Reeve (writer). Cinematographer: Jerome Ash. Original Music: Heinz Roemheld and Sam Perry (uncredited). Production Company and Distributor: Universal Pictures. Production Dates: August–September 1930 (24-day shooting schedule). Cost: $428,040. Release Date: October 23, 1930. Genre: Crime Drama. Running Time: 75 minutes. Black and White. Language: English. Cast: **Lupe Vélez** (**Ming Toy**), Lew Ayres (Billy Benson), Edward G. Robinson (Charlie Yong), E. Alyn Warren (Lo Sang Kee), Tetsu Komai (Hop Toy), Henry Kolker (Mr. Benson), Mary Forbes (Mrs. Benson), Edgar Norton (Thomas), Charles Middleton (Dr. Fredericks), Jean Hersholt (Man).

The *Lima News* (April 20, 1932) reported that *East is West* was:

[a] racially charged film, Lupe plays Ming Toy, a little Chinese girl who is purchased from a love boat in China by an American youth, played by Lew Ayres, and set free in the United States. Here she falls in love with her benefactor and he with her. The natural complications and prejudices against an inter-racial marriage are raised by the boy's wealthy family but they're eventually won over by the genuine sweetness and charm of Ming Toy....

Eight years earlier, Constance Talmadge played Ming Toy in the silent version of *East Is West*. George Burns and Gracie Allen were close friends with Edward G. Robinson and *East Is West* was their favorite film. They often did a sidesplitting parody of Robinson and Lupe's characters from the film.

Fay Bainter played Ming Toy in the Broadway play of the same name. It ran for three years.

Reviews:

The *Los Angeles Record* (November 14, 1930):

He's conceited, funny and entertaining, and in his characterization, Edward G. Robinson plays one of the best roles of his screen career in *East Is West*....

Playing with him, and doing some splendid acting is Lupe Vélez, as Ming Toy. Ming Toy is believed to be Chinese, is rescued from a Chinese love nest, then sold to Charlie Yong to keep her from being returned to China.

Lewis Ayres, as Billy Benson, falls in love with Ming Toy and wishes to marry her, but Charlie Yong is equally as anxious for that honor, and decides to kidnap the girl. Miss Vélez's portrayal of the Chinese girl trying to become Americanized is very good, and her broken English furnishes many laughs.

Kenneth R. Porter of the *Los Angeles Examiner* (November 14, 1930):

The charm of Lupe Vélez is reflected in the cleverly played Oriental role of Ming Toy, white girl reared by a Chinese family. Lupe's dark hair and eyes enhance the sparkling beauty of her flapperish Oriental characterization. Her accent, too, is quite befitting the part....

Taglines:

Lupe Vélez as Ming Toy, sold into bondage when the love boat sailed!

You will smile with the smiles of little Ming Toy, sob with her sobs, hate with her hates, love with her loves!

**Oriente y Occidente** (1930) Directors: George Melford, Enrique Tovar Ávalos. Producers: Paul Kohner and Carl Laemmle Jr. Writers: John B. Hymer, Samuel Shipman (play), Baltasar Fernández Cué, Tom Reed, Winifred Reeve (writers). Cinematographer: George Robinson. Original Music: Heinz Roemheld. Production Company and Distributor: Universal Pictures. Release Date: December 26, 1930. Genre: Crime Drama. Running Time: 93 minutes. Black and White. Language: Spanish. Cast: **Lupe Vélez** (**Ming Toy**), Barry Norton (Billy Benson), Tetsu Komai (Hop Toy), Manuel Arbó (Charlie Yong), Daniel Rea (Lo Sang Ki), José Soriano Viosca (Sr. Benson), André Cheron (Tomas), Lucio Villegas (Dr. Fredericks), Marcela Nivón, James Wong.

*Oriente y Occidente* is the Spanish-language ver-

sion of *East Is West* (1930). It was filmed immediately following the completion of the latter. Lupe played the role of Ming Toy in both films. This was her first all-talking Spanish feature.

**Resurrection** (1931) Director: Edwin Carewe. Producers: E. M. Asher, Edwin Carewe, Carl Laemmle Jr. Writers: Finis Fox (screenplay), Leo Tolstoy (novel *Resurrection*). Cinematographers: Robert Kurrle, Al Green (uncredited). Art Director: Herman Rosse. Original Music: Dimitri Tiomkin. Production Company and Distributor: Universal Pictures. Release Date: January 27, 1931 (New York City), February 2, 1931 (general U.S. release). Genre: Drama. Running Time: 81 minutes. Black and White. Language: English. Cast: John Boles (Prince Dmitri Nekhludoff), **Lupe Vélez** (**Katusha Maslova**), Nancy O'Neil (Princess Marya), William Keighley (Captain Schoenbock), Rose Tapley (Princess Sophya), Michael Mark (Simon Kartinkin — Innkeeper), Sylvia Nadina (Simon's Wife), George Irving (Judge), Edward Cecil (Smelkoff the Merchant), Mary Forman (Beautiful Exile), Grace Cunard (Olga), Dorothy Flood (Princess Hasan).

Director Edwin Carewe (1883–1940) and screenwriter Finis Fox (1884–1949) were brothers. *Resurrection* was one of Carewe's last films prior to his death of a heart ailment. *Resurrection* and the alternate Spanish language version, *Resurrección,* were the last two films that Fox were involved with prior to his death. Carewe insisted on Lupe as his female lead in *Resurrection*. Citing her as a "peasant girl at heart," he was confident in his choice, realizing early on that she would understand better than any contemporary star the thoughts and passions which motivate the tragic Katusha ("Lupe Vélez to Be Tried in Tragic Role." *The Milwaukee Sentinel*, February 8, 1931).

*Resurrection* was heavily touted as the successor to Universal's Academy Award–winning Best Picture, *All Quiet on the Western Front* (1930). Russian-Jewish composer Dimitri Tiomkin (1894–1979) was signed to write the score, not only because of his extraordinary talent, but also because of his knowledge of Russian culture, history and music. In late October of 1930, the *New York Morning World* reported: "Tiomkin, now living on Catalina Island and working on his score, regards his task as heaven sent. The resultant picture is expected to be the nearest approach to an original opera the screen has offered since it first lisped from a scratchy sound-track."

Tiomkin previewed a sample of a wistful lullaby and a poignant love song for the press. The final result was a score that blended with the emotions of the story so well that his compositions were as much a part of the storytelling as the actors were. However, Tiomkin was less than pleased with what happened next. In his 1959 autobiography *Please Don't Hate Me*, he wrote, "My score was massacred. It was fortissimo when it should have been a whisper, and vice versa: drowned out by noisy sound effects when it should have been expressive. You couldn't hear the Cossack song for the thunder of the horse hooves. It was my first experience of the constant war between music and sound effects...." Tiomkin also humorously recalled that a large colony of White Russian exiles in the Los Angeles area were recruited as extras, and some of them were terrified by the Cossack uniforms. Tiomkin was lavish in his praise for Lupe's performance and her conception of good music as well as her depth and understanding of his compositions (*Hollywood Daily Citizen*, September 23, 1930). During Tiomkin's five-decade career, he received nearly two dozen Academy Award score and song nominations, culminating in four Oscar wins (www.dimitritiomkin.com).

On May 23, 2004, Kessinger Publishing released a 544-page edition of *Resurrection* illustrated with photos from this film. The synopsis reads:

> Prince Nekhlyudov (John Boles) is rich and idle. Called to serve on a jury, he recognizes the accused woman as a girl he seduced years earlier. The seduction ruined her; rejected by those who had brought her up, she was reduced to prostitution. Though innocent of the murder she is accused of, Maslova (Lupe) is found guilty through a legal error. Overcome with remorse and seeing himself as the original cause of Maslova's degradation, Nekhlyudov vows to reform his life (www.amazon.com).

Carewe also directed the previous silent version of *Resurrection* in 1927. Dolores del Rio played Katusha Maslova and Rod La Rocque played Prince Nekhludov.

Lupe played the female lead in both English and Spanish versions of the film. Both were shot in 1931. When she autographed a photograph of herself from the film to her co-star, John Boles, she used the same fountain pen that Tolstoy used

in writing his famous love epic. When Tolstoy died, his eldest son, Count Ilya Tolstoy, inherited the pen. Later, he presented the pen, bearing his father's name, to a friend in Los Angeles, as a token of his regard. The pen was one of the few remaining articles that played a major part in the writings of Tolstoy ("Tolstoy Pen Thrills Lupe Vélez," *Los Angeles Evening Express,* October 8, 1930).

Reviews:

The *Los Angeles Evening Herald* (February 20, 1931):

> Upon Miss Vélez's untamed shoulders fall the quieting responsibility of being the second Hollywood actress [Dolores del Rio starred in the silent version] to essay Katusha.... Few will object to the manner in which Miss Vélez has played Katusha for the talkies.... More than any role Lupe has played, this one marks her as having the stuff stars are made of....

The *Independent Daily News* (February 20, 1931):

> Miss Vélez, who has cast aside much of her frivolous manner, has emerged in this film a serious and capable actress....

The *Reading Eagle* (May 28, 1931):

> [One] of the most gripping all-talking films of the season.... [I]t is a drama of human souls lost in passion and redeemed love. This great love epic by Tolstoy, telling of life in Russia, is one of the masterpieces of the screen."

Taglines:

> Banned from Love ... Banned from Marriage ... Sentenced to Prison for a Crime She Did Not Commit ... And the Guilty Man Goes Free!

> Youth aflame with first love! A drama overwhelming in power! A gigantic masterpiece of literacy comes to vivid life on the talking screen.

> Lupe Vélez in the screen's supreme dramatic achievement.

> Break your engagements to see this Immortal Film Epic!

**Resurrección** (1931) Directors: Eduardo Arozamena and David Selman. Producer: Paul Kohner. Writers: Baltasar Fernández Cué, Finis Fox (writers), Leo Tolstoy (novel *Resurrection*). Cinematographer: Robert Kohner. Original Music: Dimitri Tiomkin (adaptations of the English version, including "Gypsy Song," refitted with Spanish lyrics). Production Company and Distributor: Universal Pictures. Release Date: March 6, 1931.

Genre: Drama. Running Time: 85 minutes. Black and White. Language: Spanish. Cast: **Lupe Vélez (Katusha Maslova)**, Gilbert Roland, billed as Luis Alonso (Prince Dmitri Nekhludov), Miguel Faust Rocha (Capitán Shenbok), Soledad Jiménez (María), Amelia Senisterra (Princess Sofia), Eduardo Arozamena, Blanca de Castejón.

This was the alternate Spanish-language version of *Resurrection* (1931). Both films starred Lupe as Katusha Maslova.

In "Este Hollywood," an April 3, 1931, article written by Gabriel Navarro and published in *La Prensa*, he compares Lupe and Dolores del Rio's versions of Katusha Maslova, favoring the latter. Though he often praised Lupe (in many ways he contributed in stereotyping her), he was less than impressed with her dramatic efforts in this Spanish-language version. Navarro said she got "too many close-ups and too much screen time," a detriment to the rest of the cast. He continued:

> We see Dolores del Rio in the role of "Katusha," indeed, while this new "Maslova" is Lupe Vélez in disguise.... [T]here is something in Lupe Vélez that overcomes the character she is playing.... [Her performance] has quite deplorable moments, like that drunkenness scene in the last reel, and in general, all tragic scenes, [drama] being banned for Lupe....

**The Squaw Man** (1931) Producer-Director: Cecil B. DeMille. Assistant Directors: Earl Haley and Mitchell Leisen. Writers: Edwin Milton Royle (play *The Squaw Man*), Lucien Hubbard, Lenore J. Coffee (screenplay), Elsie Janis (dialogue). Cinematographer: Harold Rosson. Gowns: Adrian. Production Company and Distributor: MGM. Production Dates: February 9–March 26, 1931. Filming Locations: Agoura Ranch, Agoura, California, Hot Springs Junction, Arizona. Release Date: September 5, 1931. Genre: Western Drama. Running Time: 107 minutes. Black and White. Language: English. Cast: Warner Baxter (Jim Wingate, aka Jim Carston), **Lupe Vélez (Naturich)**, Eleanor Boardman (Lady Diana Kerhill), Charles Bickford (Cash Hawkins), Roland Young (Sir John "Johnny" Applegate), Paul Cavanagh (Henry, Earl of Kerhill), Raymond Hatton (Shorty), Julia Faye (Mrs. Chichester Jones), DeWitt Jennings (Sheriff Bud Hardy), J. Farrell MacDonald (Big Bill), Mitchell Lewis (Tabywana), Dickie Moore (Little Hal Carston), Victor Potel (Andy), Frank Rice (Grouchy), Lilian Bond (Babs), Luke Cosgrave (Shanks),

Frank Hagney (Deputy Clark), Lawrence Grant (General Stafford), Harry Northrup (Meadows, the Butler), Ed Brady (McSorley, Hawkins' Henchman), Chris-Pin Martin (Spanish Pete, Hawkins' Henchman). Availability: An accessible 35mm print is located at the George Eastman House Motion Picture Collection in Rochester, New York.

The play debuted in New York City's Wallack's Theatre on Broadway on October 23, 1905. It closed on April 1, 1906, after 222 performances. William S. Hart played Cash Hawkins and William Faversham played the lead, Jim Carston. The play had four Broadway revivals (1907, 1908, 1911 and 1921); the 1911 revival with Dustin Farnum in the lead closed after only eight performances. The 1921 revival once again starred William Faversham and ran for fifty performances at the Astor Theatre.

According to studio records, *Squaw Man* star Warner Baxter earned $5,000 per week (approximately $75,000 in 2011); Lupe earned $2,500 per week (approximately $37,500 in 2011). Roland Young earned $2,000 per week (approximately $30,000 in 2011) and J. Farrell MacDonald earned $1,000 per week (approximately $15,000 in 2011).

Due to rising costs and declining economic times, the president of Loews, Inc., Nicholas Schenck, attempted to step in and stop production before completion. DeMille told him they'd lose more money by shutting the film down and Schenck reluctantly agreed to allow DeMille to continue. *The Squaw Man* was considered a box office flop. The film marked the end of DeMille's contract with MGM.

Two silent versions of *The Squaw Man* were made in 1914 and 1918 (the former was the first feature film made in Hollywood). In the 1914 version, Naturich was played by Red Wing, a Native American actress. Ann Little took on the female lead in 1918.

Reviews:
Mordaunt Hall of the *New York Times* (September 9, 1931):

> Skillfully acted by a dozen good players, handsomely produced as to scenery and technical excellence, it makes an interesting entertainment — one that is too somber in its story to be called amusing and too neatly carpentered in its plot to be called a genuine tragedy.

**The Cuban Love Song** (1931) Director: W. S. Van Dyke. Producer: Albert Lewin. Writers: C. Gardner Sullivan, Bess Meredith (screenplay), John Lynch (adaptation), John Colton, Gilbert Emery, Robert E. Hopkins, Paul Hervey Fox (additional dialogue). Cinematographer: Harold Rosson. Gowns: Adrian. Art Director: Cedric Gibbons. Original Music: Herbert Stothart. Production Company and Distributor: MGM. Filming Locations: Scott ranch, Santa Monica, California. Release Date: December 5, 1931. Genre: Musical-Comedy-Romance. Running Time: 86 minutes (Turner Library print). Black and White. Languages: English and Spanish. Cast: Lawrence Tibbett (Terry Burke), **Lupe Vélez** (**Nenita Lopez**), Ernest Torrence (Romance), Jimmy Durante (O.O. Jones), Karen Morley (Crystal), Louise Fazenda (Elvira), Hale Hamilton (John), Mathilde Cornont (Aunt Rose), Philip Cooper (Terry Jr.), Ernesto Lecuona and the Palau Brothers' Cuban Orchestra (Orchestra).

Reviews:
The *San Jose News* (November 5, 1931):

> Miss Vélez is one of the screen's liveliest and most capable screen stars. Her earlier pictures have established her as an actress who can take a fiery role and make it 100 per cent perfect.... In *Cuban Love Song*, she has a picture which brings out all her abilities as a romantic breaker of hearts....

*The Brownsville Herald* (November 11, 1931):

> Lupe Vélez, as the fiery little Cuban charmer, has a role such as she has not had in a long time, and her captivating manner, piquant charm, and clever dancing in the Cuban episodes are outstanding....

Winifred Aydelotte of the *Los Angeles Record* (November 12, 1931):

> Well, I've heard Lawrence Tibbett sing "The Peanut Vendor," and I've seen Lupe Vélez do the rumba, and now I can go home and write my memoirs and not leave out a thing. Life can hold no more. It all happens in *The Cuban Love Song*, which opened yesterday at Loew's State, and inspired the audience, at these two spots, almost to cheering. The rest of the picture goes on, beautifully directed and beautifully photographed, but it just goes on.
>
> Tibbett, Ernest Torrence and Jimmy Durante are three marines who spend all of their time out of the brig getting into more trouble. Lupe Vélez is the little Cuban girl whom Tibbett can't forget even after all the excitement of the war and 10 years of happy marriage with Karen Morley.
>
> It must be fun working with Miss Vélez. She pounces on an emotion with a lovely Latin thor-

oughness, wrings it out with a tender, devastating understanding and leaves a delighted audience to hang it up to dry. She is perfectly and captivatingly charming in this role.... There's a lot to overlook in this film, but no matter. The comedy is so funny, the high spots so high, Miss Vélez so lovely, and Tibbett's voice so gorgeous, that the picture could have many more faults and still be priceless.

The *Spokane Daily Chronicle* (January 22, 1932):

> [Vélez] contributes a thoroughly enjoyable characterization to the film offering. Her role is considered one of the strongest she has had in recent seasons and in no manner does she fail to take advantage of the dramatic opportunities to develop it to the fullest extent....

Lupe was a favorite star amongst the prop boys, electricians and extras, so much so that when shooting on *The Cuban Love Song* finished, the prop boys presented her with a hand-carved makeup box. Lupe kissed them all on both cheeks and brought them to tears when she thanked them by saying, "Every man offer Lupe diamond, which she no take, but no man ever made anything for her with his own hands" (*Photoplay*, January 1932).

The Scott ranch in Santa Monica was transformed into a tropical environment for the fiesta scene. Car loads of imported tropical fruits, transplanted palm and mango trees, along with a myriad of extras of all nationalities, including Spanish, Mexican, Chinese and Cuban, were all on hand to make the atmosphere as authentic as possible. It was estimated that over 1,000 people were in attendance for the Cuban feast scenes. Barbeque ovens were erected for roasting whole pigs, and fruits and international delicacies were piled high on tables; one of the most comedic action sequences of the film occurs when Ernest Torrence and Jimmy Durante are struck with coconuts by an irate monkey ("*The Cuban Love Song* Has Exotic Tropical Background," *The Florence Times Daily*, November 21, 1931).

On January 1, 1932, *The Lewiston Daily Sun* reported that the Moving Picture Exhibitors' Union of Havana had declared a boycott on all MGM films until *The Cuban Love Song* was withdrawn from the market. Prominent Cubans who viewed the film in New York City returned to their home country with indignant protests. They were concerned because the film depicted Cuba as an "uncivilized country, where the natives are half-clothed and bare-footed, and magistrates impose absurd penalties on foreigners."

***Hombres de Mi Vida*** (1932) Directors: Eduardo Arozamena and David Selman. Writers: Samuel Hopkins Adams (novel *Men in Her Life*, written under the pen name Warner Fabian), René Borgia (writer). Production Company and Distributor: Columbia Pictures. Production Dates: December 1931–January 1932. Release Date: February 12, 1932. Genre: Romance Drama. Black and White. Language: Spanish. Cast: **Lupe Vélez (Julia Clark)**, Gilbert Roland (Jaime Gilman), Ramón Pereda (Andres Brennon), Carlos Villarías (Bray), Paul Ellis (Count Ivan Karloff), Luis Alberni (Gaston), Virginia Ruiz, Luana Alcañiz.

This is the Spanish-language version of the December 10, 1931, U.S. release *Men in Her Life* starring Lois Moran, Charles Bickford, Victor Varconi, Don Dillaway, Luis Alberni, Adrienne D'Ambricourt and Barbara Weeks. Moran played the lead female role of Julia Cavanaugh in the English-language version, while Lupe played Julia Clark (same character, different surname) in this foreign equivalent that was theatrically released two months later, on February 12, 1932.

***The Broken Wing*** (1932) Director: Lloyd Corrigan. Writers: Paul Dickey, Charles W. Goddard (play), Grover Jones, William Slavens McNutt (writers). Cinematographer: Henry Sharp. Original Music: Rudolph G. Kopp (uncredited), John Leipold (uncredited). Production Company and Distributor: Paramount Pictures. Release Date: March 25, 1932. Genre: Romantic Drama. Running Time: 71 minutes. Black and White. Language: English. Cast: **Lupe Vélez (Lolita)**, Leo Carrillo (Captain Innocencio Dos Santos), Melvyn Douglas (Philip "Phil" Marvin), George Barbier (Luther Farley), Willard Robertson (Sylvester Cross), Claire Dodd (Cecelia Cross), Arthur Stone (Justin Bailey), Soledad Jiménez (Maria), Julian Rivero (Bassilio), Pietro Sosso (Pancho), Chris-Pin Martin (Mexican Husband), Charles Stevens (Chicken Thief), Joe Dominguez (Captain).

Louella O. Parsons reported in her *Los Angeles Examiner* (June 16, 1931) column that Lupe's lover, Gary Cooper, would be playing the lead in *The Broken Wing* opposite Lupe's often-touted rival, Dolores del Rio. But, everything changed after a

scheduling conflict forced del Rio to drop out and Lupe was cast as her replacement. Cooper was scheduled to start filming upon his arrival home from a rest and recreation tour of Europe; for a brief moment, it looked as though the off-screen lovers would once again be teamed on screen. The excitement was short-lived, however, when soon after the switch in female leads was made, Cooper was out and Fredric March was announced as his replacement (*Hollywood Citizen News*, December 10, 1931). As it happened, March also lost the role. The part of Phil Marvin, an aviator who crashes his plane in a sleepy Mexican village, suffers a bout of amnesia and is nursed back to health by Lupe's Lolita, was eventually filled by Melvyn Douglas. Probably, the imminent breakdown of Lupe and Gary's personal relationship had a lot to do with the change in leading men.

The original play of the same name opened on Broadway at the 48th Street Theater on November 29, 1920. It closed in April of 1921 after 171 performances. There was also a 1923 silent film version. Lupe reprised her character of Lolita in the hour-long *Lux Radio Theater* broadcast of *The Broken Wing* that aired on Sunday, April 14, 1935.

The film was banned in Mexico and at the request of the Mexican minister it was also suppressed in Panama City. It had been approved by the Panama board of censors, but a showing was only halfway done when the order to cease the screening was issued. Admission fees were returned to the 400 irate audience members (*The Oakland Tribune*, July 16, 1932).

Reviews:

Mordaunt Hall of the *New York Times* (March 26, 1932):

> Melvyn Douglas does good work as the aviator. George Barbier is thoroughly pleasing as Farley. But the brunt of the story is borne by Leo Carrillo and Miss Vélez and with their spirited encounters and bright and colorful dialogue they succeed in making the utmost of their roles.

Winifred Aydelotte of the *Los Angeles Post-Record* (March 25, 1932):

> That *The Broken Wing* accomplishes its main purpose was proved yesterday by the crowds at the Paramount who enjoyed the film down to the last flap, but the picture executes another coup on its way with carefree ease. It proves just one more time that Lupe Vélez is one of the most versatile, charming, intriguing and exciting actresses on the screen today. Even with Leo

Carrillo at his dialected best as the jealous, humorously vengeful suitor, the picture would have lacked in charm and essential color without Miss Vélez, what it never could have made up in plot or any other way. She plays the role of the little senorita who puts a good bit of importance on cards and fortune telling and love potions, and who believes that the young American aviator who crashes in her garden is a direct gift from heaven.

***Kongo*** **(1932)** Director: William J. Cowen. Assistant Director: Errol Taggart (uncredited). Writers: Chester De Vonde, Kilbourn Gordon (play), Leon Gordon (screenplay). Cinematographer: Harold Rosson. Art Director: Cedric Gibbons. Production Company and Distributor: MGM. Production Dates: August 4–September 1932. Release Date: October 1, 1932. Genre: Horror Drama. Running Time: 86 minutes. Black and White. Language: English. Cast: Walter Huston (King "Deadlegs" Flint aka Rutledge), **Lupe Vélez** **(Tula)**, Conrad Nagel (Dr. Kingsland), Virginia Bruce (Ann Whitehall), C. Henry Gordon (Gregg aka Whitehall), Mitchell Lewis (Hogan), Forrester Harvey (Cookie Harris), Curtis Nero (Fuzzy). Availability: The Warner Archive Collection released the film on DVD in May 2011.

This is a remake of MGM's *West of Zanzibar* (1928). Walter Huston previously played Flint in the Broadway stage play Kongo, which opened at the Biltmore Theatre in New York City on March 30, 1926. After 135 performances, it closed in July 1926 (www.ibdb.com).

Virginia Bruce married John Gilbert during the first week of production on the film. In October of 1931, newspaper reports suggested that it was Lupe who would marry Gilbert. They never got to the altar. Bruce and Gilbert's marriage was short-lived. They failed to celebrate their second wedding anniversary, divorcing on May 25, 1934. They had one child, Susan Ann Gilbert.

In a late 1930 interview, Lupe's leading man Walter Huston said that girls like Lupe were "born to act." Lupe agreed with him, saying, "What I do on the screen is just what I did when I was a baby. Acting and life to me are both play." All throughout the filming of *Kongo*, director William J. Cowen kept chiding her for playing pranks. When she wasn't smearing paint on the face of a cameraman, she would put "Queenie," the chimpanzee, up to some serious monkey business ("Act-

ing Child's Play, Lupe Vélez Believes," *Appleton Post-Crescent*, October 22, 1932).

Reviews:

Ned Pedigo of the DeLuxe Theatre in Garber, Oklahoma, submitted his comments to the "What the Picture Did for Me" column published in the *Motion Picture Herald* (May 6, 1933):

> A terrible conglomerated mess of nothing. Had a lot of walkouts.... [W]hen one pays two bits to see this one, he doesn't forget when he comes out. Hand him 30 cents back. Beg his pardon and I doubt if that will square it.

## The Half-Naked Truth (1932)

**The Half-Naked Truth** (1932) Director: Gregory La Cava. Assistant Director: Hugh Walker (uncredited). Producers: Pandro S. Berman, David Selznick. Writers: Gregory La Cava, Corey Ford (screenplay), Ben Markson, H. N. Swanson (story), David Freedman, Harry Reichenbach (book *The Anatomy of Ballyhoo: Phantom Fame*). Cinematographer: Bert Glennon. Original Music: Max Steiner (uncredited). Special Effects: Harry Redmond Sr. Production Company and Distributor: RKO Radio Pictures. Release Date: December 16, 1932. Genre: Comedy-Romance-Musical. Running Time: 77 minutes. Black and White. Cast: **Lupe Vélez (Teresita, La Belle Sultana and Princess Exotica)**, Lee Tracy (Jimmy Bates), Eugene Pallette (Achilles), Frank Morgan (Merle Farrell), Shirley Chambers (Ella aka Eve), Franklin Pangborn (Hotel Clerk), Robert McKenzie (Colonel Munday), Mary Mason (Farrell's Secretary). Availability: A 16mm print is located at the George Eastman House Motion Picture Collection in Rochester, New York.

This movie features the only screen appearance by composer Max Steiner. He's seen briefly as a bandleader. Watch for the way Lupe throws the Chihuahua around. The tiny dog is grabbed and tossed around like an unwanted purse!

Taglines:

> Any moment her gun might point at the prominent man of this town who had done her wrong!

> This astonishing comedy drama has all the thrills you'd expect from the most spellbinding drama, and all the laughs you'd expect from the maddest of comedies!

> Just another publicity stunt.... Her agent was full of 'em!

> A million candlepower romance loaded with laughter.

*Half-Naked Truth* will startle you with its sensational scandal!

> Come! You'll See the Best Picture That Lupe Vélez or Lee Tracy Ever Made!

Reviews:

*The Lima News* (May 30, 1933):

> A lively comedy-drama that exposes the ballyhoo racket, *The Half-Naked Truth* is based on the exploits of Harry Reichenbach, perhaps the most spectacular press agent Broadway ever knew. Lee Tracy plays the role of the press agent. Lupe plays opposite him as the girl who becomes famous thru high-pressure publicity.

Bert Silver of the Silver Family Theatre in Greenville, Michigan, submitted his comments for the "What the Picture Did for Me" column published in the *Motion Picture Herald* (May 13, 1933): "This is a good entertaining picture. Story good, cast fair and both stars great."

## Hot Pepper (1933)

**Hot Pepper** (1933) Director: John G. Blystone. Writers: Barry Conners, Philip Klein (writers), Dudley Nichols (story). Cinematographer: Charles G. Clarke. Costumes: Earl Luick. Art Director: Joseph C. Wright. Production Company and Distributor: Fox Film Corporation. Genre: Comedy. Running Time: 76 minutes. Black and White. Language: English. Working Title: *Hell to Pay*. Cast: Edmund Lowe (Harry Quirt), **Lupe Vélez (Pepper)**, Victor McLaglen (Jim Flagg), El Brendel (Olsen), Lilian Bond (Hortense), Boothe Howard (Trigger Thorne), Gloria Roy (Lily), André Cheron (Maitre d').

Not one to be a mere spectator at a good fight, Lupe couldn't bear sitting out an on-screen fight either. During the filming of a brawl in *Hot Pepper*, she got so excited that she jumped in and joined the action.

Lupe plays the role of Pepper, a nightclub dancer and singer. Racketeers make their move on Harry (Edmund Lowe) and his Broadway nightclub and Jim (Victor McLaglen) and Olsen (El Brendel) were to come to the rescue. As *The Oakland Tribune* reported: "[Lupe] rushed into the mob of swinging huskies, grabbed a chair leg and did her level best in contributing to what is believed to be Hollywood's best fight scene. The Mexican actress got pushed around somewhat herself but did not complain" ("Lupe Uses Leg of Chair with Wicked Effect," January 1, 1933). *Hot Pepper* was Lupe's only film for the year.

Reviews:

Harrison Carroll of the *Los Angeles Evening Herald and Express* (January 20, 1933):

> [Lupe] is impudent, provocative and boisterous. Victor McLaglen and Edmund Lowe have to step fast to keep her from stealing the spotlight....

Harriet Parsons of the *Los Angeles Examiner* (January 20, 1933):

> Lupe Vélez, in a role that fits her so perfectly she doesn't have to act, gives the film its name. Playing a fiery little hoyden from South America, she gets a chance to kick, scream and vamp. In other words Lupe's in her element....

*Film Daily* (January 21, 1933) wrote:

> Throughout the picture, [Quirt and Flagg] are rivals for the smiles of Lupe Vélez, who handles her part of a Mexican hell-cat to perfection. At the RKO Roxy, the audience laughed throughout and applauded time and time again.

Horn and Morgan of the State Theatre in Hay Springs, Nebraska, submitted comments to the "What the Picture Did for Me" column in the *Motion Picture Herald* (May 6, 1933):

> Not nearly as "hot" as we had been led to believe when we read reviews and some exhibitors' remarks. It was rather suggestive in some spots and the dancing was quite torrid....

Thomas B. Orr of the Liberty Theatre in Attalla, Alabama, submitted his "What the Picture Did for Me" comment a week later:

> Too hot for small towns. We got by with it, but there is no excuse for parts of this picture. A certain class like it, but it is not the class that will keep you in business.

**Palooka** (1934) Director: Benjamin Stoloff. Assistant Director: Joe Cooke. Producer: Edward Small. Writers: Ham Fisher (comic strip), Jack Jevne, Arthur Kober, Gertrude Purcell (screenplay), Murray Roth, Ben Ryan (additional dialogue). Cinematographer: Arthur Edeson. Art Director: Albert S. D'Agostino. Production Company: Edward Small Productions. Distributor: United Artists. Production Date: October–November 1933. Release Date: January 26, 1934. Genre: Comedy. Running Time: 86 minutes. Black and White. Language: English. Alternate Titles: *Joe Palooka* (USA), *The Great Schnozzle* (UK). Cast: Jimmy Durante (Knobby Walsh), **Lupe Vélez** (**Nina Madero**), Stuart Erwin (Joe Palooka), Marjorie Rambeau (Mayme Palooka), Robert Armstrong (Pete "Goodtime" Palooka), Mary Carlisle (Anne), William Cagney (Al "Mac" McSwatt), Themla Todd (Trixie), Gus Arnheim (Orchestra Bandleader), Franklyn Ardell (Doc Wise), Tom Dugan (Whitey, Joe's Trainer), Louise Beavers (Crystal, Mayme's Housekeeper), Fred "Snowflake" Toones (Smokey), Guinn "Big Boy" Williams (Slats). Availability: VHS and DVD.

Reviews:

Mordaunt Hall of the *New York Times* (February 28, 1934):

> Mr. Durante volleys wisecracks throughout the film. He is his inimitable self, boasting one moment of his profile and the next trying out his singing voice on the public. Lupe Vélez is vivacious as the siren Nina. Marjorie Rambeau plays Palooka's mother in a satisfactory fashion. Mary Carlisle personates the girl back home who is idiotic enough to fall in love with Palooka.

This movie was spun off into a series of "Joe Palooka" films (*Joe Palooka, Champ* [1946], *Gentleman Joe Palooka* [1946], *Joe Palooka in the Knockout* [1947], *Joe Palooka in Fighting Mad* [1948], *Joe Palooka in Winner Take All* [1948], *Joe Palooka in the Big Fight* [1949], *Joe Palooka in the Counterpunch* [1949], *Joe Palooka Meets Humphrey* [1950], *Joe Palooka in Humphrey Takes a Chance* [1950], *Joe Palooka in the Squared Circle* [1950], *Joe Palooka in Triple Cross* [1951] and the TV series *The Joe Palooka Story* (1954–1955). Following his stint in the "Mexican Spitfire" series, Leon Errol took on Jimmy Durante's role of Knobby Walsh in seven of the *Joe Palooka* films between 1946 and 1950.

Lupe would go on to have a relationship with Guinn "Big Boy" Williams and by November of 1940 she officially announced her engagement to him (he had an uncredited role as Slats in this film). Lupe was a foot and a half shorter and 150 pounds lighter than "Big Boy" but that didn't stop her from physically assaulting him. Despite his reputation as a mauler, if his feelings were hurt, "Big Boy" would cry like a baby. With Lupe he would fight hard and cry harder. Errol Flynn once commented that they were the oddest couple he had ever seen. Ironically, it was at Flynn's house where their rocky relationship ended. In a fit of rage, Lupe picked up a large, framed photograph of "Big Boy" and smashed him over the head with it, repeatedly, until she broke the frame. She then took out the photo, tore it into pieces,

Lupe in costume as "Slim Girl" with two of her beloved Chihuahua dogs, relaxing in between scenes for *Laughing Boy* (1934).

threw them on the floor, and urinated on the pile. Lupe screamed a tirade of Spanish insults during the entire incident. Needless to say, the engagement was off (Conner, *Lupe Vélez and Her Lovers*).

***Laughing Boy*** (1934) Director: W. S. Van Dyke. Producers: Hunt Stromberg, W. S. Van Dyke. Writers: Oliver La Farge (novel), John Colton, John Lee Mahin (screenplay), John Huston (original screenplay adaptation [uncredited]). Cinematographer: Lester White. Wardrobe: Dolly Tree. Art Director: Edwin B. Willis. Original Music: Herbert Stothart. Production Company and Distributor: MGM. Filming Location: Navajo Indian Reservation, Arizona. Production Dates: November 1933–January 31, 1934. Release Date: April 13, 1934. Genre: Drama-Romance. Running Time: 79 minutes. Black and White. Language: English. Cast: Ramon Novarro (Laughing Boy), **Lupe Vélez (Slim Girl)**, William B. Davidson (George Hartshone), Chief Thunderbird (Laughing Boy's Father), Catalina Rambula (Laughing Boy's Mother), Harlan

Knight (Wounded Face), Philip Armenta (Yellow Singer), Deer Spring (Jesting Squaw's Son), Pellicana (Red Man). Availability: Long thought to have been a "lost" film, *Laughing Boy* prints have been found and restored over the years.

Director William Wyler wrote Lupe a letter on April 12, 1933, and in a postscript he wrote that he saw "where you got your wish since Johnny [Weissmuller] will be doing *Laughing Boy* after all and I know he'll be very good." It wasn't to be. Ramon Novarro ended up with the lead role.

In his 1980 autobiography *An Open Book*, John Huston revealed that he had written the script for *Laughing Boy* after reading the 1929 Oliver La Farge novel of the same name. The novel won the 1930 Pulitzer Prize and Huston convinced Universal Studios head Carl Laemmle Jr. to buy the rights. The picture was delayed for one reason or another, and finally Universal sold the rights to MGM. Huston said, "[MGM] proceeded to make a wretched, vulgar picture out of it in 1934, starring Ramon Novarro and Lupe Vélez. It should be done again."

The film cost $518,000 (approximately $8.5 million in 2011). Its domestic gross was $180,000; the foreign gross $84,000. In the days before DVD distribution, box office receipts were the only chance studios had to regain their production costs. *Laughing Boy* bombed — big time. After domestic and foreign grosses were tallied, the studio was over a quarter of a million dollars in the red (Ellenberger, *Ramon Novarro: A Biography of the Silent Film Idol*).

Novarro was so embarrassed by the film, he couldn't sit through it. Likewise, Oliver La Farge was so angered by the bastardization of his Pulitzer Prize–winning novel that when he met screenwriter John Lee Mahin following the film's release,

he threw his drink (glass included) in Mahin's face (Soares, *Beyond Paradise: The Life of Ramon Novarro*).

*Variety* (May 15, 1934) noted that certain parts of the film, including the scene where Lupe's character Slim Girl and Novarro's character Laughing Boy camp out together, were deemed offensive by the New York Censor Board. The controversial scenes were deleted before all screenings in that state. The version viewed by the author had this scene included.

Reviews:

*Variety* (May 15, 1934):

> *Laughing Boy* is below average entertainment despite the handsome production and care it has received. For one thing, the simulation of Indian accents, notably by Ramon Novarro, leaves something to be desired. Most of the time the star sounds like Maurice Chevalier.

Elizabeth Yeaman of the *Hollywood Citizen News* (May 18, 1934):

> [*Laughing Boy*] is handicapped at the outset by flagrant miscasting of the title role [Novarro].... Lupe Vélez fares a little better in the role of Slim Girl. Her interpretation may deviate from that of the book, but at least it is interesting and fairly credible....

The *Los Angeles Evening Herald and Express* (May 18, 1934):

> In the title role of *Laughing Boy*, Ramon Novarro plays with fine understanding and sincerity.... Slim Girl, the civilized Navajo maiden, who finds she cannot live entirely in the white man's nor her native world, is given an appealing interpretation by Lupe Vélez. The difficult role is a natural for Lupe and she does it in the approved Vélez manner....

*Prescott Evening Courier* (June 8, 1934):

> The sparkling vigor of Lupe Vélez was never more vividly presented than as Slim Girl, the Indian girl who knows love in the civilized reservation towns but still craves the primitive men of her tribe.... More than a thousand Navajos were used during the filming.

J. J. Medford of the Orpheum Theatre in Oxford, North Carolina, submitted his comments to the "What the Picture Did for Me" column published in the *Motion Picture Herald* (September 1, 1934):

> Entirely too sexy even for adults and all of my patrons were displeased. This could have been a great picture with a few changes, but Metro does not care to please the public. Played on bargain day to poor business....

A traditional Native American blanket that Novarro has wrapped around him in some scenes very clearly has the controversial swastika symbol pattern on it. This is historically correct. The ancient symbol was adopted by Adolf Hitler for the Nazi Party in 1920 and to this day, it is notoriously known throughout the Western world as a representation of hate, war, anti–Semitism and death; but prior to the German ruination of the symbol, it had quite the opposite meaning. The swastika represented peace, sun, strength, good luck and good fortune. Native Americans (mostly Navaho), Asian culture and several Indian religions such as Hinduism, Buddhism and Jainism, commonly used the swastika in a peaceful way for centuries. But, despite being used in a positive (and religious) light by many people for thousands of years, the swastika's original meaning has been forever stigmatized by Nazi Germany. The symbol is now outlawed in Germany.

***Strictly Dynamite*** (1934) Director: Elliott Nugent. Producers: Pandro S. Berman, H. N. Swanson. Writers: Robert T. Colwell, Robert A. Simon (play), Jack Harvey, Milton Raison, Ralph Spence, Maurine Dallas Watkins (writers). Cinematographer: Edward Cronjager. Costumes: Walter Plunkett. Choreographers: Hermes Pan (uncredited). Special Effects: Harry Redmond Sr. Production Company and Distributor: RKO Radio Pictures. Release Date: May 11, 1934. Genre: Comedy-Musical. Running Time: 71 minutes. Black and White. Language: English. Cast: Jimmy Durante (Moxie Slaight), **Lupe Vélez (Vera Mendez)**, Norman Foster (Nick Montgomery), William Gargan (Georgie Ross), Marian Nixon (Sylvia Montgomery), Eugene Pallette (Sourwood Sam), Sterling Holloway (Elmer Fleming), Minna Gombell (Miss LeSeur), Leila Bennett (Miss Mary Hoffman), Franklin Pangborn (Mr. Bailey), Berton Churchill (Mr. Rivers), Irene Franklin (Mrs. Figg), Jackie Searl (Robin Figg), Stanley Fields (Puss — Bodyguard), Tom Kennedy (Junior — Bodyguard), Donald Mills, Harry Mills, Herbert Mills, John Mills (The Mills Brothers). Availability: The Warner Archive Collection released the film on DVD in May 2011.

Review:

The *Mason City Globe Gazette* (July 2, 1934):

Jimmy Durante and Lupe Vélez put on the sort of performance one would expect in *Strictly Dynamite*, aided and abetted considerably by a good supporting cast and the Four Mills brothers.

The LP Disc (Soundtrack) *Playboy of Paris, The Way to Love, The Beloved Vagabond, Strictly Dynamite, The Singing Kid* (Label/Issue No: Caliban 6013) includes, "Hot Patatta," "I'm Putty in Your Hands," "Money in My Clothes," "Oh Me, Oh My, Oh You, " and "Swing It Sister," performed by Jimmy Durante, Lupe Vélez and the Mills Brothers. No liner notes.

Taglines:

The title describes this one! It's loaded with comedy T.N.T. The cast ignites the fuse, which explodes with laughter.

Romance and Uproarious Comedy Combined in a Colorful Behind-the-Scenes Broadcasting Satire.

## *Hollywood Party* (1934)
Directors: Richard Boleslawski (uncredited), Allan Dwan (additional sequences — uncredited), Edmund Goulding (uncredited), Russell Mack (uncredited), Charles Reisner (uncredited), Roy Rowland (uncredited), George Stevens (comic segments — uncredited), Sam Wood (uncredited). Producers: Howard Dietz, Louis Lewyn, Harry Rapf (all uncredited). Writers: Howard Dietz (screenplay), Arthur Kober (screenplay), Richy Craig Jr. (comedy dialogue — uncredited), Herbert Fields (dialogue — uncredited), Edmund Goulding (contributor to screenplay), Edgar Allan Woolf (story — uncredited). Cinematographer: James Wong Howe. Art Director: Frederic Hope. Costumes: Adrian. Original Music: William Axt (uncredited). Production Company and Distributor: MGM. Release Date: May 24, 1934 (New York City), June 1, 1934 (general U.S. release). Genre: Comedy-Musical. Running Time: 68 minutes. Black and White with Technicolor Animated Sequence. Language: English. Alternate Titles: *Hollywood Revue of 1933* and *Star Spangled Banquet* (working titles). Cast: Stan Laurel (Stan), Oliver Hardy (Ollie), Jimmy Durante (Himself/Schnarzan), Jack Pearl (Baron Munchausen), Polly Moran (Henrietta Clemp), Charles Butterworth (Harvey Clemp), Eddie Quillan (Bob Benson), June Clyde (Linda Clemp), Mickey Mouse (Himself), **Lupe Vélez (The Jaguar Woman/Jane in Schnarzan Sequence/Herself)**, George Givot (Liondora aka Grand Royal Duke), Richard Carle (Knapp), Robert Young (Himself/Radio Announcer/Cameo Appearance [uncredited]). Availability — VHS and DVD.

In May 1934, despite many big names being involved in its production (writers, producers, and directors), *Hollywood Party* premiered almost incognito. There were no producer or director credits to be seen because no one wanted their names attached to it. This was a clear declaration of failure by the studio. A choppy mess of a film, it was salvaged (barely!) and released in an attempt to recoup what money had already been spent after irate MGM boss Louis B. Mayer shut it down in mid-production.

The tit-for-tat egg-breaking routine between Laurel and Hardy and Lupe Vélez is a Hollywood gem and reason enough to watch for this scene alone. Along with Lupe's amusing "Schnarzan" parody with Jimmy Durante, these two brief moments of hilarity are about the only glue that holds this weak production together. This was Lupe and Jimmy Durante's fourth and last film together. Durante's real-life wife, Jeanne Olsen, has a cameo towards the end.

Harrison Carroll reported in his *Los Angeles Evening Herald and Express* column (February 5, 1934) that during the filming of *Hollywood Party*, Lupe was required to hang upside down by her knees from a crossbar on set. After a minor technical difficulty, Lupe was left hanging for longer than expected. Getting redder by the second, Lupe shouted, "Hurry up there, I'm no Tarzan, I'm only his mate!"

## *The Morals of Marcus* (1935)
Director: Miles Mander. Assistant Director: Arthur Barnes. Producer: W. J. Locke. Writers: Guy Bolton, Miles Mander, H. Fowler Mear (writers), W.J. Locke (play). Cinematographer: Sydney Blythe. Art Director: James A. Carter. Production Company and Distributor: Gaumont British Picture Corporation. Filming Location: Twickenham Film Studios, St. Margarets, Twickenham, Middlesex, England. Genre: Comedy. Running Time: 75 minutes. Black and White. Language: English. Cast: **Lupe Vélez (Carlotta)**, Ian Hunter (Marcus Ordeyne), Adrianne Allen (Judith), Noel Madison (Tony Pasquale), J.H. Roberts (Butler), H.F. Maltby, Arnold Lucy, Frank Atkinson (Ship Steward), D.J. Williams, James Raglan, Agnes Imlay, Johnny

Lupe holds her own with Stan Laurel and Oliver Hardy in the hilarious egg-breaking scene from *Hollywood Party* (1934). This skit is the definite highlight of a weak mishmash of a production.

Nitt (Nightclub Tap Dancer). Availability: A viewing copy is available at the British Film Institute.

The earlier movie versions of W.J. Locke's play were *The Morals of Marcus* (1915) and *Morals* (1921). In this version, Lupe plays Carlotta, a half–English, half–Syrian harem girl who takes refuge in the cabin of Marcus (Ian Hunter), a middle-aged archaeologist. Upon being discovered, she explains that she's escaping an arranged marriage. He sympathizes with her plight and takes her to his home. She falls in love with him, but her amorous feelings are at first rebuffed. When Judith (Adrianne Allen), a society divorcee who loves Marcus tries to get rid of Carlotta, Marcus realizes he's in love with her after all.

Reviews:

The *New York Times* (January 13, 1936):

> Despite its moments of exhilarating comedy, the film manages to be aggressively dull when Lupe Vélez is not busy exercising her fiery temper or

being unconsciously amusing in her attempts to scale the proverbial dramatic heights.

*Film Daily* (January 14, 1936):

> Fairly entertaining romantic comedy aided by the sprightly work of Lupe Vélez plus good support....

*Kinematograph Weekly*, April 4, 1935:

> Lupe Vélez is exceedingly good as the wild Carlotta, her volatility is delightfully feminine and she manages to win much sympathy.... [G]ood story [and] excellent acting by box office stars.

***Gypsy Melody*** (1936) Director: Edmond T. Gréville. Assistant Director: John "Pinky" Green. Producers: Leon Hepner and Emil E. Reinert. Writers: Irving LeRoy, Dan Weldon. Cinematographer: Claude Friese-Greene. Production Company: British Artistic Films. Distributors: Wardour Films. Filming Location: UK. Release Date: July 27, 1936. Genre: Comedy-Musical. Running

Time: 77 minutes. Black and White. Language: English. Cast: **Lupe Vélez (Mila)**, Alfred Rode (Captain Eric Danilo), Jerry Verno (Madame Beatrice), Raymond Lovell (Count Chamberlain), Margaret Yarde (Grand Duchess), Fred Duprez (Herbert P. Melon). Availability: In recent years, a print of this movie was found and donated to the BFI by the French national archive. It is missing approximately five minutes of footage (www.britishpictures.com).

In June 1935, director Edmond T. Gréville established his own London-based company, British Artistic Films. It was not a successful venture. *Gypsy Melody*, a remake of *Juanita* (1935), was its only feature production (www.screenonline.org.uk).

*Monthly Film Bulletin* (August 1936) wrote, "Lupe Vélez's portrayal of a gypsy [dancer] is definitely musical comedy-ish.... [T]he music constitutes the film's major appeal...."

**Stardust** (1937) Director: Melville W. Brown. Producer: William Rowland. Writers: John E. Harding (story), John Meehan (screenplay). Cinematographers: Jack A. Marta and John Stumar. Special Effects: Len Lye. Production Company: William Rowland Productions. Distributor: British Lion Film Corporation in the UK, Grand National Pictures in the U.S. Filming Location: UK. Genre: Comedy-Musical-Romance. Running Time: 75 minutes (UK), 67 minutes (USA). Black and White. Language: English. Alternate Titles in the U.S.: *Mad About Money* and *He Loved an Actress*. Cast: Ben Lyon (Roy Harley), **Lupe Vélez (Carla de Huelva)**, Wallace Ford (Peter Jackson), Jean Colin (Diana West), Harry Langdon (Otto Schultz), Mary Cole (Peggy), Cyril Raymond (Jerry Sears), Ronald Ward (Eric Williams), Arthur Finn (J.D. Meyers), Philip Pearman (Prince), Andreas Malandrinos (Ambassador), Olive Sloane (Gloria Dane), Peggy Novak (Secretary), John Stobart (Headwaiter), Ronald Hill (Attorney), Albert Whelan (Judge), Alan Shires (Dance Partner). Availability: DVD.

This movie was originally filmed in an experimental color process that was so substandard, the film was released in black and white (*Variety*, May 25, 1938). *Today's Cinema* (November 30, 1938) wrote that it was a "cut-to-pattern story" of film production presumed to be financed by alleged wealthy cattle queen Carla de Huelva (Lupe). The story was called "bemusing," and the song-and-

dance scenes (of Busby Berkeley proportions) provided "aural and ocular appeal." Lupe doesn't appear until the twenty-one-minute mark.

**High Flyers** (1937) Director: Edward F. Cline. Producer: Lee S. Marcus. Writers: Bert Granet, Byron Morgan, Benny Rubin (writers), Victor Mapes (play *The Kangaroos*). Cinematographer: Jack Mackenzie. Costumes: Renié. Art Directors: Field M. Gray, Van Nest Polglase. Original Music: Roy Webb. Special Effects: Vernon L. Walker. Production Company and Distributors: RKO Radio Pictures. Production Dates: August–September 1937. Release Date: November 26, 1937. Genre: Comedy. Running Time: 70 minutes. Black and White. Language: English. Alternate Titles — *Fall Guys* (working title). Cast: Bert Wheeler (Jeremiah "Jerry" Lane), Robert Woolsey (Pierre Potkin), **Lupe Vélez (María Juanita Rosita Anita Moreno del Valle)**, Marjorie Lord (Arlene Arlington), Margaret Dumont (Martha Arlington), Jack Carson (Dave Hanlon), Paul Harvey (Horace Arlington), Herbert Clifton (Stone, the Butler), Charles Judels (Mr. Fontaine), Lucien Prival (Mr. Panzer), Herbert Evans (Mr. Hartley), George Irving (Chief of Police).

The *Hammond Times* (June 22, 1937) reported that Lupe had been signed as the feminine lead in the latest Wheeler and Woolsey comedy *Fall Guys*. (*Fall Guys* was the working title of *High Flyers*.) Marjorie Lord played Arlene Arlington in the film and she remembered Lupe's colorful language very well, saying:

> Oh, my God. I'd done that play, *The Old Maid*, with Helen Menken, who had a foul mouth, but Lupe Vélez, she was full of energy, and her language was something. She was an exhibitionist ... she went right through you! I liked her, but she took over. You knew she was there! (www.classicimages.com).

Lupe had a gift for mimicking people flawlessly and she showcased her flair in this film by doing impersonations of Simone Simon, Dolores del Rio, and even Shirley Temple! Lupe begins to sing, then mid-way through the song she wraps a shawl over her head, purses her lips and sings to imitate del Rio. With ease, she switches to the more demure persona of Simon, then straight into a Spanish-accented version of Temple's signature song "On the Good Ship Lollipop," complete with a bonnet and curls! At parties, Lupe would also do a contemptuous, sidesplitting impersonation of Adolf

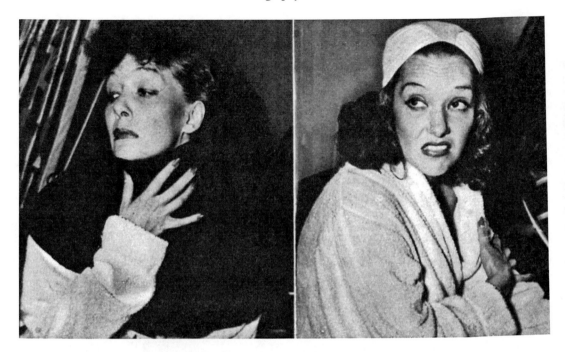

**Lupe was a natural mimic and her Hollywood peers were all fair game. At left she's seen impersonating Katharine Hepburn; at right she transforms herself into Gloria Swanson.**

Hitler. She also does the Hitler impersonation in *Honolulu Lu* (1941).

Aside from Lupe's solo number, Robert Woolsey does a couple of dance routines with Lupe, including a cute number complete with well-timed tambourines. Bert Wheeler does a lengthy Chaplin impersonation, followed by an appearance in the now politically incorrect blackface that is cringe-inducing by today's standards. These musical snippets are the brief highlights in an otherwise weak story (consisting of manic mish-mash and too much double-talk) that goes nowhere.

Sidney Skolsky of *Hollywood Citizen News* (August 23, 1937) reported that when Lupe wasn't working in a scene, she was asked to leave the set because she made too much noise. A follow-up story in the same paper (August 25, 1937) said that Lupe was much quieter than she used to be, but she still managed to be the noisiest person at the RKO studio. She would often be seen riding her bicycle between scenes, usually with a dog or two in the basket up front. She had no bell, she'd just yell at people to "get out of the way" if a collision was imminent. And whenever she visited a film executive, she wouldn't park her bike, she'd take it right into the office with her. She explained that it wasn't

because she didn't trust people at the studio, it was simply because she loves her bicycle so much.

Shortly after filming ended on *High Flyers*, Robert Woolsey, one half of the popular comedy team Wheeler and Woolsey, was bedridden with a kidney complaint that would take his life just over a year later. He died on October 31, 1938. He was 49 years old. Bert Wheeler continued in show business as a solo performer but he never again reached the success that he enjoyed with his longtime partner. He died of emphysema on January 18, 1968. He was 72 years old.

Review:

*Film Daily* (December 15, 1937):

> This is a very slapstick production, done in the traditional Wheeler-Woolsey technique of goofy nonsense, and given some comedy class with the fine work of Lupe Vélez. The laughs come right through the footage, so that this is the answer to the critics who sniff at this type of low comedy…. Lupe Vélez proves herself a real comedienne, and very delightful….

**La zandunga** (1938) Director: Fernando de Fuentes. Co-Director: Miguel M. Delgado. Producer: Pedro A. Calderón. Writers: Fernando de Fuentes, Rafael M. Saavedra (dialogue and screen-

In the Wheeler and Woolsey comedy *High Flyers* (1937), Lupe received third billing behind the long-standing, popular comedy duo, and the lead female role. *High Flyers* was Robert Woolsey's final film.

play), Salvador Novo (dialogue). Cinematographers: Ross Fisher, Alex Phillips. Costumes: Marissa. Art Director: Jorge Fernández. Original Music: Lorenzo Barcelata, Max Urban. Choreographer: Felipe L. Obregón. Production Company: Films Selectos. U.S. Distributor: Cinexport Distributing (Spanish language with English subtitles). Filming Location: Mexico City. Release Dates: March 17, 1938 (USA), March 18, 1938 (Mexico). Genre: Drama-Romance. Running Time: 100 minutes. Black and White. Language: Spanish. Cast: **Lupe Vélez (Lupe)**, Rafael Falcón (Ramón Miranda), Arturo de Córdova (Jauncho), Joaquín Pardavé (Don Catarino, the Mayor), Carlos López (The Secretary), María Luisa Zea (Marilú), Manuel Noriega (Don Eulogio), Rafael Icardo (Don Atanasio), Carmen Corrés (Petra), Antonio Mendoza (Pedro), Enrique Carillo (Juan), Álvaro González (José Antonio), Jesús Melgarejo (El Número Doce), Hernán Vera (Don Manuel), David Silva, José Elías Moreno. Availability: DVD.

Miguel M. Delgado was credited as co-director on the film because he stepped in to complete the production after director Fernando de Fuentes bowed out due to illness. Delgado had been married to Lupe's sister Josephine (aka Josefina) for a number of years; by the time *La zandunga* was released, they were divorced. No doubt Lupe pulled a few strings to get Delgado his position on *La zandunga*. In fact, in Hollywood, she had helped him every step of the way, as she consistently did with all members of her family.

In 1929, soon after moving to the United States, Lupe got Delgado (her brother-in-law) a job as her boyfriend Gary Cooper's secretary. He went on to work as an assistant director to Henry Hathaway but later returned to his native Mexico where he became an actor, screenwriter and prolific director. Between 1941 and 1990, he directed 139 films. He died on January 2, 1994, at age 88.

By 1938, Lupe's sister Josephine had entered the United States once again. On her handwritten en-

**A beautifully lit promotional shot of Lupe in *La zandunga* (1938). Photograph courtesy of the Agrasánchez Film Archive.**

trance document (similar to a visa and used for people entering the U.S. on foot or by car), she listed herself as a divorcee and stated she was entering for "6 months as a singer." She went on to marry Pvt. Gordon Anderson. At the time of Lupe's death in 1944 and all throughout probate proceedings regarding Lupe's estate, she was referred to as Mrs. Josephine Anderson.

Lupe's salary for *La zandunga* was $12,500 per week (approximately $195,000 in 2011). The premiere of *La zandunga* fell on the same day (March 18, 1938) that Mexican President Lázaro Cárdenas announced the expropriation of foreign oil companies into Mexico. It was a celebratory day for the Mexican people and there were huge fiestas. Still, the theater was filled to capacity for the premiere of *La zandunga*. It spoke volumes for Lupe's popularity in her home country. This is the only film in which Lupe's character name is also Lupe.

By 1944, Lupe was engaged to her *La zandunga* co-star, Arturo de Córdova. They never married.

*La zandunga* was so popular with audiences that it enjoyed countless revivals in theaters all the way into the mid–1950s.

***The Girl from Mexico*** (1939) Director: Leslie Goodwins. Assistant Director: Sam Ruman (uncredited). Producer: Robert Sisk. Writers: Lionel Houser (story and screenplay), Joseph Fields (screenplay). Cinematographer: Jack Mackenzie. Costumes: Renié. Art Director: Van Nest Polglase. Original Music: Albert Hay Malotte, Harry Tierney, Roy Webb (all uncredited). Production Company and Distributor: RKO Radio Pictures. Production Date: March 1939. Release Date: June 2, 1939. Genre: Comedy-Romance-Musical. Running Time: 71 minutes. Black and White. Language: English. Cast: Lupe Vélez (Carmelita Fuentes), Donald Woods (Dennis "Denny" Lindsay), Leon Errol (Uncle Matthew "Matt" Lindsay), Linda Hayes (Elizabeth Price), Donald MacBride (L.B. Renner), Edward Raquello (Tony Romano),

Elisabeth Risdon (Aunt Della Lindsay), Ward Bond (Mexican Pete). Availability: DVD (part of the "Mexican Spitfire: Complete 8-Movie Collection"). A four-DVD set, it was released by the Warner Archive Collection in May 2011.

RKO boss George Schaeffer personally picked Lupe for the lead role. Her name appeared above the title, with Donald Woods and Leon Errol receiving second and third billing, respectively.

In one scene, Lupe is resisting Edward Raquello's romantic advances. As they're struggling on a bed, Donald Woods storms into the room to rescue her. He takes a swing at Raquello and he in turn gives Woods a left hook that knocks him out of camera range and onto a mattress on the floor. Not one to miss out on a good fight, Lupe hops off the bed and smashes a breakaway vase over Raquello's head. The scene called for this rough 'n' tumble physicality; however, Lupe hit Raquello so hard, he was seriously dazed. As Raquello lay groaning on the floor, still not quite knowing what hit him or even where he was, Lupe clapped her hands and laughed hysterically, saying, "We do it again, please? Thee sees fon!" (Harrison, Paul. "That Fiery Lupe Vélez Is Fizzing Firecracker on Movie Set," *San Jose Evening News,* April 11, 1939).

Made on the cheap, the "Mexican Spitfire" series were considered B-films and mostly shown as the second billed feature with a bigger-budgeted counterpart. Ironically, they often proved more popular with audiences than the much-hyped feature presentation.

Lupe's most noted Hollywood nickname, "The Mexican Spitfire," was inspired by this series. Throughout her career, she was also called "The Mexican Hurricane," "The Mexican Wildcat," "The Mexican Madcap," "Whoopee Lupe" and "The Hot Tamale," just to name a few. But, to her pals, she was simply "Loop."

Mexican-born Max Wagner (1901–1975) was a bit-part actor who would play the mostly uncredited roles of a Cab Driver, Thug, Gangster, Delivery Man, Sailor, Janitor, Policeman, Reporter, Guard, etc. He appeared in over 300 films during his long Hollywood career. He usually played a bartender-waiter-type in the "Mexican Spitfire" series, and he was also required to monitor Lupe's manic Spanish ad libs for profanity. While most English-speaking audiences had no clue what Lupe was yelling during one of her Spitfire rages, she

still wasn't allowed to curse. Despite Wagner's acting scenes being minimal, he was paid for the duration of the production to just sit on the set and listen to Lupe yell ("Lupe Vélez Is Censored on the Set," *Hammond Times*, March 12, 1939).

Reviews:

Joseph Gray of Gray Theatre, Pennsylvania, submitted his comments for the popular "What the Picture Did for Me" column published in the *Motion Picture Herald* (December 14, 1940): "Just the type for our patronage. Everyone seemed to enjoy it. This girl Lupe puts action into this picture. Very good supporting cast. Good show any day."

Taglines:

Caramba! Cyclone! Fireworks!

Oh, how she loves! She's dynamite! He lights the fuse!

Here Come the Fireworks!

See the sights! Love-fights—"mike" fright! Don, the big "ad" man—and luscious Lupe, sizzling sagebrush senorita!

***Mexican Spitfire*** (1940) Director: Leslie Goodwins. Producers: Lee S. Marcus, Cliff Reid. Writers: Joseph Fields (story and screenplay), Charles E. Roberts (screenplay). Cinematographer: Jack Mackenzie. Costumes: Renié. Art Director: Van Nest Polglase. Production Company and Distributor: RKO Radio Pictures. Production Dates: Began late September 1939. Release Date: January 9, 1940 (New York City), January 12, 1940 (general U.S. release). Genre: Comedy-Romance. Running Time: 67 minutes. Black and White. Language: English. Cast: **Lupe Vélez (Carmelita Lindsay)**, Leon Errol (Uncle Matt Lindsay/Lord Basil Epping), Donald Woods (Dennis Lindsay), Linda Hayes (Elizabeth Price), Elisabeth Risdon (Aunt Della Lindsay), Cecil Kellaway (Mr. Chumley), Charles Coleman (The Butler). Availability: DVD (part of the "Mexican Spitfire: Complete 8-Movie Collection").

The first official *Mexican Spitfire* film was released just six months after the success of *The Girl from Mexico* (1939), which inspired the series. Starting with this film and continuing through until the last film in the series, Lupe Vélez and Leon Errol's names appear side by side (with Lupe's name first) before the title of the film.

For the first time, Errol introduces the audience to the befuddling British character Lord Epping. Errol is still very much involved in the story as

Uncle Matt, but his ongoing impersonation of the whiskey-swilling nobleman makes for an extremely mixed-up identity crisis, followed by a chain of events that leads to a full-on food fight — all of which involve Carmelita (Lupe), of course. As Lord Epping, Errol created a hilarious walk best described as a bow-legged penguin with podiatry issues! It's a visual not soon forgotten. Director Leslie Goodwins cleverly worked several long shots of "the walk" into the "Mexican Spitfire" series for additional laughs.

Review:

The *Sarasota Herald-Tribune* (December 29, 1939) wrote:

> [*Mexican Spitfire* is] a slapstick, farce, burlesque. It is utterly silly, ridiculous and slaphappy. It has no rhyme, and its only reason is laughter. It draws most of the latter from the comic antics of limber-legged Leon Errol, in a dual role, and most of its situations spring from the hackneyed mistaken identity flub-dub.

Stanley Lambert of the Rialto Theatre in Racine, Wisconsin submitted his comments for the popular "What the Picture Did for Me" column published in the *Motion Picture Herald* (July 13, 1940):

> "Here is a comedy just loaded with belly laughs.... [T]he comedy never lets up and the audience was in stitches. This one is a cinch to please."

Tagline:

> Viva! Viva! Vélez!

**Mexican Spitfire Out West** (1940) Director: Leslie Goodwins. Assistant Director: Kenneth Holmes. Producers: Lee S. Marcus, Cliff Reid. Writers: Charles E. Roberts, Jack Townley. Cinematographer: Jack Mackenzie. Costumes: Renié. Art Director: Van Nest Polglase. Special Effects: Vernon L. Walker. Production Company and Distributor: RKO Radio Pictures. Production Dates: Mid-July–August 13, 1940. Release Date: October 29, 1940 (New York City), November 29, 1940 (general U.S. release). Genre: Comedy-Romance. Running Time: 75 minutes. Black and White. Language: English. Alternate Titles — *Lord Epping Out West* (working title). Cast: **Lupe Vélez (Carmelita Lindsay)**, Leon Errol (Uncle Matt Lindsay/Lord Basil Epping/Higgins), Donald Woods (Dennis "Denny" Lindsay), Elisabeth Risdon (Aunt Della Lindsay), Cecil Kellaway (Mr. Chumley), Linda Hayes (Elizabeth Price), Lydia

Bilbrook (Lady Ada Epping), Charles Coleman (The Butler), Charles Quigley (Mr. Roberts), Eddie Dunn (Mr. Skinner), Grant Withers (Withers), Tom Kennedy (Taxi Driver). Availability: DVD (part of the "Mexican Spitfire: Complete 8-Movie Collection").

This movie features the third and last appearance for Donald Woods as Carmelita's (Lupe) husband Dennis Lindsay. A popular movie and TV actor for over 50 years, Woods appeared in at least 100 stage productions and was prolific in radio and television. He was also a pioneer in live television, hosting variety shows. Upon his retirement he moved to Palm Springs and became a successful real estate broker. He was married to his college sweetheart Josephine Van der Horck for over 60 years; they had two children, Linda and Conrad. Woods died on March 5, 1998. He was 91 years old. He has a star on the Hollywood Walk of Fame that honors his contribution to Television.

Reviews:

The *Motion Picture Herald* (October 12, 1940):

> Previewed at the RKO Hillstreet, Los Angeles, where the seats prevented the audience from rolling in the aisles.

The *Los Angeles Examiner* (October 19, 1940):

> Don't miss Lupe Vélez and Leon Errol in *Mexican Spitfire Out West*.... [T]he two stars are so funny ... and there's something amusing going on every minute. What the feature picture lacks in laughs is more than made up for in the Vélez-Errol funfest.

On December 20, 1941, the *Motion Picture Herald* published the opinion of H. M. Gerber of the Roxy Theatre in North Dakota in their "What the Picture Did for Me" column: "Terrible. It should never be taken out of the can. It's not funny; it's foolish."

**Six Lessons from Madame La Zonga** (1941) Director: John Rawlins. Producer: Joseph Gershenson. Writers: Ben Chapman, Marion Orth, Larry Rhine, Stanley Rubin. Cinematographer: John W. Boyle. Gowns: Vera West. Art Directors: Jack Otterson, Harold H. MacArthur. Original Music: Everett Carter, Milton Rosen. Production Company and Distributor: Universal Pictures. Production Dates: December 6–late December 1940. Release Date: January 17, 1941. Genre: Comedy-Musical. Running Time: 62 minutes. Black and White. Language: English. Cast: **Lupe Vélez (Madame La Zonga)**, Leon Errol (Señor Alvarez/Mike Clancy), William Frawley (Beheegan),

Helen Parrish (Rosita Alvarez), Charles Lang (Steve), Shemp Howard (Gabby), Eddie Quillan (Skat), Guinn "Big Boy" Williams (Alvin), Danny Beck (Danny), Frank Mitchell (Maxwell), Johnny Bond (Pony), Richard Reinhart (Tex), Jimmy Wakely (Jim), Wade Boteler (Captain), Eddie Acuff (Steward).

Despite being in the middle of the "Mexican Spitfire" series, Lupe and Leon Errol signed individual contracts with Universal to appear in this film. Naturally, the studio hoped to cash in on the "Spitfire" success as well as the current success of the song "Six Lessons from Madame La Zonga."

During shooting, Lupe and "Big Boy" Williams were engaged. In one scene she yells at him, "I wouldn't marry you if you were the last man on earth!" From "reel life" to "real life," Lupe's words came true: She *didn't* marry him.

Review:

The *New York Times* (February 19, 1941):

> The latest in the Leon Errol-Lupe Vélez duets deviates hardly a hair's breadth from their previous ventures. This time Mr. Errol is a spurious señor, Havana-bound on the trail of some easy money, and Miss Vélez is the loud-mouthed nightclub proprietress who happens to be in need of it.... Miss Vélez is noisier than ever....

## The Mexican Spitfire's Baby (1941)

Director: Leslie Goodwins. Producer: Cliff Reid. Writers: Jerome Cady, Charles E. Roberts. Cinematographer: Jack Mackenzie. Costumes: Renié. Art Director: Van Nest Polglase. Production Company and Distributor: RKO Radio Pictures. Production Dates: May 21–June 11, 1941. Release Date: November 28, 1941. Genre: Comedy-Romance. Running Time: 69 minutes. Black and White. Language: English. Cast: **Lupe Vélez (Carmelita Lindsay)**, Leon Errol (Uncle Matt Lindsay/Lord Basil Epping), Charles "Buddy" Rogers (Dennis Lindsay), Zasu Pitts (Miss Emily Pepper), Elisabeth Risdon (Aunt Della), Fritz Feld (Lt. Pierre Gaston de la Blanc), Marion Martin (Fifi), Lloyd Corrigan (Mr. Chumley), Lydia Bilbrook (Lady Ada Epping), Vinton Haworth (Hotel Clerk). Availability: DVD (part of the "Mexican Spitfire: Complete 8-Movie Collection").

This "Mexican Spitfire" installment was the supporting feature for the film that many critics regard as the greatest of all time, *Citizen Kane*. It was originally slated to be the last film in the series; however, box office receipts were so strong that

RKO decided to continue the series, and four more films were made.

Charles "Buddy" Rogers takes over the role of Dennis Lindsay, Carmelita's (Lupe) husband. He continued in the role for two more films, *Mexican Spitfire at Sea* and *Mexican Spitfire Sees a Ghost*. ZaSu Pitts plays a likable busybody of a hotel manager, Miss Emily Pepper. She reprised the role in *Mexican Spitfire at Sea* (1942).

Review:

*Sheboygan Press*, February 21, 1942:

> Back again and funnier than ever, Lupe Vélez and Leon Errol lead a patrol of talented funsters through a barrage of laughter....

## Honolulu Lu (1941)

Director: Charles Barton. Producer: Wallace MacDonald. Writers: Eliot Gibbons, Paul Yawitz. Cinematographer: Franz Planer. Production Company and Distributor: Columbia Pictures Corporation. Production Dates: September 19, 1941–October 10, 1941. Release Date: December 11, 1941. Genre: Comedy-Musical. Running Time: 72 minutes. Black and White. Language: English. Cast: **Lupe Vélez (Consuelo Cordoba)**, Bruce Bennett (Skelly), Leo Carrillo (Don Estaban Cordoba), Marjorie Gateson (Mrs. Van Derholt), Don Beddoe (Bennie Blanchard), Forrest Tucker (Barney), George McKay (Horseface), Nina Campana (Aloha), Roger Clark (Bill Van Derhoolt), Helen Dickson (Mrs. Smythe), Curtis Railing (Mrs. Frobisher).

In this film, Lupe does the hula, a dance she learned from a Hawaiian-born classmate during her convent days in San Antonio, Texas. Charles Barton, the director of the film, said that Lupe was being a good girl on his set, that she hadn't indulged in any temper tantrums, that she hadn't called anybody any bad names, and that she kissed him and cameraman Franz Planer every morning when she came to work (*Hollywood Citizen News*, October 7, 1941).

The timing (and title) of the film couldn't have come at a worse time: It was released four days after the surprise Japanese attack on Pearl Harbor, when nothing about Honolulu was funny. Box office receipts reflected America's mood. Lupe's performance was reviewed positively.

Review:

The *Lima News* (February 22, 1942):

> [A] devastating explosion of mirthful dialogue and situations, offering Miss Vélez ample op-

portunity to reveal her versatile abilities and, further, to do a hula-hula with a Spanish accent! ... Miss Vélez swings a wicked skirt, a wicked song, a wicked fist. She is, in other words, slightly terrific!

Lupe impersonates Marlene Dietrich, Gloria Swanson, Katharine Hepburn and Adolf Hitler in the film.

***Playmates*** (1941) Director: David Butler. Assistant Director: Fred Fleck. Producer: David Butler. Writers: James V. Kern, M. M. Musselman (story), James V. Kern (screenplay), Arthur Phillips (additional dialogue). Cinematographer: Frank Redman. Gowns: Edward Stevenson. Art Directors: Carroll Clark and Albert S. D'Agostino. Original Music: Roy Webb (uncredited). Special Effects: Vernon L. Walker. Production Company and Distributor: RKO Radio Pictures. Filming Location: Pasadena, California. Production Dates: July 22– early September 1941. Release Date: December 26, 1941. Genre: Comedy-Musical. Running Time: 96 minutes. Black and White. Language: English. Cast: Kay Kyser (Himself), John Barrymore (Himself), **Lupe Vélez** (**Carmen del Torro**), Ginny Simms (Herself), May Robson (Grandma Kyser), Patsy Kelly (LuLu Monahan), Peter Lind Hayes (Peter Lindsay), Kay Kyser Band (Themselves), Harry Babbitt (Himself), M.A. Bogue (Ish Kabibble), Sully Mason (Himself).

John Barrymore plays himself in a hilarious parody. In his usual dry-witted fashion, he said, "I must say this is the most fascinating character I ever played" (*Corpus Christi Times*, August 6,

Lupe negotiates with an ailing John Barrymore in a scene from *Playmates* (1941). On Lupe's right hand is a horseshoe-nail-ring (handmade for her) that she treasured, and always wore. She was gifted the simple ring by a Pittsburgh man as a thank you for helping him and his family out of a financial hole.

1941). This movie features the *only* existing film footage where Barrymore recites Hamlet's "To be or not to be" soliloquy. It also marked Barrymore's last screen appearance. He died on May 29, 1942. He was 60 years old.

Costume designer Edward Stevenson produced a luxurious wardrobe of gowns and costumes especially for Lupe's character of Carmen del Torro. Lupe's onscreen role was that of an untamed female bullfighter and the costumes reflected her fiery character to perfection. The detail is apparent, but the black and white imagery obviously fails to showcase the vibrancy of the wardrobe to its fullest.

A lemon yellow crepe afternoon dress with same-colored fringe attached at the left shoulder, brought down through the draped, girdled hipline to hang five inches below the hem, was one of the two day dresses designed. A silver-fringed beaded evening gown was the most outrageous costume made for the film.

All of Lupe's dresses had a strong Mexican flavor; however, her bolero suit of black wool, embroidered with gold thread and sequins, was a true replica of a real Mexican bullfighters jacket, with less embroidery to cut the weight. A genuine bullfighter's jacket could weigh upwards of 50 pounds — half of Lupe's body weight! With the elaborate jacket, Lupe wore a slim black wool skirt, slit at the hem, an ivory crepe blouse with a scarlet sash. The outfit was completed with a black velour bullfighter's cap with gold embroidery. Lupe loved the outfit so much, she stepped straight off the set in her bullfighter's costume and went directly to Ciro's for dinner one evening. The patrons gasped as she entered the establishment — just the reaction Lupe was hoping to get.

Additional costumes consisted of a bolero dress with a fringe-trimmed, chartreuse bolero, wine skirt and red sash. However, Lupe's absolute favorite was one of the three strapless rumba dresses. Made of gold lace tissue, it had a skirt of one continuous piece of material, pleated at the waist, running between her feet and slit at the sides. "Look," Lupe said as she swished gaily around in her dressing room. "Look at me — see how cheec, how superb! Thees Eddee [Edward Stevenson], he ees vonderful!" ("Lupe Vélez Hits Headlines As Leader of Fashion," *Reno Evening Gazette*, November 1, 1941).

The elaborate lace gown worn by Lupe in the bullring sequence was her own. Once again designed by Stevenson, it was made by Lupe's secretary (who did most of her sewing). Twenty-five yards of antique Spanish lace (purchased by Lupe in Granada two weeks prior to the revolution in Spain) was used in the making of the dress. Lupe had worn it once, socially, and since it fit the scene (and her) perfectly, RKO agreed for her to wear it. Lupe didn't charge the studio rental for using her own wardrobe, but the studio gave her a $15,000 insurance policy on the gown, valid for one year, to cover the cost of the irreplaceable lace, should it be ruined in any way (Harry Crocker, "Behind the Makeup," *Los Angeles Examiner,* September 13, 1941). Her lucky horseshoe nail ring is visible in several scenes.

Lupe was hoping two of her Chihuahua dogs could be used in the production. Director David Butler gave in to Lupe's pleas and tried using them in a restaurant scene. One of the dogs jumped into Kay Kyser's lap and proceeded to lick him all over the face. The other one knocked a glass of water onto Lupe's gown. "I ought to make tamales out of you," she threatened (*Los Angeles Evening Herald and Express*, September 1, 1941). One of the dogs must have taken the threat seriously; it behaved itself long enough to be featured in a scene where it's walked on a leash along the street (by Kyser, with Lupe in tow) at the fifty-one-minute mark.

***Mexican Spitfire at Sea*** (**1942**) Director: Leslie Goodwins. Producer: Cliff Reid. Writers: Jerome Cady, Charles E. Roberts. Cinematographer: Jack Mackenzie. Costumes: Edward Stevenson. Art Directors: Albert S. D'Agostino, Walter E. Keller. Production Company and Distributor: RKO Radio Pictures. Production Dates: October–November 1941. Release Date: March 13, 1942. Genre: Comedy-Romance. Running Time: 72 minutes. Black and White. Language: English. Cast: **Lupe Vélez (Carmelita Lindsay)**, Leon Errol (Uncle Matt Lindsay/Lord Basil Epping), Charles "Buddy" Rogers (Dennis Lindsay), Zasu Pitts (Miss Emily Pepper), Elisabeth Risdon (Aunt Della Lindsay), Florence Bates (Mrs. Baldwin), Marion Martin (Fifi Russell), Lydia Bilbrook (Lady Ada Epping), Eddie Dunn (Mr. George Skinner), Harry Holman (Mr. Joshua Baldwin), Marten Lamont (Purser). Availability: DVD (part of the "Mexican Spitfire: Complete 8-Movie Collection").

Review:

*Film Daily* (January 8, 1942):

Hectic comedy.... [T]he latest adventures of Lupe Vélez and Leon Errol resolves itself into such a confused labyrinth of story structure that even the laughs have a hard time finding their way out.

**Mexican Spitfire Sees a Ghost** (1942) Director: Leslie Goodwins. Assistant Director: William Dorfman (uncredited). Producer: Cliff Reid. Writers: Charles E. Roberts, Monte Brice. Cinematographer: Russell Metty. Gowns: Renié. Art Directors: Carroll Clark, Albert S. D'Agostino. Production Company and Distributor: RKO Radio Pictures. Production Dates: January 28–February 1942. Release Date: June 26, 1942. Genre: Comedy-Romance. Running Time: 75 minutes. Black and White. Language: English. Alternate Titles — *Mexican Spitfire and the Ghost* (working title). Cast: **Lupe Vélez (Carmelita Lindsay/Maria)**, Leon Errol (Uncle Matt Lindsay/Lord Basil Epping/Hubble), Charles "Buddy" Rogers (Dennis Lindsay), Elisabeth Risdon (Aunt Della Lindsay), Donald MacBride (Percy Fitzbadden), Minna Gombell (Edith Fitzbadden), Don Barclay (Fingers O'-Toole), John Maguire (Luders), Lillian Randolph (Hyacinth), Mantan Moreland (Lightnin'), Harry Tyler (Bascombe), Marten Lamont (Mr. Harcourt). Availability: DVD (part of the "Mexican Spitfire: Complete 8-Movie Collection").

Surprisingly, this "Mexican Spitfire" installment (the weakest of the series) was the *main* feature on a double bill. The second-billed film during its premiere showing in Pomona, California, was the Orson Welles classic *The Magnificent Ambersons* (1942).

*Mexican Spitfire Sees a Ghost* was the third and last appearance in the series for Charles "Buddy" Rogers as Dennis Lindsay. In this installment, Lupe makes her first appearance by swinging dangerously on a painter's scaffold outside the Lindsays' apartment window. She's been spying on people, and after happily divulging what secrets she's found out about the other building residents, she swings inside to safety and plops down with a thud on the carpet. Given Lupe's early death, the lines that follow in this particular scene are certainly goosebump-producing:

DENNIS: As we grow older we must become more dignified.
CARMELITA: You mean I got to be old and dignified?
DENNIS: Well, yes.

CARMELITA: Oh ... Ahhhh, like Aunt Della?
DENNIS: Well, of course. You wouldn't see her doing a thing like that, would you?
CARMELITA: Oh nooo, Dennis. Well, if I got to be old like Aunt Della and dignified, then I don't want to be dignified, because I don't want to be old! You go 'head, you get old. Not me, I'm gonna be young all my life.

*Motion Picture Herald* published the comments of F.E. Shipley of the State Theatre in Lenox, Iowa, in the popular "What the Picture Did for Me" column (November 7, 1942): "Another entertaining programmer in the *Spitfire* series. Audiences like them."

**Mexican Spitfire's Elephant** (1942) Director: Leslie Goodwins. Assistant Director: Ruby Rosenberg. Producer: Bert Gilroy. Writers: Charles E. Roberts (story and screenplay), Leslie Goodwins (story). Cinematographer: Jack Mackenzie. Costumes: Renié. Art Directors: Albert S. D'Agostino and Feild M. Gray. Production Company and Distributor: RKO Radio Pictures. Release Date: September 17, 1942. Genre: Comedy-Romance. Running Time: 64 minutes. Black and White. Language: English. Cast: **Lupe Vélez (Carmelita Lindsay)**, Leon Errol (Uncle Matt Lindsay/Lord Basil Epping), Walter Reed (Dennis Lindsay), Elisabeth Risdon (Aunt Della Lindsay), Lydia Bilbrook (Lady Ada Epping), Marion Martin (Diana De Corro), Lyle Talbot (Reddy), Luis Alberni (Luigi), Arnold Kent (Jose Alvarez). Availability: DVD (part of the "Mexican Spitfire: Complete 8-Movie Collection").

In this movie, Walter Reed replaces Charles "Buddy" Rogers as the third and last Dennis Lindsay. Marion Martin switches characters in this installment. Twice having played the role of the French blonde bombshell Fifi, here she plays Diana De Corro, the female half of a jewel smuggling racket.

Review:

The *Hammond Times* (Hammond, Indiana, December 29, 1942):

> The series was amusing for a time but shows signs of petering out. The latest episode can best be described as a rehash of others that preceded it. There should be something else a comedian of [Leon] Errol's talents can do.

*Motion Picture Herald* published the comments of M. Bailey of the Strand Theatre in Dryden, Ontario, Canada, in this "What the Picture Did

for Me" column (January 9, 1943): "The few who came didn't care for it. Many walked out."

Taglines:

> MAMMOTH MIRTH MYSTERY! The thrill-and-laugh-hit of the series!

> MASTODONIC MIRTH! A larcenous lovely has Lupe furious and Leon loopy in the thrill-and-laugh hit of the series!

> IT'S A ROAR FROM SHIP-TO-SHORE! Lupe and Leon on a maelstrom of smoothie smugglers, man-hunting T-Men, and a pink elephant with green spots!

> PANDEMONIUM With A PACHYDERM! A misplaced elephant tangles Lupe and Leon in their laughiest hit!

> IT'S THE LAST GASP IN LAUGHS! MAMMOTH FUN! Lupe and Leon trapped between T-Men, gem-runners and a misplaced pachyderm!

***Ladies' Day*** (1943) Director: Leslie Goodwins. Assistant Director: Ruby Rosenberg. Producer: Bert Gilroy. Writers: Dane Lussier, Charles E. Roberts (writers), Robert Considine, Edward C. Lilley, Bertrand Robinson (play). Cinematographer: Jack Mackenzie. Gowns: Renié. Art Directors: Albert S. D'Agostino, Feild M. Gray. Original Music: Roy Webb. Production Company and Distributor: RKO Radio Pictures. Production Dates: Mid-July–early August 1942 (additional scenes began shooting on January 20, 1943). Release Dates: March 25, 1943 (New York City), April 9, 1943 (general U.S. release). Genre: Comedy-Sports. Running Time: 62 minutes. Black and White. Language: English. Cast: **Lupe Vélez (Pepita Zorita)**, Eddie Albert (Wacky Waters), Patsy Kelly (Hazel Jones), Max Baer (Hippo Jones), Jerome Cowan (Updyke), Iris Adrian (Kitty McClouen), Joan Barclay (Joan Samuels), Cliff Clark (Dan Hannigan), Carmen Morales (Marianna D'Angelo), George Cleveland (Doc), Jack Briggs (Marty Samuels), Russ Clark (Smokey Lee), Nedrick Young (Tony D'Angelo), Eddie Dew (Spike McClouen), Tom Kennedy (Dugan, the House Detective), Ralph Sanford (Field Umpire).

Tagline:

> He's a sucker for a curve ... especially when a dame throws them ... his way!

***Redhead from Manhattan*** (1943) Director: Lew Landers. Assistant Director: William A. O'Connor. Producer: Wallace MacDonald. Writers: Joseph Hoffman (screenplay), Rex Taylor (story). Cinematographer: Philip Tannura. Costumes: Travilla. Production Company and Distributor: Columbia Pictures. Production Dates — January 18–February 8, 1943. Release Date: May 6, 1943. Genre: Comedy. Running Time: 64 minutes. Black and White. Language: English. Alternate Titles — *Redhead from Rio* (working title). Cast: **Lupe Vélez (Rita de Silva/Maria de Silva aka Elaine Manners)**, Michael Duane (Jimmy Randall), Tim Ryan (Mike Glendon), Gerald Mohr (Chick Andrews), Lillian Yarbo (Polly), Arthur Loft (Sig Hammersmith), Lewis Wilson (Paul), Douglas Leavitt (Joe), Clancy Cooper (Policevrman), Johnny Mitchell (Marty Britt).

Lupe appears in blackface and speaks with a Southern jive accent while impersonating Elaine's African American maid Polly (Lillian Yarbo). Sandra Lynn was Lupe's double for a number of years prior to *Redhead from Manhattan*. She is seen in

**Lupe on the left and her double Sandra Lynn on the right. This photograph was taken when Sandra doubled for Lupe in *Redhead from Manhattan* (1943).**

several scenes where Lupe was required to play a dual role and they were so alike, even cast and crew had trouble telling the difference between them. The similarity was only skin deep, though. Lupe was loud and boisterous. Sandra quiet and subdued, yet they became close friends. So many people had told Sandra she looked the spitting image of Lupe Vélez that, on a lark, she showed up at the studio unannounced and asked, "Do you need a double for Lupe?" The story goes that Lupe saw her from a distance and yelled, "Holy Doodle! How you like that! That girl over there, he look jost like me. You! What your name?" That was the beginning of a friendship and working relationship that lasted right up until Lupe's untimely death.

Sandra had a secondary career as a photographer and would travel to Palm Springs for the social season, then come back to work as Lupe's double when needed. Before filming on *Redhead from Manhattan* began, Lupe called Sandra in Palm Springs and said, "Keedo, I'm lonesome. You come back. We have fun." It was an offer Sandra couldn't refuse. After all, Sandra thought of her photography as "work" and of being with Lupe in Hollywood as more of a vacation ("Lupe's 'Twin' Having Fun in Filmland," *The Pittsburgh Press*, April 19, 1943).

Tagline:

"Song and Dance ... Swing and Romance ... To Knock You for a *Lupe!*"

***Mexican Spitfire's Blessed Event*** (1943) Director: Leslie Goodwins. Producer: Bert Gilroy. Writers: Dane Lussier (screenplay), Charles E. Roberts (screenplay and story). Cinematographer: Jack Mackenzie. Art Directors: Albert S. D'Agostino, Walter E. Keller. Production Company and Distributor: RKO Radio Pictures. Production Dates: March 24–April 14, 1943. Release Date: July 17, 1943. Genre: Comedy-Romance. Running Time: 63 minutes. Black and White. Language: English. Cast: **Lupe Vélez (Carmelita Lindsay)**, Leon Errol (Uncle Matt Lindsay/Lord Basil Epping), Walter Reed (Dennis Lindsay), Elisabeth Risdon (Aunt Della Lindsay), Lydia Bilbrook (Lady Ada Epping), Hugh Beaumont (George Sharpe), Aileen Carlyle (Mrs. Pettibone), Alan Carney (Navaho Room Bartender), Marietta Canty (Verbena — Carmelita's Maid). Availability: DVD (part of the "Mexican Spitfire: Complete 8-Movie Collection").

Charles Coleman had played the role of butler to the Lindsays in previous "Spitfire" installments, but in *Mexican Spitfire's Blessed Event*, without explanation, Coleman plays Lord Epping's loyal servant ... but he's not the *same* character! This time he goes by a different name, Parkins.

This was the eighth installment in the "Mexican Spitfire" series, *The Girl from Mexico* included. It was also the last. A few years later, reporter Lloyd L. Sloan of *Hollywood Citizen News* (May 13, 1947) spoke to Leon Errol about working on the *Spitfire* series. Errol said working with Lupe was "a pleasure" and that the films made a lot of money and everyone was happy until one of the studio executives decided he could shoot the scripts in eighteen days. Errol said everyone was so tired at the end of the fourth day, they were all ready to quit. "The guy had us running from one side of the room to the other to save time on takes," he explained. "We looked like a track team." Needless to say, the new producer didn't last too long.

RKO once announced a spin-off series based on Leon Errol's popular Lord Epping character but it never came to fruition. The character was reprised in a short that was made quite a few years following the last *Mexican Spitfire* film; it rehashed the old mistaken identity shtick with Errol playing two parts. *Lord Epping Returns* (1951) was released less than a month before Errol's October 12 death. He was 70 years old. One month after Errol's death, on November 10, 1951, Charles E. Roberts, film veteran and writer of the "Mexican Spitfire" series, as well as dozens of Leon Errol two-reelers, died of a heart attack at his home. He was 57 years old.

Shortly before completing this last film in the "Mexican Spitfire" series, Lupe turned down a part in the screwball comedy *Hi Diddle Diddle* (1943). "I read the script," she explained, "and it is not for me" (*San Antonio Light*, April 7, 1943).

Tagline:

Funny Enough to Make a Stork Squawk!

Memorable Quotes:

Lady Epping (Lydia Bilbrook) to her absent-minded husband Lord Epping (Leon Errol): "Somehow you look so incomplete."
Lord Epping: "Have you ever found me wanting in anything!"
Lady Epping: "Frankly, I have...."

***Nana*** (1944) Directors: Roberto Gavaldón, Celestino Gorostiza. Producers: C. Camacho Corona,

Alberto Santander. Writers: Roberto Gavaldón, Alberto Santander (writers), Celestino Gorostiza (dialogue), Émile Zola (novel). Original Music: Jorge Pérez. Cinematographer: Alex Phillips. Costume Design: Alberto Vázquez Chardy and Western Costume (Hollywood). Filming Location: The Azteca Film Studios, Mexico. Production Date: Filming began on October 11, 1943. Release Dates: June 2, 1944 (Mexico premiere), September 17, 1944 (Los Angeles premiere). Running Time: 87 minutes. Black and White. Language: Spanish. Genre: Drama. Cast: **Lupe Vélez (Nana)**, Miguel Ángel Ferriz (Muffat), Chela Castro (Rosa Mignon), Crox Alvarado (Fontan), Elena D'Orgaz (Satn), José Baviera (Van Doeuvres), Sergio Orta (Impresario), Isabelita Blanch (Nana's Aunt), Jorge Reyes (Fauchery), Mimi Derba (Bebe's Mother), Roberto Corell (La Falloise), Virginia Zuri (Bebe), Pepe del Rio (Bebe), Clifford Carr (Steiner), Luis Alcoriza (De Fauchery), Conchita Gentil Arcos (Zoe), Victorio Blanco (Marques), Rafael Beltrán (Felipe), Hernán Vera (Prefect). Availability: The Universidad Nacional Autónoma in Mexico and the Mary Pickford Institute for Film Education in Los Angeles. The rights to the film are held by the Agrasánchez Film Archive, in Harlingen, Texas.

On August 9, 1943, gossip columnist Louella O. Parsons reported (*Los Angeles Examiner*) that Lupe had just received word from the film company in Mexico that she *must* make *Nana,* the picture she had already agreed to do for them. "Not only *Nana,*" said Lupe, "but two others [*Anna Karenina* and *La dama de las camelias,* aka *The Lady of the Camellias*]. They send me back my money when I send it back to them." By late September (*Los Angeles Examiner,* September 27, 1943), there was no mention of the additional two films that she had seemingly been paid in advance to do. In fact, she told Parsons that when she finished *Nana,* she would retire from the screen, and announced that she would become the wife of actor Arturo de Córdova. The marriage never eventuated.

Author Gabriel Ramírez wrote of Lupe's erratic and disjointed behavior on the set: "[Her] angry outbursts became intolerable.... [S]he progressively became more depressed and exalted; her mood swings left her out of control." Once filming was complete, Lupe returned to the United States and celebrated her saint's day, in honor of Our Lady of Guadalupe, with a big party and feast at her house on North Rodeo Drive (December 12, 1944).

Commemorating this historically religious day is very important for most Mexicans, and especially so for namesakes like Lupe. It is a day of feast and festivities to honor the miracle of the image of the Virgin of Guadalupe appearing on the cloak of Juan Diego (1474–1548), an indigenous peasant, on December 12, 1531, upon the hill of Tepeyac near Mexico City. The miracle of the apparition had a major influence on the spread of the Catholic religion in Mexico; the Roman Catholic Church canonized Juan Diego in 2002. He is now officially known as Saint Juan Diego Cuauhtlatoatzin.

Lupe invited "many Mexicans in the industry, employed and unemployed, wealthy and poor" to celebrate the annual event. At the get-together, she was "nervous, confused and visibly disconcerted" (Ramírez, *Lupe Vélez: la mexicana que escupia fuego*).

According to a December 13, 1943, *Los Angeles Evening Herald and Express* article by Harrison Carroll, Lupe worked obscenely long hours on the *Nana* set, with days beginning at 5:45 A.M. and not ending until 10 P.M. She also played some of the scenes "with a fever of 103 degrees."

The *Los Angeles Times* (September 19, 1944) wrote:

> Oh, Lupe, come on back and just be your spitfire, comedienne self! ... But, Miss Lupe is undeniably lovely in a long blond wig and her singing and dancing are bewitching. She wears many different costumes of the hoopskirt period and her lovely figure sets them off to advantage....

The lackluster reception of *Nana* in Mexico (both critically and publicly) may have affected its American release a few months later. In San Antonio, Texas, it premiered as a midnight movie, a bad sign. At the time, there were several theaters in the area catering to Spanish-speaking audiences, so a midnight screening, especially for a premiere, indicated it wasn't regarded as a box office magnet. In contrast, Lupe's 1938 film *La zandunga* was a huge success, with countless runs from its initial release, right up until the mid–1950s. Prints were screened until they were in nearly unwatchable condition. Theaters asked for replacement reels. *Nana* did not enjoy the same adulation.

Six months after the release of *Nana* in Mexico and about two months after its release in Los Angeles, Lupe committed suicide. Despite reports to

the contrary, Lupe did *not* attend a premiere of *Nana* on the evening prior to her death. This story appears to have been yet another attempt at further dramatizing an already tragic event. In reality, the film opened in Los Angeles (at the California and Mason theaters) on September 17, a little under two months *prior* to her suicide.

At the time of her death, Lupe was signed to a $4,000-per-week (approximately $50,000 in 2011) personal appearance contract that was scheduled to begin on December 28, 1944, in Albany, New York, and continue on through the East and Midwest for twelve weeks. She had signed yet another lucrative contract for radio broadcasts (*The Bill-board*, December 23, 1944) and she was also scheduled to begin a war bond sale drive in the East.

Alternate versions and adaptations of *Nana* were produced long before and long after Lupe's version: There were *Nana*s in 1914, 1926, 1934, 1955, 1970, 1981, 1985, 1999 and 2001.

The film was banned from New York by the New York State Film Board, who declared that the picture had "a low moral tone, and excepting for a few opening and closing scenes, [it] portrays immortality and licentiousness in an attractive manner. It is, therefore, denied a license for public exhibition according to Section 1082 of the Education Law of the State of New York."

# *Appendices*

## I: Lupe's Other Lost Productions (1929–1944)

Lupe was linked with the following productions but for various reasons, they proceeded without her (or did not proceed at all). Any "Lost Lupe Productions" that were mentioned within the previous pages are *not* listed below.

***The Squall*** (1929) Louella O. Parsons reported (*Los Angeles Examiner,* June 13, 1928) that First National had their eye on Lupe for the lead female role of Nubi, the Gypsy girl in *The Squall.* Myrna Loy ended up with the role.

**A United Artists movie, 1929** Lewis Milestone was to direct Lupe in a film for UA; however, he jumped ship and took the helm of *New York Nights* (1929), a Norma Talmadge–Gilbert Roland production (*Los Angeles Record*, March 27, 1929).

***Under a Texas Moon*** (1930) Doris Denbo (*Hollywood Daily Citizen,* May 15, 1929) wrote that Monte Blue and Lupe Vélez were both scheduled to appear in this Michael Curtiz–directed production, but now *out* of it. Frank Fay, Raquel Torres and Myrna Loy were the lead actors in the final film. Lupe and Monte appeared in *Tiger Rose* (1929) together.

***Blind Raftery*** (1929) The *Rochester Evening Journal* (September 17, 1929) reported that Lupe was cast as "the Spanish wife of a blind, wandering bard" in this Irish-themed romance, written by Donn Byrne. George Fitzmaurice was slated to direct and newcomer Donald Novis was signed to play opposite Lupe. It never happened.

***Argentina*** (stage, 1931) Louella O. Parsons reported (*Los Angeles Examiner,* February 10, 1931) that Lupe was close to accepting David Belasco's offer to play the lead role in *Argentina*, a play written by Belasco for Lenore Ulric a few years before.

***Hypnotized*** (1932) On February 20, 1932, *Hollywood Citizen News* reported that Mack Sennett had

been working on the script for *Hypnotized* since June 1931. Up to twenty writers had collaborated with him and at the time of the article it was estimated that $100,000 (approximately $1.6 million in 2011) had already been invested in the production. W.C. Fields and Charles Mack had been signed and Sennett was said to be looking for more stars to complete the cast, including Clara Bow and Lupe. On July 15, 1932, Elizabeth Yeaman of *Hollywood Citizen News* announced that Marjorie Beebe had been signed for the second feminine lead, with Fifi Dorsay, Maria Alba or Lupe Vélez still in contention for the lead female role of Princess Mitzi; Alba got it. Despite a solid cast, *Hypnotized* received lackluster reviews. W.C. Fields did not appear in the cast.

***The Son-Daughter*** (1932) Elizabeth Yeaman of *Hollywood Citizen News* (September 5, 1932) reported that MGM had bought the film rights to the David Belasco play *The Son-Daughter.* Jacques Feyder had been assigned to direct and Lupe was the female lead. The film was released on December 23, 1932. Directed by Clarence Brown, it starred Helen Hayes, Ramon Novarro, Lewis Stone, Warner Oland, Ralph Morgan, Louise Closser Hale and H.B. Warner.

***Paprika*** **and a Will Rogers movie** Harrison Carroll of the *Los Angeles Evening Herald and Express* (December 21, 1932) reported that Erich von Stroheim was writing the story *Paprika* for Lupe. In the same article, Carroll mentioned that Lupe had been signed by Fox to star alongside Will Rogers in a movie that was supposed to have started work on May 1, 1933.

**Malibu** Harrison Carroll of the *Los Angeles Evening Herald and Express* (June 17, 1933) wrote that *Malibu* was scheduled for Lupe but "will not be ready for some time."

***The Prizefighter and the Lady*** (1933) The *Los Angeles Examiner* ("Society Sees Ring Fight Filmed," September 19, 1933) reported that the Max Baer–Myrna Loy feature *The Prizefighter and the Lady* would have a climactic fight scene that included an all-star audience. Those who turned up for the scene included Clark Gable, Walter Huston, Robert Montgomery, Marino Bello, Jean Harlow, Helen Twelvetrees, Adrienne Ames, Lionel Barrymore, Ramon Novarro, Bruce Cabot, Frank Woody, John Huston, Jack Pearl, Jean Hersholt, George Givot, Mark Cohen, and Lupe. No stranger to boxing matches, Lupe cheered, booed and did her customary ringside air punches, just as she would at the Hollywood Legion fights every Friday evening. She wore a brown tweed sports coat with a beige woolen dress and a small beige hat. Unfortunately, she's not seen in the existing print. At one time, Lupe was in the running for the female lead, as was Norma Shearer, Joan Crawford, June Knight and Ginger Rogers.

***In Old Louisiana*** (1934) Harrison Carroll of the *Los Angeles Evening Herald and Express* (January 13, 1934) noted that Lupe's husband Johnny Weissmuller had put the kibosh on Lupe's imminent personal appearance tour; instead, she was going to "stay on in Hollywood to do the picture, *In Old Louisiana*, for MGM."

***Turea*** (1934) Harrison Carroll of the *Los Angeles Evening Herald and Express* (March 7, 1934) wrote that MGM was looking to send Lupe and husband Johnny Weissmuller to the South Seas to do the film *Turea*. It was being developed for the screen by John Farrow, based on a story by the late F.W. Murnau. Talking about the possibility of the production going ahead, a grinning Weissmuller said, "It looks like a field day for Lupe. I'll get away from the Tarzan yell, but my lines probably will be reduced to a couple of grunts."

***The Girl Friend*** (1935) Harrison Carroll reported (*Los Angeles Evening Herald and Express*, July 14, 1934) that Lupe was in rehearsals for the new Columbia musical *The Girl Friend*. On December 10, 1934, George Lewis of the *Los Angeles Post-Record* reported that Lupe had started work on the film. Ann Sothern ultimately appeared as the female

lead in the film. Jack Haley played the male lead. Russell Mack was originally slated to direct but the job was instead given to Eddie Buzzell.

**Casino de Paris (Parisian stage revue, 1935)** Lupe refused $4,000 per week (approximately $65,000 in 2011) to appear with Maurice Chevalier at the Casino de Paris because she didn't want to learn French and because she was tired of the theater ... for the time being, anyway.

***Wrecks of Paradise*** (French, 1935) In December of 1935, Lupe was scheduled to travel to Paris for the French production *Wrecks of Paradise*. Production and money problems ensued and Lupe returned home after a few weeks abroad.

***Seven Up*** (play, 1937) Louella O. Parsons wrote (*Los Angeles Examiner*, September 17, 1937) that Lupe was still deciding between returning to her native Mexico for a film role and going back east for a stint in the Broadway play *Seven Up*. She chose the film, which was *La zandunga* (1938).

***7/11*** (play, 1937) Elizabeth Yeaman of the *Hollywood Citizen News* (November 23, 1937) wrote that Lupe was two weeks late filming *La zandunga*, and the production delay prevented her from going to New York for her role in the Broadway play *7–11*. Lupe was to star as a Mexican nightclub entertainer. Louella O. Parsons reported (*Los Angeles Examiner*, December 19, 1937) that *La zandunga*'s delays also prevented Lupe from playing a role in Simone Simon's new film, most likely *Josette* (1938).

**More Douglas Fairbanks movies (1939)** After her breakout role in *The Gaucho*, Douglas Fairbanks had always planned for Lupe to star in more of his films; however, his death on December 12, 1939, prevented both of the planned projects from eventuating. Fairbanks reportedly had Lupe earmarked for a biopic about Spanish entertainer Lola Montes as well as a film about Hernán Cortés, with Lupe playing the role of La Malinche (www.austinfilm.org).

***Serenade*** (1940) The 1940 version of *Serenade* never happened, but when it was being planned, Louella O. Parsons reported (*Los Angeles Examiner*, January 26, 1940) that Lupe was excited about the film. She wrote, "[Lupe] is really crazy to play the role of the Mexican senorita." *Serenade* was later made in 1956 with Mario Lanza, Joan Fontaine, Sara Montiel and Vincent Price.

***The Marines Are Ready*** (1941) *The New York Times* (July 18, 1941) reported that Lupe was signed for the female lead in RKO's *The Marines Are Ready*, scheduled to start shooting on August 1, 1941. Edmund Lowe and Victor McLaglen were signed to star. Anne Shirley was announced as the female lead, but then RKO announced that they were replacing her with Lupe. The film was going to be produced by Howard Benedict and directed by Leslie Goodwins. It never eventuated.

McLaglen and Lowe starred together in *Call Out the Marines* (1942) the following year; they're the only names in common with the cast and crew of *The Marines Are Ready*. Some newspapers reported that Lupe was assigned for the lead in this film, then due to a scheduling conflict was replaced by British-born Binnie Barnes.

***The Men in Her Life*** (1941) As early as 1934, *Film Weekly* (December 21, 1934) wrote that Lupe was suggested for the female lead in the film adaptation of Lady Eleanor Smith's novel *Ballerina*. Released seven years later, *The Men in Her Life* starred Loretta Young as Lina, a circus performer turned ballerina, and (as the title suggests) the various men in her life. This film is in no way affiliated with *Men in Her Life* (1931) or its Spanish-language adaptation (starring Lupe), *Hombres de mi vida* (1932).

***Panama Hattie*** (stage, 1942) The *Los Angeles Evening Herald and Express* (November 17, 1941) wrote that Lupe was mulling over a deal to replace Ethel Merman in the Broadway comedy-musical *Panama Hattie*. The play opened at the 46th Street Theater in New York on October 30, 1940, and closed on January 3, 1942, after 501 performances. Ethel Merman played Hattie (www.ibdb.com).

***Tampico*** (1942) Louella O. Parsons wrote (*Los Angeles Examiner,* January 4, 1942) that Lupe had tested for *Tampico*. A wartime drama of the same name was released in April 1944, starring Edward G. Robinson, Lynn Bari and Victor McLaglen.

***Next Comes Love*** aka ***The Big Show-Off*** (1944) Louella O. Parsons wrote (*Los Angeles Examiner*, April 11, 1944) that Lupe would star in *Next Comes Love* (working title), an original story by László Vadnay, for Republic. Had Lupe appeared in this production, later released as *The Big Show-Off,* it would have been her last film, released posthumously on January 22, 1945. Arthur Lake, Dale Evans, Lionel Stander, George Meeker, Paul Hurst and Marjorie Manners starred.

# II: Appearing as Herself (1928–1941)

***Screen Snapshots #5*** (1928) Genre: Documentary Short. Studio: Columbia. Language: English. Black and White. Running Time: 10 minutes. Release Date: Mid-March 1928.

This short takes audiences on a ten-minute tour of Hollywood. There is a fight between Carroll Nye and a dog with Rin-Tin-Tin coming to the rescue, the auction block scene from *The Love Mart* (1927), a visit to various film sets, a comedy skit by Joe Rock and the rescue of Lupe Vélez from fire by Rod La Rocque.

The *Screen Snapshots* series ran from 1922 to 1958. It showcased the stars doing regular things away from the screen, as well as highlights from selected films.

***Hollywood Snapshots #11*** (1929) Producer: Jack Cohn. Genre: Documentary Short. Black and White. Language: English. Release Date: January 1, 1929. Cast: Eddie Lambert (Himself—Host/Narrator), Clara Bow, Joan Crawford, Rosetta Duncan, Vivian Duncan, Douglas Fairbanks Jr., Ralph Graves, Jack Holt, Edward Everett Horton, Al Jolson, Carl Laemmle Jr., Ted Lewis, Jeanette Loff, Eddie Quillan, Harry Richman, **Lupe Vélez**, Paul Whiteman (Themselves).

The long-running *Hollywood Snapshots* series showcased Hollywood's best-loved actors at home, playing sports, on vacation, interacting with their pets—being "normal."

***Screen Snapshots Series 9. No. 11*** (1930) Director: Ralph Staub. Genre: Documentary Short. Running Time: 10 minutes. Language: English. Black and White. Production Company and Distributor: Columbia Pictures. Release Date: January 1930. Cast: Eddie Lambert, Douglas Fairbanks Jr., Joan Crawford, Carl Laemmle Jr., Paul Whiteman, Edward Everett Horton, Eddie Quillan, Clara Bow, Rosetta Duncan, Vivian Duncan, Ralph Graves,

Johnny Hines, Jack Holt, Al Jolson, Ted Lewis, Jeanette Loff, Harry Richman, **Lupe Vélez** (Themselves).

This installment is particularly noteworthy for showing newlyweds, Douglas Fairbanks Jr. and Joan Crawford returning from their honeymoon.

*Voice of Hollywood* (1931) Genre: Documentary Short. Running Time: 8 minutes. Black and White. Language: English. Production Company and Distributor: Tiffany Productions. Cast: Don Alvarado, John Boles, Betty Compson, Bebe Daniels, Mickey Daniels, Louise Fazenda, Mary Kornman, Tom Mix, Ruth Roland, **Lupe Vélez** (Themselves).

Hollywood stars are seen at a film premiere, each speaking into a microphone for Don Alvarado, who's playing a host on the STAR radio station. Mickey Daniels and Mary Kornman, two original "Our Gang" members all grown up, do a comedy skit and dance number. Lupe does a brief intro and sings a Spanish song from her latest film, *The Cuban Love Song* (1931).

*The Voice of Hollywood No. 13 — Second Series* (1932) Director: Mack D'Agostino. Producer: Louis Lewyn. Genre: Documentary Short. Production Company: Louis Lewyn Productions. Distributors: Tiffany Productions. Release Date: January 17, 1932. Running Time: 12 minutes. Language: English. Black and White. Cast: Allen "Farina" Hoskins, George Bancroft, El Brendel, Gary Cooper, Jackie Cooper, Thelma Todd, **Lupe Vélez**, John Wayne (Themselves).

More stars, more cameos, more publicity for the studios and their famous players.

*Hollywood on Parade No. A-12* (1933) Producer-Director: Louis Lewyn. Genre: Documentary Short. Production Company: Louis Lewyn Productions. Distributor: Paramount Pictures. Release Date: June 30, 1933. Running Time: 10 minutes. Language: English. Black and White. Cast: Constance Bennett, Joan Bennett, Gary Cooper, Claudia Dell, Cliff Edwards, Jean Harlow, Harry Langdon, Carole Lombard, Clarence Muse, William Powell, Raquel Torres, **Lupe Vélez**, Bert Wheeler, Alice White, Warren William, Robert Woolsey (Themselves).

More candid footage of the stars of 1930s Hollywood. Cliff Edwards (best known as the voice of *Pinocchio*'s Jiminy Cricket) hosts this installment. Jean Harlow is seen playing golf, and several stars are seen at a racetrack. A Mexican mariachi band serenades a poster of Lupe from *Wolf Song* (1929); after a moment, the poster comes to life with the scene from the film of Lupe dancing with Gary Cooper. Edwards joins the mariachi band and plays his ukulele as they march off screen.

*Mr. Broadway* (1933) Director: Johnnie Walker. Writers: Abel Green (writer), Ed Sullivan (story and screenplay). Cinematographer: Fred Zucker. Genre: Comedy. Filming Locations: New York City. Production Company: Broadway-Hollywood Productions, Ltd., and Malcomar Productions. Distributors: Arthur Greenblatt Distribution Service and Broadway-Hollywood Productions, Ltd. Release Date: September 12, 1933. Running Time: 63 minutes. Language: English. Black and White. Cast: Ed Sullivan, Jack Dempsey, Ruth Etting, Bert Lahr, Hal Le Roy, Josephine Dunn, Ted Husing, Blossom Seeley, Benny Fields, Lita Grey, Joe Frisco, Jack Benny, Mary Livingstone, Gus Edwards, Jack Haley, **Lupe Vélez**, Frank H. Gard, Nils T. Granlund, Eddy Duchin, Ernst Lubitsch, Primo Carnera, Max "Slapsie Maxie" Rosenbloom, Johnnie Walker, Tony Canzoneri, Isham Jones, Abe Lyman (Themselves), Dita Parlo (The Girl), William Desmond (First Suitor), Tom Moore (Second Suitor).

Ed Sullivan aka "Mr. Broadway" takes viewers on an hour-long tour of various trendy New York nightclubs to spy on celebrities at play.

Review: *Film Daily* (September 15, 1933): "Broadway night-life travelogue with interest centered on array of well known personalities. A rather difficult subject to stretch out to feature length, and more or less beset with technical handicaps, this nevertheless is an interesting novelty with both entertainment and fan interest in sufficient quantity to justify itself...."

**"A Hollywood Bridge Game" (London, March 23, 1934)** While Lupe isn't exactly appearing as "herself" on this 78 RPM recording, the mimicry tables are turned and for once *she's* impersonated, by British comedienne-actress-entertainer Florence Desmond (1905–1993). Several comedic sketch-type records like this one were made by Desmond in the 1930s. The situations consisted of a group of Hollywood stars in a social situation, at a party or a card game, etc. Marlene Dietrich, Greta Garbo, Gracie Fields, Marie Dressler and Tallulah Bankhead were all regularly imitated in Desmond's comic routines. In the 1934 recording "A Hollywood

Bridge Game," Desmond impersonates the voices of Jimmy Durante and ZaSu Pitts. "Jimmy" teaches "ZaSu" how to cheat their opponents "Mae West" and **Lupe Vélez**" in a game of bridge.

***Toyland Premiere*** (1934) Producer-Director: Walter Lantz. Writers: Walter Lantz, Victor McLeod. Original Music: James Dietrich. Animators: George Grandpré, Laverne Harding, Frank Kelling, Lester Kline, Fred Kopietz, Bill Mason, Manuel Moreno. Song Composers: James Dietrich, Walter Lantz, Victor McLeod. Presenter: Carl Laemmle (Universal "Cartune" Classics). Release Date: December 7, 1934. Color (Two-strip Technicolor). Language: English. Running Time: 9 minutes. Genre: Animated Short. Production Companies: Universal Pictures, Walter Lantz Productions. Distributor: Universal Pictures.

Oswald the Lucky Rabbit, Santa Claus, Frankenstein's Monster, Tarzan (aka Johnny Weissmuller), **Lupe Vélez (as herself in animated form)**, Shirley Temple, Al Jolson, Bing Crosby and Laurel and Hardy greet Santa at a department store reception following the pre–Christmas Toyland Parade. Laurel and Hardy get into all sorts of mischief by dressing up in a dragon costume in an attempt to steal the lavish chocolate cake. When the sight of the dragon causes Tarzan to faint, Lupe picks him up and swings the limp jungle man to safety on the light fixtures of the department store. She lets out her own version of the legendary Tarzan-like scream as she goes. Availability: DVD.

***The CooCoo Nut Grove*** (1936) Director: Friz Freleng. Producer: Leon Schlesinger. Writer: Sid Marcus. Sound Effects Editor: Treg Brown (uncredited). Animators: Robert McKimson, Sandy Walker. Character Designer: T. Hee (uncredited). Music Director: Carl W. Stalling. Orchestrator: Milt Franklyn. Running Time: 7 minutes. Language: English. Technicolor. Genre: Animated Short. Production Companies: Leon Schlesinger Studios, The Vitaphone Corporation. Distributors: The Vitaphone Corporation, Warner Bros. Pictures. Release Date: November 28, 1936 (USA). Vocal Talent: Bernice Hansen (Dionne Quintuplets), Verna Deane, Peter Lind Hayes, Ted Pierce, The Rhythmettes. Availability: DVD.

Johnny Weissmuller and **Lupe Vélez** are seen in cartoon form as Tarzan and his date.

***Recordar Es Vivir*** (1941) Director: Fernando A. Rivero. Genre: Documentary Short. Filming Location: Mexico. Language: Spanish. Release Date: January 15, 1941. Cast: Cantinflas, Sara Garcia (Ella misma), **Lupe Vélez.**

A documentary short about the Mexican film industry and its stars.

# III: Noted Stage Work (1932–1944)

*Hot-Cha!* (1932) Musical comedy. Music: Ray Henderson. Lyrics: Lew Brown. Book: Mark Hellinger, H.S. Kraft, Ray Henderson, Lew Brown. Story: H.S. Kraft. Musical Direction: Al Goodman. Orchestrator: Robert Russell Bennett. Choreographer: Bobby Connolly. Scenic Designer: Joseph Urban. Costume Designer: John Harkrider. Directors: Edgar J. MacGregor, Edward C. Lilley. Producer: Florenz Ziegfeld Jr. Theatre: Ziegfeld Theatre, New York. Opening: March 8, 1932. Closing: June 18, 1932 (119 performances). Description: A musical in two acts. Setting: New York and Mexico. Cast: Iris Adrian, Louise Allen, Mary Ann, Nick Basil, Miriam Battista, Herman Belmonte, Leonard Berry, Virginia Biddle, Joan Burgess, Alice Burrage, Tito Coral, Mary Coyle, Jack Daley, Dorothy Day, Antonio De Marco, Renee De Marco, Louis Delgado, Alan DeSylva, Marion Dixon, Dody Donnelly, Betty Dumbris, Prudence Edgar, Georgia Ellis, Jules Epailly (Store Keeper Manuel), Harriet Fink, Marjorie Fisher, Dorothy Flood, John Fulco, Robert Gleckler, Pearl Harris, Patty Hastings, Florence Healy, Hernandez Brothers, Theo Holley, Jean Howard, Stanley Howard, Mercedes Hughes, Alfonso Iglesias, Dorothy Kal, Gloria Kelly, Tom Kelly, June Knight, Frances Kruger, Charles La Torre, Bert Lahr (Alky Schmidt), Jane Lane, Rose Louise, Evelyn Lowrie, Neva Lynn, June MacCloy, Frances Markey, Edwin Marsh, Mary Joan Martin, Lorelle McCarver, Lou Ann Meredith, Rosalie Milan, Vic Monroe, Grace Moore, Pauline Moore, George O'Brien (Ensemble), Ethel O'Dell, Catherine O'Neil, Lester Ostrander, Lynne Overman (Hap

Wilson), Arthur Page, Sherry Pelham, Theo Phane, Lilyan Picard, Eleanor Powell (Dancer), Basil Prock, Polly Ray, Carol Renwick, Mary Alice Rice, Wilburn Riviere, Buddy Rogers (Jack Whitney), Alma Ross, William Ruppel, Mina Ruskin, Marion Santre, Roy Sedley, Gertrude Sheffield, Marie Stevens, Kay Stewart, Thomas Thompson, **Lupe Vélez (Conchita)**, Veloz and Yolanda, Efim Vitis, Marion Volk, Molly Wakefield, Diana Walker, Lorraine Webb, Mildred Webb, Marjorie White.

Florenz Ziegfeld sent columnist Louella O. Parsons a lengthy telegram to explain Lupe's role in the play. He wrote:

> Lupe remains with the Follies as co-star with Bert Lahr. She has an Equity contract for the run of the play and it will be a long time before she is able to make another picture. She has taken her audiences by storm. And this is remarkable because she only had four days to get up her part.

He went on to announce that Lupe (here making her Broadway debut) would reprise her Follies role in a film but the project never materialized. The play closed about two and a half months after Ziegfeld's enthusiastic telegram was sent (*The Fresno Bee-Republican*, April 1, 1932). On July 22, 1932, just a few days after *Hot-Cha!* closed, Ziegfeld succumbed to pleurisy. He was 65 years old.

According to author Charles Higham (*Ziegfeld*, 1972), behind the scenes, Lupe gave Ziegfeld more than his fair share of concerns. One time when she failed to show up for a matinee performance, Ziegfeld sent Goldie, his private secretary, to fetch her. The audience was in place and the curtain was held for one hour. When Goldie arrived at Lupe's hotel, she heard a commotion in the room. When the door opened, Goldie was astonished to see Lupe's sister giving the star of *Hot-Cha!* a high colonic irrigation on the carpet! "I've got a hangover!" Lupe said rather shakily. Goldie immediately dragged her to her feet and slapped her face. She then hauled her down the stairs and put her in a taxi. They got her on stage and the show did go on, but she struggled with that particular performance due to her inebriated condition.

Bert Lahr recalled Lupe rehearsing for the play in the nude. She found the tight-fitting costumes too confining so she'd strip off and continue with rehearsals as though she was fully clothed. While Lahr was amused, albeit a little distracted, by his co-star's uninhibited behavior, Flo Ziegfeld was in awe of Lupe's rehearsal technique. Not surprisingly, he showed up on time for each and every run through (Henry Jenkins, "You Don't Say That In English!, http://web.mit.edu/cms/People/henry3/lupe.html).

Lahr and Lupe developed a tight bond during the course of the show. He played a matador and she played his girlfriend. As for the plot, there wasn't much of one. A few jokes, some songs thrown in here and there, that was about it. Thirteen years her senior, Lahr was amused by Lupe's quick wit and enamored by her charm. Lupe felt the same about Lahr. They knew exactly where each other's funny buttons were and they pushed them — often! Lahr said:

> Working with Lupe was quite an experience. She couldn't laugh. She cackled — like a duck. I'd say things under my breath to her on the stage and she'd start to cackle.... [W]hen she'd go to the Mayfair or somewhere she'd just put on a dress. Nothing under it — nothing! [John Lahr, *Notes on a Cowardly Lion: The Biography of Bert Lahr*].

On stage, Lupe would chew a wad of gum and let it hang out one side of her mouth so that only Lahr could see it. When she wasn't on stage, Lupe would watch the show from the wings and laugh so loudly, the audience could hear her. Even when she *wasn't* on stage, she still managed to steal the show.

Lahr's future wife Mildred Schroeder (they were married in 1940) actually fainted with despair as the lovestruck Lahr left her side to rush through a revolving door in order to greet Lupe. When Lupe was asked about her feelings for Lahr, she said, "I love him" (Conner, *Lupe Vélez and Her Lovers*).

One night, Lupe realized that it was silly for her to own sixteen fur coats, so she told each chorus girl to write her name on a slip of paper and drop it into a hat. Then she drew a slip. The girl whose name was drawn was given one of her fur coats (*Modern Screen*, September 1932).

A 1932 radio performance of Lupe singing "Conchita" was released on LP disc (Label/Issue No: JJA Records 19779), Album Title — *The Music of Broadway: 1932* (Reissues of 78s). LP disc (Label/Issue No: Mark56 Records 737), Album Title — *Ziegfeld Follies on the Air* (Also titled — *Florenz Ziegfeld and the Ziegfeld Follies*).

Elizabeth Dickson of *Collier's* magazine (undated, circa 1932) gave Lupe one of the biggest compliments of her career:

The [*Hot-Cha!*] stage seems empty when [Lupe] isn't on.... [O]n she comes, and the topmost row in the balcony gets a shot in the arm. Talking, singing, dancing, imitating, this girl from over the border is having such a perfectly swell time herself that the gulf between the audience and performer closes up. This isn't technique. It's a gift.

***Strike Me Pink*** (1933) Musical revue. Producers: Ray Henderson, Lew Brown, Waxey Gordon. Sketches: Lew Brown, Ray Henderson. Additional Dialogue: Mack Gordon, Jack McGowan, Richard Jerome. Lyrics: Lew Brown. Music: Ray Henderson. Musical Director: Al Goodman. Orchestrator: Edward Powell. Production supervisors: Ray Henderson, Lew Brown. Sketches Directed by Jack McGowan. Dances and Ensembles Staged by Seymour Felix. Theater: Majestic Theatre (New York). Opening: March 4, 1933. Closing: June 10, 1933 (122 performances). Description: A revue in two acts. Cast: Aber Twins, Mary Ann, Claiborne Arms, Roy Atwell, Gracie Barrie, Emmy Bock, Helane Brown, James Brown, Norma Butler, Barbara Caswell, Mary Chappelle, Hal Clyne, Frank Conlon, Wilma Cox, Dorothy Dare (Son's Wife), Marguerite De Coursey, Ruth Dod, Dorothy Dodge, Bill Douglas, Johnny Downs, Elsie Duffy, George Duke, Jimmy Durante, Geraldine Dvorak, Mabel Ellis, Louise Estes, Peggy Fish, Alex Fisher, Peggy Gallimore, Eleanor Garden, Eddie Garr, Ruth Grady, Lula Gray, Jack Harcourt, Pearl Harris, Ruth Harrison, David Johns, Daniel Johnson, Charlotte Joslin, Leoda Knapp, Leslie Laurence, Charles Lawrence, Hal Le Roy (Bobby), Betty Lee, Clark Leston, Phyllis Lynd, Diana Lynn (Dancer), Barbara MacDonald, Mary Joan Martin, Earl Mason, Rosalie McCallion, June McNulty, Jack Moore, Mary Moore, Jewel Morse, George Murray, Ricky Newell, Carolyn Nolte, Olaf Olson, Lillian Pertka, Leonore Pettit, Jack Ross, Jean Ryan, Jimmy Ryan, Ted Schultz, Louise Sheldon, Jackie Sherman, Madeline Southworth, **Lupe Vélez**, Matthew Vodnoy, George Dewey Washington, Davenie Watson, Milton Watson, George Weeden, Roberta West, Gil White, Marguerite Wiley, Hope Williams.

*Strike Me Pink* opened at the height of the Great Depression. Times were tough, so much so that when the show opened, the banks closed. Production supervisor Lew Brown told everyone they had to take cuts or the show would be shut down. He wanted to take $250 a week out of Lupe's salary.

She emphatically answered, "No!" He flew into a rage and told her she couldn't refuse without putting 300 people out of work. She told him to take *$500* out of her salary, so long as he promised that no chorus girl would be cut. He agreed and the show opened.

Lupe had long been a favorite of the chorus girls. After she made it in America and had everything that money could buy, she loaned them her dresses, shoes and jewelry when they had a special date planned or a man to impress. She lovingly called chorus girls "her hobby," because she saw how hard they worked for such little reward. They rehearsed at least six weeks before the main stars in the show, usually from six in the morning to nine at night. Lupe often saw them with their toes bleeding. Before a show even opened, they were in debt; they never got credit, they never got respect. So Lupe made it her job to fight for them and everyone listened to Lupe. She often joked that she could sit in the front row of any New York show and ruin it. The chorus girls would see her and forget their lines or their steps. They'd wave and yell out, "Oh, hulloa, Lupe!" Their mothers would send Lupe cakes and pastries as a thank you for watching out for their daughters. Earning $1500 a week, Lupe said that the $500 pay cut made little difference to her, but taking two or three dollars out of the $55 that a chorus girl gets is the difference between enough to eat and not enough to eat. And Lupe always remembered what having not enough to eat felt like (The Gladys Hall Papers, the Margaret Herrick Library).

> The show was backed by gangster Waxey Gordon.... [O]pening-night top was $25 (outrageous for those dark days), and the tickets were printed on gold stock.... [T]he result was neither a flop nor a smash, but a pleasant run of 122 performances [www.playbill.com].

> The play would have continued indefinitely and only closed because both Lupe and Jimmy Durante were bound to film contracts and were required to fulfill their obligations in Hollywood (*Syracuse Herald*, March 8, 1934).

***Transatlantic Rhythm*** (1936) Opened at London's Adelphi Theatre on October 1, 1936. Producer: James Paul ("Jimmy") Donahue. Main Cast: **Lupe Vélez**, Ruth Etting, Lou Holtz, Buck and Bubbles.

While first-night crowds jostled London Bobbies outside the Adelphi Theatre, behind the curtain the milling cast of *Transatlantic Rhythm*

threatened a walkout unless producer James Paul ("Jimmy") Donahue Jr., 23-year-old heir to part of the Woolworth fortune, paid their back salaries. High-strung showgirls had dressed and undressed several times during the to and fro of negotiations, and veteran stage and screen star Ruth Etting had threatened to quit on the spot. Lupe claimed she was also owed $7,250 (approximately $115,000 in 2011). Lupe managed to calm the masses by jumping onto a chair and crooning "Ah, Sweet Mystery of Life" to the fretful chorines. Somehow, she persuaded them to put on the $110,000 revue without pay, but it didn't last (*Time*. October 12, 1936).

The show opened in Manchester, England. By the time it reached London, it was heavily in debt and two weeks behind in cast salaries. When it was all said and done, Donahue lost a little less than $50,000 in the failed revue show. The venture did little to diminish his enthusiasm and he claimed it was a "valuable experience." Etting left the show after opening night in London. Though she was still owed a week's salary, upon her return to New York on the *Normandie*, she was photographed with her arm around Donahue to show there were no hard feelings (*Rochester Journal*, October 13, 1936). *The Times of London* (undated, 1936) called the show, writing, "It turned out to be a brilliantly hollow entertainment."

During her time with *Transatlantic Rhythm*, Lupe was miserable, mainly because her marriage to Johnny Weissmuller was crumbling. The only reason she took the job abroad was to give them a much-needed break. She thought it may help bring them back together. After a time, Weissmuller flew to London to visit her, but it didn't take long to realize that nothing had changed. In an extensive interview in 1938, she told reporter Gladys Hall that she would spend her weekends in London in castles, being entertained by royalty, being fawned over by the public, yet in her own home, there was nothing but heartache (The Gladys Hall Papers, the Margaret Herrick Library).

**Vaudeville tour (1936)** Lupe's vaudeville tour with husband Johnny Weissmuller earned them $5,500 per week (approximately $86,000 in 2011) between the two of them. Lupe sang, danced and once again showcased her talent for impersonating her peers; Gloria Swanson, Dolores del Rio and Katharine Hepburn were mimicked to raucous laughter from the sell-out audiences. Lupe also performed a comedic Tarzan skit with Weissmuller.

***You Never Know* (stage, 1938)** Lupe performed in this play on tour prior to its New York opening. Tryouts began March 3, 1938, at the Shubert Theatre in New Haven; March 7, 1938, at the Shubert Theatre, Boston; March 21, 1938, at the National Theatre, Washington, D.C.; March 28, 1938, at the Forrest Theatre, Philadelphia; April 18, 1938, at the Nixon Theatre, Pittsburgh; April 24, 1938, at the Cass Theatre, Detroit; May 1, 1938, at the Grand Opera House, Chicago; May 22, 1938, at the Shrine Auditorium, Des Moines; May 23, 1938, at English's Theatre, Indianapolis; May 27, 1938, at the Hartman Theatre, Columbus; May 29, 1938, at the Erlanger Theatre, Buffalo; September 16, 1938, at the Bushnell Theatre, Hartford. A musical comedy in two acts, it opened at the Winter Garden in New York on September 21, and closed on November 26 after 78 performances. It was produced by Lee and J. J. Shubert and based on the play *By Candlelight* by Siegfried Geyer. Directed by Rowland Leigh and George Abbott. Music and lyrics by Cole Porter. Additional music by Dana Suesse, Robert Katscher, Rowland Leigh, Alex Fogarty and Edwin Gilbert. Choreography by Robert Alton. Cast: Clifton Webb (Gaston), Libby Holman (Mme. Baltin), Rex O'Malley (Baron Ferdinand de Romer), Toby Wing (Ida Courtney), **Lupe Vélez (Maria)**.

Rehearsals were so out of control, director Rowland Leigh walked out and refused to return until Libby Holman and Lupe resolved their differences. The fireworks started when Holman announced that all she wanted was a small part and "perhaps one little song." She got more than she wished for. After being assigned two new Cole Porter numbers, Lupe had something to say and for various reasons (see biography portion) she threatened to kill Holman (*The Abilene Reporter-News*, August 31, 1938). The Lupe-Libby feud aside, Holman was so hated by the crew, they referred to her as "The Jewish Witch."

Due to a serious riding accident in October 1937, Porter's legs were in plaster during casting and rehearsals. A serious infection and multiple operations would be the cause of lifelong medical problems, including drug and alcohol addictions to numb the pain. After thirty-four operations,

his right leg was amputated and replaced with an artificial limb in 1958. Porter died of kidney failure on October 15, 1964. He was 73 years old.

Whether she was on stage in Mexico or a Hollywood star with the world at her feet, Lupe enjoyed making fun of her contemporaries. Much of the impersonating was all good-hearted fun; however, when the occasion called for it, she'd often use her mimicking talent to publicly humiliate her rivals. Lupe had three very bitter female feuds during her Hollywood years: Jetta Goudal, Libby Holman and Lilyan Tashman.

One time, while Lupe was dining at the Embassy club, she spotted Lilyan Tashman from across the room. Lilyan was wearing long white gloves, so Lupe proceeded to wrap napkins around her arms and make fun of her for all to see. People snickered at Lupe's impromptu show but Lilyan wasn't laughing. On that occasion, both ladies were restrained before a physical altercation could happen. But sarcastic, bitchy remarks flew back and forth between Lupe and Lilyan for ages. Then came the culmination of years of pent-up frustration and the feisty pair came to blows on the powder room floor in the Montmarte Café in Hollywood. They clawed, punched and kicked at each other and by all accounts, Lupe won a clear decision. A few years later, Lilyan Tashman died (1896–1934) of stomach cancer. She was 37 years old (Conner, *Hollywood's Most Wanted: The Top Ten Book of Lucky Breaks, Prima Donnas, Box Office Bombs, and Other Oddities*).

Close to a dozen well-known theater and film stars were considered for Lupe's role of Maria. Those on the short list were Marlene Dietrich, Tallulah Bankhead, Miriam Hopkins, Gloria Swanson, Mary Ellis, Peggy Conklin, Genevieve Tobin, Margo, Joan Crawford and June Knight ("Cole Porter Musical Is Coming Here," *The Pittsburgh Press*, February 5, 1938).

Lupe appeared as Maria in Boston, Washington, Pittsburgh, Detroit, Chicago and Indianapolis. The *Los Angeles Examiner* ("Show Stopped By Lupe Vélez," March 8, 1938) reported on the opening night's performance at the Shubert Theatre in Boston (March 7):

Lupe Vélez stopped the show tonight as she made her first musical comedy appearance since 1932 in ... *You Never Know* ... Displaying her talents as a comedienne, with the aid of Porter's clever lyrics, the Mexican actress won ovations

for her singing and dancing opposite Clifton Webb, whose performance was no less ingratiating. Lupe showcased her impersonations once again.... [S]he transformed herself from Katharine Hepburn, Gloria Swanson, Simone Simon and Shirley Temple...."

Just prior to the Washington opening of *You Never Know*, Lupe arrived in town and said she wanted a ninth floor suite and that nothing else would suffice. She was quietly informed that no hotel in Washington was higher than eight stories due to a building ordinance. Lupe didn't care about building regulations, she still wanted the ninth story. A very patient hotel manager showed Lupe a luxurious third floor suite which she loved. As she looked at the room number, 306, she squealed with delight. "Look," she yelled to the manager, pointing to the number on the door. "Three and seex — eet make nine. That's same as these nine floor, eh? Nobody fool Lupe" ("Whoopee Lupe," *The Pittsburgh Press*, March 29, 1938).

Reviews: *Time* (April 11, 1938): "Clifton Webb's versatility, Lupe Vélez's high spirits, Libby Holman's low register, *You Never Know* has sex & sophistication, somewhat less breath & bounce. Riding high are Vélez and Webb as a manservant and lady's maid who doll up in their employers' togs. Libby Holman, featured in the billing, is slighted in the show."

*Vogue* (undated, 1938): "Lupe Vélez has no more dignity than a donkey."

John Mason Brown of the *New York Post* (September 1938): "You might think that with Cole Porter on hand to supply music and lyrics for such performers as Webb, Vélez and Holman, the results would be sprightly, but in spite of what you may have thought, permit me to report you are wrong."

By all accounts, the show put on behind the scenes was far more entertaining than anything brought to the stage. After it closed, Lupe was ill from the demands of the show and the stresses of the daily battles with Holman. She was sick and exhausted. Her doctors ordered her to rest (Gladys Hall Papers, the Margaret Herrick Library).

**The Paramount Theater, New York City (1940)**
Lupe headlined an in-between movies show with Red Skelton and Tommy Dorsey and His Orchestra. It was originally slated to run for one hour, but there was so much ad libbing going on, it wasn't unusual for the performance to run an hour

and a half. With three performances a day, the schedule was grueling, but the show proved so popular that the initial two-week run turned into six weeks. While the live show was only supposed to go on "between" films, Lupe and Red would often come out onto the stage and heckle the actors on the screen. They particularly enjoyed making fun of the wacky sci-fi horror-fest, *Dr. Cyclops* (1940).

**Glad to See You** (stage, 1944) On October 13, 1944, Lowell E. Redelings of *Hollywood Citizen News* reported that Lupe had withdrawn from rehearsals for Dave Wolper's new musical comedy *Glad to See You* since the role "wasn't to her liking." In reality, she was a few months pregnant and grappling with what to do; two months later she was dead.

A month to the day after Lupe announced that she was dropping out of the production (November 13, 1944), *Glad to See You* opened at the Schubert Theatre in Philadelphia. It closed at the Opera House in Boston on January 6, 1945, and never made it to Broadway. The cast included Jane Withers, Eddie Davis, June Knight, Kenny Bowers, Sammy White, Joseph McCauley, Gene Barry, Nancy Donovan, Jayne Manners, Charles Conoway, Eric Roberts, Patsy O'Shea, Alexis Rotov, Gloria McGehee, Lew Eckels, Walter Rinner, Michael Mauree, Sid Lippe, Jack Harney, Peter Kehrlein, John (Red) Kullers, Slam Stewart, Valerie Bettis, María Monez, Paul Mario, Nancy Newton, Farley and Lunick, Whitney Sisters and Betty Jane Hunt (www.kennybowersfanclub.com).

# IV: Noted Radio Work (1930–1940)

**February 25, 1930** Lupe appeared as the guest artist on the Paul Whiteman Old Gold radio hour, singing "Caribbean Love Song" over the air on the Columbia Broadcasting System in Los Angeles. *The Evening Independent* (St. Petersburg, Florida, February 25, 1930) explained that Lupe's voice would be carried via 3000 miles of wire lines to station WABC in New York, and it would then be distributed to the Columbia network. While Lupe sang in Los Angeles, Whiteman directed his famous band in San Diego. This was the first time a national broadcast was sent out of the coast city. The Mexican Marimba band of Agua Caliente were also showcased during the broadcast.

**April 3, 1932** Ziegfeld stars both past and present appeared on *Ziegfeld Follies of the Air*, the inaugural presentation, featuring Florenz Ziegfeld, Lupe Vélez, Eddie Dowling and Al Goodman's orchestra, direct from New York. Billie Burke (Mrs. Ziegfeld) and daughter Patricia appeared from Los Angeles in the new weekly series. Aside from KHJ, seventy additional stations of the Columbia network heard the 5 P.M. broadcast.

**October 12, 1934** Lupe walked out on a British radio broadcast because they wanted her to sing "The Peanut Vendor Song" and she wanted to talk instead. As eager listeners awaited Lupe's performance, an announcer said, "We were expecting Miss Vélez to sing but I am afraid she has disappointed

us." Lupe later explained that she was disappointed herself, but in reality, her contracts would not permit her to sing anyway, even if she wanted to ("Lupe Vélez Walks Out on British Radio Co.," *Dunkirk Evening Observer*, October 13, 1934).

**May 24, 1937** Lupe appeared on the *Lux Radio Theater* episode "Under Two Flags." Herbert Marshall, Olivia de Havilland and Lionel Atwill also loaned their voices to tell a story of the Foreign Legion in this one-hour broadcast. Cecil B. DeMille was also featured, making the introductory and closing remarks. Lupe played the role of Cigarette, a French girl.

**August 14, 1937** Lupe was interviewed on KNX's *Hollywood in Person* at 9:45 A.M.

**August 19, 1937** Lupe and George Raft, along with Frederick Jagle of the operatic field, were *Music Hall* guests at 6 over KFI. They performed "Way Out West on West End Avenue" from the 1937 Broadway musical *Babes in Arms*. The film version of the same name (directed by Busby Berkeley) was released in 1939 and starred Judy Garland and Mickey Rooney.

**February 1, 1938** Lupe appeared as a guest star on Jack Oakie's broadcast at 6:30 P.M. on KNX.

**January 26, 1939** Lupe appeared on *Tune Up Time*. Edward Everett Horton, Hugh Herbert, Willie Howard and Rudy Vallee also appeared on the show.

**March 28, 1939** Lupe appeared on the air with Bob Hope at 7 P.M. on KFL.

**October 10, 1940** Lupe was one of the guest stars on *Let Yourself Go*, Milton Berle's KECA program at 7:30 P.M.

# V: Pop Culture (1949–2012)

**Unmade Lupe Vélez Biopics** On February 7, 1949, Erskine Johnson of the *Los Angeles Daily News* announced that an indie producer was trying to clear the rights to do the life story of Lupe Vélez, with Marquita Rivera in the lead role.

In early March 1966, Cuban-born actress Estelita Rodriguez was cast, and enthusiastically preparing for, her role of Lupe Vélez in a Vélez biopic. By March 12, 1966, 37-year-old Estelita was dead, on the kitchen floor of her North Hollywood home. Her cause of death wasn't made public, although some sources say she died of influenza.

In July 1969, a film based on the life of Lupe was once again talked about. Puerto Rican–born actress Rita Moreno was announced as being signed in the lead role. However, for the third time in two decades, the seemingly cursed project once again failed to get off the ground. It is somewhat surprising that Moreno even signed on to play her in the first place. Soon after winning her Academy Award for *West Side Story*, Moreno told interviewer Bob Thomas ("U.S. Films Don't Appeal to Moreno," *Corpus Christi Times*, May 1, 1963) that there were few, if any, post–Oscar roles that she considered worthy of accepting. She also blamed Lupe for stereotyping Latin women:

"...Oh, I've had offers for film roles," she said. "Latinas. You know the kind I mean — spitfires, girls with wild tempers. Look — I don't mind playing a Latin. I am one. I'm a girl with dark hair and large, flashing brown eyes.... Anita in *West Side Story* was a Latin, and she had a temper. But she also had depth of character. The roles I am offered don't." She sighed, "Lupe Vélez! She's the one who started this Hollywood thinking. She never knew what we poor Latins have had to face, following her."

Three years earlier, again in an interview with Thomas, Moreno wasn't nearly on handn "I'd like to have known [Lupe]. I'm sure she wasn't really a spitfire but a warm human being" ("Typing Latins as 'Sexpots' Is Called 'Silly,'" *Meriden Journal*, November 18, 1960).

*Lupe* (1965) Artist-filmmaker Andy Warhol shot the film *Lupe* with Edie Sedgwick in the title role during December 1965. Playwright Robert Heide said, "I conferred with Andy about writing *The Death of Lupe Vélez* for Edie who was anxious to play the role of the Mexican Spitfire, found dead in her Hollywood hacienda with her head in a toilet bowl. I met Edie [and I] mentioned the script I was working on. Edie said innocently, 'Oh, we already filmed that this afternoon. It's in the can ... in Technicolor.' Nothing was said when Andy arrived, although he did astonish me that evening by asking, 'When do you think Edie will commit suicide? I hope she lets me know so I can film it'" ("Village'65 Revisited, Letter to the Editor," *Village Voice*, July 27, 1982). Warhol's glib prediction came true a few years later, only he wasn't there to film it. Sedgwick was 28 years old when she died on November 16, 1971. The coroner ruled her death as "undetermined/accident/suicide"; the cause of death was "probable acute barbiturate intoxication" (Stein and Plimpton, *Edie*). Warhol's film did nothing to dispel Lupe's supposed "toilet death," each segment ends with a visual of Sedgwick with her head in the toilet.

*Lupe* (1967) Producer-Director: José Rodriguez-Soltero. Genre: Comedy-Musical. Running Time: 60 minutes. Release Date: January 30, 1967. Color. Language: English. Production Company and Distributor: Film Makers' Cooperative. Cast: Mario Montez (Lupe Vélez), White Pussy (A Cat), Salvador Cruz, Dorrie, Charles Frehse, Norman Holden, Charles Ludlam, Maxwell Reid, Medea Reid, Bill Vehr.

Puerto Rican–born experimental filmmaker José Rodriguez-Soltero (1943–2009) produced this follow-up homage to Warhol's 1965 film of the same name, complete with Mario Montez, a drag queen (and Warhol favorite) in the title role as Lupe Vélez. *The Village Voice* (June 17, 2008) described the film as a "persistent mess set to a mix of schmaltzy Spanish ballads, the Rolling Stones, flamenco, and Vivaldi...." With that said, it is to

this day considered an "art film." With all its wacky weirdness, it falls under the "cult classic" banner.

**Sleazy Scandals of the Silver Screen #1 (Comic, 1974)** Underground comic artist Jim Osborne (1943–2001) had a brief but memorable career from 1968 to the mid–1970s. His fascination with the macabre and gruesome gained him notoriety. Ironically, his personality was a stark contrast to the shocking work he produced; by all accounts, he was a quiet, unassuming man. Osborne suffered acute asthma and kidney problems. He retired from professional drawing, and into relative obscurity, for the last 25 years of his life. Lupe's last few hours of life is artfully depicted in *Sleazy Scandals of the Silver Screen #1* (January 1, 1974). Entitled "Hollywood Tragedy: The Suicide of Lupe Vélez," the story (by Lawrence La Fey) and art (Osborne) is inspired by the Kenneth Anger "died with her head in the toilet" tale. The comic is explicit and in bad taste, but with that said, it's still very well illustrated. Lupe is drawn *sans* clothes throughout.

**Children of Light by Robert Stone (1986 novel)** A schizophrenic actress describes a suicide-by-drowning scene that she just performed as "Lupe Vélez takes a dunk."

**"The Mexican Spitfires" (Band, 1988)** In 1988 the Sydney, Australia–based indie-pop group The Mexican Spitfires released their first six-track 12-inch EP, aptly titled *Lupe Vélez*.

**Frasier (1993 sitcom episode)** In the pilot episode of the award-winning *Frasier*, "The Good Son," Frasier Crane's (Kelsey Grammer) producer Roz Doyle (Peri Gilpin) tries to improve Frasier's outlook on his life by telling him the story of Lupe Vélez:

> ROZ: Ever heard of Lupe Vélez?
> FRASIER: Who?
> ROZ: Lupe Vélez, the movie star in the '30s. Well, her career hit the skids, so she decided she'd make one final stab at immortality. She figured if she couldn't be remembered for her movies, she'd be remembered for the way she died. And all Lupe wanted was to be remembered. So, she plans this lavish suicide — flowers, candles, silk sheets, white satin gown, full hair and makeup, the works. She takes the overdose of pills, lays on the bed, and imagines how beautiful she's going to look on the front page of tomorrow's newspaper. Unfor-

tunately, the pills don't sit well with the enchilada combo plate she sadly chose as her last meal. She stumbles to the bathroom, trips and goes head-first into the toilet, and that's how they found her.
> FRASIER: Is there a reason you're telling me this story?
> ROZ: Yes. Even though things may not happen like we planned, they can work out anyway.
> FRASIER: Remind me again how it worked for Lupe, last seen with her head in the toilet.
> ROZ: All she wanted was to be remembered. Will you ever forget that story?

**Torture-Tech Overdrive (1994)** A compilation CD ("If It Moves...") featuring the song "Lupe Vélez" by Jimmy Jazz. The song is about the illogicality of attempting to create a "beautiful suicide."

**The Simpsons (1997 sitcom episode)** In an episode titled "Homer's Phobia" (February 16, 1997), guest star John Waters gives several Simpson family members a driving tour of Springfield's shopping district. During the trip, he points out the store where Lupe Vélez reportedly bought the toilet she drowned in.

**The Assumption of Lupe Vélez (1999)** Directed by Rita Gonzalez, this 22-minute short is a mix of recreation scenes taken from Warhol and Rodriguez-Soltero's films about Lupe (1965 and 1967, respectively). Starring Latino drag queen La Lupe, it recreates Lupe's last night alive through to her evolvement into an underground cult icon.

**The Amazing Adventures of Kavalier & Clay by Michael Chabon (2000 novel)** Lupe Vélez is mentioned in this Random House novel, which won a 2001 Pulitzer Prize for fiction.

**Glamorous Latin Film Stars Paper Dolls by Tom Tierney (2003 book)** An eclectic mix of sixteen stars (with thirty-two costumes), from classic Hollywood right up until modern day, are featured within this Dover publication dedicated to actresses-performers with Hispanic roots. Famed paper doll artist Tom Tierney draws Lupe in outfits from *The Gaucho* (1927) and *Mexican Spitfire's Elephant* (1942).

**Forever Lupe (2007)** Mexican film director Martín Caballero made this critically acclaimed short film starring Mexican actress Marieli Romo as Lupe Vélez. In an interview with the author, Caballero said,

> In my opinion, she was more talented than Dolores del Rio because Lupe worked with the most important film directors of her time. She

was the first Mexican actress to work on Broadway as a leading star, she played comedy and dramatic roles.... [F]or me, she was a true star and a true diva. The most important thing is that she was so proud of being a Mexican woman. She represents my country as an extremely talented star.

**Lupe Book Optioned for Biopic:** December 20, 2007, actress Roselyn Sanchez optioned Floyd Conner's *Lupe Vélez and Her Lovers*, a full-length biography published in 1993 by Barricade Books. At the time, Sanchez was also interested in playing the lead role of Lupe Vélez. The biopic is yet to be made (*Los Angeles Times*, December 20, 2007).

***Return to Babylon*** **(2008)** This Alex Monty Canawati–directed homage to silent Hollywood was bogged down with varying post-production problems for many years. However, following Canawati's August 21, 2010, appearance on the A&E series *My Ghost Story* where he and the cast of the film spoke of varying degrees of paranormal activity

experienced during the production, Canawati teamed up with filmmaker Matt Riddlehoover to complete, re-edit and distribute the film.

It was authentically filmed with 1920s hand-cranked movie cameras (with black and white film). Many stars of old Hollywood features are included as characters and an impressive cast of talented modern actors portrayed them. Maria Conchita Alonso gets top billing as Lupe Vélez.

**Lupe Vélez Paper Doll (2010)** Internationally renowned paper doll artist Gregg Nystrom designed and created a beautifully detailed Lupe Vélez paper doll in September of 2010.

**Lupe Vélez Biopic (2012)** In May 2012, it was announced that actress Ana de la Reguera will produce and star (as Lupe) in a biopic about the life and career of Lupe Vélez. Oscar nominated director Carlos Carrera is slated the write the treatment and direct the film. Tentatively titled *Lupe*, the U.S. and Mexican co-production is scheduled to start filming by early 2013.

# Chapter Notes

## Chapter 1

1. Gabriel Ramírez, *Lupe Vélez: la mexicana que escupia fuego* (Mexico: Cineteca Nacional).

2. During the war, Lupe's father Colonel Villalobos was nicknamed "El Gallo," aka "The Rooster." He fought against General Pancho Villa in the long, complicated and very bloody Mexican Revolution (*Verdad y Mito de la Revolución Mexicana, Vol. 2 (Truth and Myths of the Mexican Revolution)*, Ignacio Muñoz, Ediciones Populares, S.A., Mexico, 1961).

3. Lupe's brother Emigdio would have been about three and a half, maybe four years old at the time, far too young to ride his own horse. However, it was discovered that Lupe had another brother. Jacobo Villalobos Reyes y Vélez (1906–1912) is buried in the El Saucito cemetery in San Luis Potosí, Mexico. It's probable that he died in the midst of the Revolution, maybe even during the incident that Lupe recounts. Following family tradition, the first-born son took the name of his father, Jacobo. And so, the story about Lupe's "father" dying in the Revolution was mistakenly started. If anyone had bothered to check the birth to death dates (1906–1912), the error would have been corrected decades ago.

4. For her entire Hollywood career, Lupe would carry her makeup around with her in a rusty fishing tackle box. She did all her own makeup, insisting that she knew her face best (*Los Angeles Examiner*, August 19, 1937).

## Chapter 2

1. "Religious Faith of Lupe Vélez Told," *Los Angeles Evening Herald and Express,* December 18, 1944.

2. Various sources spell the name differently, yet all variations are incorrect. Lupe would sometimes alternatively pronounce his name as "Mil-a-tone" or "Meelton"; however, the correct Spanish spelling of the name is Melitón. In English, the translated name would closely resemble Milton.

## Chapter 3

1. Gladys Hall Papers, Margaret Herrick Library.

## Chapter 4

1. Fernando Curiel, *Paseando por Plateros* (M. Casillas Editores and Cultura SEP, 1982).

2. Lupe's father Jacobo was eventually found alive, but he was near death from several bullet wounds and he needed extensive medical attention. The months following his return were crucial and it took an extended period of care for him to recover completely.

3. One night, after a party, Jorge Loyo was traveling as a passenger in a car driven by Lupe when a group of policeman mistook them for bandits. Shots were fired and Loyo was slightly wounded. Lupe stopped the car and when the police caught up she gave them a tongue-lashing that reportedly "made the public guardians look like children" (*La Prensa*, May 22, 1935).

4. The producer of Lupe's debut show, Pablo Prida Santacilia, wrote in his book *Y se levanta el telón: mi vida dentro del teatro* (1960) that a suggestive costume (costing 40 pesos) was specially made (by Paquita) for Lupe's stage debut. While Lupe maintains her debut costume was homemade, it's entirely likely that it initially was, but then following the scandal of the Actors' Guild ban and the subsequent build-up to Lupe's debut following the ban being lifted, the sell-out crowd, etc., a professional costume was made for her to replace it.

## Chapter 5

1. Unidentified snippet, 1927.

2. The feminine form of "mestizo," meaning a person who has both native American and European blood.

3. Lupe's debut at the Teatro Principal took place on either March 11 or April 1, 1925 (sources vary). She was still only sixteen at the time. A few months later, by the time she was seventeen, she was performing at the Teatro Lírico. Her Chihuahua "La Pluma" ("The Feather") went everywhere with her, even to the theatre. Her first song, "Charlie, My Boy," was part of the "No lo tapes" (meaning "Do not cover it") revue show (*Y se levanta el telón: mi vida dentro del teatro,* Pablo Prida Santacilla, Editorial Botas, México, 1960, 1st edition, and www.austinfilm.org)

4. "Beneficio" was a theatre show that paid the artist a bonus. "Beneficios" were for very popular artists; in some cases, also for artists in need.

5. Lupe continued to do this, even after her Hollywood success; she would not put on airs or think herself better than anyone with less money or less success than herself. In California, she would attend Mexican colony celebrations and charitable events.

## Chapter 7

1. *Los Angeles Evening Herald,* August 3, 1931.

2. Lupe's first Hollywood contract is an extremely complicated matter. On March 12, 1927, Lupe signed an exclusive contract with theatrical agent Frank A. Woodyard (alternatively referred to as Frank A. Woodward in main text), who would act as her manager. She was to give him twenty-five percent of her earnings. Just two days after signing with Woodyard on March 14, 1927, Lupe was loaned to Hal Roach Studios. In turn, Lupe was loaned to Douglas Fairbanks Pictures Corporation for her breakout role in *The Gaucho* (1927). Lupe insisted she was underage when signing the contract with Woodyard, making their agreement invalid. Woodyard claimed otherwise. As a result of their dispute, Woodyard brought two actions to the California Supreme Court, one against Lupe and another against Lupe and Cecil B. DeMille Pictures Corporation, the company next wanting to use her services (for 1928's *Stand and Deliver*). Woodyard's November 1927 application for an injunction to prevent Lupe from working with anyone else pending settlement of the contract with him was denied by the court. By January 5, 1928, an out of court settlement was agreed upon. Woodyard received $50,000 in compensation and Lupe was released from the contract she signed with him.

3. In an interview with *El Herald de México* (November 13, 1927), Lupe said, "[Douglas Fairbanks] is crazy for me — on the screen, of course, not in real life, because he has his adorable Mary Pickford, and I have Mr. [F. Richard] Jones, my fiancé and presently my director [on *The Gaucho*]." The article states that "marriage is so close and it worries Lupe."

4. Del Rio's well-publicized romance with Orson Welles (they never married) ended her marriage to Cedric Gibbons and the couple were divorced in 1941. Del Rio died of liver disease, April 11, 1983, at age 77.

## Chapter 8

1. Floyd Conner, *Lupe Vélez and Her Lovers* (Fort Lee, NJ: Barricade, 1993).

2. The *Appleton Post-Crescent* (June 25, 1929) ran a picture of Lupe holding two turtles with the

letters of "L" and "G" painted onto their shells. The letters stood for "Lupe" and "Gary" (Cooper). The photo sparked a nationwide trend, and children all across America asked their parents for turtles with their initials painted on the shells.

## Chapter 9

1. Carolyn Roos Olsen and Marylin Hudson, *Hollywood's Man Who Worried for the Stars: The Story of Bö Roos* (Indianapolis, IN: Authorhouse, 2008).
2. If Lupe's relationships with Mil-a-tone in Mexico and F. Richard Jones (director of *The Gaucho*) were as serious as she suggested, then she was engaged five times. Though she was reportedly engaged to John Gilbert, neither of them publicly confirmed it.

## Chapter 10

1. *Los Angeles Evening Herald and Express*, December 16, 1944.

## Chapter 11

1. *San Jose Evening News,* October 30, 1933.

## Chapter 12

1. *Rochester Evening Journal*, February 5, 1934.
2. Hortensia Elizondo was better known among Spanish-speaking people living in the United States than in her own country. She despised Mexican cinema in general; praise from her pen was a rare occurrence. But she did compliment *La zandunga*.
3. In 1927, Lupe told reporter Loreley (aka María Luisa Garza) of *El Heraldo de México*, "I have just bought this car and would like to crash it, since I like it so much." Driving her car at high speeds gave Lupe a great thrill, and she sped around Beverly Hills with little regard for the laws of the road. She had no fear of the police. Aside from her limousine, convertibles were Lupe's cars of choice. She'd put the top down and feel her hair fly wildly around in the wind. In April 1929, Lupe's freewheeling road escapades were halted when she was hit with a speeding ticket. She was cited on Wilshire Boulevard for going forty miles an hour in a twenty-mile zone, and also for not having a driver's license. In a burst of temperament befitting Lupe, she tore up the summons and flung it in the officer's face, got back in her car and drove away. After failing to appear at a May hearing for the offense, a summons for her arrest was issued. She voluntarily surrendered to the police later that month and was released on $30 bail (approximately $275 in 2011), pending a further hearing. It was just one instance where the law caught up with "lead foot Lupe," but it did nothing to deter her from continuing to drive by her own rules ("Police Catch Up with Lupe Vélez." *Los Angeles Times,* May 23, 1929). Journalist Don Alvarado published a story (*La Prensa*, May 22, 1935) about a colonel (he remained nameless) who challenged Lupe to be a passenger in his speeding car. He told her she'd be afraid of the speed his car could reach. Lupe assured him she would not. Lupe got in and the colonel put his foot down. The more the colonel sped up, the more Lupe shouted, "Faster, colonel, faster!" The car was zigzagging along the roadway, seemingly moments away from crashing, yet Lupe was in her element. No fear was shown by Lupe, and the colonel lost the bet.
4. In 1971, Johnny legally adopted the biological daughter of his last wife, Maria. Lisa Weissmuller Gallagher died on May 14, 2007. She was 66 years old.
5. Hugh Munro Neely, film historian and curator of the Mary Pickford Institute, interviewed Gates for a planned documentary project, a dual biography on the life and careers of Dolores del Rio and Lupe Vélez. He said, "I liked the idea that their careers appeared to run parallel for such a long time, and then diverged so dramatically." Neely said Gates confessed to him that Weissmuller always had a "soft spot for Lupe," and that he worried about her and was "sick over her death." However,

when she learned that the scandal of Lupe's death would be a significant part of Mr. Neely's story, he said, "She cut me off and refused to talk to me again."

## Chapter 14

1. Clayton Moore, *I Was That Masked Man* (Lanham, MD: Taylor, 1998).

## Chapter 15

1. www.imdb.com.

2. *Los Angeles Evening Herald and Express* (November 6, 1939) reported that Lupe and Art Laschelle dressed in old clothes and stood unnoticed among film fans for the premiere of *The Real Glory* (1939). Whenever an actress came along whom Lupe didn't like, she gave her the Bronx cheer. Incidentally, the star of the film was Gary Cooper.

## Chapter 16

1. *Los Angeles Examiner*, October 3, 1938.

2. John Barrymore's elder brother Lionel Barrymore chuckled for an hour when he heard what Lupe said about him: "He's not like a Hollywood actor at all. Why, the man fairly reeks of common sense" (*Los Angeles Evening Herald Examiner*, August 5, 1932).

## Chapter 17

1. *Los Angeles Evening Herald and Express*, June 1, 1943.

2. Although Arturo de Córdova was married, rumors swirled about his sexuality. Lupe's second cousin Pedro Quintanilla Gómez-Noriega said:

As far as I remember about my grandmother's account of Lupe's life, Arturo de Córdova was *never* Lupe's boyfriend, let alone her lover. It was always rumored that in fact he was gay and that his association with Lupe (Lupe being a great friend to her friends) was to hide that fact. Lupe was instrumental in his entering the entertainment business, through her forcing the makers of her film *La zandunga* to hire him. That film catapulted him to stardom. About six years later, their "romance" was reported in all the Hollywood papers, for the sole purpose of boosting his career in America. In the end, de Córdova proved to be a questionable friend to Lupe, having forgotten what she did for him and shunning her in the latter part of her life.

## Chapter 18

1. *Los Angeles Evening Herald and Express*, November 27, 1944.

2. The average U.S. *yearly* wage in 1943 was $2,000. In comparison, Ramond was earning a very healthy $2,400 *per month* (www.thepeoplehistory.com).

## Chapter 19

1. "Seek To Bury Lupe In Mexico." *Los Angeles Evening Herald and Express,* December 16, 1944.

## Chapter 20

1. *Hollywood Citizen News*, June 23, 1945.

2. Josephine had attempted her own acting career in Hollywood. She made her screen debut in *Her Man* (1931) as an uncredited cigarette girl. A year later she appeared as Grace, the nurse, in *Dracula* (1931), again uncredited. Lastly, she took the role of Juanita in *The Ridin' Fool* (1931). She

rode the coattails of her famous sister, taking the Vélez name, but despite her similarity in appearance with Lupe, her career went nowhere.

3. One hundred thousand dollars seems like a very low estimate on Lupe's *entire* collection of jewelry. After all, in 1934, her most expensive piece, a convertible necklace, had an estimated worth of $75,000 alone. Of the eighteen jewelry pieces auctioned, that same necklace was listed as her most valuable item. Given Lupe's extravagant tastes, it's unlikely that the remaining seventeen pieces of jewelry would have such a lowly value of $25,000 combined.

## Filmography

1. In 1935, Lupe turned down $4000 per week to appear with Maurice Chevalier at the Casino de Paris. In 1938 she turned down a $4500 per week, four-picture deal in Mexico. *La zandunga* (1938) was an exception; Lupe received $12,500 a week for her services on the Mexican production. Additionally, she was still in high demand in Argentina and she often turned down lucrative personal appearance tours and picture deals in the South American region. *If* Lupe's Hollywood career dried up, and it certainly hadn't, internationally her career was far from over.

2. Lupita is a term of endearment for Guadalupe or Lupe. The closest English translation would be "Little Lupe."

# Bibliography

## Newspapers

*The Abilene Reporter-News*, August 7, 1937; August 31, 1938; December 15, 1944.

*Appleton Post-Crescent*, June 25, 1929; no date, 1930; November 29, 1930; October 22, 1932.

*The Argus*, December 4, 1937.

*The Berkeley Daily Gazette*, March 19, 1928.

*The Brisbane Courier*, August 6, 1930.

*The Brownsville Herald,* April 14, 1929; November 11, 1931; August 19, 1934; September 27, 1937.

*The Brownsville Herald Ten-Year Review*, December 28, 1933.

*The Chronicle Telegram*, February 27, 1948.

*Classic Images*, April 1999.

*Corpus Christi Times,* August 6, 1941; May 13, 1948; May 1, 1963.

*The Courier Mail*, February 15, 1934.

*Daytona Beach Morning Journal*, December 23, 1944.

*The Deseret News,* December 19 and December 28, 1944.

*Dunkirk Evening Observer*, October 13, 1934; November 14, 1940; October 28, 1941.

*The El Paso Herald Post,* December 15, 1944.

*Ellensburg Daily Record*, December 16, 1944.

*Evening Herald Examiner,* June 24, 1932.

*The Evening Independent,* February 25, 1930; October 24, 1943.

*Film Daily,* November 27, 1927; April 8, 1928; December 29, 1929; February 23 and August 24, 1930; January 21 and September 15, 1933; January 14, 1936; December 15, 1937; May 17, 1939; October 9, 1940; February 2 and September 4, 1941; January 8, May 6, and October 5, 1942; March 24, 1943.

*The Florence Times*, December 15, 1944.

*The Florence Times Daily*, November 21, 1931.

*The Frederick Post,* July 15, 1929.

*The Fresno Bee,* December 5, December 15 and December 16, 1944.

*The Fresno Bee-Republican*, April 1, 1932.

*Hammond Times,* June 22, 1937; March 12, 1939; October 23, 1940; December 29, 1942.

*Herald-Journal,* November 12, 1937.

*El Heraldo de México*, October 3, 1925; November 1, 1925; November 13, 1927.

*Hollywood Citizen News*, December 23, 1931; February 20, July 15, August 5, and September 5, 1932; September 28 and November 4, 1933; May 18, 1934; August 23, August 25, and November 23, 1937; October 7 and November 10, 1941; October 13, 1944; June 23, 1945; May 13, 1947.

*Hollywood Daily Citizen*, March 1 and May 15, 1929; February 25, February 28, September 3, and September 23, 1930.

*The Independent Daily News,* February 20, 1931.

*Jefferson City Post-Tribune,* August 8, 1941

*Kentucky New Era,* October 22, 1940, and November 15, 1944.

*Kinematograph Weekly,* April 4, 1935.

*Laredo Times,* January 1941.

*The Lewiston Daily Sun,* January 1, 1932.

*The Lewiston Evening Journal,* December 19, 1944.

*Lima News,* April 20, 1932; May 30, 1933; November 9, 1940; February 22, 1942; December 15, 1944.

*Lincoln State Journal,* August 16, 1938.

*Los Angeles Daily News,* January 10, 1945; February 7, 1949.

*Los Angeles Evening Herald,* March 3, March 22, August 15, and November 14, 1930; January 10, and February 20, 1931.

*Los Angeles Evening Herald and Express,* August 7, 1930; April 2, December 21, and December 23, 1932; January 20, January 28, June 17, and October 7, 1933; February 5, February 8, March 7, April 16, May 18, June 13, and July 14, 1934; February 21, 1937; February 16, 1938; January 5, 1940; September 1 and November 17, 1941; June 6, 1943; January 14, November 27, December 15, and December 17, 1944.

*Los Angeles Examiner,* June 1, June 4, and June 13, 1928; March 2 and March 29, 1929; March 27, July 8, and November 14, 1930; February 10, June 16, and November 12, 1931; January 20, September 19, October 3, and October 30, 1933; May 20, September 17, September 23, and December 19, 1937; March 8 and July 18, 1938; April 23, 1939; January 26 and October 19, 1940; September 13, 1941; June 4, 1942; August 9, 1943; April 11 and December 15, 1944; July 7, 1945.

*Los Angeles Independent Daily News,* August 15, 1930; September 28, 1934; January 14, 1943.

*Los Angeles Post-Record,* March 25, 1931; March 25 and undated, 1932; June 10 and undated, 1933; July 14 and December 10, 1934.

*Los Angeles Record,* March 27 and March 29, 1929; March 15, June 17, and November 14, 1930; February 20, November 12, and undated, 1931.

*Los Angeles Times,* May 23, 1929; August 15, 1930; undated, 1942; April 18, September 19, December 10, and December 19, 1944; June 10, 1949; December 20, 2007.

*The Lowell Sun,* January 19, 1945.

*Mason City Globe,* December 14, 1944.

*Mason City Globe Gazette,* July 2, 1934.

*The Meriden Daily Journal,* February 17, 1934.

*Meriden Journal,* November 18, 1960.

*The Miami News,* December 19 and December 29, 1944; June 20, 1945.

*The Milwaukee Journal,* December 26, December 27, and December 28, 1944.

*The Milwaukee Sentinel,* February 8, 1931.

*Modesto Bee,* December 5, 1944.

*The Montreal Gazette,* December 15, 1944.

*The Morning Herald,* May 8, 1928.

*The Morning Leader,* July 29, 1927.

*Motion Picture Herald,* May 6 and May 13, 1933; September 1, 1934; July 13, October 12, and December 14, 1940; December 20, 1941; November 7, 1942; January 9 and July 10, 1943.

*New Castle News,* December 17, 1937.

*New York Morning World,* October 1930.

*The New York Post,* September 1938.

*The New York Times,* November 22, 1927; April 2, 1928; March 11, 1929; March 28, August 23, and undated, 1930; September 9, 1931; March 26 and December 31, 1932; February 28, 1934; January 13, 1936; February 19 and July 18, 1941; December 15, December 21, and December 29, 1944; January 11, June 9, June 22, and September 20, 1945.

*News-Palladium,* December 20, 1944.

*Northern Territory Times,* April 12, 1932.

*The Norwalk Hour,* August 17, 1933.

*The Oakland Tribune,* July 16 and December 25, 1932; January 1 and August 26, 1933; September 11, 1936.

*La Opinión,* January 23 and January 31, 1929.

*Ottawa Citizen,* December 23, 1944.

*The Owosso Argus-Press,* July 28, 1950.
*Oxnard Press-Courier,* June 21, 1945.
*The Palm Beach Post,* December 29, 1939.
*The Palm Beach Post-Times,* August 16, 1970.
*Pittsburgh Post-Gazette,* December 15, 1944.
*The Pittsburgh Press,* March 29, September 23, and December, 1929; July 11, 1934; September 8, 1937; February 5 and March 29, 1938; April 19, 1943; December 21, 1944; June 22, 1945.
*Port Arthur News,* June 22, 1945.
*La Prensa,* October 2, 1925; February 8 and April 3, 1931; May 22, November 6, and December 17, 1932; May 12 and May 22, 1935; February 10, 1936; April 4 and September 25, 1938; June 29, 1941; December 28, 1944.
*Prescott Evening Courier,* June 8, 1934.
*The Reading Eagle,* May 28 and November 23, 1931.
*Reno Evening Gazette,* December 7, 1932; November 1, 1941.
*The Rochester Evening Journal,* March 25 and September 17, 1929; October 7, 1933; February 5, 1934.
*Rochester Journal,* October 13, 1936.
*The Rock Hill Herald,* February 25, 1928.
*San Antonio Express,* March 2, 1940.
*San Antonio Light,* April 7 and September 5, 1943; December 16 and December 18, 1944; January 2 and November 25, 1945.
*San Francisco Chronicle,* December 29, 1935.
*San Jose Evening News,* October 30, 1933; April 11, 1939.
*San Jose News,* November 5, 1931; October 23, 1941; December 27, 1944.
*Sarasota Herald-Tribune,* December 29, 1939; December 22, 1944.
*Sheboygan Press,* October 20, 1928; April 9, 1929; February 3, 1930; February 21, 1942.
*The Southeast Missourian,* August 18, 1933.
*The Spartanburg Herald-Journal,* October 17, 1937.
*Spokane Daily Chronicle,* January 22, 1932.
*The Sun,* January 18, 1942.
*The Sunday Morning Star,* June 17, 1928.
*Syracuse Herald,* June 19, 1927; July 14, 1929; January 10, 1932; March 8, 1934.
*The Times of London,* undated, 1936.
*The Toledo News-Bee,* December 3, 1936.
*Toronto Daily Star,* June 20, 1945.
*Tyrone Daily Herald,* December 11, 1936.
*El Universal Ilustrado,* 1925; January 11 and January 18, 1937.
*Variety,* May 15, 1934; May 25, 1938.
*The Vidette Messenger,* December 15, 1944.
*The Village Voice,* July 27, 1982; June 17, 2008.

## Magazines

*The Billboard,* December 23, 1944.
*Cinema Reporter,* April 1943.
*Collier's,* undated, 1932.
*Exhibitors Herald-World,* undated, 1930.
*Film Weekly,* December 21, 1934.
*Modern Screen,* September 21 and October 1931; September 1932; January 1941
*Monthly Film Bulletin,* August 1936; December 1938.
*The Morning Leader,* July 29, 1927.
*Motion Picture Magazine,* July 1928.
*New Movie,* 1932.
*Photoplay,* 1928; February 1929; undated and December 1930; 1931; January and June 1932.

*Revista de Revistas*, undated ,1925; February 12, 1928.
*The Saturday Evening Post*, 1956.
*Screen Book Magazine*, February 1934.
*Screen Romances*, January and November 1933.
*Screen Secrets* (#48) March 1929; (#49) April 1929; (#50) May 1929; (#51) June 1929.
*Shadoplay Magazine*, October 1934.
*Sleazy Scandals of the Silver Screen* #1, January 1, 1974.
*Smart Set*, undated, 1929.
*Time*, October 12, 1936; April 11, 1938; December 25, 1944; July 25, 1960.
*Today's Cinema,* November 30, 1938.
*Vogue*, undated, 1938.

## Books

Anderson, Clinton H. *Beverly Hills Is My Beat.* New York: Popular Library, 1960.
Anger, Kenneth. *Hollywood Babylon.* San Francisco: Straight Arrow, 1975.
Ankerich, Michael G. *The Sound of Silence: Conversations with 16 Film and Stage Personalities Who Bridged the Gap Between Silents and Talkies.* Jefferson, NC: McFarland, 1998.
Arce, Hector. *Gary Cooper: An Intimate Biography.* New York: Bantam, 1980.
Bakish, David. *Jimmy Durante: His Show Business Career, with An Annotated Filmography and Discography.* Jefferson, NC: McFarland, 1995.
Balogh, Laura Petersen. *Karl Dane: A Biography and Filmography.* Jefferson, NC: McFarland, 2009.
Birchard, S. Robert. *Cecil B. DeMille's Hollywood.* Lexington: University Press of Kentucky, 2004.
Blake, Michael F. *Lon Chaney: The Man Behind the Thousand Faces.* Vestal, NY: Vestal, 1993.
Bradshaw, Jon. *Dreams That Money Can Buy: The Tragic Life of Libby Holman.* New York: William Morrow, 1985.
Carr, William. *Hollywood Tragedy.* Robbinsdale, MN: Fawcett, 1976.
Conner, Floyd. *Hollywood's Most Wanted: The Top Ten Book of Lucky Breaks, Prima Donnas, Box Office Bombs, and Other Oddities.* Chicago: Potomac, 2002.
Conner, Floyd. *Lupe Vélez and Her Lovers.* Fort Lee, NJ: Barricade, 1993.
Curiel, Fernando. *Paseando por Plateros.* Mexico: M. Casillas Editores and Cultura SEP, 1982.
Ellenberger, Allan R. *Ramon Novarro: A Biography of the Silent Film Idol, 1899–1968.* Jefferson, NC: McFarland, 1999.
Eyman, Scott. *Empire of Dreams: The Epic Life of Cecil B. DeMille.* New York: Simon & Schuster, 2010.
Fleming, E. J. *Carole Landis: A Tragic Life in Hollywood.* Jefferson, NC: McFarland, 2005.
Flynn, Errol. *My Wicked, Wicked Ways.* New York: G.P. Putnam, 1959.
Hemming, Roy. *The Melody Lingers On: The Great Songwriters and Their Movie Musicals.* New York: Newmarket, 1986.
Higham, Charles. *Ziegfeld.* Chicago: Henry Regnery, 1972.
Hotchner, A. E., and Doris Day. *Doris Day: Her Own Story.* New York: William Morrow, 1976.
*How I Broke Into the Movies*, facsimile ed. Video Yesteryear, 1984.
Huston, John. *An Open Book.* New York: Knopf, 1980.
Jacobson, Laurie. *Dishing Hollywood: The Real Scoop on Tinseltown's Most Notorious Scandals.* Nashville: Cumberland House, 2003.
Keylin, Arleen. *Hollywood Album 2: Lives and Deaths of Hollywood Stars from the Pages of* The New York Times. New York: Arno, 1979.
Lahr, John. *Notes on a Cowardly Lion: The Biography of Bert Lahr.* Berkeley: University of California Press, 2000.
Lanza, Joseph, and Dennis Penna. *Russ Columbo and the Crooner Mystique.* Los Angeles: Feral House, 2002.
Lennig, Arthur. *The Immortal Count: The Life and Films of Bela Lugosi.* Lexington: University Press of Kentucky, 2003.

Mann, William J. *Behind the Screen: How Gays and Lesbians Shaped Hollywood, 1910–1969*. New York: Viking, 2001.

McNulty, Thomas. *Errol Flynn: The Life and Career*. Jefferson, NC: McFarland, 2004.

Mendible, Myra. *From Bananas to Buttocks: The Latina Body in Popular Film and Culture*. Austin: University of Texas Press, 2007.

Moore, Clayton. *I Was That Masked Man*. Lanham, MD: Taylor, 1998.

Muñoz, Ignacio. *Verdad y Mito de la Revolución Mexicana, Vol. 2 (Truth and Myths of the Mexican Revolution)*. Mexico: Ediciones Populares, S.A., 1961.

Olsen, Carolyn Roos, and Marylin Hudson. *Hollywood's Man Who Worried for the Stars: The Story of Bö Roos*. Indianapolis, IN: Authorhouse, 2008.

Onyx, Narda. *Water, World and Weissmuller: A Biography*. Los Angeles: Vion, 1964.

Ralston, Esther. *Some Day We'll Laugh: An Autobiography*. Metuchen, NJ: Scarecrow, 1985.

Ramírez, Gabriel. *Lupe Vélez: la mexicana que escupia fuego*. Cineteca Nacional Mexico, 1986.

Ramos, Vázquez Marisol. *Yo, Marga: Memorias de Marga López*. Mexico: Grupo Olimpa Editores, 2005.

Riva, Maria. *Marlene Dietrich*. Chicago: Ballantine, 1994.

Robinson, Edward G., and Leonard Spigelgass. *All My Yesterdays: An Autobiography*. New York: Hawthorn, 1973.

Santacilia, Pablo Prida. *Y se levanta el telón: mi vida dentro del teatro*. Mexico: Editorial Botas, 1960.

Schulberg, Budd. *Moving Pictures*. Harmondsworth: Penguin, 1981.

Shearer, Stephen Michael. *Patricia Neal: An Unquiet Life*. Lexington: University Press of Kentucky, 2006.

Skaerved, Melene Sheppard. *Dietrich (Life and Times Series)*. London: Haus, 2003.

Smith, H. Allen. *Life in a Putty Knife Factory*. Philadelphia: Blakiston, 1945.

Soares, André. *Beyond Paradise: The Life of Ramon Novarro*. Jackson: University Press of Mississippi, 2010.

Stein, Jean, and George Plimpton. *Edie: American Girl*. New York: Knopf, 1982.

Swindell, Larry. *Last Hero: A Biography of Gary Cooper*. New York: Doubleday, 1980.

Tiomkin, Dimitri, and Prosper Buranelli. *Please Don't Hate Me*. Garden City, NY: Doubleday, 1959.

Tolstoy, Leo. *Resurrection*. Whitefish, MT: Kessinger, 2004.

Usai, Paolo Cherchi. *Griffith Project: Volume 10: Films Produced in 1919–46*. London: BFI, 2006.

Vance, Jeffrey, and Tony Maietta. *Douglas Fairbanks*. Berkeley: University of California Press, 2008.

Various. *Writing the Range, Race, Class, and Culture in the Women's West*. Norman: University of Oklahoma, 1997.

Walker, Alexander. *The Shattered Silents: How the Talkies Came to Stay*. New York: William Morrow, 1979.

Wayne, Jane Ellen. *Cooper's Women*. New York: Prentice Hall, 1988.

Weissmuller, Johnny Jr., W. Craig Reed, and William Reed. *Tarzan, My Father*. Toronto: ECW, 2008.

# Internet

http://eh.net/hmit/ (Economic History Association).

http://rinconar.blogspot.com (Adrián René Contreras, San Luis Potosí expert).

http://twitchfilm.com/ (14th Annual San Francisco Film Festival; filmmaking process for a scene in *The Gaucho*).

http://web.mit.edu/cms/People/henry3/lupe.html (Henry Jenkins, "You Don't Say That In English!"

www.allmovie.com.

www.amazon.com.

www.austinfilm.org.

www.britishpictures.com.

www.classicimages.com.

www.dimitritiomkin.com.

www.familysearch.org.

www.filmsite.org.
www.ibdb.com.
www.imdb.com.
www.independent.co.uk.
www.ishof.org.
www.kennybowersfanclub.com.
www.lorenzhart.org.
www.moviemorlocks.com.
www.peoplehistory.com.
www.playbill.com.
www.pictureshowman.com.
www.screenonline.org.uk.
www.tcm.com.
www.thehumanmarvels.com.
www.thisdayinquotes.com.
www.trademarkia.com (/tarzan-74162760.html).
www.zillow.com.

## Archives, Institutions, Individual Correspondence, and Key Documents

American Film Institute.
Agrasánchez Film Archive.
Beverly Hills Police Department (Archives).
British Film Institute.
Census (1930), Beverly Hills, California.
Dick Moore, letter to the author.
Family History, Photographs and Correspondence from Pedro Quintanilla Gómez-Noriega (Lupe Vélez's second cousin). Including two trips to Mexico City (December 2010 and January 2011) to photograph Lupe's grave.
The *Frasier* Files: Transcripts—1.1, "The Good Son," Original airdate, September 16, 1993.
George Eastman House.
Hal Roach Studio Files (documents, letters and contracts).
Library of Congress (Recorded Sound Reference Center).
Los Angeles County Coroner's Office (Lupe Vélez Coroner's Register).
Lupe Vélez Death Certificate (Filed January 22, 1945).
Lupe Vélez Last Will and Testament (Filed December 15, 1944).
Manifests for Alien Passengers into the United States (various years; for Lupe Vélez and several family members).
Margaret Herrick Library (Special Collections: Sammy Cahn Papers, Gladys Hall Papers, Henry King Papers and William Wyler Papers).
Mary Pickford Institute.
Miles, John P., D.W. Griffith Corp. *Lady of the Pavements* press release, August 1928.
New York Public Library for Performing Arts — Music Division (The Lawrence Tibbett Papers).
New York State Film Board.
Our Lady of the Lake University (archive material).
*Strictly Dynamite* (1934) Press Book.
Studio records (MGM).
Twentieth Century–Fox Film Corporation.
University of Monterrey (UDEM).
University of Washington Libraries (Special Collections).
Various scrapbook clippings from fan magazines (1928–1944).

# Index

Numbers in **bold** italics indicate pages with photographs

235